MW01630099

Mexico and American Modernism

Mexico and American Modernism

Ellen G. Landau

YALE UNIVERSITY PRESS | NEW HAVEN AND LONDON

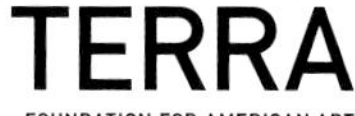

This publication is made possible through support from the Terra Foundation for American Art.

Published with assistance from the National Endowment for the Humanities. Any views, findings, conclusions, or recommendations expressed in this publication do not necessarily reflect those of the National Endowment for the Humanities.

yalebooks.com/art

Designed by Susan Marsh
Set in Plantin Light type by Tina Henderson
Printed in China through Oceanic Graphic International, Inc.

Library of Congress Cataloging-in-Publication Data
Landau, Ellen G.
  Mexico and American modernism / Ellen G. Landau.
     pages cm
   Includes bibliographical references and index.
  ISBN 978-0-300-16913-3 (hardback)
  1. Art, American—20th century. 2. Modernism (Art)—United States.
  3. Art, Mexican—Influence. I. Title.
  N6512.5.M63L36 2013
  709.73'0904—dc23   2012041635

Jacket illustrations: (*front*) Robert Motherwell, *Pancho Villa, Dead and Alive*, 1943 (fig. 83); (*back*) Jackson Pollock, *Male and Female*, 1942–43 (fig. 93).

A catalogue record for this book is available from the British Library.

This paper meets the requirements of ANSI/NISO Z39.48–1992 (Permanence of Paper).

10 9 8 7 6 5 4 3 2 1

Contents

Mexico and American Modernism presents a related set of interdisciplinary cross-cultural case studies charting the impact of aesthetic connections to Mexico and Mexican art on four important mid-twentieth-century American artists. Major contributions by Isamu Noguchi, Philip Guston, Jackson Pollock, and Robert Motherwell were sparked in decisive ways by their links to Mexican artistic achievements and, in three instances, to unique opportunities available south of the border. The little-known Mexican mural experiences of Guston and Noguchi both foreshadowed and nourished central tenets of their mature artistic production. For example, the curious turn to what we now term "identity politics" so evident in Guston's late figurative style makes much more sense in light of the complex autobiographical narrative embedded in *The Struggle Against Terrorism*, the epic fresco he created in Morelia in 1934–35 with Reuben Kadish. Noguchi's Mexico City project is often marginalized in accounts of his career. Yet its style and imagery drew closely upon his nascent association with famed choreographer Martha Graham, providing a foretaste of their successful twenty-two-year theatrical collaboration, while referencing simultaneously his sister's parallel participation in radical leftist dance. Numerous analogues in organization, bodily metaphor, and polemical content connect the design and iconography of Noguchi's *History as Seen from Mexico, 1936* to the dialectic of Manhattan's socialist dance troupes. Jackson Pollock had close encounters with the explosive work of Mexican muralists José Clemente Orozco and David Alfaro Siqueiros in Los Angeles and New York (he actually knew Siqueiros well), and Robert Motherwell spent the second half of 1941 living first in Taxco and then in a Mexico City suburb, interacting respectively with Roberto Matta Echaurren and Wolfgang Paalen, expatriate Surrealists. A close reading of some of the most innovative early works by Pollock and Motherwell reveals critical thematic and technical dimensions unlikely without their having synthesized a Mexican impetus. Whereas French Surrealist founder

André Breton saw Mexico and Mexican art somewhat reductively—he is presented here as a kind of foil to the Americans—these artists were catalyzed by its power, and they knew it.

Prior scholarship on Abstract Expressionism (the so-called "triumph of American painting" which developed in the early years of the second World War) has only scratched the surface in analyzing Mexican implications for U.S. creativity. Cross-fertilization with the extraordinary flowering of Mexican art that took place in the early twentieth century and the broadening effect of its tumultuous social circumstance continued to open new avenues for North American achievement well into the 1940s. Sharpened and refined interrogation of this phenomenon can add new perspective on the cultural impact of globalization, a key twenty-first-century directive of humanistic studies. One aim of this book is to complicate the primarily Eurocentric context within which U.S. goals and accomplishments in the visual arts are so often framed and to expose, in four key instances, alternate parameters of a modernist dialogue rooted in Western Hemisphere hybridity. For the artists in this study, admiring and accepting Mexican impetus led to corollary immersion with a much wider range of contexts—in addition to radical dance, philosophy, rhetoric, psychology, politics, and religious history, for example.

Each of the first four chapters of *Mexico and American Modernism* revolves around one central character. Chapter 5 brings Pollock and Motherwell together to explore further the intersection of artistic subjectivity with global concerns and elucidate what one artist subject termed the "humanly meaningful" goals of abstraction. The book is divided into two thematic sections with somewhat differently focused, but interrelated, arguments. Chapters 1 and 2, on Noguchi and Guston, track their social and political sympathies developing in the context of Depression-era left-wing radical thought. For them, working in Mexico in the mid-1930s allowed the communication of sympathies for the downtrodden too extremist up north. Even temporary displacement would have a profound longterm stimulus effect on each. In Chapters 3 to 5 a more comprehensive argument is formulated and its consequences played out through specific examples, not all made in Mexico. Here emphasis is placed on the Mexican-related iconographic and technical experiments of Pollock in New York and, especially, the formation of Motherwell's style and aesthetic within the crucible of the Surrealists' various expatriate circles. For Motherwell, working closely with Matta and Paalen in Mexico provided an impetus to explore "the question of identity as a moral problem," and, concurrently, to develop a more internationalist outlook. The impact of Motherwell's encounters with notable cultural figures, including, among others, Breton, Meyer Schapiro, Lionel Abel, and Kurt Seligmann, played a decisive role in his ability to maximize cross-border interchange.

Chapter 1 explicates Noguchi's case, uncovering explicit links between the unusually strident cement relief he sculpted for Mexico City's publicly funded Mercado Abelardo L. Rodríguez and the contemporaneous radical-ization in New York of avant-garde dance. Noguchi's extraordinary series of stage sets for Martha Graham's company was initiated immediately prior to his beginning this Mexican work; these have been mostly studied by dance historians who are somewhat less interested in formulating connections with his sculptural oeuvre. Authors discussing *History as Seen from Mexico, 1936* typically note its embedded Marxist symbolism, but none explore the obvi-ous traces in it of Noguchi's identification with the agenda of activist dance, or establish how his Mercado mural encapsulates many of the premises underpinning his much-celebrated secondary career of designing for the stage. The great passion for Mexico that Graham and Noguchi shared needs to be considered in any evaluation of their collaboration. A principal aspect of the chapter on Noguchi involves parsing the sculptor's obvious knowledge of the effectiveness of bodily metaphor to express polemical content.

An earlier version of Chapter 2, featuring Philip Guston, was published in the Smithsonian American Art Museum's scholarly journal *American Art* as "Double Consciousness in Mexico: How Philip Guston and Reuben Kadish Painted a Morelian Mural" (Spring 2007), winning the 2008 Patricia and Philip Frost Award. This chapter challenges the accepted notion that Guston and Kadish's monumental 1934–35 epic *The Struggle Against Ter-rorism,* had no visible connection to its Mexican setting. I explain how the theme of this fresco (conceived and executed near a former Inquisition site in Michoácan that had, by the early thirties, been transformed into a hotbed of anticlericalism) was firmly rooted in local historical reality, and in a way that could intersect with the personal agenda of its young Jewish painters. Subsidiary sections of the Morelia composition, hardly ever discussed, are tied to the artists' previous experience in Los Angeles when portable murals made to protest the fate of the Scottsboro Boys were destroyed by red-baiting police, and to Guston's fixation with the Ku Klux Klan that came full circle in his influential late paintings.

Chapter 3 originated in arguments first proposed in an essay for a joint Pollock/Siquieros retrospective held in Düsseldorf, Germany, in 1995, and subsequently refined as "Mexico and American Modernism: The Case of Jackson Pollock" in *Abstract Expressionism: The International Context* (Rut-gers, 2007). This material has been additionally revised, including greatly expanded documentation. During the late 1930s, emulating Orozco's pow-erful social vocabulary in accordance with his own private archetypes aided Pollock in redirecting his admiration for the heroics of Michelangelo into a more modernistic context. While Orozco's compelling iconography helped point Pollock toward a complex psychological and artistic identification with Picasso, Siqueiros's polemically based experimentation with materials suggested the more groundbreaking potential of a "subversive alternate arrangement." The Mexican master's example of machismo, more extreme than that of Pollock's teacher Thomas Hart Benton, also played a central role in his psychic development.

Exposing a legacy of malefaction and intolerance from biblical times to the present, Guston and Kadish's mid-1930s Morelia mural referenced by implication a confluence of insecurity, persecution, and ritual violence considered at that time a characteristic of Mexico, equally powerful to its great sensuousness and natural beauty. Such dramatically stark contrasts also appealed to filmmaker Sergei Eisenstein as well as to Mexico's revolving-door contingent of displaced Surrealists in the early years of the following decade; the country's émigré clique during the war (including, at various junctures, Paalen, Matta, Gordon Onslow-Ford, and Breton) attracted into its orbit Robert Motherwell, another virtual unknown. Chapters 4 and 5 address the impact of Motherwell's half-year experience in Mexico in 1941, expressed upon his return home through Pancho Villa's fetishization and conversion to stark abstraction of the country's whitewashed walls and blinding sunlight, and eventually contributing to development of the artist's signature series, *Elegies to the Spanish Republic*, begun in 1949. Just how thoroughly his evolution of art and theory was connected to the deep attraction that Motherwell confessed with the "continual presence of sudden death" and other singular aspects of Mexico that "seized" his imagination compels more detailed explanation. In Chapter 5, divining the extent and impact of Mexico's aesthetic implications allows for new ways to read the embedded tropes critical to Motherwell and Pollock's early successes at Peggy Guggenheim's Manhattan gallery, Art of This Century. Dialogue with Mexican artistic accomplishment is exposed as a crucial spur to Abstract Expressionism's move away from narrative without discarding the essence of allegorical intent. Prior assessments of Surrealism's incorporation into New York School innovation have not adequately interpreted the active role that Mexico played in this process.

Up to now, the primary source for information about the Mexican impact on American mid-twentieth-century art has been *South of the Border: Mexico in the American Imagination, 1914–1947*. This comprehensive catalogue was published to accompany a 1993 traveling exhibition organized by the Yale University Art Gallery. *South of the Border* emphasized the folkloric and pictorialist aspects of the "enormous vogue of things Mexican" that reached its peak between the two world wars, and its curators ably surveyed interrelationships between more than sixty American and Mexican artists. Pollock, Motherwell, Noguchi, and Guston were all included, but—of necessity in such a large group—their ties to Mexico could only be sketched. In *Mexico and American Modernism* I redress this through a targeted set of correlated case studies and a concluding chapter that zeroes in on and fast-forwards the main protagonists into their modernist (and, in Guston's case, postmodern) futures. Although approaching Mexican accomplishment through the eyes of four U.S. artists intensely stimulated by it, my aim is not to present one side as "significant" and one as "other." As the final quotation by Octavio Paz implies, a more discursive framework is suggested for a fuller exploration of the complex and intriguing ramifications of this fascinating instance of bi-national cross-fertilization.

Acknowledgments

This project could not have been realized without the significant help of a number of people and institutions. I am particularly grateful for the support of the College of Arts and Sciences, the Department of Art History and Art, and the Baker-Nord Center for the Humanities at Case Western Reserve University, as well as the School of Historical Studies at the Institute for Advanced Study in Princeton. Much of the Guston chapter was written at the IAS in spring 2004, when I was in residence as the Agnes Gund and Daniel Shapiro Member. A "We the People" fellowship from the National Endowment for the Humanities, for projects that "explore significant events and themes in our nation's history and culture," allowed me to take an entire sabbatical year to complete this book during the 2010–11 academic year. Help in production and subventing the illustrations was provided by CAS dean Cyrus Taylor at CWRU, the university's Baker-Nord Center for the Humanities, as well as the Society for the Preservation of American Modernists and the Terra Foundation for American Art. I would like to thank the following research institutions for facilitating access to needed materials (often primary sources): the Getty Research Library; Archives of American Art, Smithsonian Institution, Washington, D.C., and New York; Dedalus Foundation; Beinecke Rare Book and Manuscript Library, Yale University; Firestone Library, Princeton University; Institute for Advanced Study Library; Laura and Alvin Siegal College of Jewish Studies Library; Ingalls Library of the Cleveland Museum of Art; Kelvin Smith Library, CWRU; and the New York Public Library for the Performing Arts.

This book would certainly not have come into being without the ideas, aid, and/or support of Irene Herner, Jürgen Harten, Patricia Fidler, Katherine Boller, and my patient, loving, and supportive husband, Howard Landau. Others especially helpful in a variety of critical ways include (in alphabetical order) Ziva Amishai-Maisels, David Areford, Joaquin Astorga, Lic. Lenía Batres Guadarrama, Karyn Behnke, Carolyn Walker Bynum,

Terese Capucilli, Claude Cernuschi, Heidi B. Coleman, John Crosse, Christine Dakin, Heidi Downey, Jack Flam, Rebecca Foster, Gary Galbraith, Ann Eden Gibson, Helen A. Harrison, Amy Hau, Arlene Sievers Hill, Dan and Carol Kadish, Ruth and Morris Kadish, the late Frank Kadish, Jonathan D. Katz, Indra Lacis, Jay Landau, David McKee, Abigail Major, Susan Marsh, Joan Marter, Mary Mayer, Musa Mayer, Arq. Eugenio Mercado López, Courtney Ruffalo Miller, Cynthia Mills, Mónica Montes, Michael Moreford, Luis Efraín Pérez Aquino, Leah Poller, Sylvia Winter Pollock, Karen Potter, Katy Rogers, Martica Sawin, Debby Tenenbaum, Marcia Tucker, Judd Tully, the late Kirk Varnedoe, Michael R. Weil, Jr., Amy Winter, Froma Zeitlin, and the anonymous readers for Yale University Press. I have definitely benefited from the prior scholarship of many astute colleagues, whose ideas are cited in text and endnotes. In particular, I could not have written this book without the excellent work already done by James Oles, Irene Herner, Ann Gibson, Stephen Polcari, Michael Leja, Martica Sawin, Robert Mattison, Dore Ashton, Gregory Gilbert, and Robert Hobbs. I would like to dedicate Part Two to the memory of Melvin P. Lader, whose work on Arshile Gorky and Art of This Century remains indispensable to all serious scholars of Abstract Expressionism.

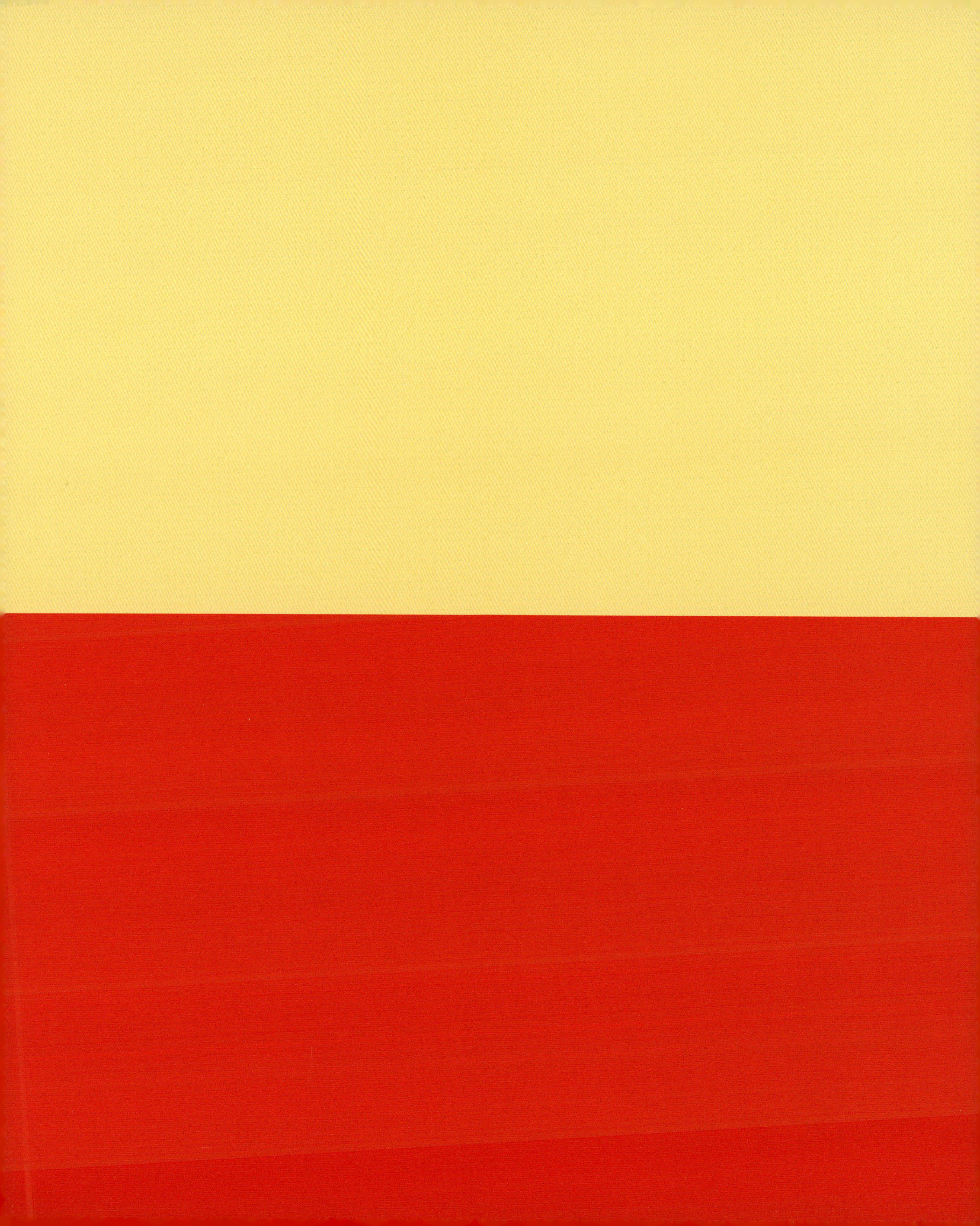

Part One

The 1930s, Mexico, Art, and Politics

Noguchi, Mexico, and Martha Graham

Standard biographies of famed sculptor Isamu Noguchi typically devote no more than a few pages to the unusual carved relief he produced at age thirty-one during the height of the depression in Mexico City (fig. 1). A major point of interest in mentioning it seems to devolve from the geographical opportunity this project provided for Noguchi's romantic affair with Frida Kahlo, enraging her notoriously philandering husband, Mexican muralist Diego Rivera, and likely unnerving the American expatriate painter Marion Greenwood.[1] Noguchi's earlier liaison with Marion, although apparently fraught, played a role in enticing him to Mexico, following her and her sister Grace.[2]

Prior to his late 1935 arrival in Mexico City, for what would turn out to be a stay of more than half a year, Isamu, the California-born son of Japanese poet Yonejirō Noguchi and American writer Leonie Gilmour, had already met several of the most important Mexican artists, or at least encountered their works. Four years earlier in New York, Noguchi had sculpted the head of José Clemente Orozco, one of Los Tres Grandes (the honorific bestowed on Rivera, Orozco, and Siqueiros), and reportedly assisted Orozco in painting his Baker Library murals at Dartmouth the following year.[3] This experience helped stimulate Noguchi's idea to create a "mural in sculpture," a number of proposals for which would be rejected by U.S. government art projects.[4] A terra-cotta version of Noguchi's Orozco, created by pressing clay into a plaster mold made from the clay original, was featured in the traveling exhibition *Drawings and Small Sculptures by Isamu Noguchi* (fig. 2). This originated in Honolulu and stopped at the Pasadena Art Institute in March 1933, prompting *Los Angeles Times* critic Arthur Millier to gush enthusiastically that Noguchi "is the possessor of a precocious ability. There are some 'correct' portraits of children, then, suddenly, one confronts the amazing head of Orozco, just a lump of earth mysteriously endowed with the Mexican painter's expression. [The artist] likes unusual people and makes

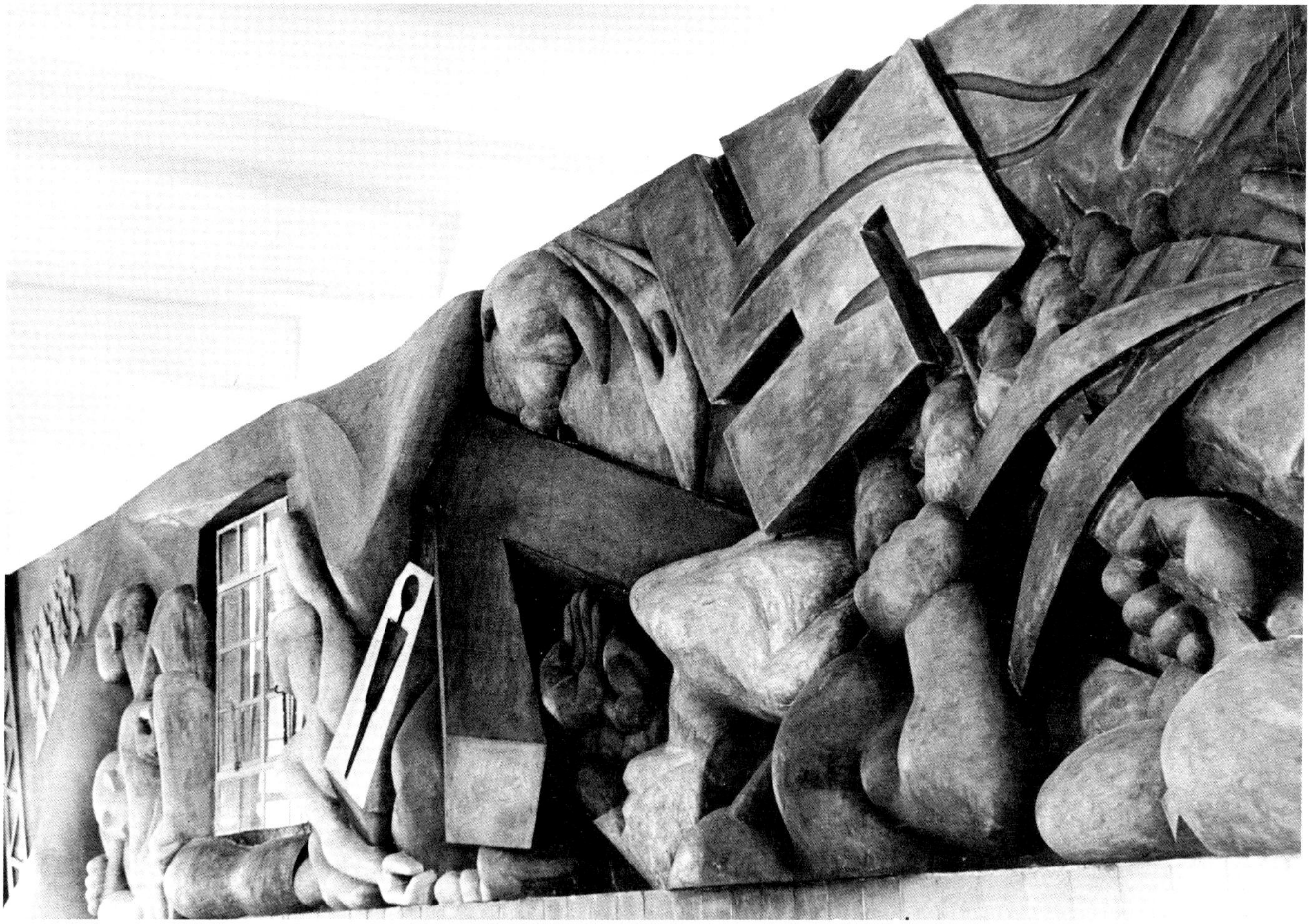

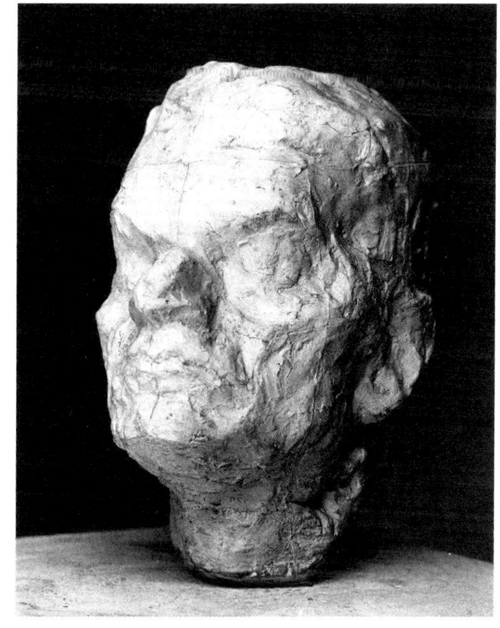

1 Isamu Noguchi, Detail from *History Mexico (History as Seen from Mexico in 1936)*, 1936. Cement, pigment, 72 ft., 2 ³⁄₁₆ in. (22 m). © 2012 The Isamu Noguchi Foundation and Garden Museum, New York/Artists Rights Society (ARS), New York.

2 Isamu Noguchi, *José Clemente Orozco*, 1931. Terra-cotta, 12 ⅛ x 8 x 10 ¼ in. (30.8 x 20.3 x 26 cm). San Francisco Museum of Modern Art. Albert M. Bender Collection, Gift of Albert M. Bender. © 2012 The Isamu Noguchi Foundation and Garden Museum, New York/Artists Rights Society (ARS), New York.

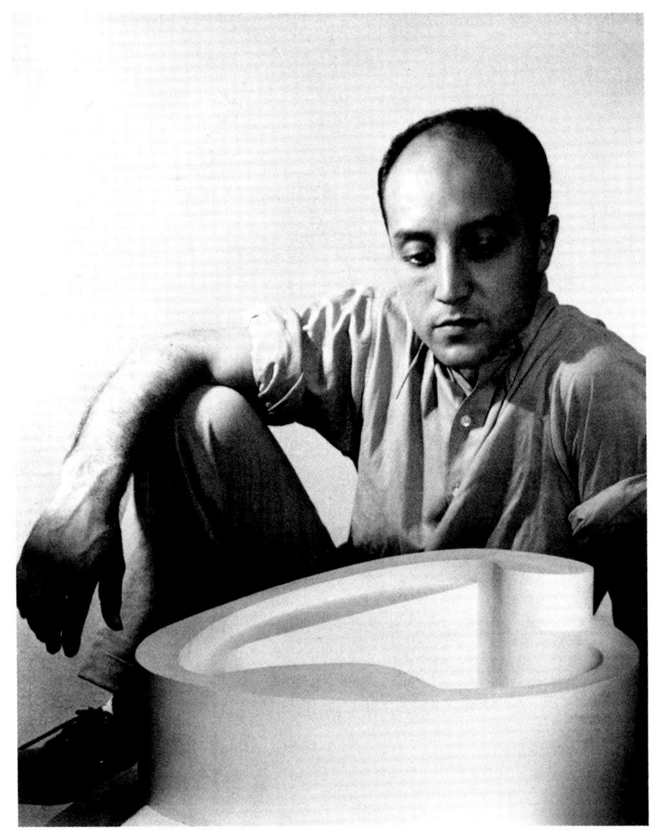

3 Photograph of Noguchi with plaster model for swimming pool (designed by architect Richard Neutra for film director Josef von Sternberg), 1935. Photo: F. S. Lincoln. Collection of the Noguchi Museum. Image courtesy of the Archives of The Isamu Noguchi Foundation and Garden Museum, New York.

them live—sometimes as expression . . . sometimes through carefully arranged forms, like the fine head of Marion Greenwood."[5] Noguchi sculpted the latter, a more severe, idealized realization, in 1929, casting Greenwood's likeness in matte-surfaced iron for a contrastingly abstract effect.

In August 1935, en route to visit the Greenwoods in Mexico and see what work he could scare up south of the border, Noguchi returned first to the city of his birth with the idea of financing his trip through portrait commissions in Hollywood. While creating a representation of actress (and future U.S. senator) Helen Gahagan Douglas, he encountered the local "Mexican art ferment," in part as a result of his association with Richard Neutra, the California modernist architect.[6] During his stay in Los Angeles Noguchi was asked by Neutra to design a pool for movie director Josef von Sternberg and constructed a model for it at the local Stendhal Galleries, but the pool was never realized (fig. 3).[7] Both Neutra and von Sternberg had a connection to Mexican muralist David Alfaro Siqueiros, whom Noguchi had met in New York.[8] Rather notoriously, Siqueiros had also resided and worked in L.A. several years before. Not only did he paint von Sternberg's portrait in 1932, but von Sternberg and Neutra ran in the same circles as another Hollywood director, Dudley Murphy, who commissioned Siqueiros to create a patio fresco for his house in Pacific Palisades.

Among the Mexican's assistants on *Portrait of Mexico Today,* installed at Murphy's home, were two young Angelenos, Reuben Kadish and Phillip Goldstein. (The latter would rename himself Philip Guston by the mid-1930s.) As Millier elucidated local readers during the Mexican's visit, "Siqueiros creates the most powerful forms that have yet to come to us from the Mexican art revolt," his judgment based on the "overwhelming effect" of the muralist's ability to "compress the idea into its most elemental form."[9] Orozco's 1930 *Prometheus* fresco at Pomona College remained a highly notable feature on the somewhat impoverished Southern California art scene (see fig. 47).[10] This had already made a strong impression on Guston and Kadish's boyhood pal Jackson Pollock, as would the later Dartmouth murals on which Noguchi assisted.

Art historian James Oles has trained a scholarly focus on the lesser known but equally powerful and dramatic wall design, six and a half feet high and seventy-two feet long, sculpted in cement by Noguchi on his own extended sojourn in Mexico City. *History as Seen from Mexico, 1936* is situated in a large second-floor room in the Mercado Abelardo L. Rodríguez, a Federal District building project completed in 1934 and named after Mexico's interim president, in office for two years before the election of Lázaro Cárdenas. Designed by the Federal District's chief architect, Antonio Muñoz, and constructed on the site of the ancient St. Gregory Convent by the Compañia de Fomento y Urbanización, the Mercado, a sizable Colonial Revival–style working commercial and cultural center, is entered at the corner of Carmen and Venezuela Streets, just a few blocks from the huge Zócalo, or central city plaza.[11] There is limited public access to the particular space (at one point used as a youth center) housing Noguchi's impressive creation.

Oles discussed Noguchi's Mercado relief in his 1995 dissertation, included illustrations of it in the 1993 catalogue *South of the Border: Mexico and the American Imagination,* and in 2001 wrote a feature article on *History as Seen from Mexico, 1936* in the scholarly journal *American Art.* All three sources provide critical documentary and stylistic information about Noguchi's Mexican mural, especially in explaining the artist's presentation of "International Themes for a Working-Class Market" and how these played out amid the complexities of a period of local and global political change. Oles discusses at length Noguchi's innovative use of materials provided by the conglomerate Cementos Tolteca, citing the relationship as an early version of corporate sponsorship, and remarks Noguchi's acceptance of the need to cooperate with the other Mercado artists in "propounding opposition to war, fascism and capitalistic abuse."[12]

Preceding Noguchi by about a year, the Greenwood sisters joined the Rodríguez market project, under the supervision of Rivera, in fall 1934.[13] Noguchi first met the free-spirited Marion in Paris in 1928 at the Académie de la Grande Chaumière. His Paris experience began in 1927 after winning a John Simon Guggenheim Foundation Fellowship; ultimately more important to his progress than afternoon studies at the Grande Chaumière and Académie Colarossi was the opportunity this presented for him to work in the mornings with Constantin Brancusi, the famed Romanian abstractionist.[14] Either while still in Paris or upon their return to the States (both have been accounted), Noguchi and Marion Greenwood engaged in a short but seemingly intense affair.

Marion Greenwood's primary Abelardo Rodríguez mural, *The Industrialization of the Countryside,* is along the entrance wall and stairway in an upper lobby near the northeast entrance to the Mercado complex (fig. 4). This is the same room as Noguchi's relief, the square footage of which was originally part of her own and Grace's allotted space. She also painted a smaller mural in the market's ground-floor foyer depicting canals as a mode

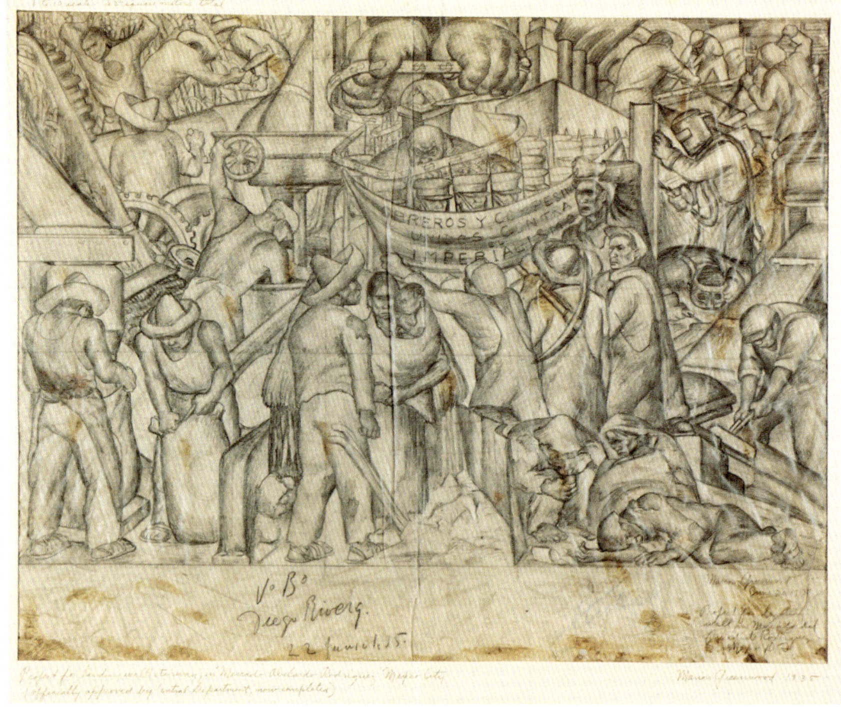

of agricultural transport. Grace Greenwood decorated the large Calle de Colombia staircase adjacent to her sister's upper-story fresco with a composition titled *Mining,* positioned directly opposite *History as Seen from Mexico, 1936.* The walls of the two stairways meet in a single panel on the second floor, painted by both women.

In 1933, along with another expatriate American artist, Howard Cook, Marion Greenwood had painted touristic frescos at Taxco's Hotel Taxqueño — the first walls covered by a female artist in Mexico — and she and Grace worked on murals in the state of Michoacán under the auspices of the University of San Nicholas Hidalgo a year before Guston and Kadish's arrival there. In January 1934, Grace completed a narrow vertical panel, *Man and Machines,* situated just outside the interior patio in Morelia's Museo Michoacano that the two Los Angeles men were destined to decorate. For a horizontal frieze along the walls of the second story arcade of a nearby college building, Marion chose a more regional topic, combining images of fishing on Lake Pátzcuaro, rural agriculture such as the harvesting of wheat, and indigenous folk art traditions.[15] Working there from October 1933 through March 1934, she specifically declined to incorporate depictions of "class-conscious" propaganda, as had been suggested. Describing to a close friend, Josephine Herbst, her thoughts for conceptualizing *Landscape and Economy of Michoacán* Marion wrote:

I'm afraid I have nothing to say, which has not been said before in the way of social significance and political attitudes, its all been said very well by Orozco and Rivera and many others. I am simply going to paint these [Mexican] people as I feel them in all their sadness, their apathy, and beauty. Hammers and sickles, and historical periods and personalities have been done to death. I have only become class-conscious in the last year, it would be an affectation for me to paint the usual propaganda at this period when I have nothing original to offer, whereas if I paint something I *feel* it might have much more significance.[16]

Of course, Marion Greenwood would not even have considered including politically inflammatory subject matter in a mural located in the United States, but this point was moot, since none were on offer. Left-wing subject matter aside, that the obviously talented Greenwood sisters were not given equivalent walls in their home country was deplored by Edward B. Rowan, head of the U.S. Public Works of Art Project. As mentioned, Noguchi experienced his own problems with Depression-era government sponsored agencies in America; all three plans he proposed in 1933 and 1934 to this forerunner of the Works Progress Adminstration (WPA) were turned down as too expensive, too abstract, or too "imaginative."[17]

"Is Sculpture a Useful Instrument of Propaganda?"

To answer the question above — posed by the *New Yorker* in February 1935 regarding Noguchi's current solo exhibition — this chapter will build on existing research concerning *History as Seen from Mexico, 1936* but provide a somewhat different slant on the roots of its iconography and its ideological underpinnings.[18] Potential sources for the obvious and surprisingly strident symbolism attacking right-wing politics, as well as the role of the capitalist system in funding and stimulating the war industry so dramatically incorporated into Noguchi's Mexico City composition, compel further amplification (fig. 5).

Although intending from the start to work in sculptural relief, Noguchi surely examined the range of socially conscious imagery in frescos in process at the Mercado by the Greenwood sisters, American émigré Pablo O'Higgins, and, perhaps to a lesser extent, the six Mexican painters working there.[19] These were Ramón Alva Guadarrama, Antonio Pujol, Miguel Tzab, Angel Bracho, Pedro Rendón, and Raúl Gamboa.[20] While Noguchi had acknowledged a special debt to the advice of Pujol and O'Higgins, his relief had a much bolder look and more strongly stated propagandistic

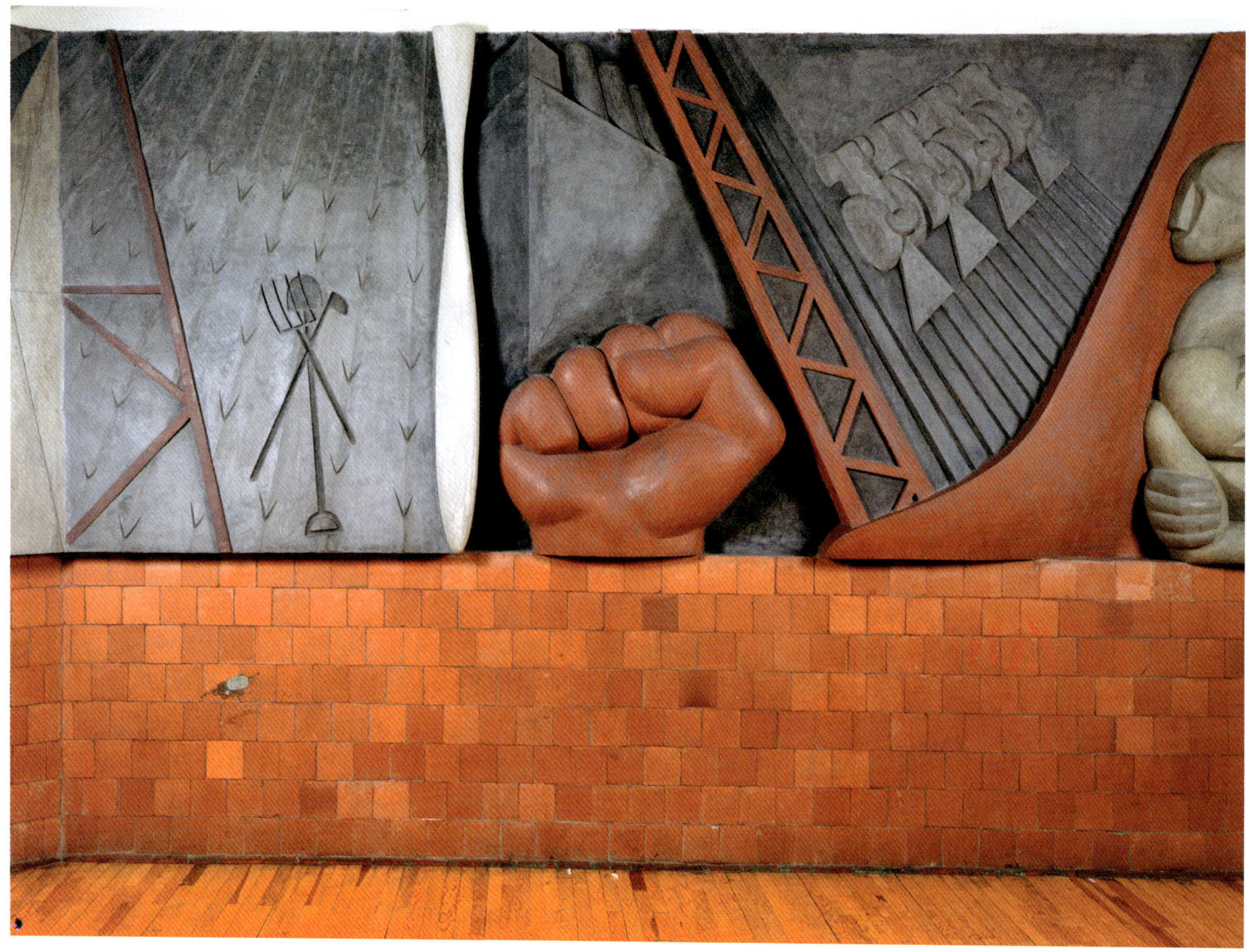

message than the predominantly genre-based narratives developed by his fellow participants.[21] Some of this difference may be ascribed to his alternate medium, a combination of tinted cement, concrete and brick at which Noguchi hacked with an ax, and possibly also to his belated and somewhat unofficial entry into the Mercado project at the Greenwood sisters' behest.[22] Apparently Noguchi had only to show a small watercolor sketch to Diego Rivera (whom he as yet barely knew) to be allowed to participate. For some reason he was permitted to bypass official endorsement and contractual obligation. Although he ultimately was paid only $88 — half of what he and the other participants were supposed to get, fourteen pesos per square meter — Noguchi raised an additional $600 from the Guggenheim Foundation.[23]

While part of a coordinated group endeavor, the forceful brand of theatrical polemics informing Noguchi's Mexico City design was linked to a reservoir of knowledge and experience unshared by the rest of the Mercado team. Crucial aspects of his achievement could be credited to Noguchi's burgeoning association with the modern dance techniques of Martha Graham and—through his sister, Ailes Gilmour (fig. 6), a former member of Graham's ensemble and an active participant in New York-based socialist dance troupes—to his unique familiarity with how bodily movement might be deployed as a "weapon" of economic and political critique.[24]

Raising Hard Questions

As surely as it fed contemporaneous proselytizers of a new form of proletarian dance, there is little doubt that a substantial level of revolutionary fervor, not simply acceptance, fueled Noguchi's design for the Mercado Abelardo L. Rodríguez. Although installed far away from Manhattan, his Mexican relief nevertheless became instantly known to New York's leftist community, including a large number in the cultural professions. In its September 15, 1936, issue, the socialist journal *New Masses* displayed a photo of the nattily attired sculptor standing before the mural's massive clenched fist, as well as four additionally striking details of *History as Seen from Mexico, 1936* (fig. 7). These accompanied a short text proclaiming, "Noguchi's polychrome relief achieves a powerful effect." Echoing the utopian rhetoric of myriad statements issued in those days, Noguchi proclaimed, "Capitalism everywhere struggles with inevitable death—all the machinery of war, coercion and bigotry are as smoke from that fire. Labor awakens with the red flag. And youth, through education, will see the world creatively more abundant, with equal opportunity for all." This somewhat naïvely miscomprehended Communistic aesthetic is one the sculptor would later regret and repudiate.[25]

That same month, Noguchi penned another article for the progressive Artists' Union house organ *Art Front,* with views of his Mercado mural illustrated. In "What's the Matter with Sculpture?" he advocated strongly for artists working in three dimensions to pay attention to the "life of today" and "today's problems."[26] Art world denizens following Noguchi's career were perhaps not as taken aback as they might have been by seeing such evidence of his clear turn away from Brancusi-inspired abstraction.[27] Prior to this Mexican sojourn, Noguchi's solo show at Marie Harriman's gallery, running from late January to mid-February of 1935, had been much talked about. As the *New Yorker* reported and most viewers agreed, "The dominating piece in the exhibition is the monumental dangling figure of a lynched Negro, conveying in its bluish glitter of steel and its bunched flesh the message of contortion, paralysis, death" (fig. 8). Noguchi later cited the construction of this alarming yet seductive work, with its echoes of the crucified peasant in Siqueiros's infamously censored 1932 Los Angeles mural (see

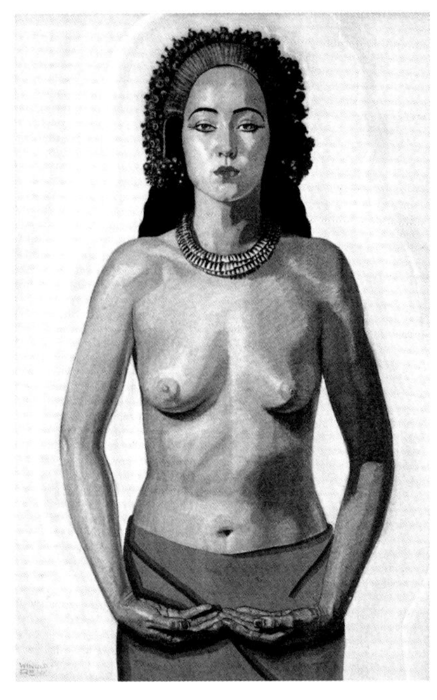

6 Winold Reiss, *Ailes Gilmour,* c. 1929. Pastel on board, 39 x 26 in. (99.1 x 66 cm). Private Collection. © Renate Reiss.

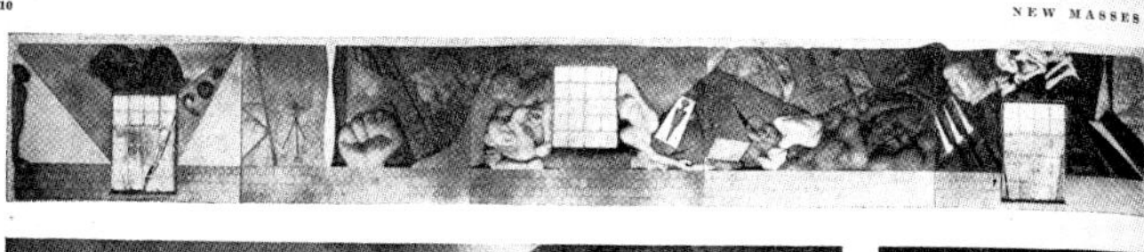
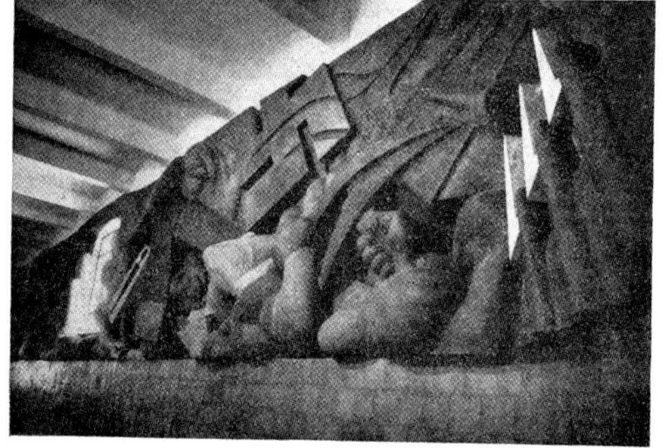
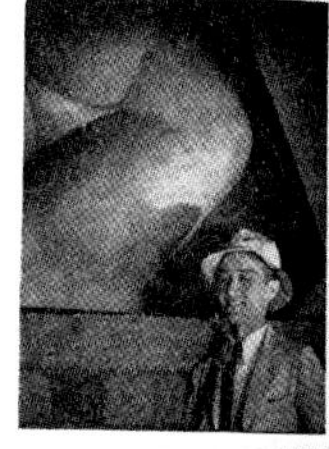
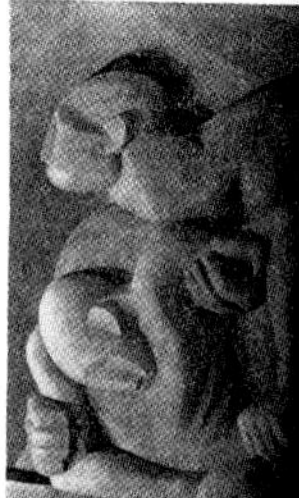
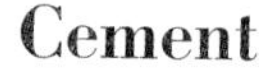
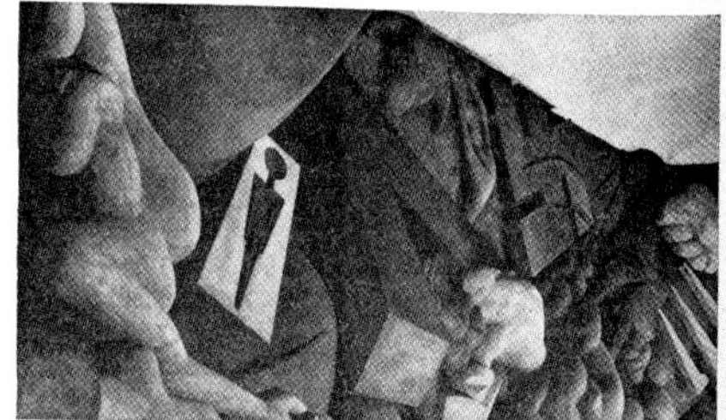

Cement

*Noguchi's polychrome relief
achieves a powerful effect*

ISAMU NOGUCHI'S sculptured wall in Mexico City's Mercado Rodriquez is perhaps the most striking thing in that unique market place. The entire area (22 meters by 2.2 meters) is done in colored cement, built up in high relief. The photograph of the artist standing below the clenched fist gives an idea of its size.

The top strip shows the complete wall. It portrays, in Mr. Noguchi's words, "history as seen from Mexico City in 1936."

"Now," says Mr. Noguchi, "our 'now' includes not only the present with the residue of the past, but the future lived already in our minds. Hope here is reality in another place, and if not in another place then in another time. No one country can any longer be historically dealt with except as an integral part of our ever more aware world. Capitalism everywhere struggles with inevitable death—all the machinery of war, coercion, and bigotry are as smoke from that fire. Labor awakens with the red flag. And youth, through education, will see the world creatively more abundant, with equal opportunity for all."

7 Isamu Noguchi, "Cement," published in *New Masses*, September 15, 1936. Beinecke Rare Book and Manuscript Library, Yale University, New Haven, Conn.

8 Isamu Noguchi, *Death (Lynched Figure)*, 1934. Monel metal, steel, wood, rope, 88¾ x 31⅞ x 22⅛ in. (225.4 x 81 x 56.2 cm). © 2012 The Isamu Noguchi Foundation and Garden Museum, New York / Artists Rights Society (ARS), New York.

fig. 23), as a direct consequence of the "influence of social consciousness" that followed "my awareness of being an American, which came in the fall or winter of 1933."[28] But how he chose to express this awareness, in a work at that time simply titled *Death*, raised "hard questions" in many minds. The anonymous *New Yorker* critic summarized some obvious dilemmas that this sculpture conjured for spectators: "Does the physiological result on the spectator contain a germ of moral effect? Granting the horror at the sight of the body, does it convey horror over the human fact of injustice and cruelty? In short, is sculpture a useful instrument of propaganda?" "I applaud Noguchi's motives," this writer observed, "but I distrust the medium and doubt the results."[29]

Protesting as a "bizarre" form of "macabre commentary" Noguchi's "presentation in an art context of a figure hanging from a real piece of rope," *Art News* noted its artist's clear "dissatisfaction" with the state of social affairs but remarked that he seemingly "still seeks some spring of vital force in the decay of civilization around him."[30] Others were not so optimistic. Before the Marie Harriman show closed, Noguchi removed *Death* and lent it to the National Association for the Advancement of Colored People and College Art Association–sponsored show *An Art Commentary on Lynching* held at the Arthur U. Newton Galleries. Due to press allegations of exploitation and "aesthetic opportunism," four days later Noguchi withdrew the work again.[31] But he did agree to show it in another exhibition opening in March, right after *An Art Commentary on Lynching* completed its run. Called *Struggle for Negro Rights*, this was organized by the Communist-led John Reed Clubs, the Artists' Union, and a variety of political action committees.[32]

Henry McBride, writing in the *New York Sun*, was the most significantly affronted by *Death* and he disapproved as well of a few additional works he also considered "leftist statements" on view at Marie Harriman. Objectionable pieces included the plaster maquette for a monument to labor leader Carl Mackley, meant for a housing development erected by the United Hosiery Workers Union in Philadelphia but never installed.[33] As Noguchi scholar Bruce Altshuler points out, "These designs were snidely described by McBride as 'wily' attempts by a 'semi-oriental' to manipulate Ameri-

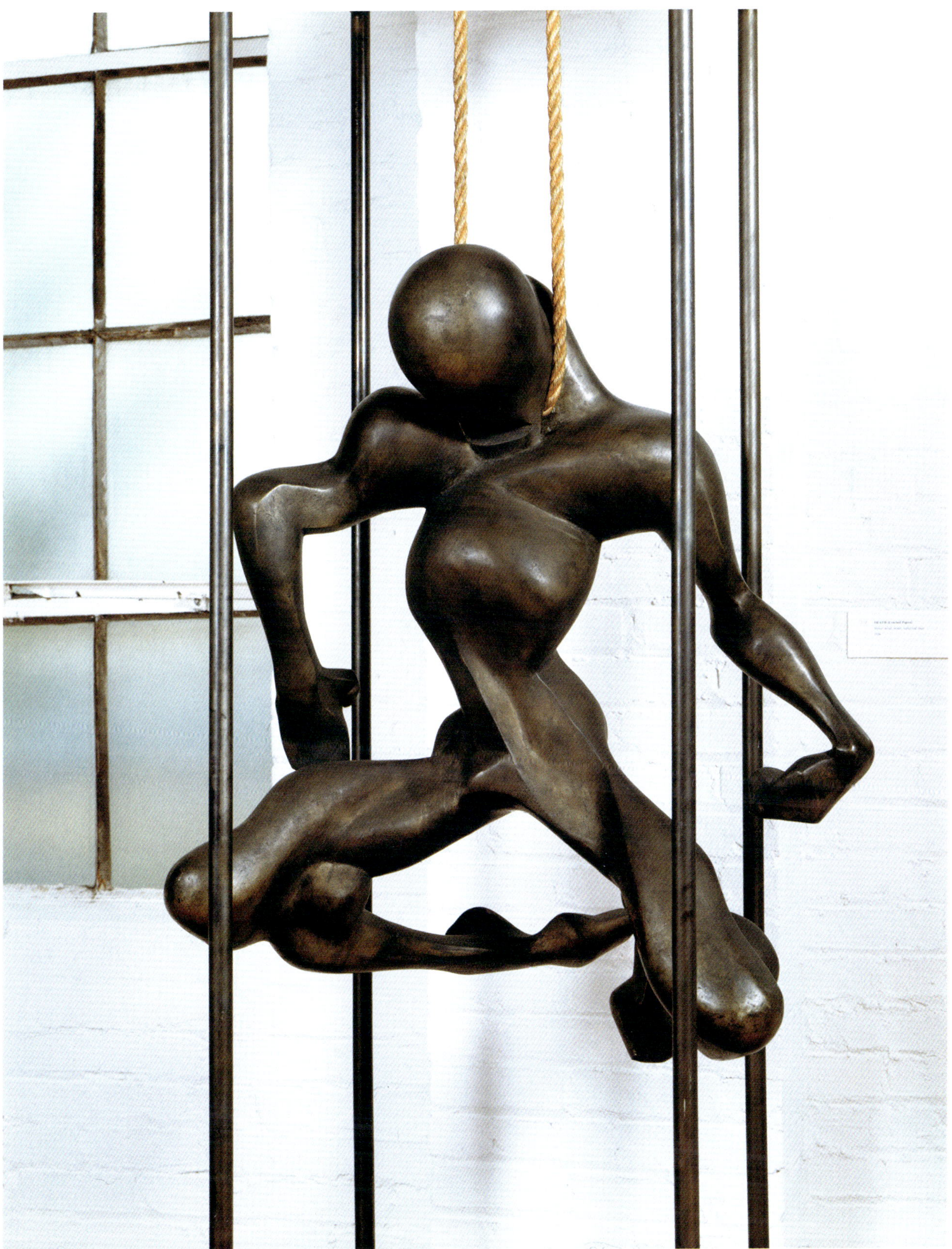

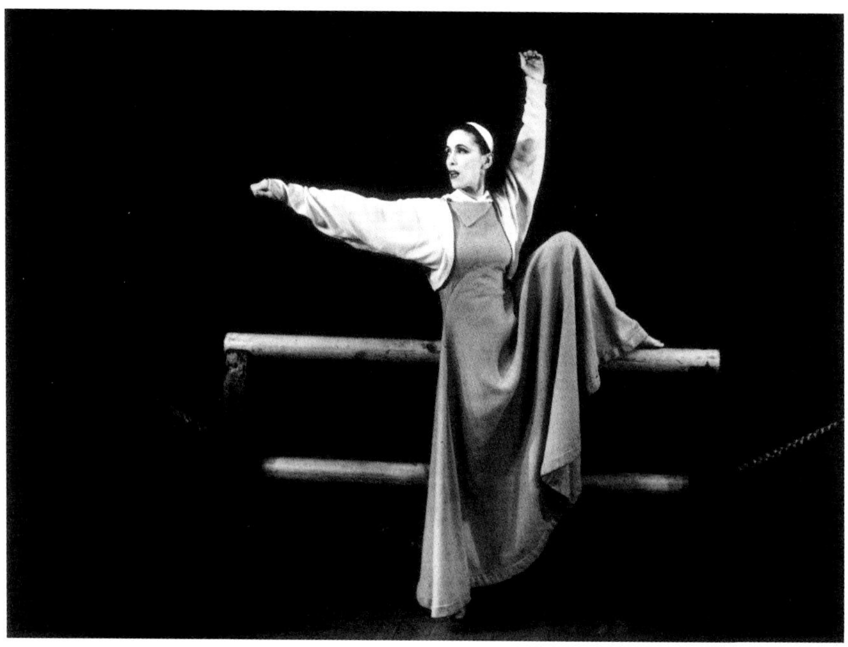

can sentiments, the consequences of Noguchi's 'studying our weakness with a view of becoming irresistible to us.'"[34] *Death* was termed by McBride "grewsome" and, much more provocatively, "just a little Japanese mistake." Another reviewer, writing in the *Christian Century,* was both attracted to and repelled by *Death* calling it "hideous and haunting": "The exact moment chosen for representation is that when the limbs of the already dead body writhed and contracted in the flames over which it had been suspended by a chain. A ghastlier subject could not well be imagined."[35] "If there is anything to make a white man feel squirmy about his color," *Parnassus* intoned, "he has it in this gnarled chromium victim jigging under the wind-swayed rope."[36]

The recognized source for *Death* (which originally had a marble counterpart, *Birth* depicting a woman in labor) was a disturbing photograph of the charred remains of George Hughes, a black farm worker lynched in Sherman, Texas.[37] This image was likely provided to the sculptor by the African American civil rights activist Walter White, who led the NAACP for almost a quarter of a century and specialized in investigating race riots and lynchings in the American South. An absolutely horrifying picture, it first appeared in June 1930 in the *Labor Defender,* and, closer to the time of Noguchi's re-presentation, it was published in the December 1934 issue of the *Afro-American* in New York. As Amy Lyford recognized, "*Death* attracted attention because of the directness with which it embodied the physical and psychic endgame of racial hatred."[38]

Dora Apel, who has also studied varying press responses to Hughes's photo and Noguchi's agonized "high tension" use of it, analyzed the ways in which he departed from the original image, producing a "rhythm of curves and planes" and a "more angular composition of positive and negative shapes" that refers to but differs from the real victim's poignant death contortions. Unlike Noguchi's sculpture, "Hughes's actual body," Apel comments, is "neither smooth nor light reflective, and does not expose sinewy muscular curves or draw itself up into a self-contained space."[39] In his autobiography some three decades later, still infuriated by the critical reaction to *Death,* Noguchi explicitly cited McBride's xenophobia as what drove him from art galleries and into the orbit of Martha Graham, the charismatic avant-garde choreographer and pioneer of modern dance (fig. 9).[40] In making *Death* Noguchi had already begun to adapt, deliberately or not, key aspects of Graham's percussive kinetics, a distinctive form of movement based on muscular contraction and release.

Reading Each Other's Lines

So far the only value of my work—if it has art value—is absolute sincerity. I would not do anything I could not feel. A dance must dominate me completely, until I lose sense of anything else.[41]

— MARTHA GRAHAM, 1920

Isamu Noguchi and Martha Graham were introduced by the Swiss-trained Japanese dancer and choreographer Michio Itō in 1926.[42] Between his extended stay in Paris and an eight month sojourn in Peking, with a side trip to Japan, where most of his childhood had been spent, by 1928 Noguchi was visiting Graham's Manhattan studio on a regular basis. "At that time," he said, Graham "was in her primitive phase, of going back to roots, to the flat foot and solar plexus, the seat of energy being lower down than in the ballet."[43] Fascinated by this, Noguchi would come frequently and "watch her dance, or rather watch her kids dancing anyway. That was my entry into the dance world that was."[44] As a result of their developing relationship, the following year Noguchi sculpted several portrait heads of Graham that he cast into bronze. Two were made because Graham was dissatisfied with the first, even commenting as late as 1989 that the "head [Noguchi] had done of me—I did not like it then and I do not like it now. It had shown a side of my face, my left side, which changes only when I work. Isamu had seen this and caught it. He had seen too deeply this time, even for me." According to Noguchi, Graham "insisted I do the second to be more as she wished; the first was too close to a reality which she aspired to rise above."[45]

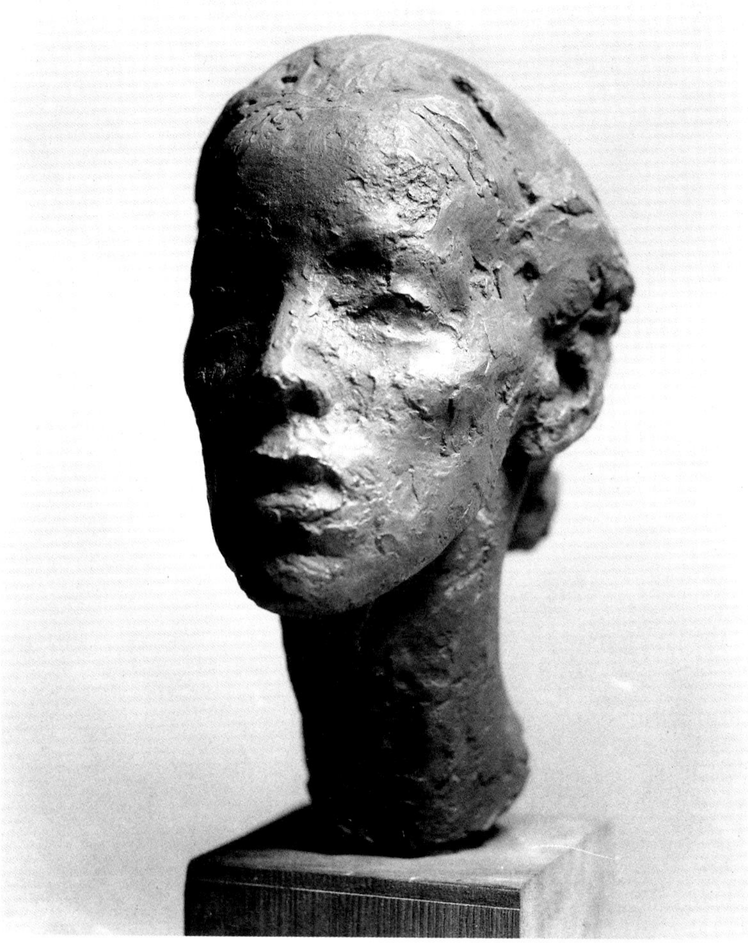

As would also be true of his likeness of Orozco (although it was as yet somewhat more refined), both of Noguchi's busts of Martha Graham feature the evident working marks associated with Rodin's *non-finito* style, which also inspired Brancusi at an important early stage. In the initial rendering, Graham tilts her face downward somewhat tentatively; its bony structure is quite pronounced and her eyes appear shaded. In the second version, her calm, more masklike countenance now facing forward and chin pointed up, Graham projects a greater confidence and sense of self (fig. 10).[46] "One of those heads," Noguchi agreed, "the first one, was rather tragic. She didn't want to be tragic. She wanted to be forward-looking and full of expectation, hope."[47]

By 1932, Noguchi was renting space in the John Murray Anderson School building, near Carnegie Hall on West Fifty-seventh Street where Martha Graham's company practiced; his sister Ailes had been dancing with Graham for two years, and their mother, Leonie, was sewing performers' costumes (she would die unexpectedly the following year). The first set design that Noguchi produced for Graham, *Frontier,* was created not long before he left for Mexico, where Graham had also traveled in 1932 using her own Guggenheim funds, the first awarded to a dancer. Graham's evident enthrallment with Mexico (which Noguchi confirmed) was captured in photographs by her traveling companion, conductor Louis Horst.[48] One affecting shot depicts her posing atop an Aztec pyramid at Teotihuacán near Mexico City, her hands raised in an incantation posture she later successfully adopted for the stage.[49] In her notebooks, Graham would describe *Dark Meadow of the Soul,* a 1946 performance choreographed and danced to music by Carlos Chavez, as an homage to Mexico directly inspired by this "hallowed" experience; Ailes Gilmour cited Mexico's characteristic religious fervor as a major stimulus for Graham's 1931 performance of *Primitive Mysteries* (fig. 11).[50] Indeed, according to Museum of Modern Art curator Rene d'Harnoncourt, who watched a tribal dance with Graham in Mexico, "she was shaken so deeply [by it] that she toppled over in a dead faint." "She was stunned," he said.[51]

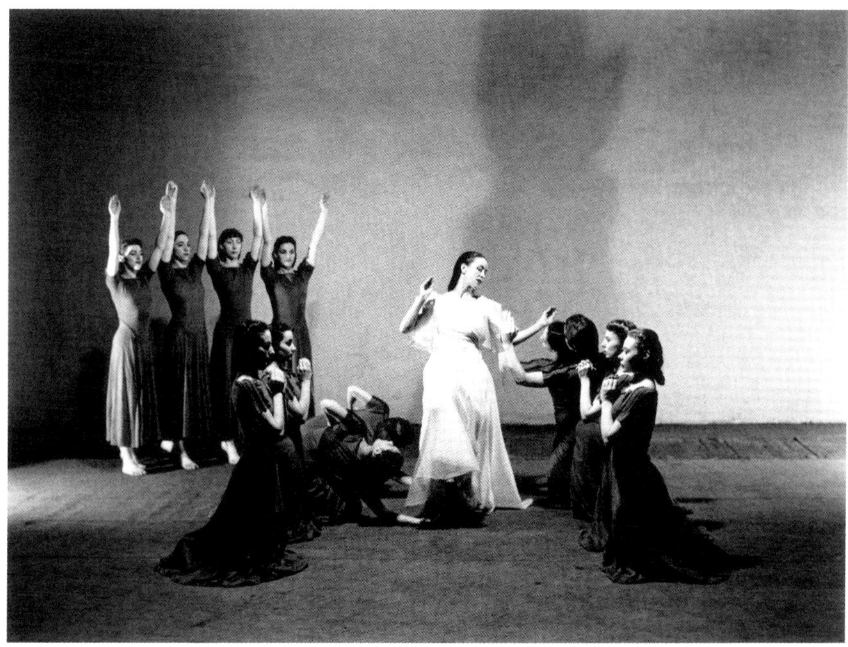

Explaining the famously stark but highly expressive rope and sawhorse fence he devised in 1935 for Graham's *Frontier,* Noguchi made several pertinent points that help us to interpret the extent of her impact on his Mercado relief.[52] "In [her] classes she was teaching this basic use of the total body rather than just the upright body . . . the collapsed body, the body in tension. . . . Since I knew all this, the spatial perspective that I created [for *Frontier*] was . . . a breathing perspective; it's not merely a visual thing but a thing you might move through. It had this sense of inward breathing."[53] Its spare nature also influenced by his knowledge of the minimalist precepts of Japanese Noh theater, *Frontier* marked a crucial beginning for Noguchi: "the genesis of an idea—to wed the total void of theater space to form and action."[54] Using just two horizontally parallel bars "placed upstage center like the barriers of a prairie outpost" and two lengths of heavy cabled rope "extending diagonally upward from both sides of the bars," he created the sense of a vast horizon, in effect, providing Graham a dynamic "volume of air" that her defiantly high kicks, leg extensions, and long, low body stretches could punctuate and activate.[55] As Noguchi asserted, in *Frontier* "it's not the rope that is the sculpture, but it is the space which it creates that is the sculpture." He continued, "It is an illusion of space. It is not flat like a painting used as a backdrop. It is a three-dimensional perspective. It bisects the theater space. Therefore it creates the whole box into a spatial concept. And it is in that spatial concept that Martha moves and creates her dances. In that sense, Martha is a sculptor herself."[56]

Art and dance historians unanimously agree that Isamu Noguchi and Martha Graham's collaboration on *Frontier,* premiering in New York City on April 28, 1935, marked a highly significant aesthetic breakthrough for each. We already know that Noguchi identified this design as the point of departure for all of his subsequent theater work. It certainly demonstrated the germ of a circumstance to be elaborated on a larger, much-heralded scale—once more in the '30s in *Sketches from Chronicle* of 1936, and then more than twenty additional times between 1944 and 1967. This was the astounding collaborative ability of two exceptionally creative minds, seemingly unprecedented in the combined art and theatrical worlds.[57] Even more interestingly, as Neil Printz clarified, "in what may now seem like an odd inversion, for the dancer this new approach would be mapped in space. For the sculptor it would be sited in the body." As if "reading each other's lines," Graham's movements took on special meaning in relation to Noguchi's stage forms, and it was also true the other way around. Their exchange was chiasmic as well as symbiotic.[58]

According to dancer May O'Donnell, many of Graham's performances at the time she and Noguchi first made contact were representative "of the social time—all of the protest, the anger—those kinds of qualities."[59] Such late 1920s through mid-'30s works as *Revolt, Immigrant (Steerage Strike),* and *Chronicle* linked physical and psychological tension onstage to Graham's passionate feelings of protest against injustice. But, moving well beyond the lyrical, decorative, and exoticist approach of her training with Ruth St. Denis and Ted Shawn, Graham's dances of this era, many of which are preserved in photographs by Soichi Sunami, demonstrate much more than simply her desire to right social inequity.[60] As phrased by another company member, Sophie Maslow, they establish that "Martha Graham had discovered something in the way the body is used—her way of making the body an expressive instrument—that nobody else had ever discovered." Maslow continued, "It was through Martha that I understood the quality of a gesture. Whatever you did had an emotional quality." Jane Dudley added, "Your whole body had to be spun to such a high level to execute Martha's technique."[61]

In accomplishing poses according to Martha Graham's evolving lexicon, the vitality and muscular energy of her dancers was repurposed to metaphorize the intensity of psychological states. At a very early age Graham had gleaned this central precept from her father, an "alienist," as physicians specializing in nerve disorders and human psychology were called at that time:

My first dancing lesson was from my father when I was about four years old. He started to discipline me because evidently I was rather willful: "Martha," he said, "movement never lies." Later when I began to understand, he elaborated: "That which you are comes out in your movement. You can cover it up to just a point, and then there comes the revealing involuntary movement that opens the whole book for anyone to read. Movement is like a barometer, a barometer of the soul's weather. It tells you what the person feels and how immediately that person is in the instant." [62]

Martha Graham's subsequent dancing and teaching opened up a new vocabulary of movement allowing, as Maslow put it, "anything in human experience" to be put onstage.

In her 1991 book focusing on Graham's dance theory and training, Marian Horosko provides a useful syllabus of Graham's recommended movements, annotated with quotations from the master teacher herself. The wording of these commentaries is often illuminating. For example, when sitting in fourth position with the front leg, knee up and foot on the floor, Graham advised her acolytes to summon up "a demonic — fierce — use of the muscles" to best perform this pose. [63] Patricia Richmond has summarized the primary tenets Graham taught: "Among the two defining aspects of Graham's technique, the first was her principle of contraction and release, an exaggeration of the body's natural breathing pattern, which, when put into action, resulted in a whip-like snap of movement from the torso out toward the limbs. The second was her emphasis on — rather than defiance of — the force of gravity in her work through the use of falls and movements weighted in a low center of gravity, sometimes from a seated base." "All falls," Graham herself explained, "are *into* the body — *into* yourself." "You were always carving a place for yourself in space. Now those were her words," recited Gertrude Shurr, a participant in *Primitive Mysteries*, "and the physicality of that was so great." [64]

Writing in 1936, the same year Noguchi sculpted his Mercado relief, Blanche Evan detailed the warm-up routine that Martha Graham put her dancers through each day, echoes of which appear in his mural (fig. 12). "Seated on the floor with legs stretched wide," she said, "we are impelled head-first into a series of complicated shapes stretching every single muscle the body possesses. The body is placed in such positions that it becomes imperative to use intense muscular power to get you from one position to another. The terminology for the torso positions consists of three words: 'release, contraction, forced release.'" [65] As is true of *Death* (now also known as *Lynched Figure*) overlaying onto *History as Seen from Mexico, 1936*, the form, technical mastery, intensity, and expressive drama built into Graham's exercises — maneuvers we know Noguchi watched avidly — adds vital nuance to understanding the formation of his trademark approach, so eloquently characterized by Printz as the "leveraging of physicality for a metaphysics of space." [66] Noguchi's remarkable understanding of the intensity and vigor

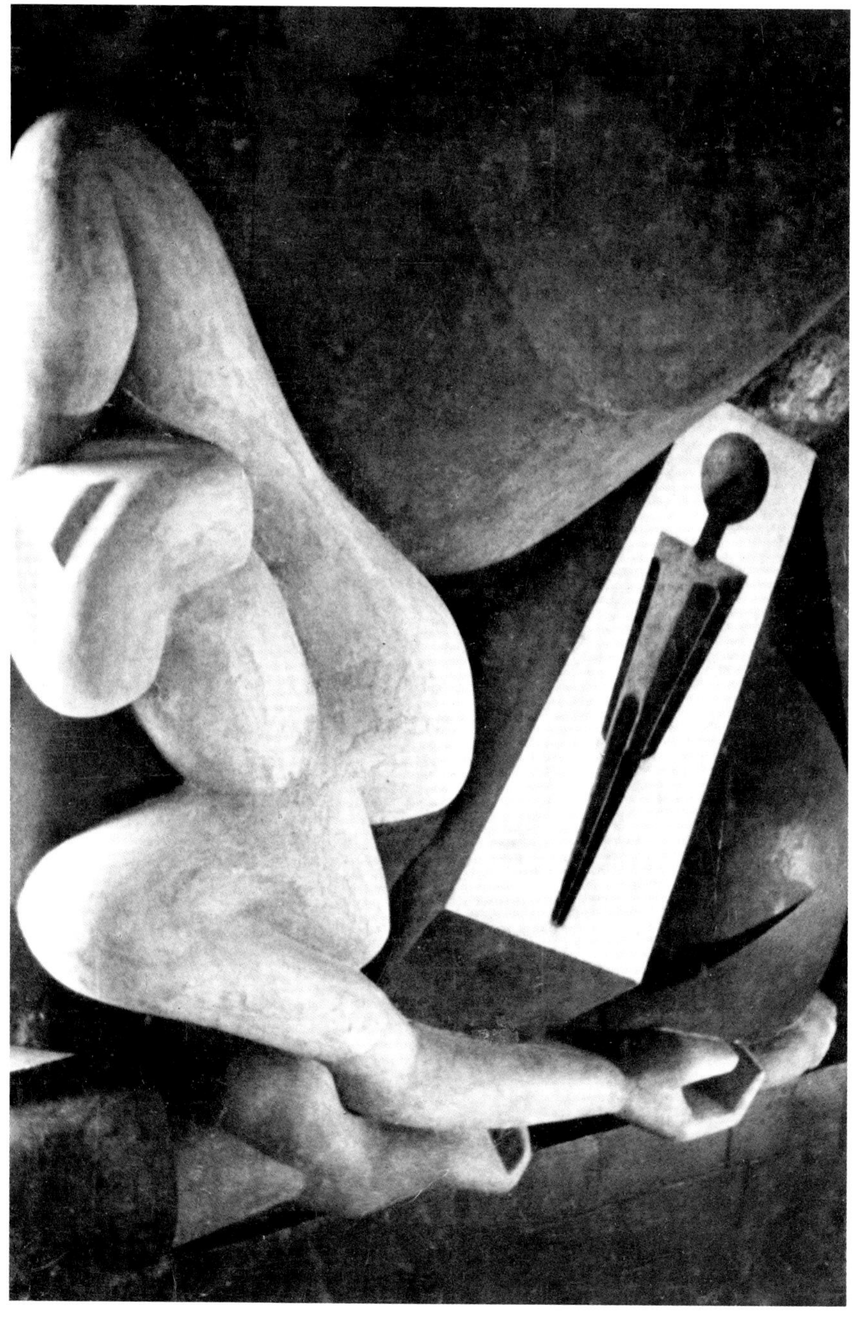

of contemporary dance is deeply implicated in the "powerful effect" of his Mercado relief. In turn, his experience in Mexico would prove foundational for advancing his later goal of developing "humanistic sculpture within a public sphere." Arguably, Noguchi achieved his greatest success at this goal when designing for the stage.[67]

Dance as a Weapon

In times like these, when revolutionary art is the banner for a class marching into power, the artist . . . speaks for and to a rising social class, and realizes he must be the crystallizer and organizer of their feelings. This places an enormous responsibility upon him. . . . In the modern dance, the task is less simple than one believes.[68]

— EDNA OCKO, 1935

Throughout the 1930s, a number of Martha Graham's company members — Sophie Maslow, Jane Dudley, and Ailes Gilmour included — also belonged to socialist dance troupes, despite the fact that participants in the latter typically "looked with distaste and even anger at the attempt of the bourgeois dancers to make the subject matter of the dance abstract."[69] With raised arms, clenched fists, and energetic lunges, leftist dancers performed in venues accessible to the common worker, such as trade union meeting halls, and at strikes and demonstrations (fig. 13). According to Horosko, Ailes (actually Noguchi's half-sister) was active with the New Dance League and Workers' Dance League, especially with Bill Matons's Experimental Unit, an offshoot of both.[70] She and Matons later danced with Helen Tamiris in WPA Federal Dance Theatre productions, including *How Long, Brethren?* and *Adelante,* in 1937 and 1939, respectively.[71] *How Long, Brethren?* based on Lawrence Gellert's collection "Negro Songs of Protest," featured a segment on the plight of the so-called Scottsboro Boys. The nationally prominent story of nine teenaged African American males wrongly accused and tried numerous times for the rape of two white women on a train traveling through Alabama was to play a dramatic role in the experiences of Guston and Kadish, discussed in Chapter 2. Along these lines, before Noguchi left for Los Angeles and Mexico, Matons's Unit performed a piece called *Lynch* at a Manhattan Dance League Festival in June 1935.[72]

Because they "found in the revolutionary movement the vitality and perspective they wanted in their dancing," participants in New York's various socialist groups were deemed, as dancer/critic Edna Ocko wrote in *New Theatre* magazine, "genteelly pink." Shared goals of comrades "stepping left" included the creation and performance of realistic sketches "bearing the message of the fighting, class-conscious proletariat" (fig. 14).[73] General agitational subjects; folk tales; songs for Soviet youth; protests against jingoism, "capitalist crimes," the arbitrary attitude of the police to the dispossessed, or Negro mistreatment; as well as militant antiwar cycles, were prominent in the early '30s. These gradually shifted to less Marxist-oriented works based on agendas of the Popular Front (especially so-called "retooled American-

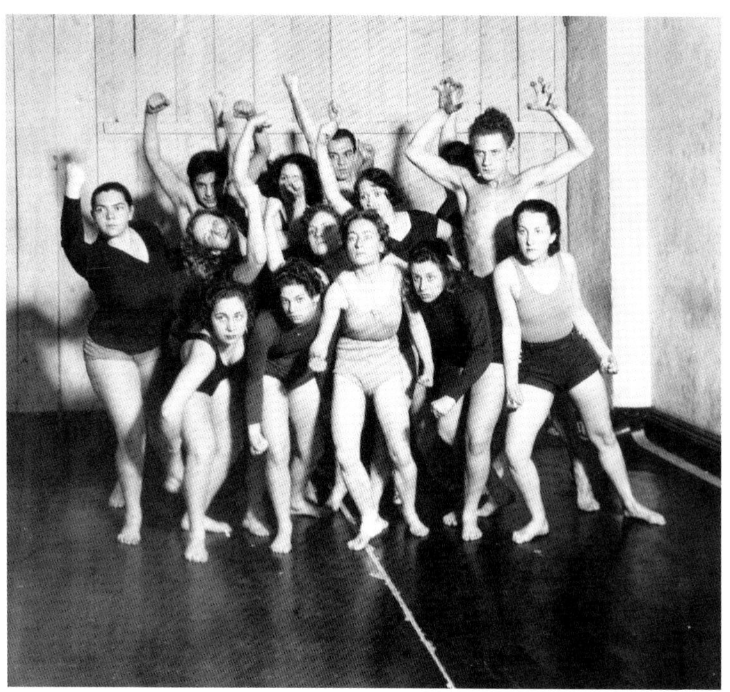

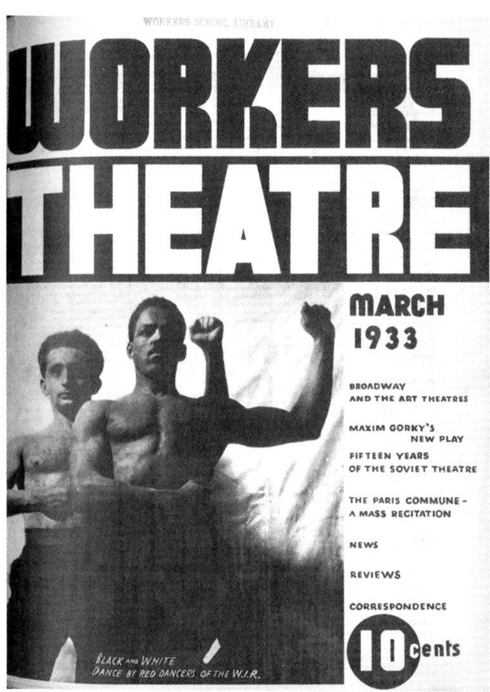

13 Members of the New Dance Group in *Improvisation*, 1932. New Dance Group Collection, Music Division, Library of Congress (017.00.00).

14 Hy Boris and Ad Bates in Edith Segal's *Black and White*, March 1933 cover of *Worker's Theatre*. Published in New York by Workers' Laboratory Theatre, 1931–33. Courtesy of Tamiment Library, New York University.

ism") and more specific themes in the news. In addition to the Scottsboro trials, popular topics included the National Recovery Act, support for the Lincoln Battalion of Americans fighting for democracy in the Spanish Civil War, and the rise of fascism and plight of the European Jews, to cite some major examples.[74]

Danced in a style more histrionic, sorrowful or satirical, heroic and/or sentimentalized than the Martha Graham Company's typical performances (Horst believed art should transcend the everyday and never proselytize), the dance leagues' adaptation of movement as a way to express and objectify deep-seated convictions and stirring revolutionary fervor often played to overflow audiences. This succeeded in introducing dance to sections of the public hitherto unacquainted with the art.[75] The importance to their militant aims of Graham's "quick, sharp, angular movements" in order to "give an impression of action, of power" was unmistakable. Reviewing the Theatre Union Group's *Anti-War Cycle*, Jean Bolan noted that Graham's technique is "eminently fitted for working class motifs," although she considered it unfortunate "that Martha Graham herself misuses them for religious ideas, serving the needs of the decadent bourgeoisie."[76] Bolan advocates that Graham's "interpretation of the Machine Age" should be "transplanted . . . to the progressive uses of a revolutionary class." Ocko, correspondingly critical in 1934 of Graham's "self-indulgent" approach, nevertheless had to grant the following year that she had become "the greatest dancer America has produced since Isadora Duncan," and was unquestionably one of the world's outstanding exponents of modern dance:

> [Graham] has developed a science of modern dance movement which seems remarkably suited to make the body a fit instrument for expression. And this rigorous training presents itself to me, at least, as an admirable technic for the revolutionary dance. It has, above all, strength and endurance; it permits of amazing gradations in dynamics; it embodies dramatic elements of militance and courage. Its most delicate moments are fraught with latent power. When the body stands, it seems immovable. The body in motion is belligerent and defiant. It seems almost impossible to do meaningless dances with this equipment.[77]

Writing admiringly of Jane Dudley's "daring conceptions" presented at a Workers' Dance League concert (inspired in part by William Gropper's anticapitalist cartoons for the magazine *New Masses*) one critic put his finger on the pluses and minuses of this alternate, more political mode of productivity, considered by many a "corrective" to Graham's rigorously defended antipropaganda stance. In Dudley's piece, Simon Hall proclaimed, she "revealed her powerful grasp of proletarian subject matter, while her imagination, steeped in understanding of the worker, evolved his life of work, war and struggle with a sympathy sheared of overemphasis or simplification."[78] This encomium, probably written in response to a 1934 Civic Repertory Theater recital by Dudley, Nadia Chilkovsky, and Miriam Blecher, contrasted with the opinion of another reviewer, Joseph Mitchell. The latter's sarcastically titled reproof in the *New York World Telegram*, "Capitalism Is Tottering, Declare Girls with a Mission, So They'll Dance and Dance Until Revolution Comes," is illustrated with pictures of Blecher and Chilkovsky posing rather fiercely. These three women and others like them intent on considering dance "a weapon for the struggling revolutionary working class," Mitchell points out, believed that technique should never be an end in itself and that ideology should be dramatized as "dictated by the idea or emotion to be expressed."[79]

It is not difficult to presume that Noguchi would have been well aware of various and sundry calls in the left-wing press for Graham to jettison more "superficial" aesthetic, mystical, and/or universalizing topics and concentrate on making good on sympathies which Ocko said—or at least hoped—were "avowedly one with the revolutionary dance."[80] In addition to *Lynch*, in which Ailes Gilmour almost certainly performed, she danced at least several times with Matons at the Mecca Temple on West Fifty-fifth Street in programs of militantly leftist propaganda content after leaving the Graham Company.[81] Noguchi might well have attended those performances, stopped in to classes given by the New Dance Group that Gilmour likely took, or visited her rehearsals with Matons's Experimental Unit, although no evidence parallel to his admission of viewing Graham's practice sessions exists to confirm this.

Nonetheless, comparison of Noguchi's narration in *A Sculptor's World* of the thematic content of *History as Seen from Mexico, 1936,* and the parallel rhetorical imagery he deployed at the Mercado Abelardo L. Rodríguez referencing the repertoire of poses prevalent in Depression-era workers' dance argues persuasively for his direct knowledge of the world in which Ailes was an active participant. In the meantime, reacting to the looming shadow of war, some of Graham's newer works—the tautly expressed anguish and despair of *Steps in the Street,* a seven-minute section of *Sketches from Chronicle* of 1936, for instance—mirrored concepts that Noguchi was developing simultaneously.[82]

How Different Was Mexico!

Now, our "now" includes not only the present with the residue of the past, but the future lived already in our minds. Hope here is reality in another place, and if not in another place then in another time. No one country can any longer be historically dealt with except as an integral part of our ever more aware world.[83]

— ISAMU NOGUCHI, 1936

Even taking into consideration his identity issues as a Japanese-American and concomitant struggle for personal acceptance, much of what Noguchi said about his participation at the Mercado Abelardo L. Rodríguez matches up with standard Depression-era leftist goals, including those of his sister's passionate activity, the workers' dance movement. "How different was Mexico!" Noguchi wrote in his memoir. "Here I suddenly no longer felt estranged as an artist; artists were useful people, a part of the community." Elsewhere asserting that he had undertaken this unusual and somewhat difficult commission to get out of the "rut" of doing portraits, Noguchi described his "Indian market" efforts in *A Sculptor's World* as "a real attempt at a direct communication through sculpture, with no ulterior or money-making motive," admitting that the version of contemporary events projected there was "no doubt biased by my bitter view."[84]

"I felt a great sense of liberty at that time," Noguchi told Paul Cummings, "and also a feeling of being with the people. I was expressing something that they could understand. When I came here I had the same feeling they had." In retrospect, Noguchi would deem working in Mexico City during the mid-1930s "marvelous" and "a privilege," because so many he met there were open to art and "artists' propaganda," even when articulated by someone from abroad. This seemed to him a very welcoming situation, an antidote, as it were, to the dispiriting feelings of outsiderness he'd experienced in New York. "I was able to shout and do what I pleased," he said, "and I was happy."[85]

Standing in front of *History as Seen from Mexico, 1936* in 1987—the only time he ever returned to the Mercado—Noguchi confirmed to Mexican Televisa that he had started this somewhat mercurial composition at the far left and worked his way over to the right. A bit counterintuitively then, what appears to be the finale of his chronicle, embodying a vision of peace and progress achieved through the wonders of science and technology, was actually created first. The gripped-fist standing kouros pose Noguchi gave to a naked Aztec boy sculpted to look as if he were standing against a limestone pilaster at the mural's farthermost edge clearly reiterates one of the compact, potent gestures that Martha Graham featured in 1931 in *Primitive Mysteries* and would use again to great effect while he was away, in *Steps in the Street* (fig. 15).

This proud youth carved in low bas-relief was evidently meant by Noguchi to encapsulate Mexico's heritage and storied past. He stares intently in the direction of stacked amoebic shapes and a working chemical beaker, items curiously preceded by Albert Einstein's famous notation for time-space. Narrating the Mercado mural's themes some three decades later, the artist included a droll political anecdote referencing both Einstein and visionary architect Buckminster Fuller that obviously still tickled his fancy. (Noguchi met Fuller in 1929 at the Greenwich Village artists' hangout Romany Marie's and had sculpted his head in a gleaming futuristic chrome-plated bronze that very same year. He would later borrow Fuller's car to get from Los Angeles to Mexico.)[86] In his Mexican relief, Noguchi wrote, "there were war, crimes of the church and 'labor' triumphant, yet the future looked out brightly in the figure of an Indian boy, observing Einstein's equation for energy. In answer to my request, Bucky Fuller had sent me a fifty-word telegram explaining the equation." But, as he added with a wink, "I could also appreciate the sardonic humor of the man who used to come by to watch me work, saying that the E=mc² really meant *Estados=Muchos Cabrones* (the State=Many SOBs)."[87]

Moving beyond Einstein's equation and past the microbe cells and chemical beaker, Noguchi next included a radio tower section (or some other girder-like structure) sketched into cement, followed by bundled farm implements, including a spade, hoe, and rake. Perhaps directly articulated as such in conversation with the artist, these were interpreted by Carlos Mérida in a 1937 guide to the Mercado complex as extolling the possibilities

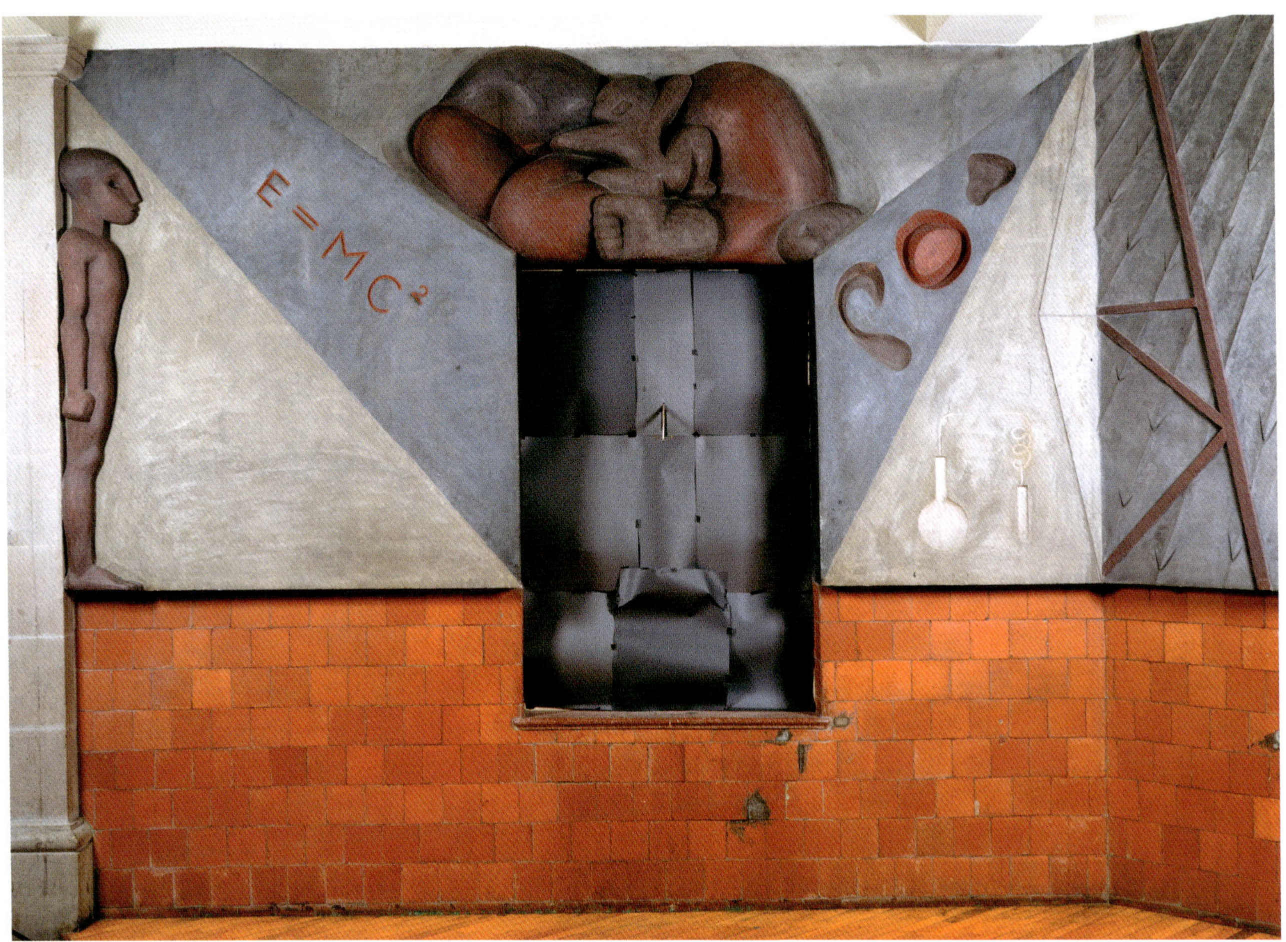

15 Isamu Noguchi, Detail from *History Mexico (History as Seen from Mexico in 1936)*, 1936. Cement, pigment, 72 ft., 2 ³⁄₁₆ in. (22 m). © 2012 The Isamu Noguchi Foundation and Garden Museum, New York / Artists Rights Society (ARS), New York.

of Socialism.[88] But an actual window intervenes between Einstein's notation and this resonant set of tools. Above it, in imitation perhaps of a decorated cathedral spandrel, Noguchi compressed an amply curving figural group into a relatively small, obliquely angled, and roughly U-shaped space.

By adding the microbe forms and test tube into his composition, Noguchi had perhaps intended another explicit allusion, in this case to a highly controversial component of Diego Rivera's 1933 Rockefeller Center mural whose desecration created an international furor. By the time Noguchi was working at the Rodríguez market, Rivera had already re-created this fresco, *Man at the Crossroads*, in Mexico City's elegant Palacio de Bellas Artes located nearby. But Rivera's inclusion of germs had a contrastingly disquieting purpose, and Noguchi's lunette perhaps more specifically addressed one of his own works perceived as censored.[89] This was *Birth*, the marble companion sculpture to *Death* he'd based on observations of the maternity ward at Manhattan's Bellevue Hospital. Whereas the subject of *Death* was

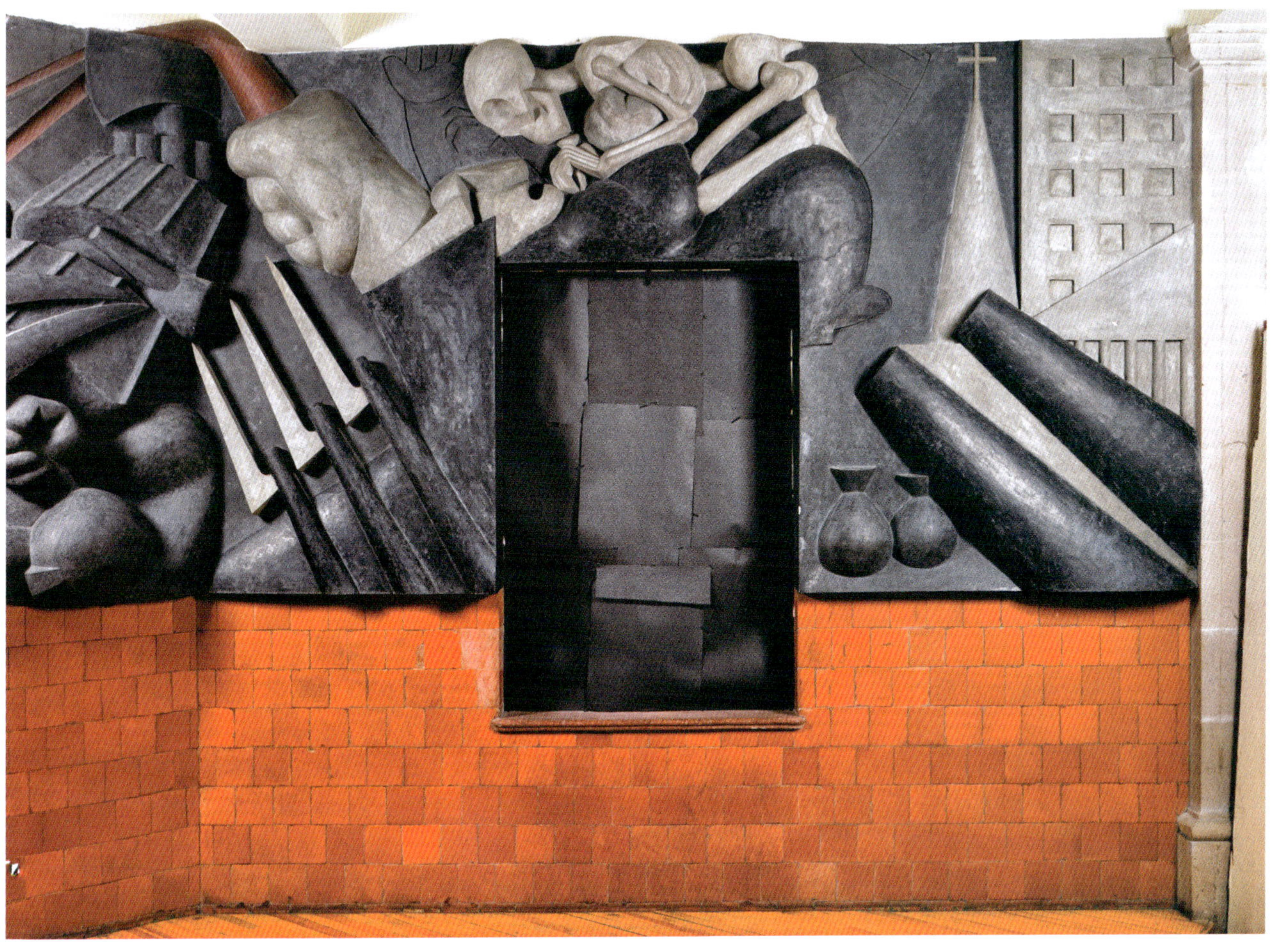

obviously shocking to many, Marie Harriman apparently deemed Noguchi's presumption to portray such an extremely intimate female activity as
even more objectionable. When she turned down *Birth* for inclusion in his
1935 New York exhibition, Noguchi, angry and frustrated, destroyed all but
the head of the original work.[90] In Harriman's opinion at least, *Death* was
"redeemed" by its social-protest qualities.

Reprising the subject of *Birth*—a topic common in Mexican murals—
Noguchi delineated an obviously indigenous newborn child. Viewed from
the rear, this baby is nestled at the crotch of his recumbent mother, her head
and upper torso hidden behind a massive stomach and thickly folded peasant legs. This vignette stands in diametric contrast to another, also placed
over a window space, located around a corner and closer to the opposite
end. "Shades of Posada!" Noguchi said, as he inserted into this section of his
Mercado composition "a fat 'capitalist' being murdered by a skeleton," a nod
to the nineteenth-century Mexican cartoonist whose mordant depictions

16 Isamu Noguchi, Detail from *History Mexico (History as Seen from Mexico in 1936)*, 1936. Cement, pigment, 72 ft., 2 $\frac{3}{16}$ in. (22 m). © 2012 The Isamu Noguchi Foundation and Garden Museum, New York/Artists Rights Society (ARS), New York.

of local politics and mores in the guise of *calaveras* were special Mexican favorites (see fig. 99).[91] Noguchi's contorted, Posada-inspired skeleton is shown locked in a deathly embrace with an overweight capitalist, identified as such by his money bags, girth, and fancy top hat (fig. 16).

The recognizable attributes of this very Marxist conceit, routinely featured in murals by Orozco and Rivera, show up elsewhere at the Mercado in the work of O'Higgins and, slightly modified, by the Greenwoods as well. But they would have been familiar to Noguchi from Gropper's illustrations in *New Masses* and countless other American leftist cartoons.[92] At his mural's right-hand edge, Noguchi provided an additionally well-known condemnatory context by including rendering in shallow relief of the Wall Street Stock Exchange. Adding a simplified outline of downtown Manhattan's Trinity Church implicates the complicity of organized religion in capitalist doings. Two cannons and three bayonets flanking the skeleton's window decry the profitability of war; before Hitler and Stalin signed their 1939 nonaggression pact, this too was a common workers' theater complaint.

In Noguchi's *History as Seen from Mexico, 1936,* cause, effect, and hopeful aftermath apparently unwind in reverse, expounded with additional force by varying levels of action, scale, and relief throughout. In some sections the mural is as much as sixty centimeters deep (more than twenty-three inches); as noted, other areas are almost flat. Although certain details strongly reflect the iconographic impact of Rivera prominent as well in panels by other members of the Mercado team,[93] as Oles points out Noguchi's decision to employ tinted cement, concrete, and brick demonstrates knowledge of the technical advances championed by Siqueiros. These relate to the latter's choice to use industrial methods developed in Los Angeles with Neutra's advice.

Noguchi's "What's the Matter with Sculpture?" recommends a number of procedural innovations pioneered by Siqueiros, with whom he had already been in contact. In April 1936 Siqueiros set up an Experimental Workshop near Union Square in Manhattan to investigate the use of new industrial methods and materials for propaganda and other artistic purposes (see fig. 57 and Chapter 3). Revealing his acquaintance with these, Noguchi writes in *Art Front,* "We must become familiar with the modern ways of handling plastic and crystalline matter (the spray-gun, pneumatic hammer, etc.)." "For any given work," he states, "we should use that precise material best suited to its size, to cost and durability," touting a "cheap and quick" characteristic of cement especially prized in poorer countries. His urging to "be not afraid to be even 'vulgar' in the use of color" likely resulted from direct experience with the brilliant hues of Mexican pueblo-style architecture.

Thanking O'Higgins and Pujol for color suggestions (the latter also incorporated concrete into a small portion of his own Mercado mural) Noguchi articulated exactly how he had fabricated and then tinted *History as Seen from Mexico, 1936* in a variety of shades of gray punctuated by black, beige, and an extraordinary reddish salmon pink. "First," he writes, "the sketch was enlarged onto the brick wall. Then bricks built in where thickness was required, then carved in and out. This took about two months. After this, cement, large marble aggregate, and lime was thrown on and the forms defined. The final coat contained fine aggregate color and cement mixed dry to assume color when applied with a trowel and polished. The job was completed seven months after starting."[94] Noguchi's imaginative disrespect for the room's oddly shaped wall angles—in some places he seems to go right through them—is another sign of his attention to the innovations of Siqueiros.[95]

Returning to the more tranquil and munificent left-hand portion of *History as Seen from Mexico, 1936*, just beyond the farm implements and right next to an upright propeller placed before a factory is where Noguchi introduced a jarring, oversized, protuberant Communist fist (see fig. 5); he would later express the most regret about highlighting this combative icon. Making allusion, she said, to "the struggle of the classes against Fascism, Imperialism and Capitalism," Marion Greenwood inserted a similar element into her industrialization narrative, which also incorporated scale inconsistencies, although much less dramatically. In some of the patio areas, O'Higgins, one of the founders of LEAR (*Liga de Escritores y Artistas Revolucionarios*, a group whose goals paralleled those of the American Communist–run John Reed Clubs), likewise featured a fist, as well as other comparably blatant propaganda and agitprop symbols (fig. 17). Articulating his own

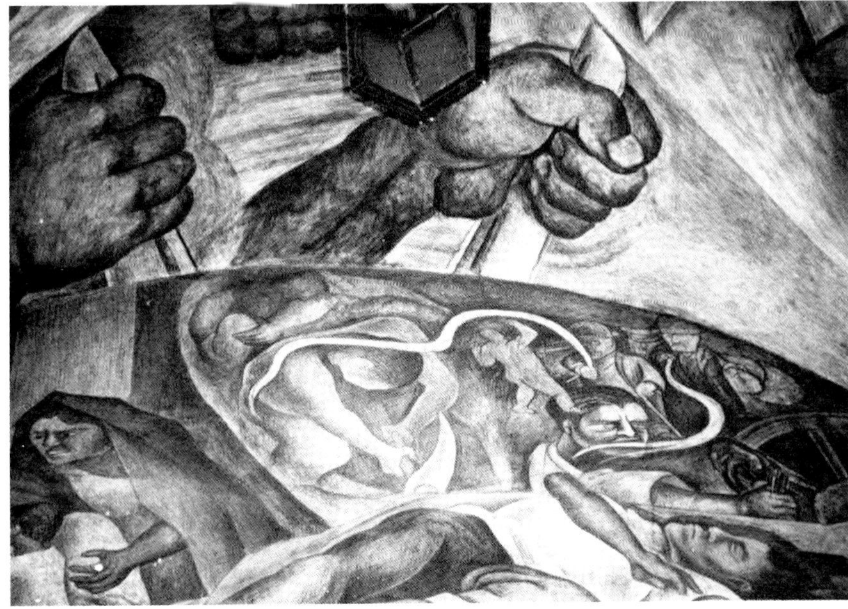

17 Pablo O'Higgins, *The Worker's Struggle Against Monopolies* (detail), 1935. Mercado Abelardo L. Rodríguez, Mexico City. Photo: Ellen G. Landau.

radical intentions, O'Higgins added the inscription "Arms for the Workers to Crush Reaction" to a ceiling vault, just as the Greenwood sisters inscribed in Spanish the Marxist slogan "Workers of the World, Unite!" on their jointly painted panel at the crest of the stairwell space.[96]

Noguchi's giant hand (the largest of several included) is followed by another engineering girder plus four angled pulleys whose parallel line of ropes suggesting technological progress demarcates a new thematic division. The ensuing central vignette surrounds another almost square window (fig. 18). Below and on both sides of it the artist sculpted figures exhibiting poses traditionally associated with lamentation, the title and subject of one of Graham's most celebrated 1930 solo works. To the left of this window a muscular male supporting, pietà-like, the arms and malnourished torso of a collapsed companion is depicted in medium relief. Bare-chested and unshod, the latter is almost fully prone; his inert legs stretch the length of a ledge situated beneath the window frame. Interestingly, Noguchi chose to place his signature on this dead (or dying) man's foot. Opposite his tragic pair, whose combined bodily manipulations restate the theme of homage to a fallen comrade popular in leftist dance, we find a small child's coffin, its inhabitant's tiny silhouette etched on top.[97] Pitched both downward and outward into the room, and tucked into space created by a grief-stricken mother's sinking back and windmilling arms, this tiny casket poignantly reminds the viewer of the corollary ravages to famine and war.

While certain aspects of Noguchi's Mercado iconography undoubtedly resemble idealistic imagery developed by others before he came, the way it is displayed emphatically does not. His "bigger," more rousing oratorical and allegorical content differs substantially from the other American and the Mexican team members' comparatively staid and conservative styles.[98] Noguchi's central supporting male facing left (perhaps intended to represent "labor awakening") might have been inspired by the Mexican anthropology museum's famous Olmec wrestler from Veracruz. But the linear tension and physical clarity of this figure's low-to-the-ground position certainly demonstrates as well the sculptor's thorough familiarity with Martha Graham's exercises and their expressive wallop employed on stage.[99] Graham featured obviously related emotivist movements in *Adolescence* of 1929, employing them even more successfully two years later in *Primitive Mysteries*.

That Noguchi's central triad of sorrowing personages reads as a stirring accusation is also due in part to his reuse of Brancusi's trademark simplification and condensation, translated to serve a more compelling dramaturgic and declamatory purpose. "The wall I did in Mexico was to be against Brancusi," he would later assert, "because not a pure, pure thing but very much related to people. If too much influenced by Brancusi, you become decorative, esoteric, separate, exclusive."[100] Rejecting the cultural populism

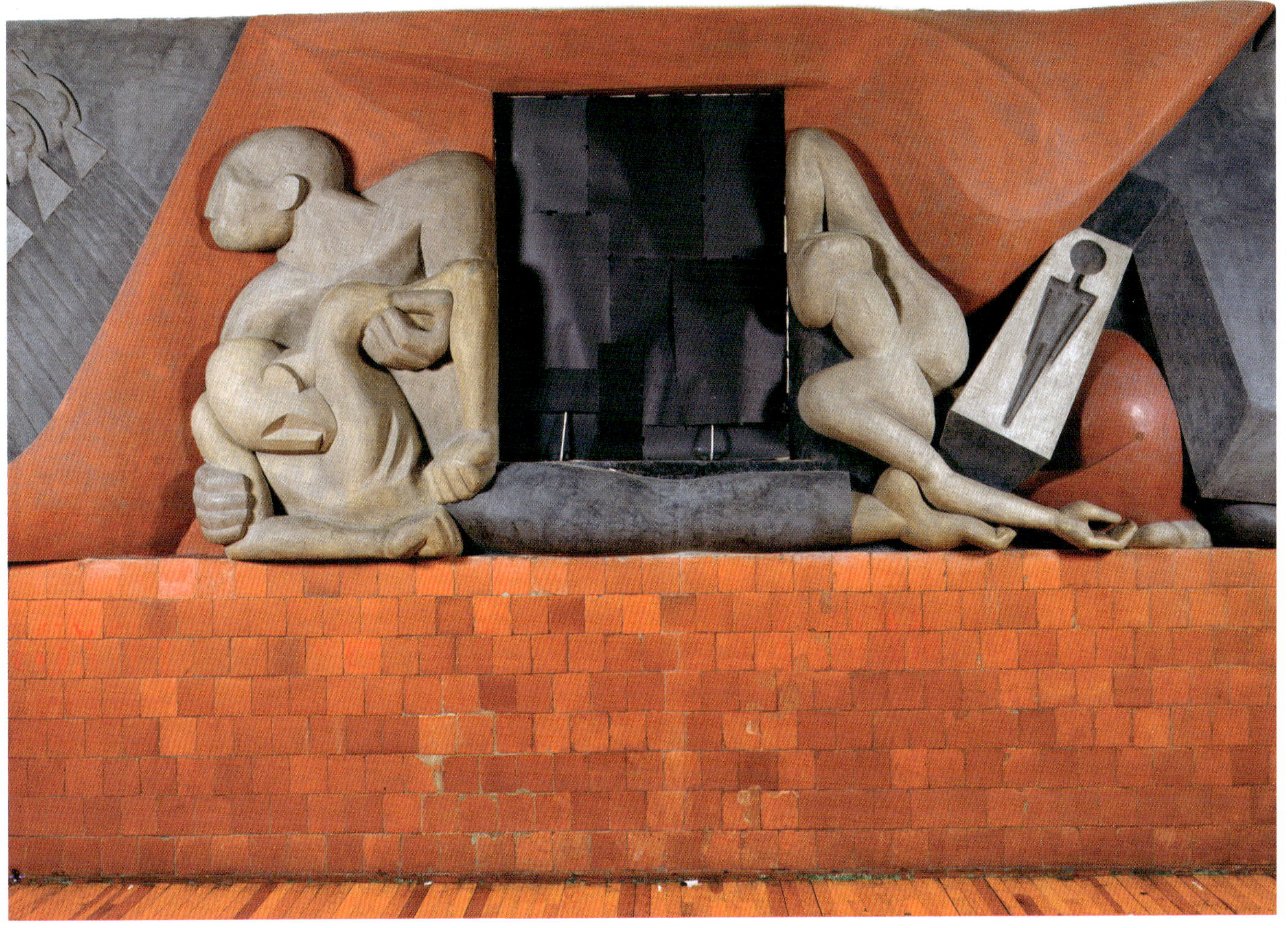

espoused by his fellow Mercado participants as too closely allied to local conditions and Cardenista government rhetoric, Noguchi adopted a more universalizing vocabulary and perspective.[101] In this—as Graham did in *Chronicle*—he more artfully reconfigured the "morally significant" fervor, sincerity, and militancy typical of socialist dance.[102]

Moving even farther to the right, Noguchi's message takes on a greatly increased plastic presence and a larger, more commanding and contemporary perspective. It is here that his ambiguous goal of communicating "history" as he saw it unfolding, in that time and from that place, finds direct fulfillment.[103]

18 Isamu Noguchi, Detail from *History Mexico (History as Seen from Mexico in 1936)*, 1936. Cement, pigment, 72 ft., 2 3/16 in. (22 m). © 2012 The Isamu Noguchi Foundation and Garden Museum, New York / Artists Rights Society (ARS), New York.

A Call for Action

Chronicle does not attempt to show the actualities of war, rather does it, by evoking war's images, set forth the fateful prelude to war, portray the devastation of spirit left in its wake, and suggest an answer.

— ORIGINAL PROGRAM NOTE, Guild Theater, New York, 1936

Figuring the trials and tribulations of the collective body politic, and articulated through reference to the grammar of modern dance, Noguchi's central figures at the Mercado Abelardo L. Rodríguez inspire a call for action against the gathering forces of evil. This invocation, produced a year before Picasso painted *Guernica,* is reinforced by the lamentation group's narrative placement literally separating war from peace — as well as presentation of a red banner wafting above. Situated between the child's coffin pointing left and the row of sharp bayonets angled right, the dominant scene to come is more striking in its assertive anti-fascist iconography and contrastingly aggressive in its engagement of actual and fictive space.

Noguchi crowded into the most deliberately complex section of his overall tableau not merely the "shades" of Posada, he also inserted a boldly delineated isometric projection that closely resembles one section of Orozco's massive Dartmouth cross.[104] This structure tapers downward toward a corpse (fallen from it?) whose egg-shaped Brancusi-like head comes to rest on an open book, possibly a signal of the impending death of knowledge. Unidentified hands are inserted between, one reaching directly toward the cross fragment's deeply shadowed cleft. Beyond the dead man's sunken ribcage (his lighter coloring draws the viewer's attention) a double line of armed soldiers, denoted by their row of helmets, marches past two outsized bulging and twisting male nudes gripping machetes. The sharpened blades of these tools for cutting grain cross the caterpillar tracks of a tank whose turret and gun are aimed to destroy the Nazis (fig. 19).

Above the mobilized fighters, at the very top of this area, Noguchi dramatically positioned a gargantuan swastika scored in blood by the tails of a whip wielded by yet another closed fist. This hand emerges from a disembodied (but suit-clad) arm raised to the left of the skeleton and right of the bayonets. An oversized hatchet or ax (one of the primary tools used in making this work) is inserted at the uppermost right. In the roughly triangular space formed where the bottom point of the instrument of Christ's sacrifice meets the Nazis' twisted cross, a bucranium or ox head (symbolic of strength since Neolithic times) and a ghostly dancer take their appointed place. The dancer's upward reaching arms re-create another signature position from *Primitive Mysteries,* one first experienced by Martha Graham atop

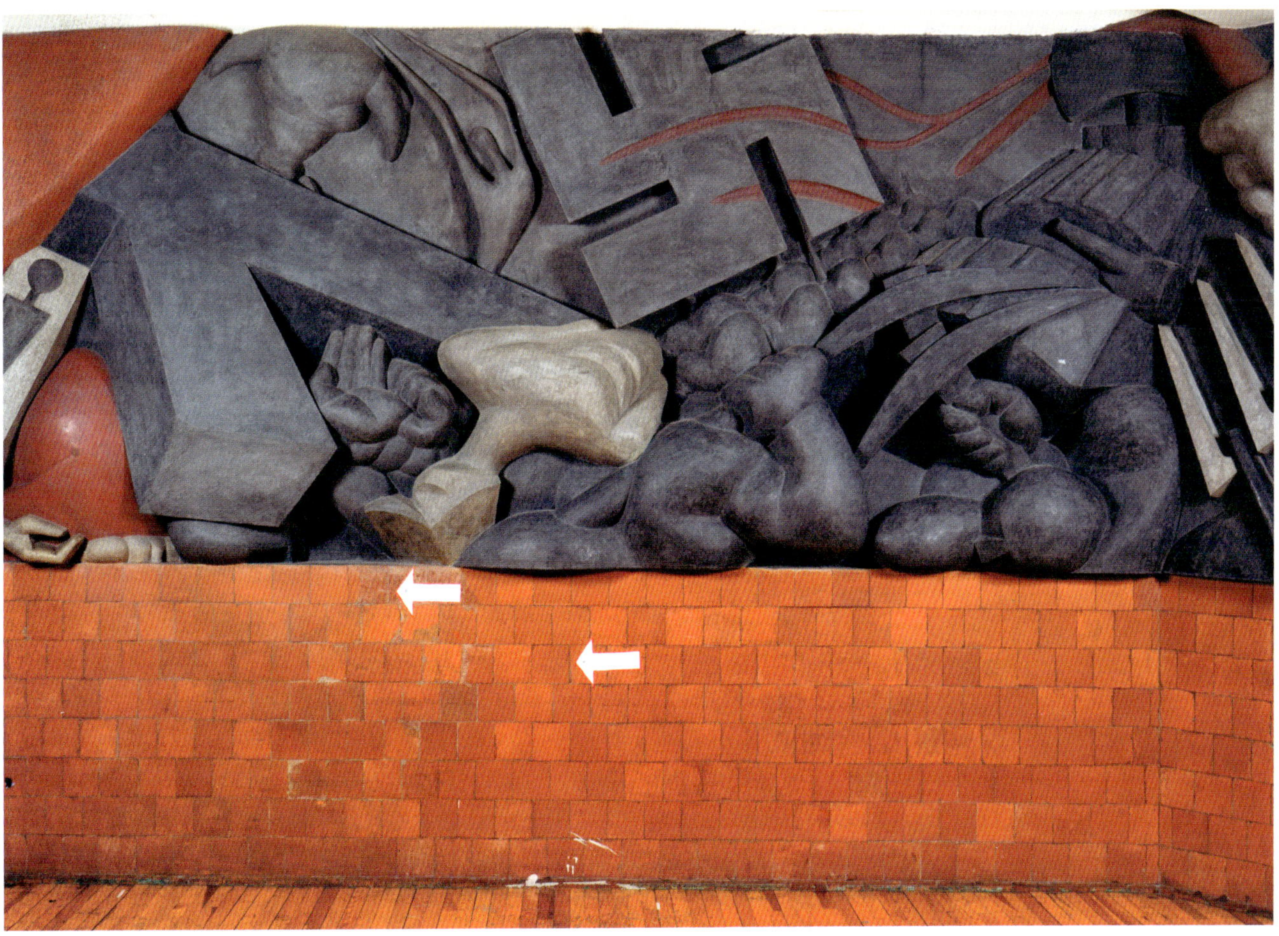

a pyramid in Mexico. The dancer's writhing posture also approximates other of Graham's virtuoso performances of the early 1930s, including *Ekstasis* and *Satyric Festival Song*.

Skillfully juxtaposing associate and dissociate imagery, united through rhythm and gesture, Noguchi's pictorially explosive antiwar montage is electric in its vitality and unambiguous in its message, a veritable blitzkrieg of conflict, impulse, and instinct. Its orchestration seems roughly to follow Jane Dudley's 1934 advice for organizing a "Mass Dance." Careful direction, Dudley explained in an article published in *New Theatre*, can "set simple but clear patterns of group movement into a form that presents our revolutionary ideas movingly and meaningfully." "Think of the possibilities," she enumerated, "marching, creeping, hesitating, rushing forward, being thrown back, the group splitting apart, scattered in all directions, uniting, coming forward, backing away, being thrown down, rising up . . ." "In this way," she articulated, "piece by piece the dance is built."[105]

19 Isamu Noguchi, Detail from *History Mexico (History as Seen from Mexico in 1936)*, 1936. Cement, pigment, 72 ft., 2 3/16 in. (22 m). © 2012 The Isamu Noguchi Foundation and Garden Museum, New York/Artists Rights Society (ARS), New York.

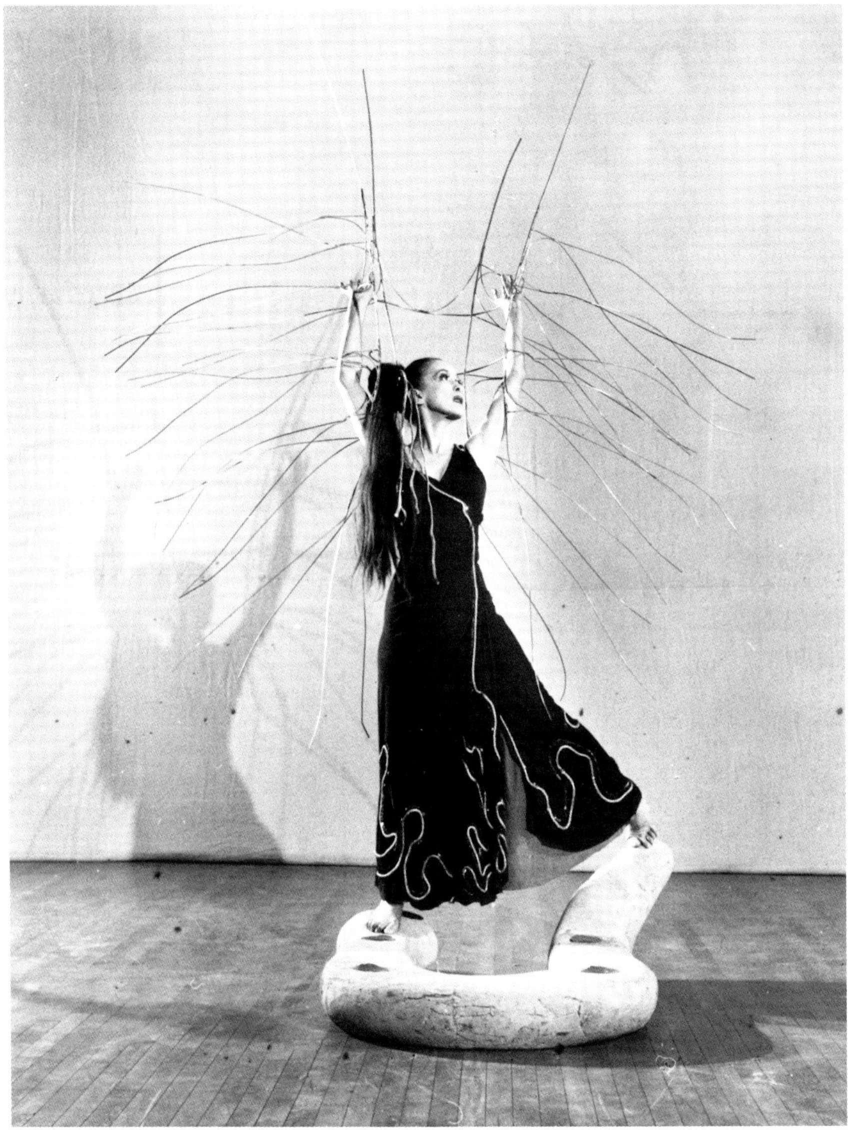

Writing himself in *A Sculptor's World,* Noguchi recalled in 1965 that his goals at the time he was in Mexico were centered on finding "a way of sculpture that was humanly meaningful without being realistic, at once abstract and socially relevant."[106] Whether planned or not, his close familiarity with the tenets of modernist dance provided a fund of imagery useful in actualizing this conviction. For greater security and stability, Noguchi's Mercado relief had to be raised one meter off the market's floor; this factor serves to increase the illusion that what takes place in *History as Seen from Mexico, 1936* unfolds as if on stage. Visual evidence endorses the assumption that Noguchi kept this appearance in mind when conceptualizing both style and iconography. The stage, he would later explain,, "is a hypothetical perfect space. Not merely space, but a space of life. My objects have a life there. They participate in the drama which is fictional but true enough for the people viewing it." [107]

Although Isamu Noguchi would identify as the only heir to his Mercado Abelardo L. Rodríguez mural, a 1940 Art Deco–inspired stainless-steel plaque titled *News*, located on the façade of Rockefeller Center's Associated Press Building, this was not exactly the case. Thinking of his exceptional work for Martha Graham over a period of twenty-two years, Archives of American Art interviewer Paul Cummings expressed a natural curiosity in 1973 about the association of Noguchi's sculptural oeuvre with dance, and he asked the sculptor outright if any of his other projects were related to the "problems that were set by the dance as [Graham] envisioned it." "Your whole involvement with Martha Graham and the stage sets—those things—the images and the objects and the space seem similar to the sculpture but yet quite different," Cummings observed. "Do you conceive of those sets as being specifically different?" (fig. 20).

While not directly meant to describe *History as Seen from Mexico, 1936*, Noguchi's response to Cummings has keen pertinence for understanding the radical formal and ideological dynamics already at work in this early, mostly underestimated creation. "Everything I do is linked," he admitted. "I've never done anything in, for instance, a theater set which I was not already involved with elsewhere somehow. The whole volume of the theater stage and how things related within it and to the people moving, was for me a sculptural problem." [108] He might also have added, "And vice-versa, of course." Calling on his unusual knowledge of and affinity for modern dance, it was in Mexico that Noguchi first imagined the potential of this intoxicating calculation.

2 | Envisioning History:

Philip Guston and Reuben Kadish in Morelia

Sightseers in Mexico touring the Museo Regional Michoacano de Morelia, a converted Baroque palazzo that was once setting to a brief sojourn by Emperor Maximilian, typically react with puzzlement when they come upon a most unusual feature, an epic mural dating to the mid-1930s that decorates a wall of one of its interior patios (fig. 21). Of course, Mexico is renowned for its murals, especially those painted by the country's famed revolutionary wall artists in the 1920s and '30s; Orozco, Rivera, and Siqueiros were celebrated throughout the world. But this mural at the Museo Michoacáno, known variously as *The Struggle Against War and Fascism, The Struggle Against Terrorism,* or *The Inquisition,* hardly seems Mexican in origin, subject, or style. Its artists, Phillip Goldstein, Reuben Kadish, and their assistant Jules Langsner (whose three signatures are barely visible at lower left) strike no chord of recognition, and this monumental work seems jarringly out of context in a museum of indigenous and Hispanic artifacts.

How did such a design, seemingly by U.S. artists of no established repute, end up in this distant place? Despite their wonderment over its origins, viewers of *The Struggle Against Terrorism,* a 1,024-square-foot saga painted in 1934–35 and uncovered in 1973 after three decades behind a fake wall, are typically riveted by the terrifying spectacle of race-hatred and intolerance throughout the ages unfolding before their eyes. Examining the mural takes spectators on an abbreviated journey from biblical times through the Middle Ages and beyond, to the rise of the Ku Klux Klan and Adolf Hitler. What they see was considered important enough at the time of its completion to be described and partially illustrated in the U.S. newsweekly *Time.*

Time's anonymous writer characterized the little-known creators of this astounding fresco as a "spectacled Kadish, 21" and "dapper Goldstein, 22," recounting in some detail how this unlikely pair from Los Angeles managed to obtain a commission to decorate "the former summer palace of Emperor Maximilian" located in Michoacán, "one of the least known of Mexico's 28

21 Philip Guston, Reuben Kadish (and Jules Langsner), *The Struggle Against Terrorism,* 1934–35. Center section of fresco at the Museo Michoacano, Morelia, Mexico. Photographed 1935, probably by Casa Lopez Articulos Fotograficos Revelado Impresion y Amplification, Morelia. Courtesy of the Reuben Kadish Art Foundation.

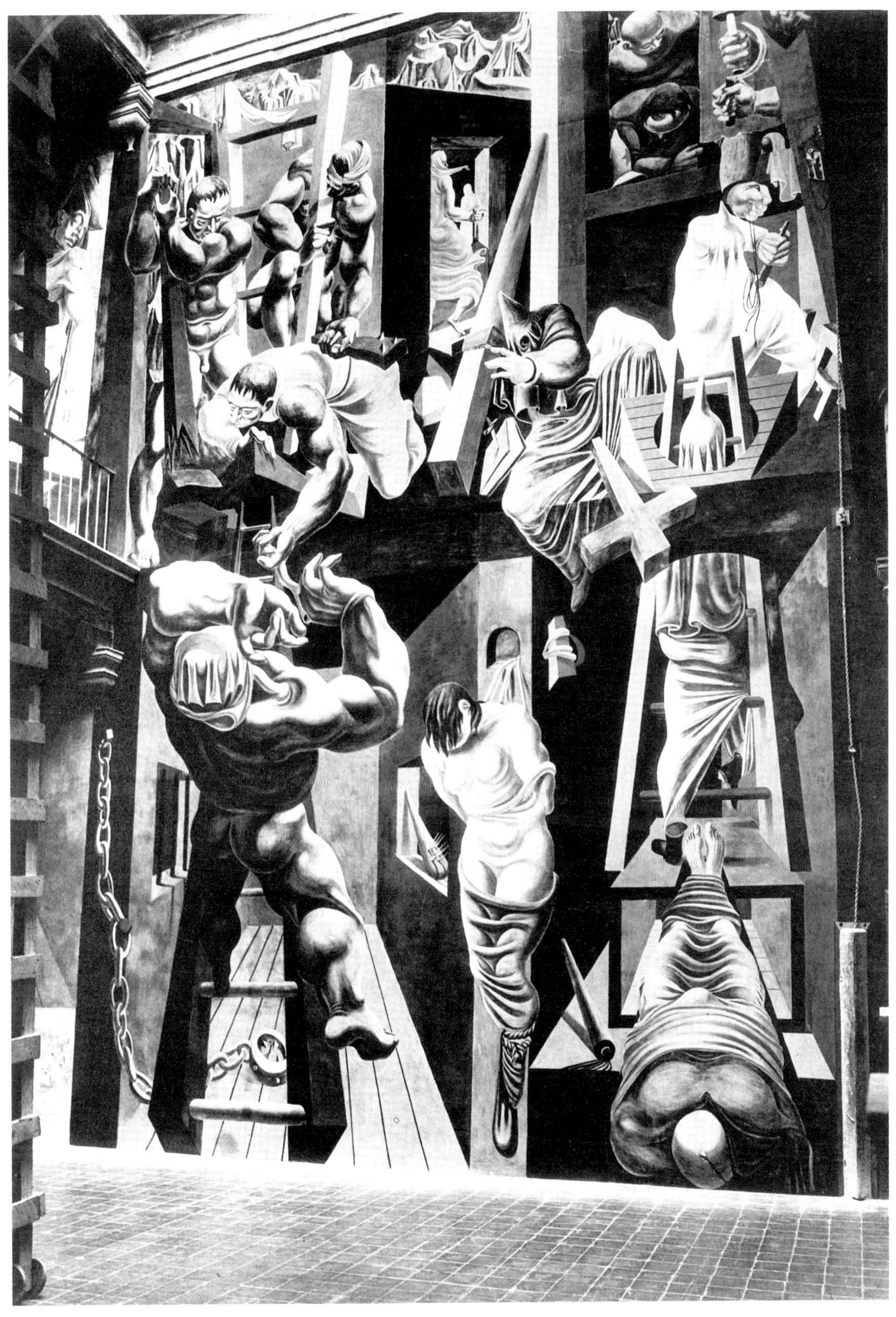

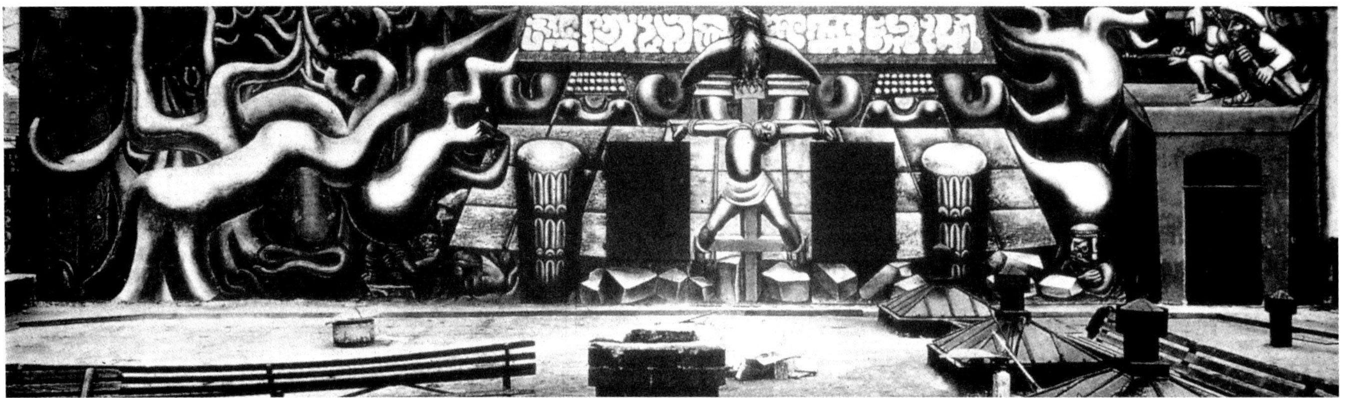

states." Their good fortune is credited primarily to support from the charismatic Siqueiros, with whom Kadish worked on *América Tropical,* his controversial outdoor mural painted in 1932 in downtown Los Angeles on folkloric Olvera Street (fig. 22). Given the opportunity to paint "On a Mexican Wall," as *Time*'s headline put it, Goldstein and Kadish demonstrated considerable skill, creating a series of colorfully painted, oversized, and foreshortened muscular figures, positioned within a complicated architectural framework. [1] The mural's protagonists appear ritualistically engaged in activities brutal, sinister, and xenophobic. According to *Time,* based on details Langsner must have provided:

> The left half of the main wall depict[s] nude workers knocking from a ladder, with splintered beam, lead pipe and spike-studded stick, a colossal figure supposed to represent the Medieval Inquisition. . . . In the centre [*sic*] is the broken-necked body of a hanged woman and above her a hooded and villainous priest. The other half of the wall is given over to the Modern Inquisition. Near the floor is the body of an electrocuted man, realistically rigid. Rising through a trap door are two hooded figures representing the Ku Klux Klan and Nazism. In the extreme upper right, Communists with sickle & hammer are rushing to the rescue. [2]

Neither expounded on nor illustrated here or in any other publication at that time, the mural features, as well, smaller side panels devised in tandem with the main composition. These are located at the far left, above and below a balcony interrupting the central space. At the top, an elderly male and female mourn a dead youth in what appears a hybrid lamentation scene; below, a strangely polemical still life features a broken colossal head, a drawing of torture, and other curious and sinister non-Mexican

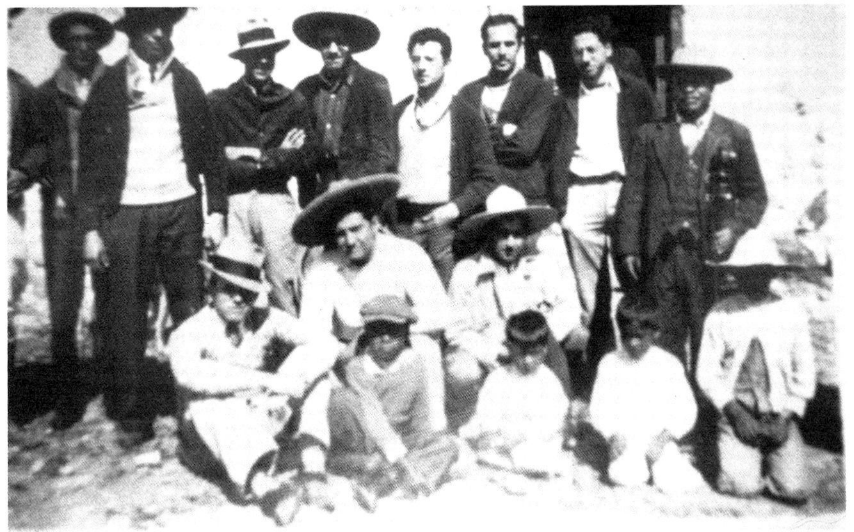

elements. Analyzing the relationship of these subsidiary scenes to the main action is crucial to understanding the Morelia mural's implicit and explicit multilayered meanings.

As evident to present-day viewers of the mural as it must have been to readers of *Time* is the fact its young painters (fig. 23) took on a very ambitious project that involved trying to summarize a worldwide historical legacy of malefaction, cruelty, and prejudice. What is not as immediately obvious perhaps is how a specific confluence of insecurity, persecution, and violence, a topos of Mexico considered equal in intensity to its natural beauty, is also ingeniously signified. Deeply encoded into the mural's iconography of evil and pain are distinct clues triggered by their own specific understanding of Mexican alterity, pertinent to the artists' sense of "otherness" and profound desire to redress the era's racial inequities. Referenced in particular is their shared relation to a heritage of Jewish persecution and ethical commitment.

Since Phillip Goldstein was perhaps primarily responsible for devising the fresco's key imagery and dictating its rhetorical tone, a study of what we would currently term "identity politics" operative in *The Struggle Against Terrorism* may prove especially significant in understanding his further accomplishments. It was not long after this Mexican experience that Goldstein became Philip Guston, now celebrated as the Abstract Expressionist whose later career turn to a sardonic, cartoon-like figurative style became so influential for postmodern developments (fig. 24). (For the sake of simplicity, his more recognized name will mostly be used throughout this chapter.) Many art historians and critics writing about Guston's distinguished career have dismissed the Mexican fresco (which the artist forswore until the 1970s) as mere juvenilia, seeing in its hyper-realistic Italianate imagery disaffection on

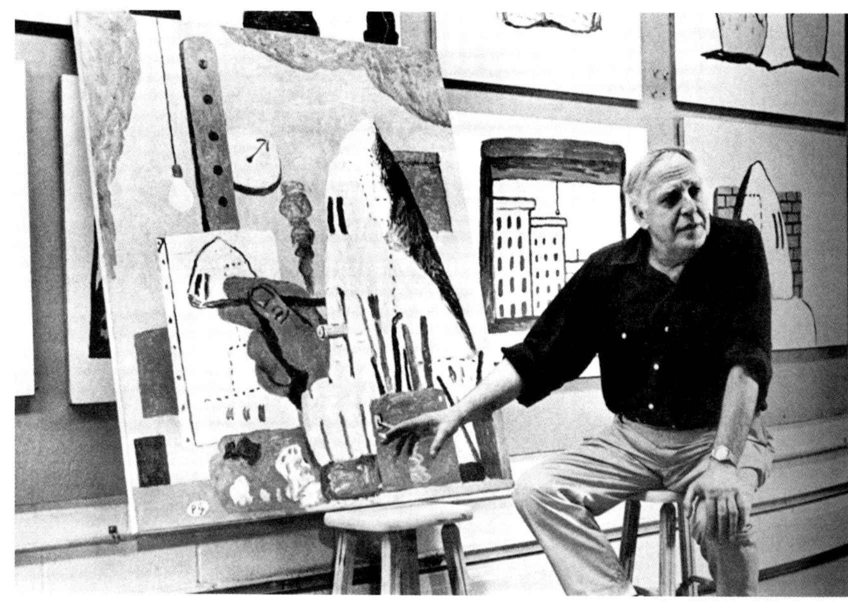

his and Kadish's part with youthfully romantic notions about Mexican art and society. Scholars have not adequately recognized how the central premises of its sprawling theatrical design were, in fact, firmly rooted in both local and global events, as well as in the painters' personal histories. Echoes of this Morelian experience would reverberate throughout their respective oeuvres.

Back home, the extreme leftist politics of Guston and Kadish had already made their art a target for hate groups. After one particularly disturbing incident they decamped for Mexico with Jules Langsner, their friend and "assistant." Described by *Time* as an "itinerant poet," Langsner took charge of such menial tasks as mixing paint, as well as promoting the Morelia mural's story to the press; he would become a distinguished West Coast curator and art critic, as well as a psychologist. The journey to creative maturity for all three men was complicated and, their 180-day sojourn in Morelia was a significant intermediate destination. This, we shall see, was particularly true for Guston.

Beginnings

As American expatriate Anita Brenner vividly described in her 1929 book *Idols Behind Altars,* the "persistence of ancient instincts and motivations" has been an important determinant of social, political, and cultural life in Mexico. Reverence for ritual and a fascination with terror and death rooted in the country's multilayered past are themes that many scholars have explored. A further clue to Mexico's prospective private resonance for Guston, Kadish,

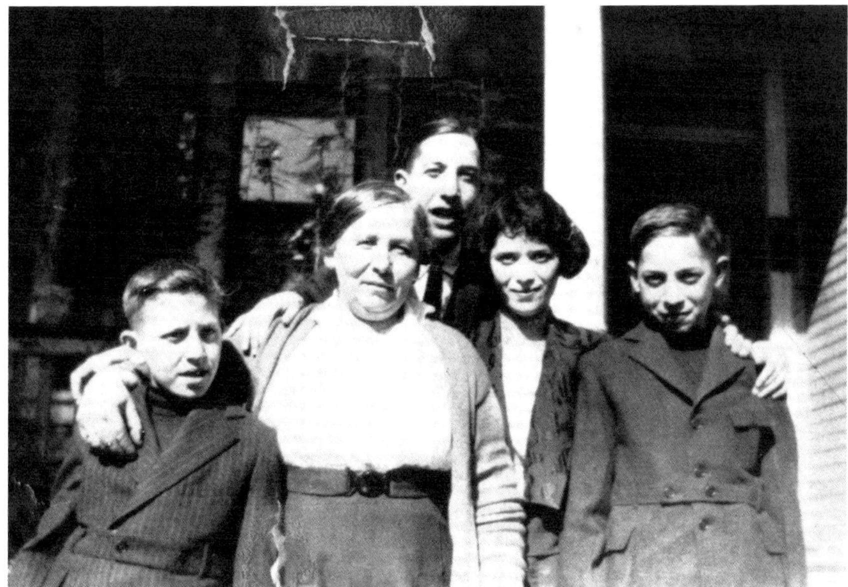

and Langsner is provided in the analysis of noted Mexican intellectual Octavio Paz. Paz proposed in his 1961 book *The Labyrinth of Solitude* that insecurity and "otherness" based on *mestizaje* (race mixing) had made a strong impact on his homeland's national character. While some contest this notion, many experts consider this collective sense of otherness a primary determinant of Mexican culture.[3] Langsner's confession that he and his friends could "integrate with strands of other cultures probably as much in our bones as American peculiarities" intimates their period-specific understanding of Mexican alterity and suggests that it had a likely effect.[4] Given their own immigrant backgrounds, these young artists seemingly approached their Mexican experience with a particular brand of "double consciousness."

Three decades before *The Struggle Against Terrorism* was unveiled, the families of the three self-styled "angry young men" who left L.A. in 1934 to try their luck in an exotic land had also fled their homes, escaping anti-Jewish pogroms and other instances of race hatred and violence in the waning days of the Russian tsars.[5] The Goldsteins departed Russia in 1905 in the wake of attacks by the Black Hundreds (antirevolutionary and anti-Semitic ruffians whose activities were unofficially sanctioned by the government) and the mutiny aboard the battleship *Potemkin* in Odessa Harbor. Phillip (the original spelling) and Reuben were both born in 1913, Julius Harold Langsner two years before. Reuben, whose father had been a Bundist in Kovno, moved from Chicago to Los Angeles at age seven.[6] By 1919 Phillip's family had also relocated to L.A. from the French-Canadian/Yiddish-speaking slums of Montreal (fig. 25). No birth certificate for the youngest of Rachel

Goldstein's seven children was ever issued. According to family gossip, Phillip's real father may not have been his mother's second husband, Lieb; the future artist was rumored to be the progeny of an affair in Odessa.[7] Haunted by the feeling that Odessa was his "true" birthplace, Phillip was raised in New World ghettos on scary stories about his terrified family hiding in Old World cellars from marauding Cossacks.

Whereas Kadish's father, Samuel, a blue-collar worker, became active in causes for political and social justice in Los Angeles, Lieb Goldstein (also known as Wolf and Lewis) would never adapt to life in America. A "brooding and doubt-racked" depressive man, he worked in Montreal as a machinist for the Canadian Pacific Railroad. Unable to find similar employment in the United States, Lieb was reduced to plying the slums in a horse-drawn wagon, picking up and reselling refuse. In 1923 or the following year Phillip discovered his humiliated father hanging from a noose slipped over the rafters of an outbuilding by their house.[8]

Phillip Goldstein and Reuben Kadish met in 1930 at the Otis Art Institute in Los Angeles, and were teenage chums of Jackson Pollock. Reuben attested to the strong competitiveness of his two buddies. Imbued with the idea of seeking "a big life," Jack and Phill worked at "living out a European fantasy" at Riverside's Manual Arts High. Expelled together for protesting funds wasted on athletics and ROTC (the Reserve Officers' Training Corps), neither would graduate.[9] After less than a year at Otis, Guston dropped out again, went to work for a radical Russian furrier, punched numbers on vests in a factory, drove a dry cleaner's truck, and, capitalizing on his good looks and flair for the dramatic, played bit parts in Hollywood. Under the tutelage of local art guru Lorser Feitelson, he and Kadish discovered avant-garde painting. They focused their study on great masters of the past and present such as Piero della Francesca, Paolo Ucello, Max Ernst, and Giorgio de Chirico. These various influences were mixed—as seen in Kadish's *Untitled (Dr. Entozoan),* completed after their return from Mexico, or Guston's earlier canvas *Mother and Child*—with cues from Post-Surrealism, most notably Feitelson's own melodramatic pastiche with strong film noir stylistic echoes (figs. 26–28).[10]

For someone with no advanced formal education, Philip Guston would become a highly literate adult. He was undoubtedly one of the most intellectually inclined of the Abstract Expressionists—certainly more so than Pollock. Dore Ashton notes Guston's early fascination with James Joyce, Ezra Pound, e.e. cummings, the French Surrealists, California novelist Nathanael West (born Nathan Weinstein), and other authors "of the Left." She mentions his later predilection for reading philosophy, especially that of Henri Bergson, Arthur Schopenhauer, Søren Kierkegaard, Friedrich Nietzsche, Carl Jung, Thomas Aquinas, and the great Jewish thinkers Baruch Spinoza and Martin

26 Philip Guston, *Mother and Child,* 1930. Oil on canvas. Private collection. © Estate of Philip Guston.

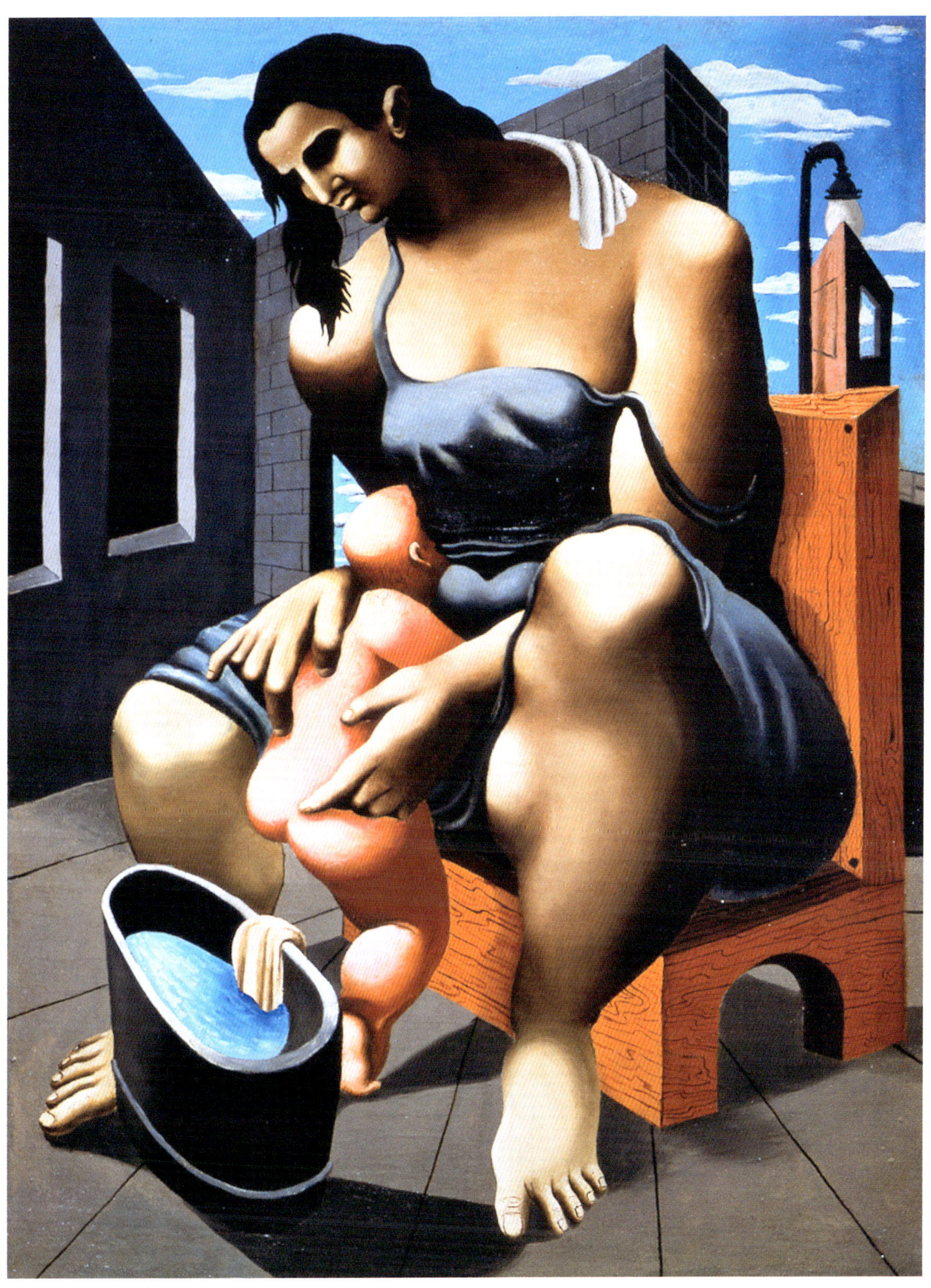

27 Reuben Kadish, *Untitled (Dr. Entozoan)*,
c. 1935. Oil and mixed media on canvas,
48¼ x 36 in. (122.6 x 91.4 cm). Los Angeles
County Museum of Art, Los Angeles, Calif.
Gift of the Reuben Kadish Art Foundation
and purchased with funds provided by
Mrs. James D. Macneil (M.2003.46). Digital
image © 2012 Museum Associates / LACMA.
Licensed by Art Resource, NY.

28 Lorser Feitelson, *Love: Eternal
Recurrence*, 1935–36. Oil on canvas.
Collection of Phoenix Art Museum.
Gift of Dr. and Mrs. Lorenz Anderman.
Photo: Craig Smith. © The Feitelson /
Lundeberg Art Foundation, Orange, Calif.

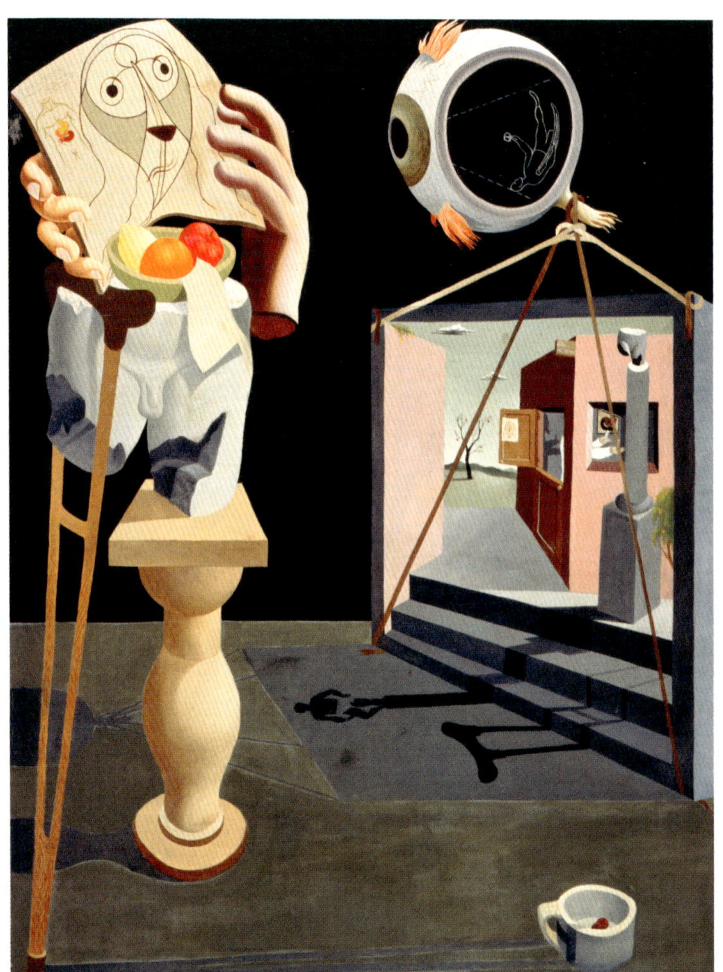

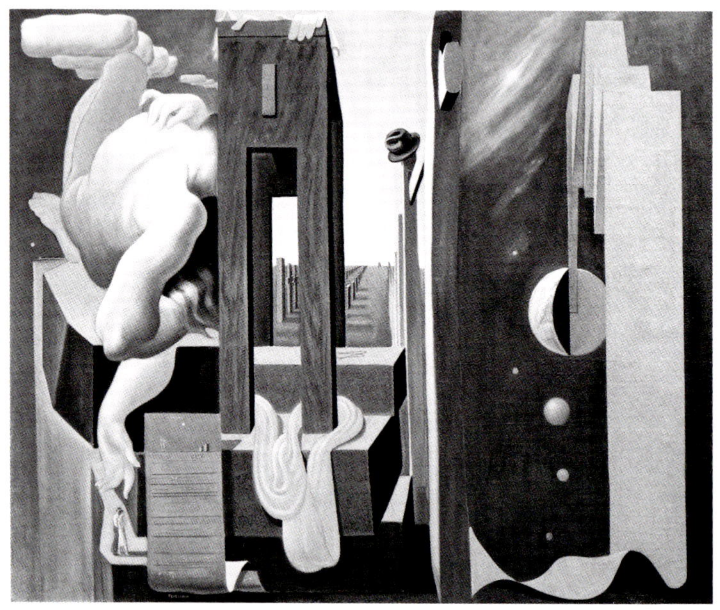

Buber. Guston's special attraction to Franz Kafka has been well detailed; this developed further after he began teaching painting in the Midwest in the early 1940s. Kafka's claustrophobic allegories of rootlessness and strangeness wrought from his own tormented Middle European Jewishness were easily absorbed into Guston's own introspective and lugubrious (very Russian) feelings of victimhood, inherited from his father.[11]

In coming to terms with his Russianness, Guston found a very pertinent model in the writings of Isaac Babel, which are more ironic and more directly connected to Judaism than are Kafka's writings. The artist admired Babel's short tales, many of which display a fervently assimilationist desire to escape ghetto life (the same life in the Pale of Settlement led by Guston and Kadish's forebears). Particularly relevant are his *Red Cavalry Stories,* based on observations made in 1920, when Babel disguised his identity to ride through Poland torching shtetls with General Budyonny's Cossack army. Such sketches have been characterized by literary scholars as saturated with their author's unshakable love/hate relation to his upbringing "nailed to the Talmud." Full of pathos, contradiction, and travesty, the *Red Cavalry Stories* display a fascination with the foibles of cruelty and violence for which Guston's works, early and late, provide a close visual parallel. These range from *Conspirators,* a now-lost canvas made in about 1932 (fig. 29), to a 1977 painting dedicated "To I. B." Babel's writings obviously stoked Guston's sense of displacement. As his poet friend William Corbett so perceptively observed, "Babel, who could never be a Cossack and could not be a Jew while he rode with the Cossacks, fit Guston and the paradoxes in his artistic life perfectly."[12]

"I like Isaac Babel," Guston pronounced in 1980, "because he deals totally with fact. There can be nothing more startling than a simple statement of fact, in a certain form. As Babel says, there's no iron that can enter the heart like a period in the right place." Annotating his own recent paintings featuring the resurgence of now more crudely drawn white-hooded figures, Guston slipped a probable reference to both *Conspirators* and *The Struggle Against Terrorism* into the following admission: "They are self-portraits. I perceive myself as being behind the hood. In the new series of 'hoods' my attempt was really not to illustrate, to do pictures of the Ku Klux Klan, as I had done earlier. The idea of evil fascinates me, rather like Isaac Babel who had joined the Cossacks, lived with them, and written stories about them. I almost tried to imagine that I was living with the Klan. What would it be like to be evil? To plan, to plot . . ."[13]

According to the social scientist Daniel Bell, it is generally believed that a man is "first of all the son of his father." But disaffection from the anxious, parochial world of their immigrant parents was a hallmark of Jewish intellectuals of Guston and Kadish's generation, and both eventually married non-Jews. In addition to masking his ethnic roots to placate the family of

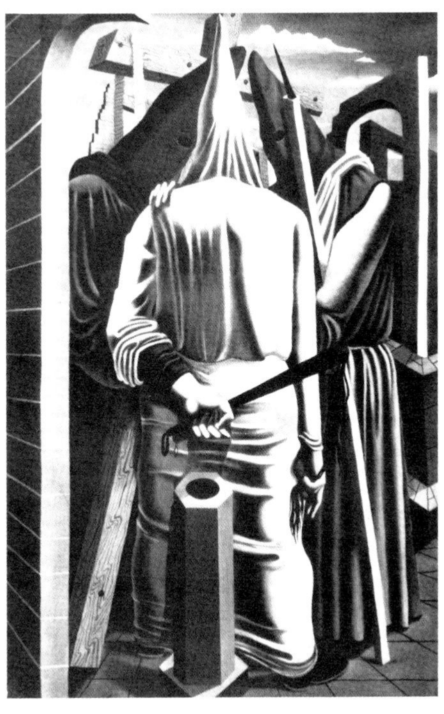

29 Philip Guston, *Conspirators,* c. 1930–32. Oil on canvas. Location unknown. Courtesy of McKee Gallery. © Estate of Philip Guston.

his Gentile wife, Guston's name change likely served to put greater distance between himself and his unsuccessful father. Musa Mayer, Guston's daughter, says she did not learn he'd had another name until she reached college; she then discovered he went so far in his deception as to repaint his signature on at least one early work (*Mother and Child*). Yet, Mayer acknowledges, Guston felt deep ambivalence and increasing guilt over this rejection of selfhood. By the end of his life, he began to re-embrace his heritage, commenting, "I have never been able to escape my family. . . . Nothing has changed in all this time. It is still a struggle to be hidden and feel strange."[14] Philip Guston's quest to understand the forces that made him who he was took its earliest convincing artistic shape in an unlikely place. To understand what happened in Morelia, it is first necessary to go back to Los Angeles and examine Guston's formative experiences with Kadish.

Los Angeles

Like Mexico, the environment that nurtured Phillip Goldstein and Reuben Kadish was marked by insecurity. Los Angeles had its own brand of restiveness based on the unusual mobility, heterogeneity, and impermanence of its population. A city located "on the edge of America," L.A. was settled in 1781 by the Spanish. Its picture-perfect weather, pseudo-Mexican architecture, and key industry, the movies, placed primary emphasis on superficiality and disposability. By the 1920s, an accentuated need for reinvention and self-validation propelled many Angelenos into eccentric fads and occult activities. Some sought an exaggerated normality, adopting paranoid and exclusionary right-wing social behaviors to achieve it. An alarming number of hate groups flourished in Depression-era Los Angeles. Bullying police and self-styled vigilantes—who were targeting vagrancy, illegal aliens, Bolshevism, union suppression, and strike-busting—regularly violated the civil rights of local citizens. Night-riding goons with hoods, nooses, and burning crosses, instead of swords and sabers, terrorized targeted constituencies with the tacit or outright approval of the government.[15] As indicated by Guston's earliest extant works, created in 1930–33, such polarities of repression were an unfortunately familiar occurrence.

Every account of the careers of Guston and Kadish features the events of February 12, 1933, when Captain William F. Hynes of the Los Angeles Police Department's notorious Red Squad, along with his American Legion posse, destroyed a set of portable murals the two artists helped create for the Hollywood branch of the Communist-affiliated John Reed Clubs. Harold Lehman, Murray Hantman, Luis Arénal (brother-in-law of Siqueiros), and other politically committed young artists were also participating in the

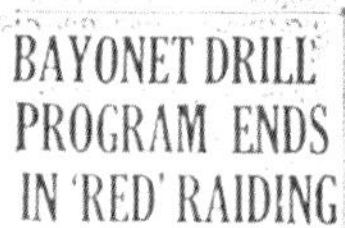
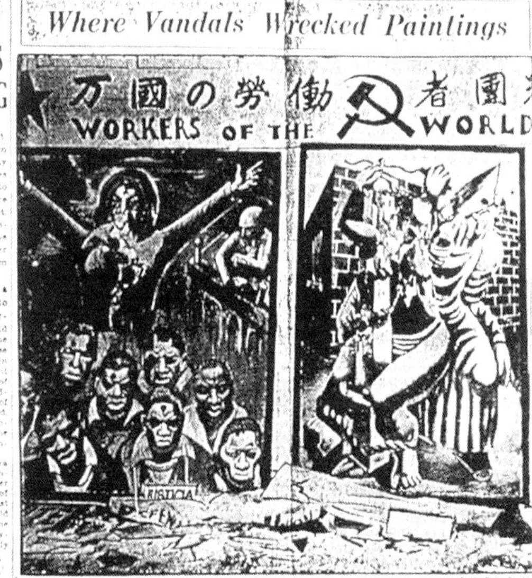

proposed exhibition, *Negro America,* meant to protest the trumped-up arrest and multiple convictions for rape of the Alabama Scottsboro Boys—a situation widely considered a "legal lynching."[16] The small frescoes painted on cement by Guston, Kadish, and friends for this show featured brutally honest if somewhat aesthetically unsophisticated images (especially in comparison to Noguchi's) deploring the recent increase in the United States of atrocities against African Americans.[17] One of the scenes they pictured, of a black man hanging by a noose from a tree, mirrored George Sherman's fate (fig. 30). Also included, among others, were the whipping of an African American by a member of the Ku Klux Klan, and a rapt white audience awaiting the imminent demise of a "boy" tied to a stake while flames licked at his feet. Hantman displayed portraits of the Scottsboro defendants under a banner advocating their freedom,[18] an important agenda item of the American Communist Party, sponsor of the John Reed Clubs nationwide.[19]

Although the Los Angeles papers went further than *Time* in describing the pair as "decidedly 'Red'" (not just "parlor pink," like New York's leftist dancers), Guston and Kadish were naïve Marxists and never card-carrying members of the party. They did gravitate into its orbit, however, after demoralizing encounters with, as Langsner put it, "rapacious, dishonest and backwards" persecutory tactics.[20] Guston was exposed to Klan rallies and abusive strike-busting after he left Otis and had to make a living. Police

30 Reuben Kadish, Portable mural for *Negro America,* Hollywood John Reed Club, 1933. Destroyed fresco. Reuben Kadish Papers, Archives of American Art, Smithsonian Institution, with permission of the Reuben Kadish Art Foundation.

31 "Where Vandals Wrecked Paintings," *Los Angeles Illustrated Daily News,* February 13, 1933. Photograph shows damaged frescoes for *Negro America* by Murray Hantman and Phillip Goldstein.

raided and ransacked the Kadish family apartment in 1928, tossing possessions and destroying books, no doubt a result of Samuel's associations with Bolshevik sympathizers in Los Angeles, and Reuben observed a cross burning in the yard of a Jewish tailor living in Santa Monica.[21] He and Guston watched in horror as sympathetic depictions of black Americans, which they and their cohort had painted on the Reed Club panels, were bashed with lead pipes and rifle butts; Guston recalled the eyes and genitals being pierced by bullets (fig. 31).[22] They were dubbed "misguided individuals" by the press when they went to court over the incident, and a reactionary judge summarily dismissed the case.[23]

Guston's portable fresco for *Negro America* was not his first presentation of a Ku Klux Klan plot. Violence had broken in 1930 out in the manufacturing plant where he worked, and, although he was not an eyewitness, as Ashton has described, Guston learned as an adolescent of the role played by the KKK and such right-wing associations as the American Legion in clearing Los Angeles of unions. In his first solo exhibition at the Stanley Rose Bookshop in 1933 (actually a two-person showing shared with Harold Lehman), he had already addressed these concerns, interweaving public events and autobiography. A number of works included there featured ropes; recall that Phillip, as a boy, found his dead father and had to cut down the noose. Much later Guston would admit to a fixation beginning at this time on the "kneeling figure with inquisitional hood" seen in Italian Renaissance paintings. "This medieval inquisition hat," he wrote, "ignited something in me." Although the now lost canvas *Conspirators* (sold by Stanley Rose) and a still-extant drawing with a similar topic are generally dated c. 1930, their shared themes suggest creation closer to the time of the aborted Hollywood John Reed Club exhibition.[24]

In view of the aggressive thematic program of *The Struggle Against Terrorism*, it seems plausible to read Guston's *Conspirators* imagery, his and Kadish's savagely mutilated Scottsboro portable compositions, and his obsessional return in the late 1960s to Klan-related subjects (in which the artist admitted he was "going back to my beginnings again") as accommodating multiple layers of personal and political significance. On a private level, Guston's lifelong desire to orchestrate "living indictments" apparently stemmed from deeply embedded emotional roots. On a more public front, the importance of the John Reed Clubs as Depression-era forums for articulation of minority opinion was noted by, among others, dealer Herman Baron, who donated space for the group exhibition similar to *Negro America*, called *Struggle for Negro Rights,* to which Noguchi contributed *Death*. "Generally," Baron, the owner of A.C.A. Galleries, observed, "unpopular minority voices [speak] for the conscience of the people[,] and the freer that minority voices are heard the more conscience there is in the nation." D. W. Griffith's incendiary film *Birth of a Nation,* revived in a talking version in

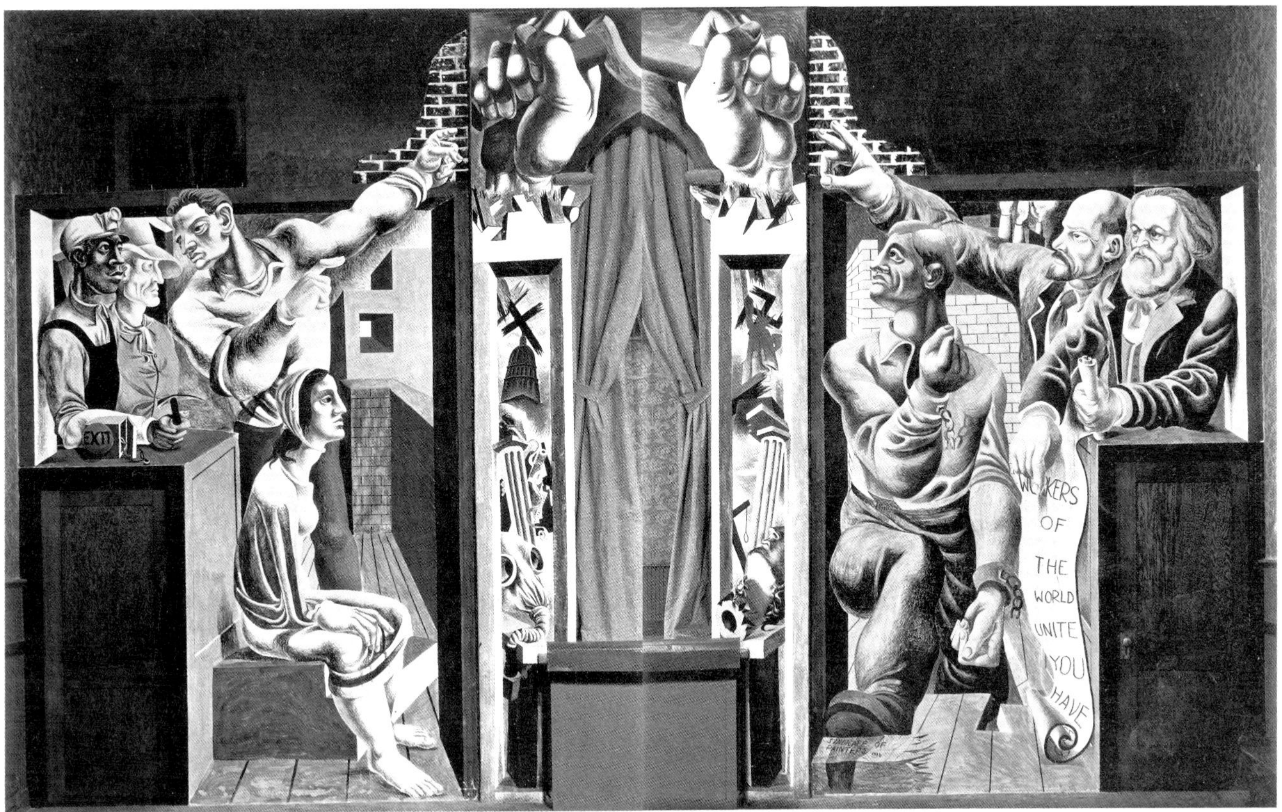

1930, made the Klan's belief in an "'alliance of degeneracy' between Jews and blacks visually explicit."²⁵

Between the time that their Scottsboro panels were destroyed and execution of their much more ambitious Morelia fresco, Guston and Kadish assisted Hantman on a Public Works of Art Project at the Frank Wiggins Trade School. More important, in early 1934 the two created another fully realized mural—completely unknown today—for the proscenium arch of the Workers Alliance Center stage in downtown Los Angeles (fig. 32). In this case, they were in charge, and their assistant was Jackson Pollock's older brother Sanford (later known as Sande McCoy). A set of installation photographs of this project, created in twenty-one days and signed merely "Syndicate of Painters," was mailed to Siqueiros. This resulted in the Mexican's promise to help any of those involved who wished to travel to his country secure a local commission.

While the Workers Alliance Center mural was strongly influenced by Siqueiros's 1932 Chouinard School fresco *The Workers' Meeting,* as well as another design created around that time for the Hollywood Reed Club auditorium, it also reflected themes made famous by Rivera and Orozco.²⁶

32 Philip Guston, Reuben Kadish, and Sanford Pollock, *Mural for Proscenium, Workers Alliance Center, Los Angeles,* 1934. Fresco. Reuben Kadish Papers, Archives of American Art, Smithsonian Institution, Washington, D.C., with permission of the Reuben Kadish Art Foundation.

As a result, it was likely the most radically left-wing composition created during the Depression by American artists painting in the United States. When Rivera included the face of Lenin at Rockefeller Center the year before, his mural was infamously destroyed. As extant photos indicate, the right-hand side of Guston, Kadish, and Sande Pollock's design featured both Marx and Lenin, one of whom gestures toward two huge fists gripping Soviet symbols, while the other points to a scroll displaying the initial phrase of the Communist Manifesto. (Some of these elements, as we've seen, were included by Noguchi, O'Higgins, and the Greenwood sisters working at the Mercado.) A laborer who has broken his shackles provides the foil to a kerchiefed female, a black miner, and two additional white members of the proletariat depicted at far left. One, a muscular youth, harangues the others to recognize the power of the party. Antiwar scenes and symbols glimpsed through two vertical openings prefigure *The Struggle Against Terrorism*'s more imaginative and explicitly antifascist iconography. While little is known about circumstances of the fresco commission at the Workers Alliance Center except that Samuel Kadish, a professional wood-grainer, played a role in the building's construction, its propagandistic fervor surely indicates that left-wing politics were more critical in the artistic educations of Reuben Kadish and Philip Guston than has yet been acknowledged. That they were motivated and empowered to elaborate this subject in 1930s Los Angeles suggests a need for further research regarding the accepted history of early twentieth-century West Coast art.[27]

Mexico

While Sande chose to join his brothers Jackson and Charles in New York, in the hope of escaping provincial and government-inspired bias against radical art at home, Guston and Kadish readily accepted Siqueros's invitation to Mexico, taking Langsner with them. To what extent did self-chosen exile from the United States serve to perpetuate or ameliorate the sense of estrangement that these not yet fully formed artists felt as a result of experiencing such traumatic incidents of prejudice in L.A.? Guston's initial letters to Lehman indicate his strong ambivalence about the aesthetics and mores of this alien environment. Exhibiting both praise and contempt, he describes their new life as "*no* cinch," further griping, "The much heralded Mexican renaissance is very much a bag of hot air. I can't explain my disappointment." Reflecting loyalty to Siqueiros, Guston heaps criticism on the opportunism of Rivera, who was at that time Siqueiros's archrival. Too "busy receiving gushing tourists," Diego Rivera did not seem to have much time to act like a true revolutionary.[28]

Things apparently changed for the better after Guston and Kadish were recommended, not just by Siqueiros but also by Rivera and Pablo O'Higgins, to decorate the interior patio of an imposing edifice in the state of Michoacán where the doomed Maximilian, Austrian emperor of Mexico under the auspices of the French, had sojourned briefly in 1864 with Empress Carlotta. The building, now run by a progressive religious institution, the University of St. Nicholas of Hidalgo, was primarily being used as a state museum. Guston, with his better Spanish skills, left Mexico City first, to negotiate with Morelia's local art commissar, Rudolfo Ayala, as well as with Gustavo Corona, the college's socialist-leaning rector. Corona had previously commissioned murals from three American women, Marion and Grace Greenwood and Ryah Ludins. Grace Greenwood's 1934 *Man and Machines* is located in the foyer that leads into the patio space allotted to Guston and Kadish. Not unlike Marion's comments to her friend Josephine Herbst, in an excited report to Lehman about his warm welcome in Morelia, Guston wrote that Corona, "the image of Lenin," wants "to make his city a modern Florence."[29]

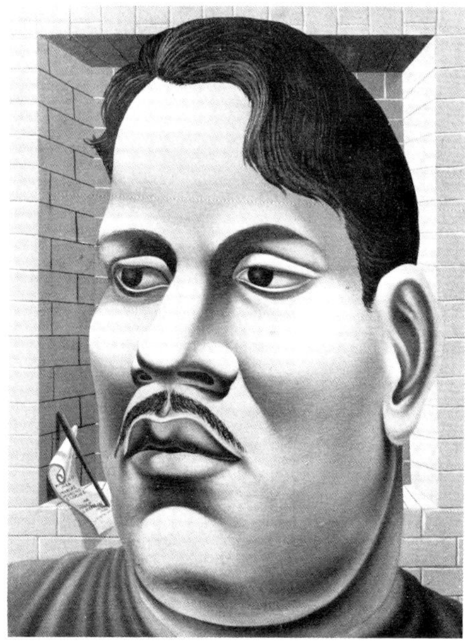

33 Philip Guston, *Portrait of Manuel Moreno Sanchez*, 1934. Location unknown. © Estate of Philip Guston.

Although the busier Mexican painters did not want to be stuck there for an extended period of time, Morelia turned out to be an interesting place for young disaffected Jewish American leftists in the mid-1930s. Located on a plateau of the "relentless" and "foreboding" Sierra Madre west of Mexico's capital, the classically Spanish provincial city of Valladolid, founded in 1541, was renamed in the nineteenth century to honor José Maria Morelos, the local rebel priest whose feats in the War of Independence were legend. (Much earlier, the native Tarascans fiercely resisted Aztec domination but were tricked into submission by the conquering Europeans.) By 1928 this Catholic stronghold had been adopted as the headquarters of future Mexican president Lázaro Cárdenas and his radical anticlericalist party. With Cárdenas then serving as governor of Michoacán, the city of Morelia, positioned near the site of a famous fifteenth-century Inquisition trial, became transformed into a hotbed of Cardenista insurgency at war with the more conservative religious factions long dominant in the region. The renegade Cardenistas opposed the "numbing effect" of Catholic fanaticism on the subsistence farm workers, known as *campesinos,* and rejected racial stereotypes that marginalized native populations. They promoted the syndical organization of the proletariat and endorsed the collective benefits of culture.[30] Portraits painted by Guston and Kadish in Morelia to make extra money indicate that the artists soon found themselves on familiar terms with some of the local politicians (fig. 33).[31] During a lull in the mural's execution, the two, plus Langsner, were even given free train passes to attend Cárdenas's December 1934 presidential inauguration in Mexico City.

The announcement in *Time* magazine of the unveiling of Guston and Kadish's mural after less than six months' gestation was hyperbolic as well

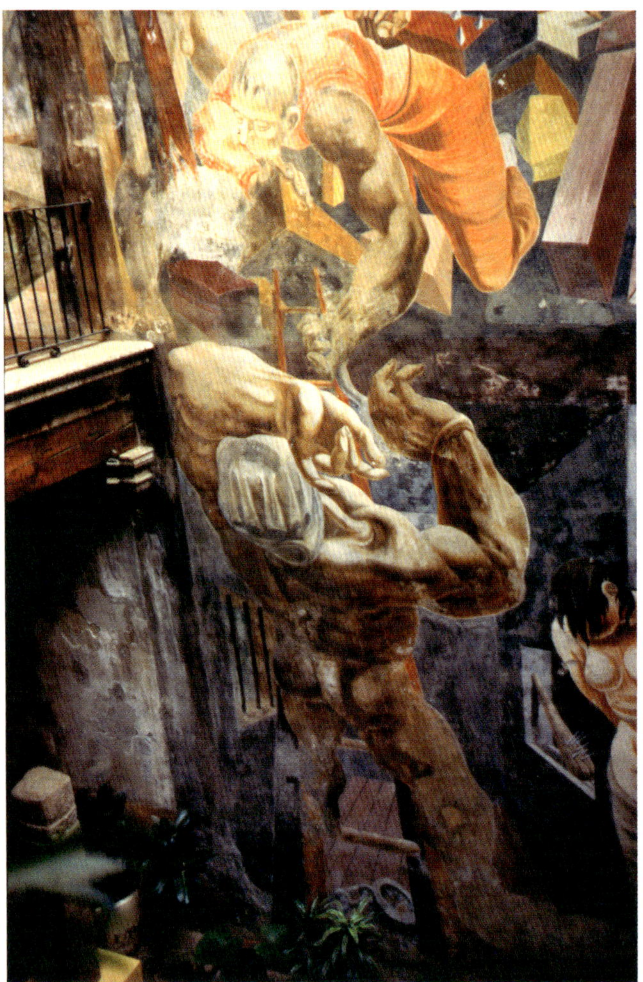

34 Philip Guston, Reuben Kadish (and Jules Langsner), *The Struggle Against Terrorism*, 1934–35. Detail of falling man from central panel. Photo: Ellen G. Landau. © Estate of Philip Guston.

as somewhat patronizing: "In that hot little place, black-coated government employees and peasants in straw sombreros gazed in open-mouthed wonder at one of the biggest, most effective frescoes in all Mexico." Improbably, it was explained, this wall painting by inexperienced Americans would now provide Mexican schoolboys with "one more reason for being conscious of Morelia," home to heroes of Mexican independence. But *Time*'s author had assuredly never seen the actual work, drawing inferences solely from information provided by Langsner. Local reaction can be much better judged by examining Benjamin Molina's three-part review, which appeared in a regional publication, *La Atalaya*, on February 1, February 16, and March 1, 1935. The specificity of his text indicates that Molina had ample opportunity to appraise firsthand the mural's distinctive effects. Indeed, he may have been part of the Mexican crew who helped create the painting.[32]

Describing "Goldstein y Kadish" as "two youths that belong to this generation and follow its tendencies," Molina focused praise on their clever resolution of a design dilemma presented by the museum patio's irregular shape. As he explains, the mural's surface spans two stories, including extensions above and below a balcony that cuts into the space; the observer's viewing angle is thus deformed from all possible positions. This distortion is especially prominent at the level of the *segundo piso* where a banister abruptly interrupts the central section. Molina praises effusively the way that these disjunctions were accommodated through physical and thematic transitions. The painters, he points out, introduced a severely foreshortened eighteen-foot-high male nude whose muscular arms, wrapped head, and thorax break the picture plane; his equipoise is being shattered by men on ladders above attacking him with torture sticks (fig. 34). Although not mentioned, Guston and Kadish made equally clever use of a lightning rod cord attached to the wall at the right perimeter to indicate another victim of terror murdered by electrocution.

Not surprisingly, considering the locale of the artists' upbringing, the astounding kinesthetic impression produced by their hurtling naked giant, whose backward fall can be reexperienced from many points of view, seems linked to cinematography.[33] Even more remarkable, the velocity of this mon-

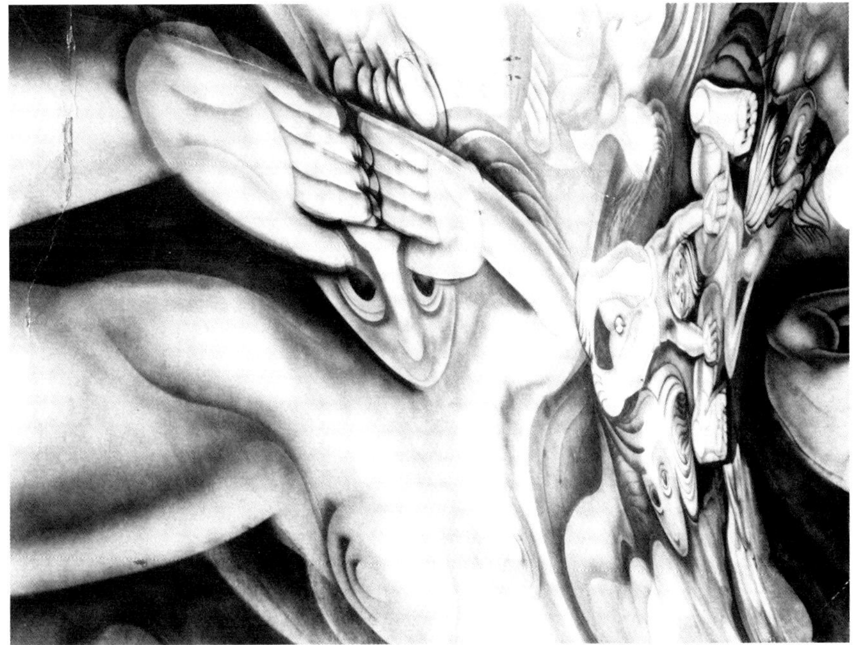

35 David Alfaro Siqueiros, *Ejercicio Plastico* (detail), c. 1933. Photograph in sepia. Basement of the Antigua Finca Los Grandos (Old Pomegrante Plantation), Buenos Aires. Photographer unknown. Courtesy of Sala de Arte Publico Siqueiros. © 2012 Artists Rights Society (ARS), New York / SOMAAP, Mexico City.

umental figure's displacement evidences the astute level at which Guston and Kadish understood the implications of polyangularity, a brand-new perspectival concept that Siqueiros had devised after learning in Hollywood to use a movie camera. Guston's letters provide a worshipful description of photographs that he and Kadish were sent of nudes Siqueiros had painted in Argentina. These, he explains to Lehman, are "very distorted so that they would appear not distorted because of the peculiar shape of the wall" (fig 35). "As the spectator moves," he elucidates, Siqueiros's figures "move and rotate with him."[34] Communicating anxiety in the guise of spatial energy, their own vertiginous version of Siqueiros's innovation further confirms its psychological and optical potency.

Glancing to the right and slightly above the catapulting giant, Morelia spectators are drawn into a solemn and ritualistic tableau of equally frightening proportions, simultaneously conservative and innovative in narrative and form. Documentary evidence in Kadish's papers indicates that this composite saga began at the extreme left, in the smaller space over the balcony.[35] In a way somewhat comparable to Noguchi's central Mercado panel, the scene of death and sorrow represented there (almost certainly painted by Guston) amalgamates traditional — in this case, Michelangelesque — pietà, deposition, and lamentation imagery (fig. 36). It directly recalls his father's suicide, as well as a drawing Guston supposedly made at age seventeen in which a black man lynched by conspiratorial Klansmen is analogized with the martyrdom of Christ. While the facial features of the muscular

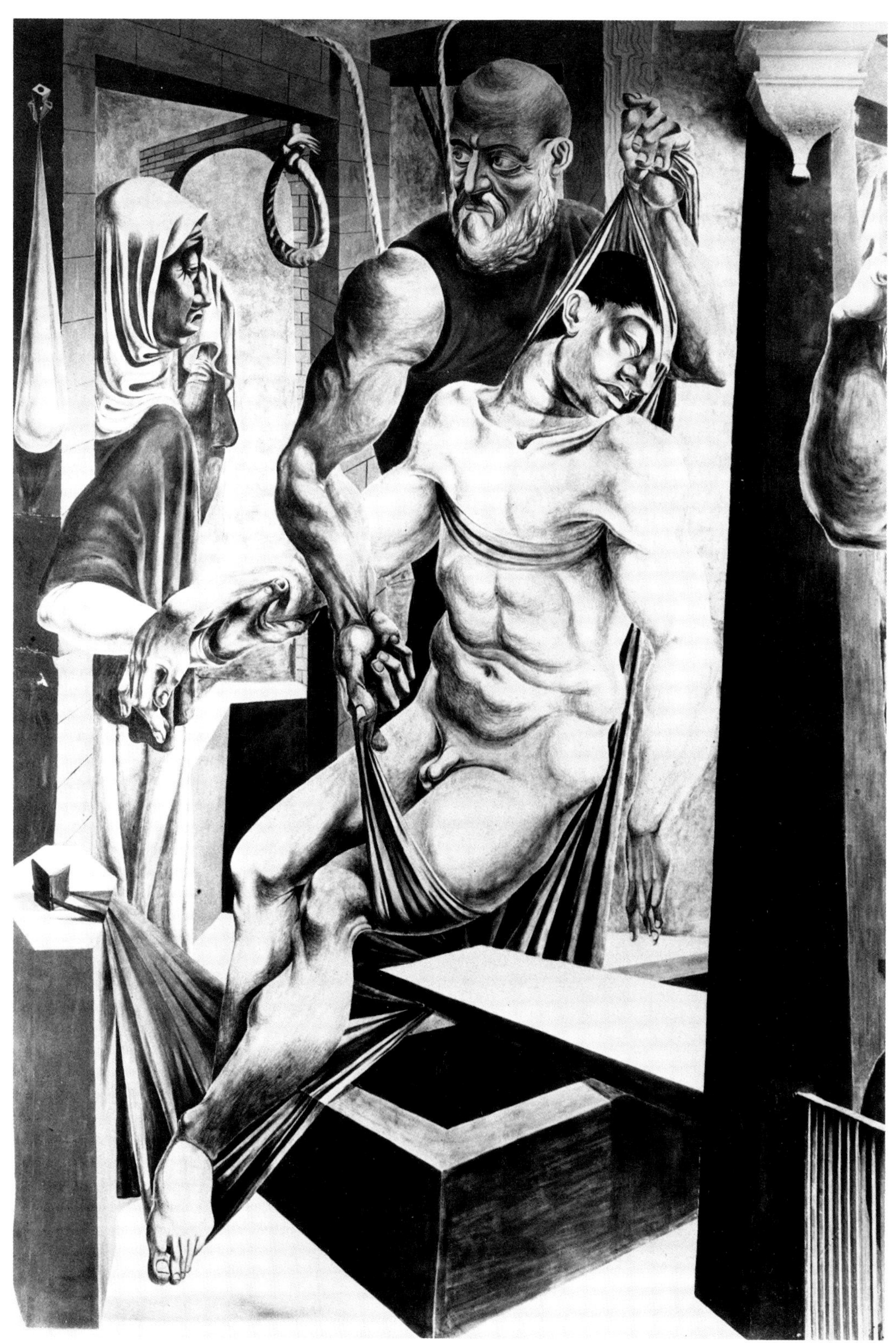

corpse suspended over an empty, open tomb might appear typically Meso-American, closer examination discloses a more conflated racial identity. Also markedly Jewish in physiognomy, the profile of this tragic youth bears unmistakable Goldstein family traits. These include Philip's hooked nose and hooded eyes, physical similarities he shared with his older brother Nat, who died tragically at a young age (fig. 37).[36]

Installation photographs taken soon after the Morelia fresco's completion, an item Langsner placed in the *Los Angeles Times,* and a letter from Kadish in Mexico to Feitelson requesting instructions, indicate that the other vignette, located directly below this lamentation scene, was meant as a somewhat pessimistic version of "subjective classicism," one of the hallmarks of Southern California's so-called Post-Surrealist style.[37] Even badly damaged by the leeching of saltpeter (which began almost immediately) this metaphysical still life à la de Chirico, one of the duo's main artistic heroes, produces an eerie effect.[38] As seen in installation photographs donated to the Archives of American Art, its original composition featured a fallen colossal sculptural head which, like the pietà figure above, is supported in a sling of tightly drawn cloth (fig. 38). This was juxtaposed with a tearful mask of tragedy hanging from a nail attached to what looks to be some kind of a wooden pain-inflicting contraption. Behind this, a tacked-up cartoon picturing yet another scene of torment was inserted into the design. Although viewers might plausibly surmise that a Hispanic codex was the inspiration for this particular section, the grisly narrative that Guston and Kadish chose to copy into a relatively inconspicuous space was actually based on an obscure European woodcut with anti-Semitic meaning (fig. 39).[39]

Limned in Italy in 1475 by a German itinerant printmaker, their source represents the *Burning of the Jews of Trent,* one episode from a series of twelve narrating the tale and consequences of the murdered and beatified baby Simon. From what may constitute the first coordinated set of graphic broadsides in art history, this example of blatant prejudice and propaganda was produced by Albert Kunne, also known as Albertus Duderstadt van Eiksvelt. Like the Scottsboro Boys almost five centuries later, the Jews of Trent were accused and convicted of a crime they did not commit. (They were set up by the disgruntled Swiss husband of one of their nursemaids.) Kunne's imagery was intended to help inflame the local populace to a frenzy by convincing Christian inhabitants of Trent that the Jews living among them—identified as such by their pointed hats—had committed the nefarious "crime" of Blood Libel (Jews were said to kill a Christian child at Passover to use his blood to make matzoh).[40]

In view of the explicitly interrelated iconographic program of *The Struggle Against Terrorism,* it is evident that Guston and Kadish (and Langsner, one presumes) were well aware of the role of hooded monks during the

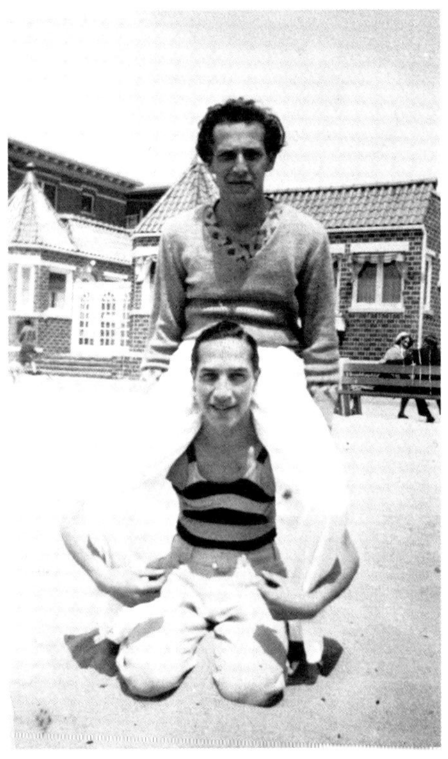

36 Philip Guston, Lamentation panel from *The Struggle Against Terrorism,* 1934–35. Reuben Kadish Papers, Archives of American Art, Smithsonian Institution, with permission of the Reuben Kadish Art Foundation.

37 Phillip [top] and Nat Goldstein on the beach in Venice, California, c. 1929. © Estate of Philip Guston.

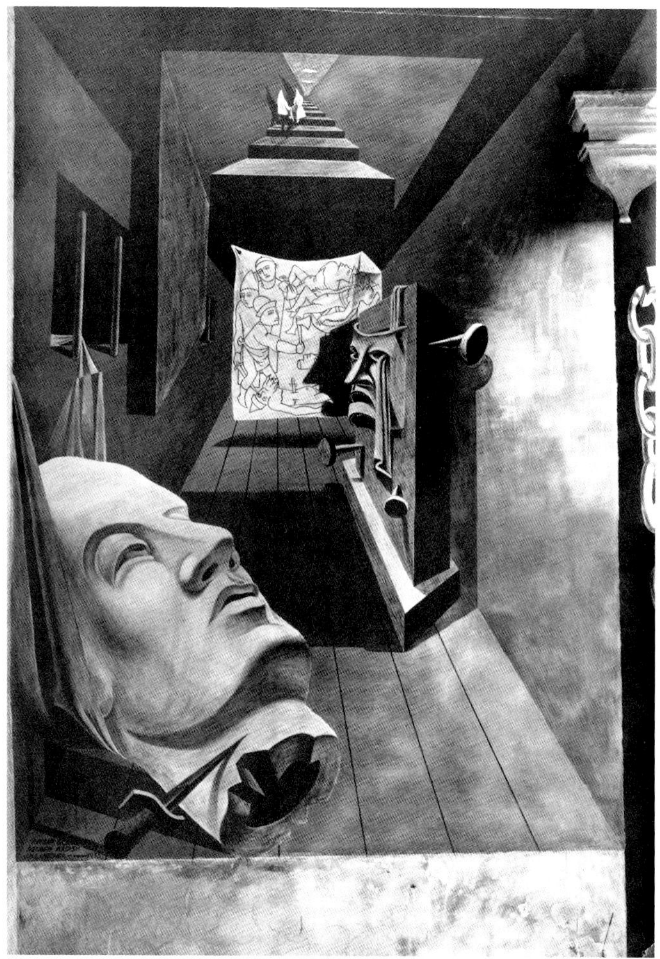

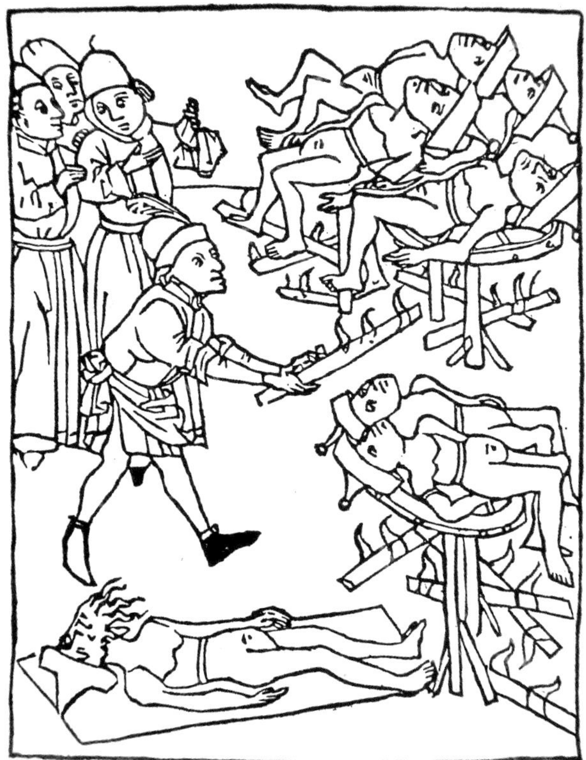

Abb. 13. Marter von Juden, die aufs Rad geflochten wurden.
Holzschnitt aus: Geschichte des zu Trient ermordeten Christenkindes.
Trient 1475. Albertus (Kune aus) Duderstat von dem Eiksvelt.
Hain 7733.

38 Philip Guston, Reuben Kadish (and Jules Langsner), Post-surrealist still life panel from *The Struggle Against Terrorism*, 1934–35. Photo from the Reuben Kadish Papers, Archives of American Art, Smithsonian Institution, with permission of the Reuben Kadish Art Foundation.

39 Albert Kunne (also known as Albertus Duderstadt von Eiksvelt), *Burning of the Jews of Trent*, 1475. Woodcut, reproduced from Georg Hermann Theodor Liebe, *Das Judentum in der Deutscher Vergangenheit* (1903), ill. 13.

Inquisition period in Europe and New Spain, enlisted as fanatical representatives of the Church Militant to harrow and oppress supposed blasphemers and heretics. Especially targeted were *judaizante*, those accused of secretly practicing Jewish rites. In 1537, the apostolic inquisitor of New Spain publicly tried Gonzalo Gómez, an important political figure in Michoacán, as a suspected judaizer.[41] Exactly how these emigrant Angelenos became familiar with an esoteric fifteenth-century leaflet created to stir up anti-Jewish sentiment in northern Italy will likely forever remain unknown. Kunne's woodcut image of the *Burning of the Jews of Trent*, a copy of which is owned by the Staatsbibliothek in Munich, appears to have been published only once before 1934, in a 1903 German text. Nevertheless, these artists knew it intimately. That Guston and Kadish increased Kunne's level of violence and affliction beyond the wheel and flame-stick, depicting the dead elder Moses being stabbed in the eye by one of the Catholic torturers (their religion is also identified through distinctive headgear), indicates their advanced level of rage.[42]

The virtual line-for-line similarity to Kunne's design of the tacked-up Morelia cartoon—today hardly visible—suggests that its injection into *The Struggle Against Terrorism* must have been cathartic for these young American Jews. Since the Mexicans would likely not have understood such a reference, Guston and Kadish used and accelerated its horror to make a secretly meaningful statement. Accusations of Blood Libel had spurred the famous Kishinev pogrom a few years before their parents left the Pale of Settlement, the arrest of Mendel Beilis in 1911 (and his notorious trial in 1913) had caused an international scandal, and the Nazis were reviving this slanderous aspersion in the propaganda periodical *Der Stürmer* at precisely the time Guston and Kadish were painting in Mexico.

Additional accessories of persecution, many associated with tactics of the Gestapo as well as of the Spanish Inquisition (these include chains, crosses, maces, nails, barred windows, ladders, flagellant whips, garrottes, and studded collars), were distributed by the painters throughout the remainder of their Morelia composition. Recalling the symbolic use by Renaissance and Baroque artists of the *Arma Christi*—instruments of the Passion, such as the nails, scourge, and crown of thorns—and the frequent depiction in Catholic art of implements employed to persecute saints, Guston and Kadish employed to great effect both the private and public connotations of this paraphernalia of pain and suffering. They underscored the timeliness of their message by including two tiny figures in Ku Klux Klan regalia dragging a dead body up a set of wide stairs in the uppermost register of the Post-Surrealist vignette.

Through metonymy, successive leaps in scale and adroit devices of internal framing, instances of infamy and corruption are conflated and telescoped into *The Struggle Against Terrorism*'s crowded main section. Overt and secretive, present and past, local and universal, the consequences of evil appear to escalate here in a subjectively organized time/space. The result is a stylized humanitarian drama expressing solidarity with the powerless and dispossessed that seems indebted to Guston's lifelong admiration for the elusive and secretive world of Piero della Francesca, one of the most celebrated Umbrian painters. What he and Kadish produced in Mexico with the help of Langsner is likewise dignified, strangely mute, elegiac, and—at certain key junctures—intensely and disturbingly phallic. By incorporating formidable modern-day totalitarian symbols into the denouement of their chronicle—a volumetric Nazi swastika and the hammer and sickle gripped in clenched Communist fists—they deliver, as did Noguchi, a jarringly effective contemporary note.

Aftermath

Oh, it is all so circular, isn't it? . . . The recent work makes me feel free to use whatever formal and plastic imagery and capabilities I may possess. I mean from my own past too—all the memories. . . . Please forgive my immodest comparison, but like Babel, I want to "paint" of things long forgotten.[43]

— PHILIP GUSTON, 1974

Conceptualized in a locale where postrevolutionary social policies were aimed at erasing the historical stigma of torture and cruelty, Guston and Kadish's 1934–35 fresco, generally referred to as *The Struggle Against War and Fascism* in English-language accounts, has been known to Morelia residents as *La Inquisición* since it was uncovered in the early 1970s. While this more charged and morally indignant title is hinted at in Langsner's description of the mural's iconography published by *Time* in April 1935, the author of "On a Mexican Wall" misleadingly dubbed it *The Workers' Struggle for Liberty. The Struggle Against Terrorism,* the version of the title adopted in this chapter, was first used in a Los Angeles newspaper notice announcing Guston and Kadish's newly finished composition several months before *Time*'s lengthier feature. While indirectly referenced, the Mexicans' alternative seems never to have been used by the artists themselves, and there is some question as to how many other names they, or Langsner, as their public relations agent, tried on for size in pitching the story. To our ears today, *The Struggle Against War and Fascism* seems too closely identified with standardized Popular Front rhetoric and, more importantly, it does not accurately indicate the empathetic direction of the mural's underlying themes. *The Struggle Against Terrorism,* considered in context with homegrown understanding of the painting's inherently antipapist tone, better reflects its overtly allegorical message while hinting at its deeply embedded, less obvious meanings.[44]

After their Mexican experience, Reuben Kadish and Philip Guston created another mural together, *The Physical Growth of Man,* in Duarte, California. Then Kadish went solo on one of the most important WPA frescoes produced in that state, *A Dissertation on Alchemy,* painted in San Francisco in 1937. But following his service in World War II, Kadish gave up painting to become a farmer.[45] He later turned to sculpture, and a considerable number of his mature works in three dimensions bear Mexican characteristics of style. How Guston's formative experience in Morelia played a crucial role in his subsequent career is a more complicated topic, one that requires preliminary recognition of the interdependence of personal authenticity and collective memory that helps define Jewishness. It turns on the notion,

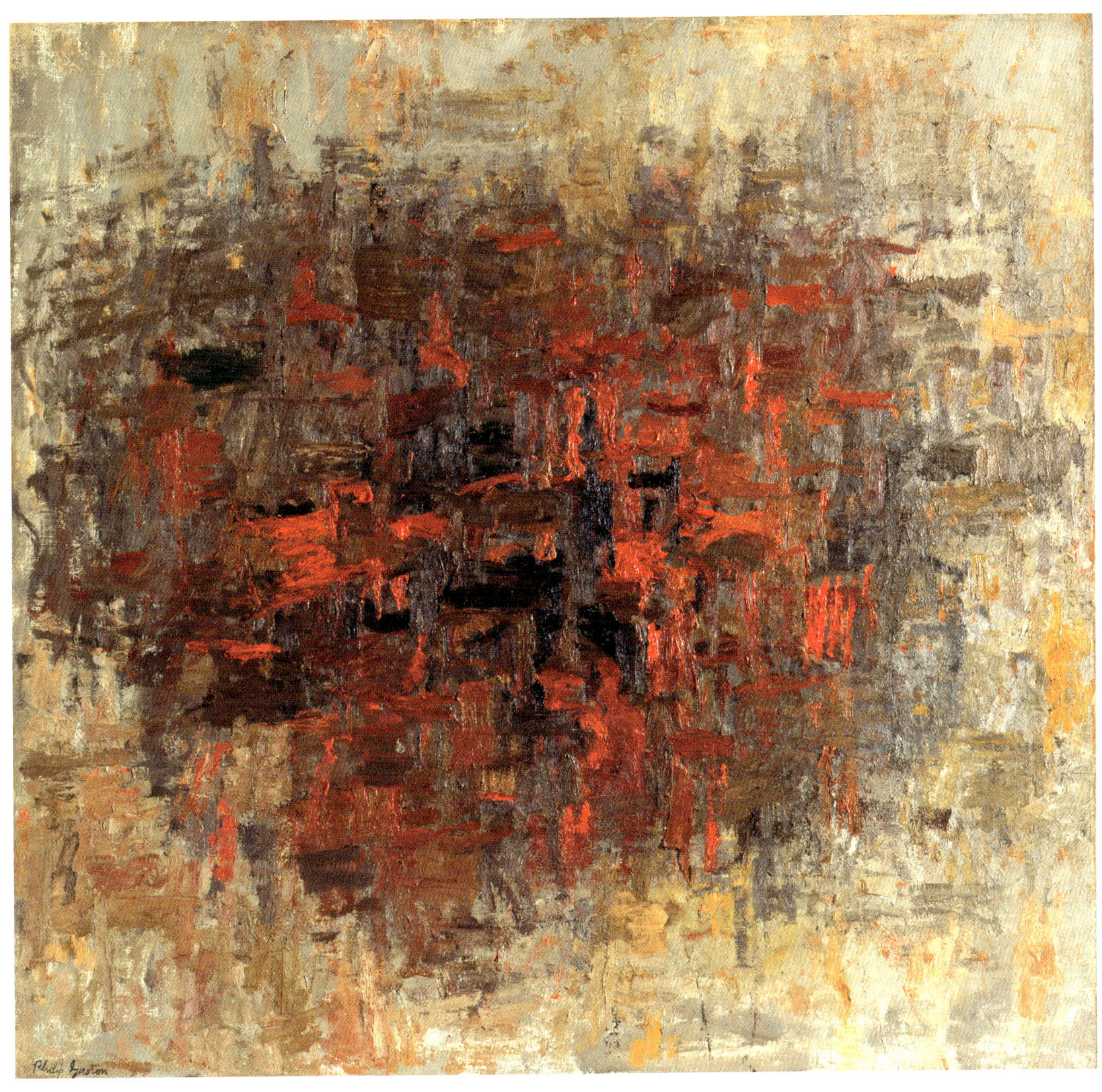

40 Philip Guston, *To B. W. T.*, 1952. Jane Lang Davis Collection, Medina, Wash. Courtesy of McKee Gallery. © Estate of Philip Guston.

described by the French theorist and philosopher Alain Finkielkraut, that an "eternal, invisible and ineffaceable" difference—one that collectively accommodates the respective lows and highs of outcast status plus greater ethical commitment—is integral to being Jewish. [46]

A clear awareness of this kind of ethnic inevitability undergirds two important critical judgments of Guston's unusual artistic trajectory. These are assessments made by the avant-garde composer Morton Feldman and the poet and novelist Ross Feld, who both knew their subject well. While cited repeatedly in the Guston literature, Feldman's and Feld's observations have not been fully connected to the artist's works and thinking process. Writing at the apogee of abstraction in both painting and music, Feldman commented in 1966 that "Guston is of the Renaissance," a possibly bewildering statement to readers of the *Art News Annual*. Why would he make such a cryptic and patently ahistoric appraisal, one that could seem unflattering in an avant-garde context? Naming as accessory another admired painter of the Italian fifteenth century, Feldman offered the following imaginative explanation: "Instead of being allowed to study with Giorgione," he wrote, Guston "observed it all from the ghetto—in the Marshes outside Venice where the old iron works were," adding somewhat mysteriously, "I *know* he was there." Due to circumstances that Feldman obviously felt no need to elaborate, Guston "brought that art into the diaspora with him." [47]

Along with his estimate of Guston's oeuvre as "the most peculiar history lesson we have ever had," Morton Feldman's deliberate choice of the charged terms "ghetto" and "diaspora," both determining facets of Jewish identity, indicates his frank recognition of Guston's artistic impetus as directly reflective of the trope of marginality that Finkielkraut so movingly defined. Indeed, as early as *The Struggle Against Terrorism*, the ineluctability of Guston's ethnicity appears crucial to his interconnected psychic and artistic preoccupations. Just as Finkielkraut admitted, it can be inferred from the artist's paintings and writings that "at every moment" of his life, he "sense[d] the coming thunder of the apocalypse."

What then should be made of the apparent commitment to nonobjectivity in Philip Guston's compositions of the 1950s and early '60s, consisting of centralized disembodied paint strokes, that helped establish his preeminence in the New York School (fig. 40)? Here Feld's opinion bears repetition. "The more I saw of the work that was coming from Guston in the late 70s," Feld explained, "the more persuaded I became that he had only *seemed* to be an abstractionist during his earlier decades." Instead, Feld surmised, "like a Marrano, a *converso,* like the underground Jews of the Spanish Inquisition [Guston had] been a secret image maker all along, coerced into abstraction but never grounded there, outwardly observing but also innerly undermining its rituals." [48] (A *converso* is a Spanish or Portuguese Jew who publicly converted to Christianity in the late Middle Ages to avoid persecution or expulsion, though often continued to practice Judaism in secret.)

Confessing that he was "tired of all that purity" and now desperately wanted "to tell stories," by 1969 Guston had shed his converso persona once and for all and returned resoundingly to figuration.[49] His explanation of this change to Dore Ashton is crucial. "Without going into details right now," Guston told her, "it feels like I am going back to my beginnings again—of why I wanted to paint and to see the images I could make. . . . I don't think anything is ever finished in a painter's life. . . . Nothing is ever forgotten." In 1978, writing from his lonely studio in rural Woodstock, New York, Guston again fell back on left-wing politics to identify and metaphorize his continuing feelings of alienation. "No one knows it," he told Feld, "but right here in the woods—I feel like Lenin or Trotsky—in Zurich plotting the revolution!—I say battlegrounds—Yes, the battle—conflict—now is showing—it's all in the open now—*we* are in the arena—exposed." Casting his spiritual lot with revolutionaries from his ancestral homeland (the latter, a Jew who concealed his ethnic-sounding name, the former rumored to be part-Jewish), Guston maintained that he was "not prepared yet—until now" to win the battle for meaning.[50]

Reviewing the twists and turns of Philip Guston's career, it appears more than evident that this "battle," still in active play so close to the end of his life, was the same one Phillip Goldstein had been waging from the start. In collaboration with Reuben Kadish, he had fired one of its first significant rounds in Mexico. No matter what name is used, their 1934–35 fresco in Morelia is far from an immature or inconsequential statement. Rather, it reveals a remarkably sure determination by idealistic young diaspora Jews to bear witness by inserting their own "post-memory" anxieties into a larger geopolitical matrix.[51] Appropriating the historic Inquisition as catalyst, they orchestrated a sophisticated pictorial structure imaginatively reflective of apprehensions and insecurities endemic to both Mexico and Los Angeles. Adding what W. E. B. Du Bois termed the "double consciousness" of the outsider, Guston and Kadish adroitly wove their immediate concerns into the global context of increasingly dangerous times. Masked behind a controlled and disquieting ambiguity, the depth and precocity of their complex moral indictment is nothing short of astonishing.

Part Two

The 1940s, Mexico, and Abstract Expressionism

Prodded by interviewers to reminisce about the start of her relationship with Jackson Pollock, Lee Krasner invariably mentioned the continuing impact of Mexican muralism on her future husband and artistic partner.[1] Indeed, it seemed to amuse Krasner to recall that it was Pollock's unusually deep admiration for David Alfaro Siqueiros that precipitated the young couple's first argument (fig. 41). Still a dedicated Trotskyite in the early 1940s, Krasner just could not believe that Pollock revered a man accused of plotting to assassinate her hero. But, she remembered, Jackson stood his ground. Pollock both idolized and idealized Los Tres Grandes, whose works he first encountered as a teenager in Southern California. A decade after moving to New York to study with Thomas Hart Benton at the Art Students League, he remained fascinated with key aspects of what they represented, both aesthetically and in terms of leftist commitment.[2]

A candid remark by Peter Busa, one of Pollock's League friends, has been widely quoted since its appearance in the artist's first biography. Benton, Busa explained, "taught Pollock about ideals of beauty; these Mexicans taught him that art could be 'ugly.'"[3] Prior to Busa's comment Pollock's earliest critical champion, Clement Greenberg, had made a similar allusion to his reliance on Mexican cues, but without identifying them as such. Reviewing his second solo show at Peggy Guggenheim's Art of This Century Gallery, Greenberg observed in April 1945, "What is thought to be Pollock's bad taste is in reality his willingness to be ugly in terms of contemporary taste." Two years earlier Greenberg had labeled the "nativeness" of Pollock's "violence, exasperation and stridency" as comparable to that of William Faulkner and Herman Melville, American literary antecedents; in his well-known 1955 essay "'American-Type' Painting," Greenberg gave Siqueiros at least a nod, listing the Mexican muralist as one of several artists whose "hints" Pollock had followed before coming out "on the other side, painting with his own brush."[4]

Typically mentioned by scholars but not often analyzed beyond demonstrating that he was introduced to freer technical methods at Siqueiros's 1936 Union Square Workshop, Pollock's debt to Mexican art (a debt that, despite its obvious impact, he never acknowledged publicly) compels further definition.[5] That Mexican experts have begun producing more nuanced interpretations of Siqueiros's rhetoric and revolutionary accomplishments is helpful in reassessing his impact on Pollock. In particular, understanding Siqueiros's innovations (both pictorial and technical) as rooted in a fundamental desire to project and promote a truer, more specific cultural identity opens fresh avenues for comparability.[6] "Both artists," as Stephen Polcari has explained, "articulate the related but different ways in which their generations went about recording, explaining and transforming their worlds," and each in his own way endeavored to "locate the human mind as a primary site of struggle and conflict."[7]

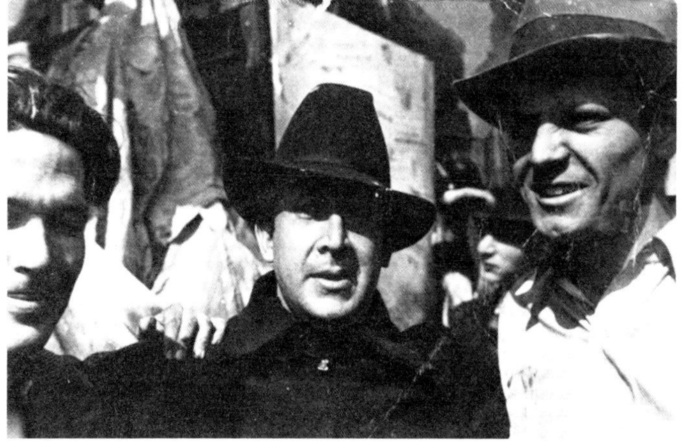

41 George Cox, David Alfaro Siqueiros, and Jackson Pollock in New York, 1936. Unidentified photographer. Jackson Pollock and Lee Krasner papers, Archives of American Art, Smithsonian Institution.

A Role Model for Action Painting

*I don't care for "abstract expressionism" . . . and it's certainly not "non-objective,"
and not "non-representational" either. I'm very representational some of the
time and a little all of the time. . . . Painting is a state of being. . . . Painting is
self- discovery. . . . Every good artist paints what he is.*[8]

— JACKSON POLLOCK, 1956

Pollock's frequently quoted, late career definition of painting as both "self-discovery" and "a state of being" signals a clear awareness on his part that his intense urge to create was motivated primarily by following an identity quest. It is hard to interpret otherwise his flat-out assertion that "every good artist paints what he is." While this therapeutic stimulus to self-expression was deeply personal, it also coincided with larger notions of democracy and individual freedom being promoted in wartime and postwar America. Whereas Siqueiros, a dedicated Stalinist for most of his life, was differently driven, to delineate Mexico's mestizo culture as the paradigm for a collective socialist utopia, Pollock was drawn to him nevertheless as a critical role model for action painting. That he found significant ways to reread (or misread) Siqueiros's achievements in paths more congruent with his own

42 José Clemente Orozco, *The Epic of American Civilization: Machine Images (Panel 12)*, 1932–34. Fresco. Hood Museum of Art, Dartmouth College. Commissioned by the Trustees of Dartmouth College, Hanover, N.H. ©2012 Artists Rights Society (ARS), New York / SOMAAP, Mexico City.

43 Jackson Pollock, *Untitled (Number 37)*, c. 1939–40. Pen and brown and black ink, graphite, and orange colored pencil on smooth coated paper, sheet 14 x 11 in. (35.6 x 27.9 cm). Hood Museum of Art, Dartmouth College, Hanover, N.H.; purchased through a gift from Olivia H. and John O. Parker, Class of 1958, the Guernsey Center Moore 1904 Memorial Fund, and the Hood Museum of Art Acquisitions Fund. © 2012 The Pollock-Krasner Foundation / Artists Rights Society (ARS), New York.

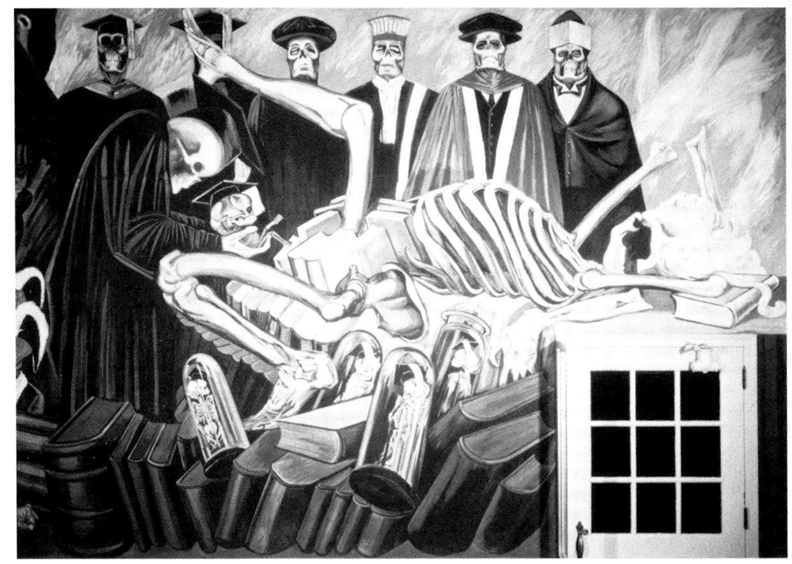

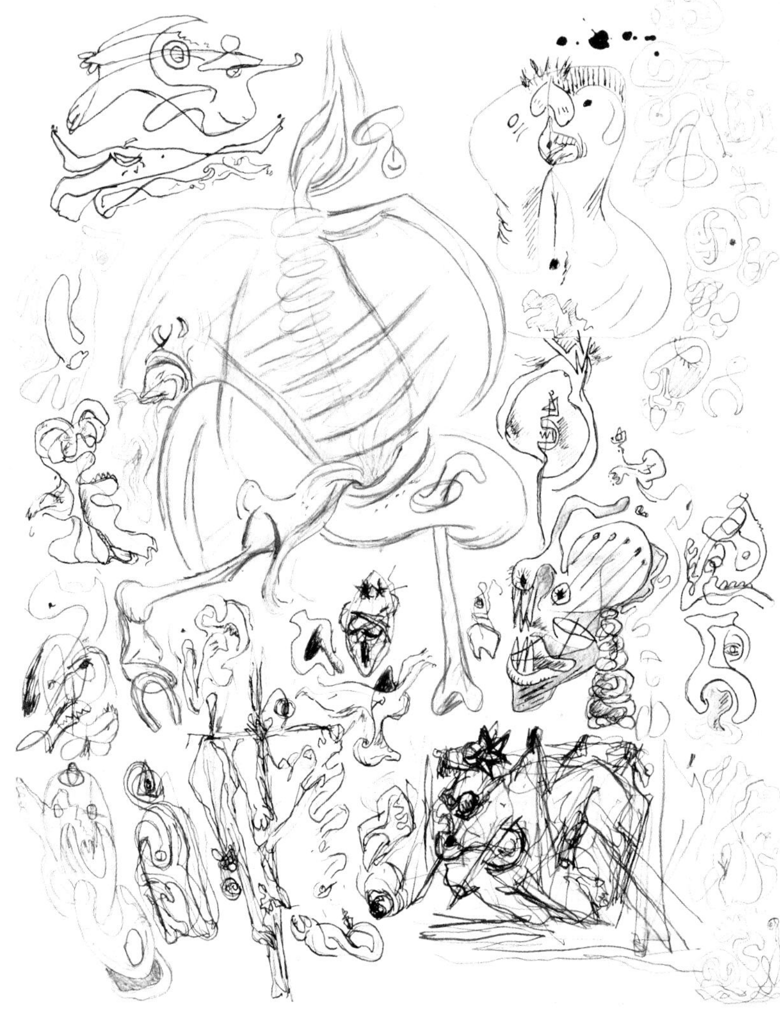

inner themes testifies to the potency of the latter's visionary aesthetic and ideological goals, as well as their powerful dialectic.

In order to situate the impact of Mexican (and other) artists on Pollock's creativity we should first recognize that by the mid-1940s many younger American artists had begun to exercise a "progression away from ways of referring in which the sensory properties of the art *look like* the referent." As Ann Gibson points out, a significant number of canvases and sculptures being created in New York at that time commenced instead to project qualities that "*functioned like*"—rather than imitated the appearance of—models in the real world.[9] While Pollock ultimately chose to prioritize perception (and experience) over representation, perhaps paradoxically, Siqueiros provided him particularly strategic clues for going about this. Siqueiros is, however, not the only protagonist in the story of Pollock and Mexican art; the fierce and passionately mythic vision of José Clemente Orozco contributed earlier and in more generative ways.

"Orozco's violence," the critic Lawrence Alloway observed, "often seems to escalate from a specifically political revolutionary cause to a 'cosmic' vision of world-wide anguish." Alloway, one of the first writers to investigate seriously Pollock's Mexican fascination, judged this apocalyptic brand of romanticism as "obviously congenial" to him.[10] The importance of the young artist's attraction to and emulation of the heroically stylized elementalism of Orozco's 1932 *Prometheus* mural at Pomona College, as well as his emotional investment in the iconography and convictions of the latter's singularly dramatic Dartmouth University Baker Library mural cycle, are evident in many of Pollock's drawings of the mid- to late 1930s (figs. 42, 43).[11] Although this influence has been identified by previous writers, Polcari and Alloway included, sizing up Orozco's impact in relation to the competing yet complementary example of Siqueiros necessitates further amplification.[12]

Actually a more overtly "violent" man than Orozco—he did not deny his part in the 1940 assault on Trotsky's residence-in-exile in the Coyocoán suburb of Mexico City and was jailed numerous times for his renegade political escapades—Siqueiros remained committed to radical ideals, culminating in his willingness to fight in the Spanish Civil War. As a result, he held up the model of a different kind of "action" to Pollock and others of his generation. While stories have circulated of young Jackson sitting around in Greenwich Village bars and cafés listening raptly as Siqueiros recounted tales of Los Tres Grandes wearing gun belts to defend their early murals and of the defiantly macho Mexican famously brandishing a revolver at his 1939 New York farewell dinner before he left for Spain, these do not embody the true essence of his example.[13] Indeed, as Mexican scholar Irene Herner has shown, the artistic expression of Siqueiros's Post-Baroque rhetorical aims, achieved primarily by inventing new media and reinventing visual space, were ultimately less aggressive than paradisiacal. Similar judgment can probably be made about Pollock, a violent man only when drunk, which was for him a noncreative state.[14]

Regarding reevaluation of the impact of Siqueiros on artistic developments in the United States, Reuben Kadish once again provided important information. Acting as Siqueiros's part-time driver in Los Angeles in 1931, he became smitten with the Mexican's charms.[15] As previously established, along with Pollock's brother Sande, Reuben joined the Bloc of Painters that Siqueiros set up to create *América Tropical* the following year (see fig.22). In reference to this highly controversial project, Il Duco would himself later remark, "From here all my methods changed on the road to a modern technology for social modern art."[16] Recalling the heady days when he and other budding West Coast artists (including Philip Guston) discovered Mexican art, Kadish declared, "Siqueiros coming to L.A. meant as much then as the Surrealists coming to New York in the forties."[17]

Unlike Noguchi, Guston, and Motherwell, Pollock had only limited contact with Mexico, making a very brief visit to Ensenada, just south of San Diego, with another League friend, Whitney Darrow, Jr., in the summer of 1932. Nonetheless, as a result of his contact with Los Tres Grandes in Los Angeles and New York — Orozco and Siqueiros in particular — Pollock's example is equally crucial in repositioning Mexico's relationship to American modernism. "The context in which Pollock is portrayed, and the company he is thought to keep has become a litmus test of scholarship, critical scruples, and changes in ideological and historical perspective," Robert Storr has pointed out. Moreover, Storr explains, no other issue "cuts closer to the root of 'the Pollock problem' in this regard than that of the place accorded the Mexican muralists."[18] While recognition of the creative possibilities inherent in neutralizing the opposition of Surrealism to Cubism is commonly described as catalytic for mid-twentieth-century American artistic innovation, how this happened was more complex, and Mexico is thoroughly implicated.

Just three months after Pollock's fatal automobile crash in August 1956, British critic John Berger targeted a core contrast between the achievements of Pollock and the Mexican muralists. "I believe that Pollock imaginatively, subjectively, isolated himself," Berger wrote in a London newspaper review. "His paintings are like pictures painted on the inside walls of his mind."[19] This aptly phrased appraisal, whether or not it was meant positively, was probably based on Pollock's own stated goals, which were already well known. Applying in 1947 for a John Simon Guggenheim Foundation fellowship (which, unlike Noguchi and Martha Graham, he did not get) Pollock had already begun to enunciate these goals with utmost precision. "I believe the easel picture to be a dying form and the tendency of modern feeling is

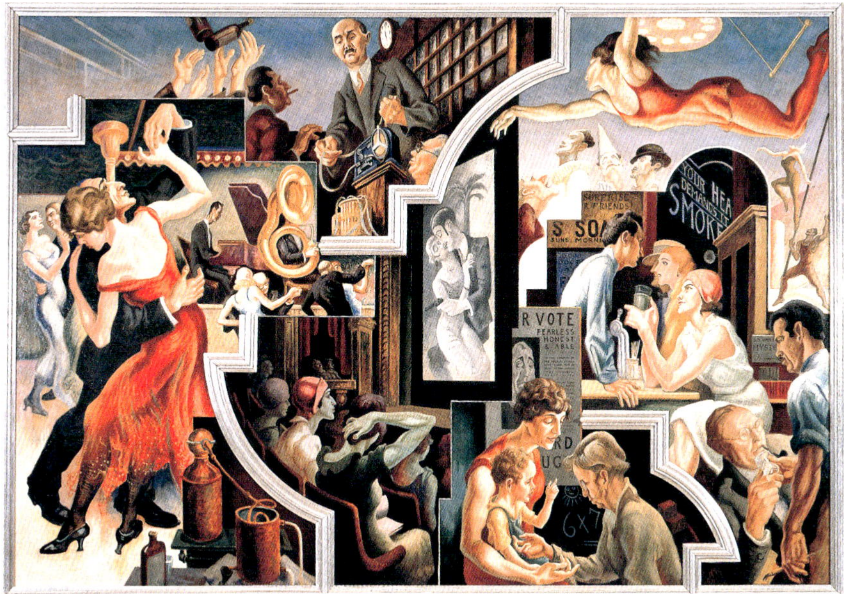

44 Thomas Hart Benton, *City Activities with Dance Hall*, from *America Today*, 1930. Distemper and egg tempera on gessoed linen with oil glaze. Collection of AXA Equitable, New York. © AXA Financial, Inc.

towards the wall picture or mural," he wrote. "I believe the time is not yet ripe for a full transition from easel to mural. The pictures I contemplate painting would constitute a half-way state, and an attempt to point out the direction of the future without arriving there completely."[20]

For a man whose verbal skills were famously lacking, this is an extremely well-phrased statement, and Pollock seemingly had help from Greenberg in preparing it. But the basic ideas expressed had been simmering for almost two decades. Seventeen years prior, Paul Jackson Pollock, a somewhat rootless youth born in Wyoming and raised in Arizona and California, had left his Los Angeles high school without graduating. He moved to New York City, making both a geographic shift and name change at the suggestion of his eldest brother. Charles Pollock, an aspiring artist, encouraged his troubled sibling to join him in studying with Regionalist Thomas Hart Benton at Manhattan's renowned Art Students League. Importantly for Jackson's development, Benton, a sort of American right-wing counterpart to the Mexicans, had also been garnering fame for major mural commissions.[21]

While claiming subscription to an isolationist refusal of foreign influence, Benton (a reformed Marxist) continued nevertheless to reference the European Old Masters he still greatly admired. In large part, as he detailed in a series of articles written during the late 1920s, Benton conceptualized his own highly mannered, rhythmic mural compositions as an "extension of muscular action patterns" (fig. 44).[22] Recognizing this as a major precept to which Pollock had early concentrated exposure is absolutely crucial to understanding his later innovations, accomplishments, and enthusiasms. Whereas

Alloway believed Pollock's stint with Benton had prepared him to accept Mexican influence, the chronology was actually reversed. Benton's was not the first wall art Pollock admired, nor probably even the most important. And certainly, by the time he submitted his Guggenheim statement, the heyday of his teacher's folksy-Baroque illustrative style had faded into history.[23]

Pollock's rather heretical intention to crossbreed progress in art by painting pictures that would "function between the easel and mural" had no doubt been clarified through ongoing conversations with Clement Greenberg, by 1947 his leading supporter. Greenberg despised Benton and everything he stood for almost or at least as much as he loathed Surrealism. In fact, Greenberg would stake his critical reputation on championing the advances in art represented by Pollock's repudiation of his teacher's anti-modern prejudices. By the time the two men likely collaborated on Pollock's grant proposal, greater receptivity to a wider variety of outside stimuli was encouraging the young artist to experiment in more novel ways. A bit ironically, perhaps, the direction of Greenberg's advocacy contributed to keeping Pollock's focus on reconfiguring an establishment art form of the past. Akin to the aims of the Mexicans, although very differently framed, the wholesale reinvention of the art-historically sanctioned "big" picture's meaning was becoming an ever more important goal for Pollock.[24]

"Little Man in Big Sea"

At the point when Pollock was trying to obtain a Guggenheim grant, Clement Greenberg was one of the very few people other than his wife invited to visit the artist's Long Island studio. The novel creative methods that Pollock initiated less than two years after moving from New York City to The Springs in late 1945 would not become better known until Hans Namuth's distinctive photos showing him at work began appearing in print a few years before Greenberg's "'American-Type' Painting" was published.[25] Wider access to Namuth's images in the early 1950s certainly allowed for a better understanding of the highly disruptive ramifications of Pollock's unusual enterprise. In particular, Namuth's extensive documentation of the making of *Autumn Rhythm: Number 30, 1950*, and other so-called "classic" allover poured pictures of that year, revealed the astounding aesthetic potential of what might be understood as Pollock's rather extremist extension of Benton's valorization of muscular process (fig. 45).

In more than five hundred black-and-white photos and two films Namuth exposes Pollock's engagement in such unorthodox means (unorthodox, that is, to anyone who had not worked with Siqueiros) as flicking, pouring, dripping, and spattering, as well as actually walking into and mov-

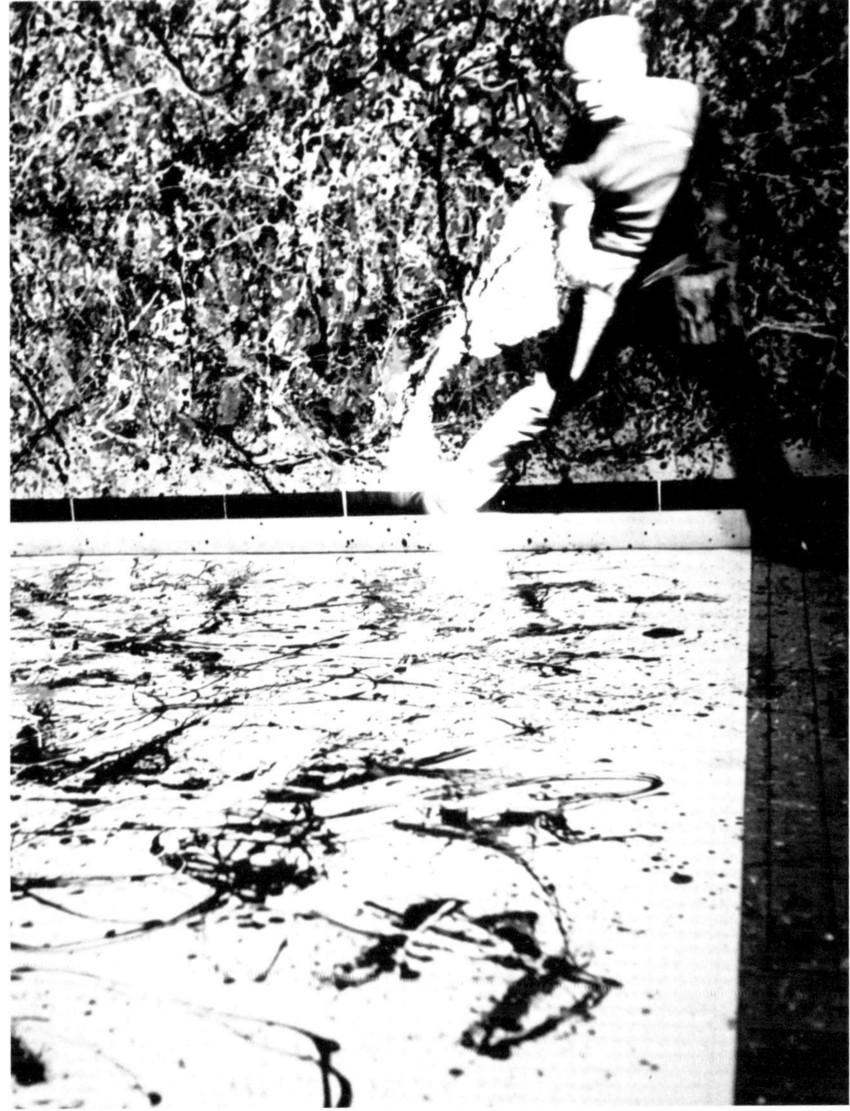

45 Hans Namuth, *Jackson Pollock*, 1950. Courtesy Center for Creative Photography, University of Arizona. © 1991 Hans Namuth Estate.

ing around his pictorial space.[26] Further delineating the impact of Pollock's attraction to the advantages of wall art, Namuth not only provides proof of Pollock's unusually physical method of generating form (based on earlier models, but significantly exceeding them), his images demonstrate the degree to which Pollock became transfixed through aesthetic and psychic transformation when surrounded by his own oversized paintings. Prompted by critic Harold Rosenberg's 1952 explanation in *Art News* that the gestural Abstract Expressionists had begun converting the canvas from a place where objects are depicted into an "arena in which to act,"[27] attention to Namuth's photographs concentrated on their dramatic revelation of Pollock's "performance" of his unconscious as he paints.[28] Namuth's images, with their well-chosen angles of vision and framing, brilliantly demonstrate the level at which Pollock's ambition to blend easel and mural conventions was capable of spectacular achievement.

Since interconnected traces of the oversight of his bodily activities playing out on the "inside walls of his mind" were displayed on the real walls around him and on the floor where his current painting rested, at work in the relatively small space of the barn on his property, Pollock immersed himself in a new visual field encompassing perpendicular directions.[29] "Little Man in Big Sea," the witty caption that Happenings innovator Allan Kaprow later appended to one of Namuth's famous photographs , captures adeptly the impression of envelopment so viscerally engendered.[30] This sensation was obviously derived from, yet also substantially subverted, the muralistic; with the possible exception of Picasso's narratively based *Guernica,* no European modernist example had yet come even close to anticipating this breakthrough. How did Pollock arrive at this extreme and exciting point, and how did the Mexicans play a role in his trajectory?

The Real Man Is Orozco

The highest, the most logical, the purest strongest form of painting is the mural. In this form alone, is it one with the other arts.[31]

— JOSÉ CLEMENTE OROZCO, 1929

Although Benton admired Orozco, Rivera, and Siqueiros (he praised all three for their initiation of a "profound and much-needed redirection of art toward its ancient humanistic functions"), Pollock's attraction to Mexican art commenced well before his attendance at Benton's classes in New York.[32] Jackson's brother Charles seems to have made the initial introduction, writing to him in 1929, "Are you familiar with the work of Rivera and Orozco in Mexico City? This is the finest painting that has been done, I think, since the sixteenth century." He continued: "Here are men with imagination and intelligence recognizing the implements of the modern world and ready to employ them."[33]

Like Kadish's and Guston's, Pollock's roots were closely tied to the cultural profile of Los Angeles between the two world wars and its distinctive political, social, intellectual, and demographic mix. He even dabbled in theosophy, attending camp meetings in Ojai to hear Krishnamurti speak. After their joint expulsion from Manual Arts High, Guston (who was, of course, still Phillip Goldstein) apparently took Pollock to meetings at the

Brooklyn Avenue Jewish Community Center, where aging Bolsheviks tried to "convert the boys" to become Communists.[34] As we've seen, in Southern California, perhaps more than anywhere else in the United States during that volatile era, Marxist sympathies frequently translated to an engagement with precepts of the Mexican revolution. Kadish's joining Siqueiros's Syndicate of Painters in 1932 and the blatant Communistic propaganda that he, Guston, and Pollock's next-oldest brother, Sande, prepared for the Los Angeles Workers' Cultural Center the following year led to Siqueiros helping obtain the Morelia commission (see fig. 32). Since young Jack had once mused to Charles about "going to Mexico City if there is any means of making a livelihood there,"[35] had he stayed out west a bit longer, it is possible that he too would have warmed to Siqueiros at that time and also joined the Syndicate; whereas Sande decided against it, he might even have gone with his friends on their year-long Mexican journey.

In any event, debilitating psychological problems with alcohol, developing in his late teens and increasing in his early twenties, would perhaps have precluded artistic success for Jackson Pollock south of the border. But moving east instead did not curb the continuing impact of Mexican innovations. Benton particularly admired Orozco, arranging shows for him in Philadelphia and at the Art Students League just before Pollock came to New York. Will Barnet, another artist starting at the League around the same time as Pollock, recalled that, even a year after Orozco's show there, "the students and faculty were still talking of the monumental forms, the sober drama of the content." Everyone at the Art Students League, Barnet said, wanted to paint murals.[36]

Alma Reed, Thomas Hart Benton's dealer in the late 1920s, championed Orozco at her East Fifty-seventh Street gallery, Delphic Studios, providing New Yorkers ample opportunity to study his style and imagery in a permanent room which, up through 1935, was devoted to Orozco's art. Benton and Orozco both painted murals at the New School for Social Research during the fall and winter of 1930–31.[37] Pollock did "action posing" for Benton on site and seems to have encountered Orozco at Benton family dinners, to which he was frequently invited. He watched Orozco and an assistant "blitzpaint" *Dive Bomber and Tank*, six three-by-nine-foot portable panels, in July 1940 at the Museum of Modern Art.[38] It is known that Pollock read the magazine *Creative Art;* an article by Reed published in September 1931 summarizes what likely drew him to the Mexican's work. "If Orozco were given to phrase-making," Reed expounded, "his definition of art would undoubtedly be: 'First, emotion; second, the power to communicate emotion; and last, the perfection of ways and means of communicating emotion.'"[39] Orozco's obsessive focus on sensation had a strong effect on Pollock's ambitions, but he would reorient this emphasis significantly.

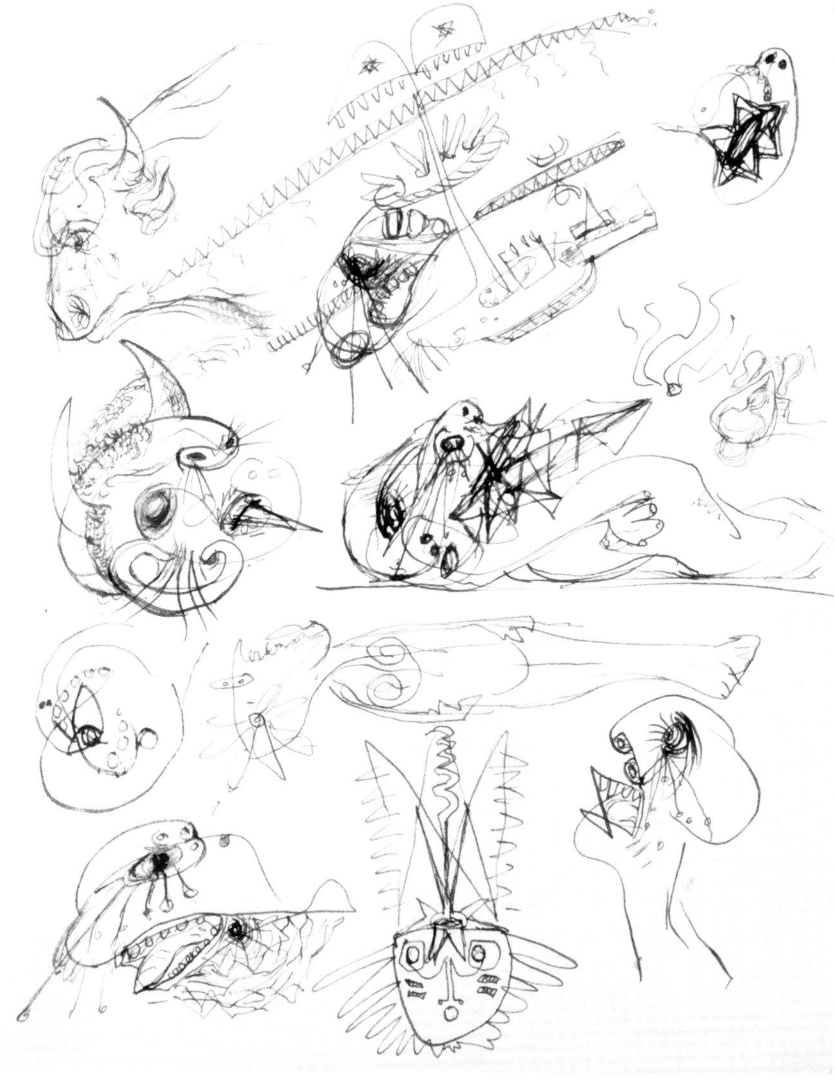

By the late 1930s, riddled with doubts about his personality and aesthetic uniqueness and under psychiatric care, Jackson Pollock initiated a concentrated attempt to mine his unconscious as a source of visual imagery.[40] Beyond Benton's influence at this point and deeply involved in a self-generated "contest" with an artist he would never actually meet, what Pollock began to conjure often resembled (as critic Hilton Kramer noted) "a Surrealist battleground on which Picasso and the Mexican muralists were fighting it out."[41] Drawings Pollock brought to his Jungian analysts during this period validate the ongoing appeal of the latter and authenticate his attempts to integrate their ideas into a wider modernist context. Interpreting these with Dr. Joseph Henderson and Dr. Violet Staub de Laszlo played a cardinal role in helping Pollock initiate his search for a personal and artistic direction to follow (fig. 46). Guston and Kadish may have played a small part in stimulating this; after their return from Morelia, the two briefly "camped out" on the floor of Sande and Jackson's Greenwich Village apartment, excitedly bringing a "renewed enthusiasm for Siqueiros's 'kinetics' and Orozco's emotional plasticity."[42]

As Kramer recognized, Pollock's growing fascination with the more abstract innovations of European avant-garde art ran parallel to his fixation with Los Tres Grandes during the late 1930s. Diego Rivera's early career had also included a Cubist phase, but, unlike Rivera, Pollock never went to Paris or knew Pablo Picasso, Cubism's primary innovator. Both Rivera and Pollock struggled first to assimilate and then to renounce Picasso, although they chose different routes to resolve this Oedipal conflict. While Pollock professed admiration for Rivera's work as early as 1928 (he wrote to Charles of his attraction to the latter's *Día de Flores*, which had just won a prize at the Los Angeles Art Museum) and a few years later he watched its author paint at the New Workers School on West Fourteenth Street, neither Rivera's Cubism nor his distinctive brand of *Mexicánidad* had any discernible repercussions on Pollock's evolving imagery.[43] By contrast, as Robert Motherwell would colorfully explain, Pollock's deep-seated need to "splash" Picasso out provided a major stimulus to his troubled creativity.[44] Indeed, Pollock's admiration for Orozco played strongly into his attraction to Picasso's more expressionistic tendencies.

Although Greenberg singled out Siqueiros as the Mexican example most consequential for Pollock's early work, most observers assign a more influential developmental role to the third revolutionary Mexican, beginning in 1961 with Alloway. Jackson and his brothers Sande and Charles all at various times described Orozco as "the *real* man,"[45] and, for an astonishingly long period, Pollock continued to cite the latter's *Prometheus* as "the greatest painting done in modern times."[46]

Pollock's development of a close and deeply responsive rapport with Orozco's 1930 *Prometheus* mural at Pomona College in Claremont was undoubtedly based in large measure on the Mexican's forceful resurrection in it of the archetypal heroics of Michelangelo, but set into a context more synchronous with modernity (fig. 47).[47] Even a half dozen years or more after moving from Los Angeles (probably c. 1938–39) Pollock filled an entire sketchbook with furiously rendered, semi-abstract compositions drawn in ink, colored pencil, and graphite paying strong homage not only to Orozco's enormously imposing California fresco but also to his Dartmouth mural cycle, which Jackson and Sande made a special trip (with Guston and two other friends), up to New Hampshire to see. In these laboriously worked-over sketches,[48] and in related c. 1938–41 paintings such as

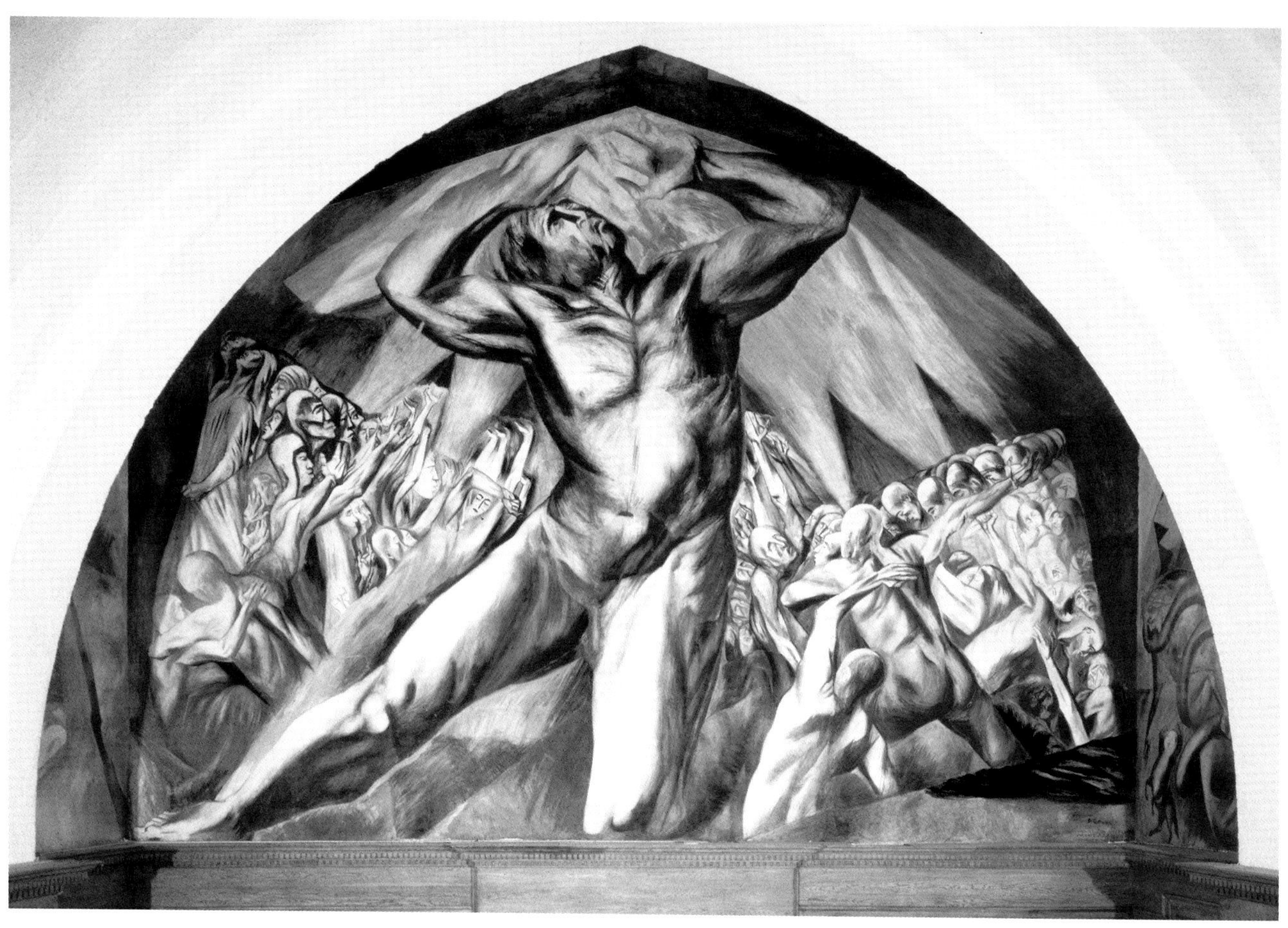

Naked Man with Knife, Pollock attempted to redefine in personal terms his profound admiration for Orozco's rigid stylization and dramatically brutal expressiveness (fig. 48).[49]

In any attempt to revise an accepted judgment it is helpful to find a model that shares certain compelling characteristics but ultimately differs in one or more suggestive ways. As such, contrasting Pollock in this nascent stage of his career to contemporaries who also regarded the search for aesthetic identity as an assimilative process can be highly instructive. Guston would seem an obvious comparative choice, not only in light of the artists' early comradeship and lifelong "friendly" rivalry, but also because his and Kadish's mural work in Mexico reflects a similar adulation of Italian Renaissance masters, including Michelangelo, in addition to assimilating Siqueiros's formidable impact. As we know, Guston and Kadish's firsthand experience with politically motivated censorship in Los Angeles played a crucial part in helping stimulate them to engender the ambitious iconography of *The Struggle Against Terrorism.* Although all three Southern California friends

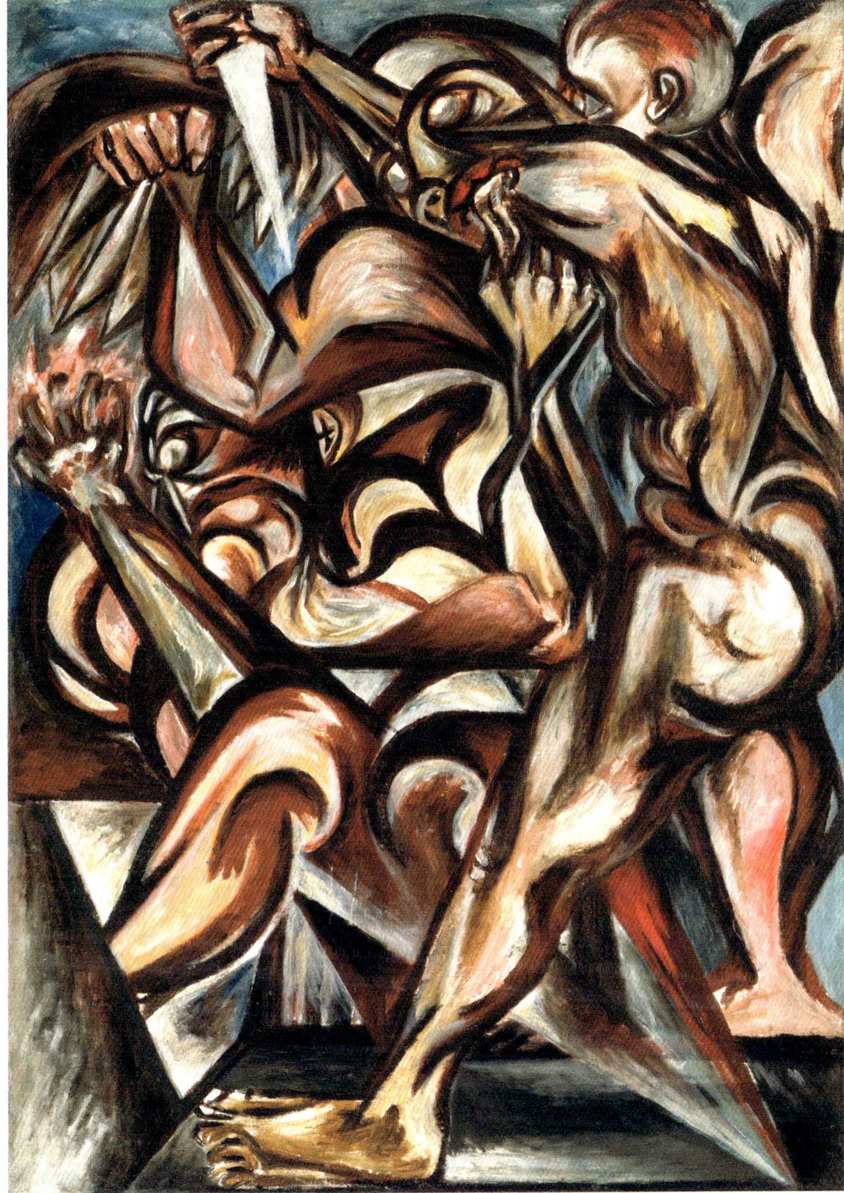

shared an interest in violence and cruelty, when set into a historical and political commentary with personal and global significance, Guston and Kadish's condemnation of inhumanity took on a different emphasis from Pollock's *Naked Man with Knife*. Their artfully painted, monumental muscular figures go about sinister-seeming activities intently but silently, and the mural's overall effect is solemn and ritualistic. Pollock's protagonists, on the other hand, inhabit a claustrophobic nightmare world, and his tension-filled composition presents a textbook case of *horror vacui*, the fear of empty space.

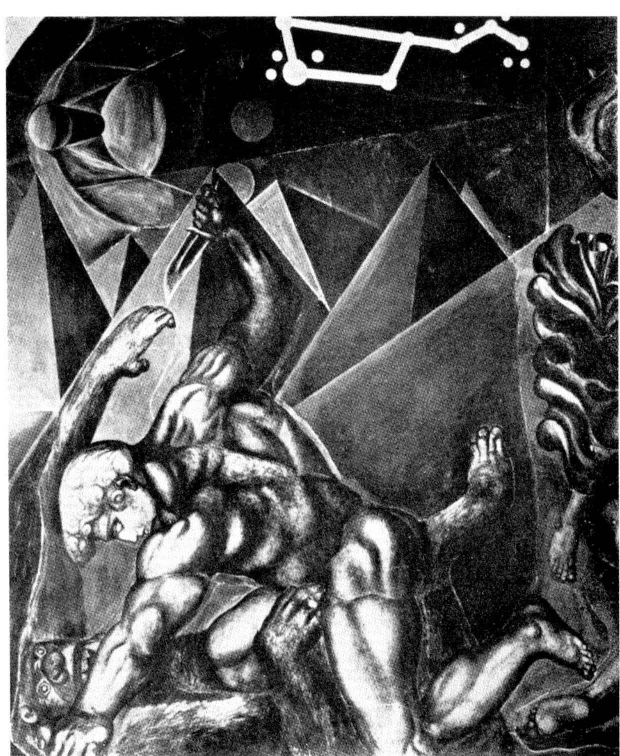

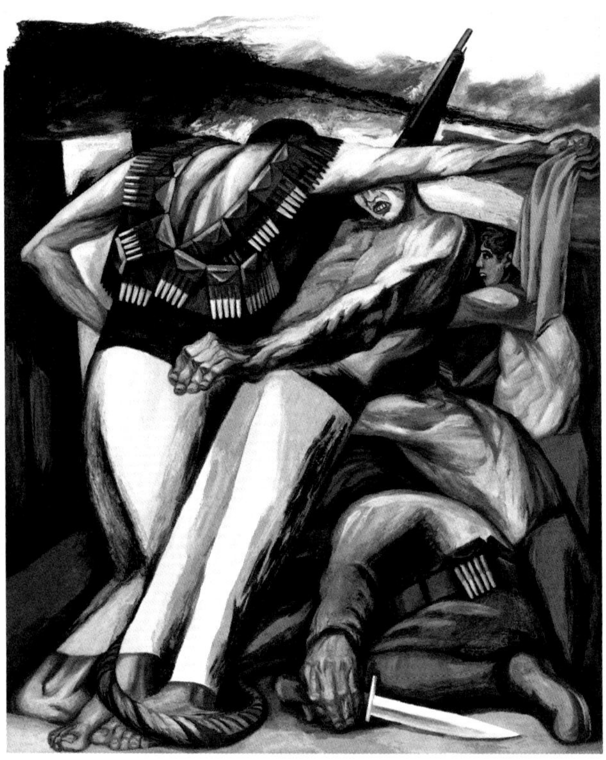

49 José Clemente Orozco, Preparatory painting for *The Two Natures of Man*, 1922 (not extant). Photography courtesy New York Public Library. © 2012 Artists Rights Society (ARS), New York/SOMAAP, Mexico City.

50 José Clemente Orozco, *Barricade*, 1931. Oil on canvas. The Museum of Modern Art, New York. Given anonymously. © 2012 Artists Rights Society (ARS), New York/ SOMAAP, Mexico City.

Based on numerous visual similarities, *Naked Man with Knife* may have been Pollock's somewhat naïve attempt to produce his own interpretation of Orozco's exclamatory panel *The Two Natures of Man,* painted in 1923–24 for the Escuela Preparatoria in Mexico City but no longer extant (fig. 49). This work, like *Prometheus,* was well known in reproduction by the late 1930s. His strong attraction to Orozco's Cain-and-Abel conception is underscored by the unusual circumstance of Pollock's having made two smaller compositions that appear to be studies for his own exaggerated version. These also resemble Orozco's 1931 easel painting *Barricade* (donated in 1937 to the Museum of Modern Art) in which a Mexican soldier or rebel wearing a bandolier reaches with his right arm to subdue a bare-chested peon (fig. 50). Interestingly, in one of Pollock's studies, a gouache, he represents a white-haired woman as being vanquished (fig. 51). Taken in combination, a revenge or wish-fulfillment motive is strongly suggested by these three works. Where this feeling may have been directed, consciously or subconsciously, is bolstered by what is known of Pollock's private fantasies through various family statements. The subsequent disposition of *Naked Man with Knife* is also pertinent—after another brother, Jay, refused it, Jackson gave it to his mother, with whom he had a highly troubled relationship.[50]

An equally indicative contrast to the one with Guston might also be

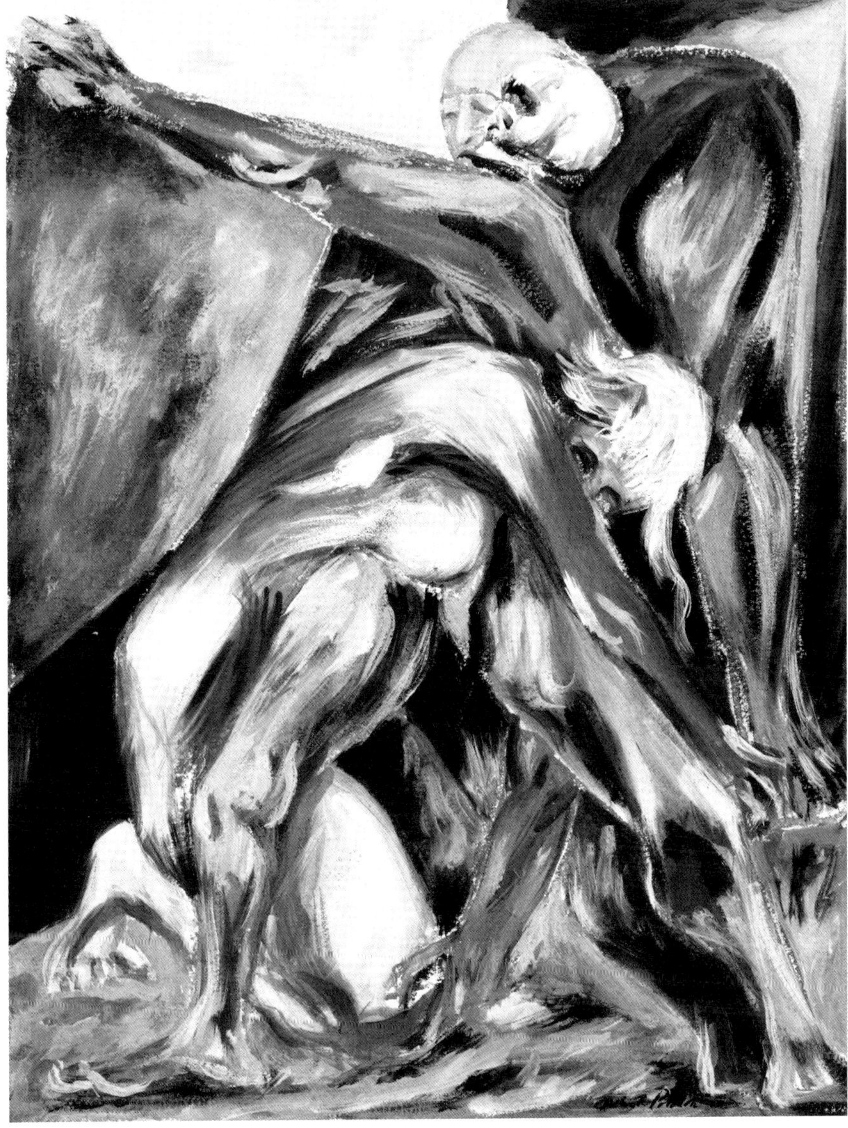

made between Pollock and Arshile Gorky, another admirer of Picasso and also a transplanted New Yorker (in Gorky's case, from Eastern Europe). Sometimes an image's identity can best be defined as residing somewhere in the gap between itself and a repertoire of other images in play.[51] Keeping this Derridean equation in mind, Gorky's early preoccupation with his mother can serve as another foil helping to explain what Pollock seems to have garnered from Orozco as a prototype. Over a ten-year period, from 1926 to 1936, Gorky created two paintings and numerous drawings based on a photograph taken in 1912 in Van City, Turkish Armenia. The young Gorky (known then as Vosdanig Adoian) stands stiffly next to his seated

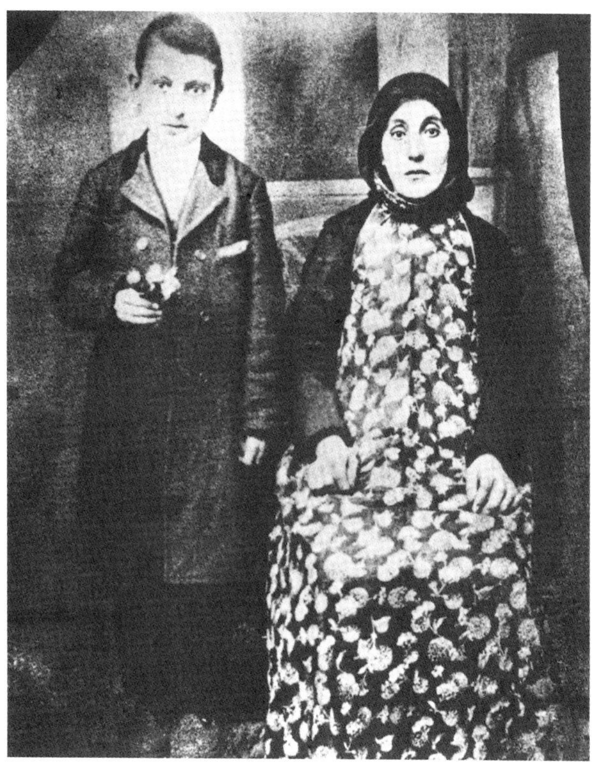

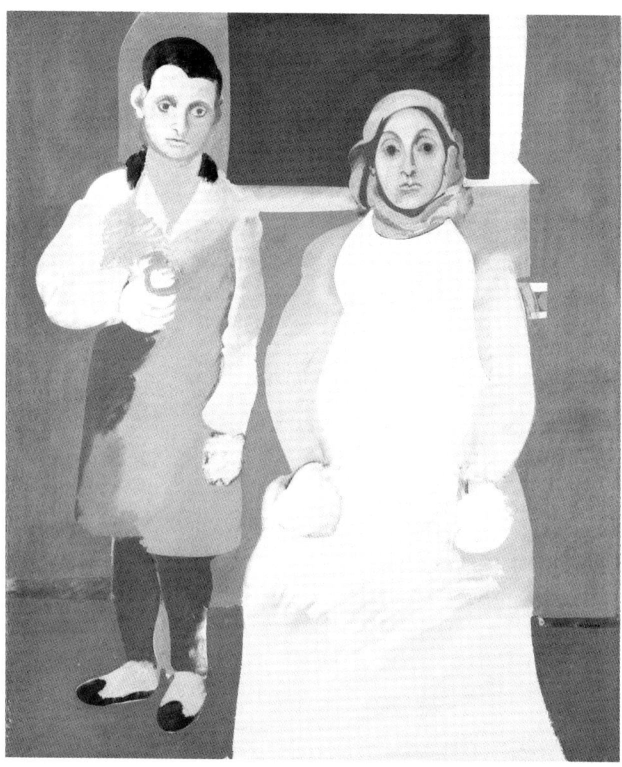

mother in this sad and moving image captured shortly before her tragic death from starvation on a march dictated by the Turks. A distant look in her eyes and the set of her lips signifies her fear, fatigue, and introspection. To modify this treasured memento for his own expressive purposes, Gorky eliminated detail and flattened space, reworking icons of the Blessed Virgin in the context of modernist innovation (figs. 52, 53).

Although the visual connection is not quite so clear-cut, Pollock may have "based" another early 1930s composition, known as *Woman,* on a family photo taken in Chico, California, in 1917, depicting mother, father and five sons. Also stiffly posed, this picture apparently underwent a far stranger metamorphosis when filtered through Pollock's differently troubled imagination. In the original, Stella Mae McClure Pollock stands in the back row, composed and robust in her sober Sunday finery. By contrast, the painting's female protagonist looms front and center with legs splayed open, naked except for pendulous earrings and high-heeled shoes. Six figures surround her; the youngest (Jackson perhaps?) attempts in vain to suckle at her breast. Whereas in the source image LeRoy Pollock and his sons are earnest and freshly scrubbed, on canvas, hollow-eyed and (in at least one case) feminized cadavers huddle around a fiercely imposing phallic matriarch (figs. 54, 55).[52]

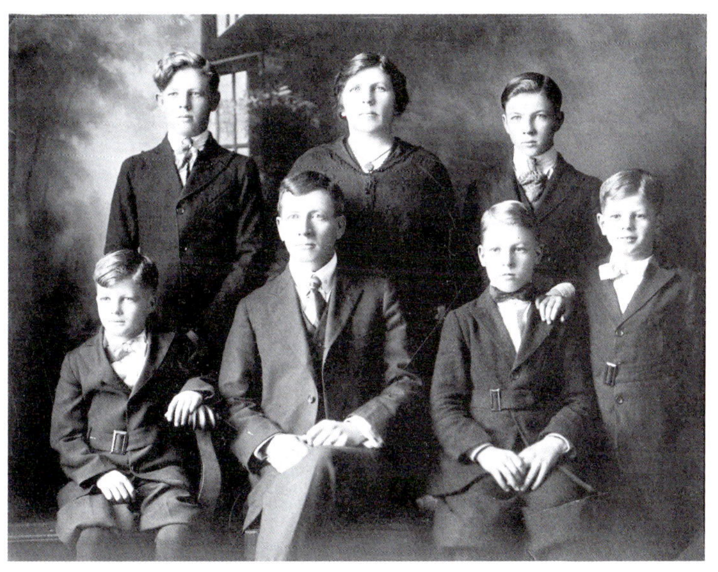

54 Photograph of the Pollock family, Chico, California, c. 1917–18. From left to right: Sanford LeRoy, Charles Cecil, LeRoy, Stella, Frank Leslie, Marvin Jay, Paul Jackson. © Charles Pollock Archives.

55 Jackson Pollock, *Untitled (Woman)*, c, 1930–33. Oil on fiberboard. Nagashima Museum, Kagoshima City, Japan. © 2012 The Pollock-Krasner Foundation / Artists Rights Society (ARS), New York.

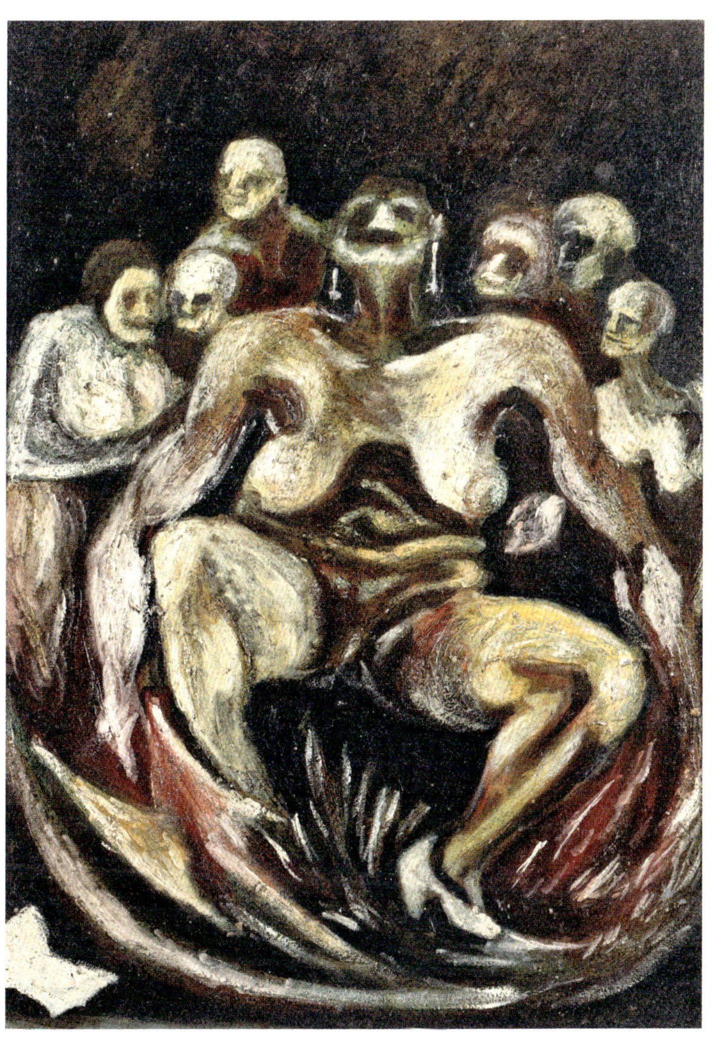

Gorky's two portraits of himself and his doomed mother have an
ephemeral and enigmatic appearance; Pollock's *Woman* likewise demonstrates unreality, but in a rather more nightmarish way. It is doubtful, moreover, that any viewer who accepts the notion that in it Pollock re-presented
his own family situation would detect a similar psychodynamic to Gorky's
at work in its creation. Pollock's attitude toward Stella could not have been
more opposed to Gorky's religious veneration of Lady Shushanik's memory.[53] Indeed, his therapists, siblings, wife, and friends were all well aware
that Jackson's conflicted feelings toward women derived from Stella's alternately remote and smothering attentiveness and his strong aversion to her
controlling personality and belittlement of his father.[54] More sexually disturbing than nostalgic, Pollock's *Woman* discloses not love and devotion but
lack of nurturance and the anxiety of castration.

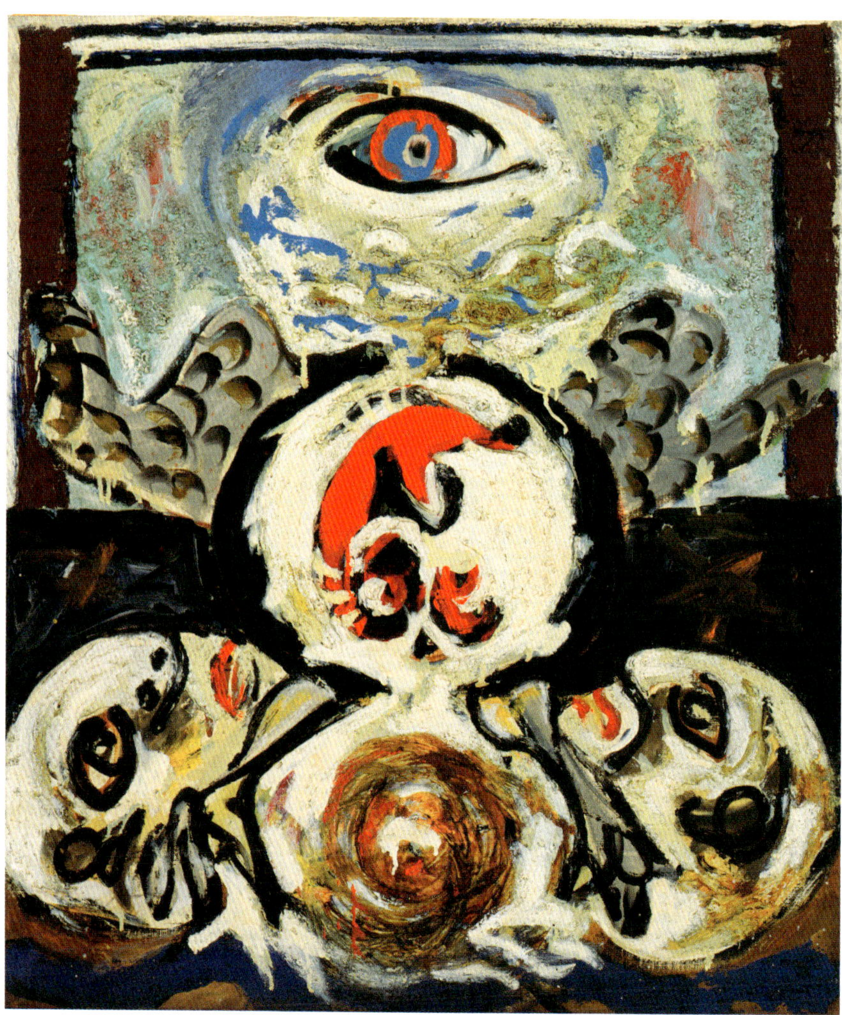

56 Jackson Pollock, *Bird*, c. 1938–41.
Oil and sand on canvas, 27¾ x 24¼ in.
(70.5 x 61.6 cm). The Museum of Modern
Art, New York. Gift of Lee Krasner in
memory of Jackson Pollock. © 2012
The Pollock-Krasner Foundation / Artists
Rights Society (ARS), New York. Digital
Image © The Museum of Modern Art /
Licensed by SCALA / Art Resource, NY.

At the time he created *Woman* (c. 1930–33), the Mexicans—particularly Orozco—would have been the only models familiar to Pollock for such compellingly suggestive deformation. Benton had certainly never made this kind of psychologically agitating work. It was not necessary to the elaboration of Pollock's private subtext for him actually to have seen Orozco's social critiques, including naked prostitutes; we know from his sketchbooks that Pollock was familiar with the latter's take-offs on José Guadalupe Posada's famously grotesque political caricatures, and that he had encountered visually similar references related to the Mexican celebration of the Day of the Dead incorporated by Orozco at Dartmouth.[55] What the literary theorist Harold Bloom might characterize as Pollock's Freudian "mis-reading" of Orozco's style and iconography aided him in producing a patently therapeutic statement in *Woman*.[56] It was certainly in large part through emulating Orozco's example that Pollock became better prepared to understand and mine the more abstractly expressive emotional potentialities he sensed in Picasso. What Orozco had to offer in the way of style and iconography seems to have been remarkably co-terminous with Pollock's aesthetic and personal needs at this crucial juncture. Could the impact of Siqueiros be characterized in any analogous way?

A New Artistic Language

Siqueiros, whom Pollock admired, splashed paint over everything.
To Pollock, having had the experience with him as well as his support,
the idea of splashing paint on a canvas as if it were a float would
come naturally. Then, at a given moment it's "Let's shoot the works."
Nobody makes such a radical invention single-handedly. But how could
a guy have the nerve to let go out of the blue like that?[57]

— ROBERT MOTHERWELL, early 1980s

Jackson Pollock had become aware of the accomplishments of David Alfaro Siqueiros at least as early as 1932, when Sande attended the Mexican's fresco class at the Chouinard School prior to joining the Olvera Street Bloc or Syndicate of Painters.[58] Technical as well as thematic echoes of *América Tropical* (reproductions of which were available at Delphic Studios) are clearly visible in such early '40s transitional works as Pollock's Jungian-inflected canvas *Bird* (fig. 56). Both material and iconographic evidence in the next stage of his artistic growth indicates that, in comparison to Orozco, Siqueiros would have an entirely different but equally important role to play.[59]

It seems likely that Pollock's widely chronicled observation of Navajo

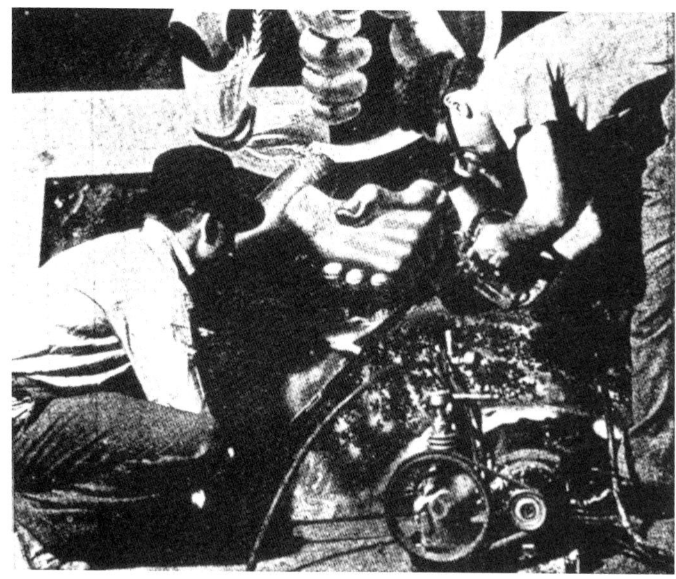

sand painters working in the galleries of the Museum of Modern Art in 1941, the year he created *Bird,* either revived or reinforced his prior attraction to the strong, gritty surfaces of Siqueiros's mural compositions in L.A.[60] The Mexican and his team had created portions of these (including the Chouinard School's *Workers' Meeting,* a fresco Pollock saw in summer 1932) by spraying Duco enamel onto a base of sand and Portland cement. Other sections were done in encaustic and then textured with drills or a blowtorch. Pollock's admixture of sand into the pigment to create a roughened texture in *Bird,* its compositional affinities with the menacing eagle in *América Tropical,* and the physiognomic similarity of his trampled-on faces with the mural's crucified peasant once again suggest a vigorous, somewhat clumsy attempt to reformulate Mexican social vocabulary in accordance with his own private archetypes.[61]

If Orozco helped direct Pollock toward a more complex psychological and artistic identification with Picasso (who also mixed sand into paint), Siqueiros's more advanced experimentation with materials now suggested, as Bloom might phrase it, the potential of a "subversive alternative arrangement" pointing a way out of the anxiety inevitably caused by Cubism's all-powerful influence.[62] Close reading of an untitled work exhibited in Pollock's 1943 debut at Peggy Guggenheim's Art of This Century, now known as *Composition with Pouring II,* can help in assessing the consequences of his ongoing Mexican interests, but some background is required first.

Asked to leave the United States in the wake of the scandal over his anti–U.S. government imagery in *América Tropical,* Siqueiros managed to return (illegally) as a delegate to the American Artists Congress, at which he gave two lectures on "The Mexican Experience in Art" in early 1936. That April he opened a workshop at 5 West Fourteenth Street near Union Square with the intent of creating art for the people. Rejecting traditional media as "archaic" and "anachronistic," Siqueiros had begun formulating in Los Angeles his theory of the "poetic role of materials in shaping a work of art."[63] The full implications of this direction—"the superposition of the objective and the subjective, of true realism and mental realism"[64]—would finally come to fruition in his New York–based activities (with which Noguchi was also familiar). Charles Pollock described the investigations that Siqueiros instigated at his Union Square "laboratory," where Jackson and Sande were now both participants.[65] Workshop assistants were instructed in the use of

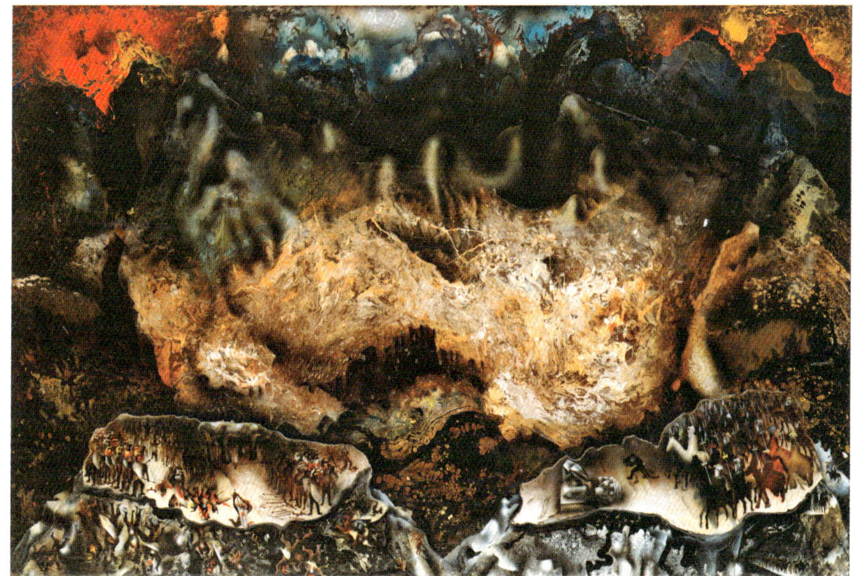

industrial nitrocellulose pigments (especially pyroxilin and Duco enamel), stencils, airbrushes (Siqueiros called these *pistol de aire*), spray guns, methods of superimposition, spontaneous and chance generation of form, including pouring, dripping, and spattering, as well as the embedding of foreign objects (wood, metal, sand, fibers, sawdust) as a way to court "controlled accidents" and increase art's politically subversive potential (fig. 57). "We were able to create the most unsuspected and dynamic things," Siqueiros wrote about his New York workshop activities. "These forms were blended and mutually destroyed, casting the synthesis of their collision into the air."[66]

Never considered ends in themselves, and primarily adopted by Syndicate members to manufacture banners, posters, and floats, including a twenty-five-foot-long collaborative work made for the May Day parade in 1936, Siqueiros also employed similar techniques on more intimate easel paintings he himself created at the Workshop.[67] While equally polemical in intent, the effects created on a smaller scale often bordered on abstraction. It is not clear whether Jackson actually observed Siqueiros making the best-known work of this series, *Collective Suicide* (fig. 58), primarily fabricated by pouring pyroxilin from a can onto a wood panel laid flat on the floor, but he definitely saw this work and similar examples after their completion in 1936.[68] To produce *Collective Suicide*, ostensibly a commentary on the Spanish conquest of the Incas, Siqueiros used sticks to flick the pigment, worked through friskets, employed an airbrush with different nozzles, and dripped lacquer thinner, encouraging accidents to generate dissolving "absorptions" of superimposed color.[69]

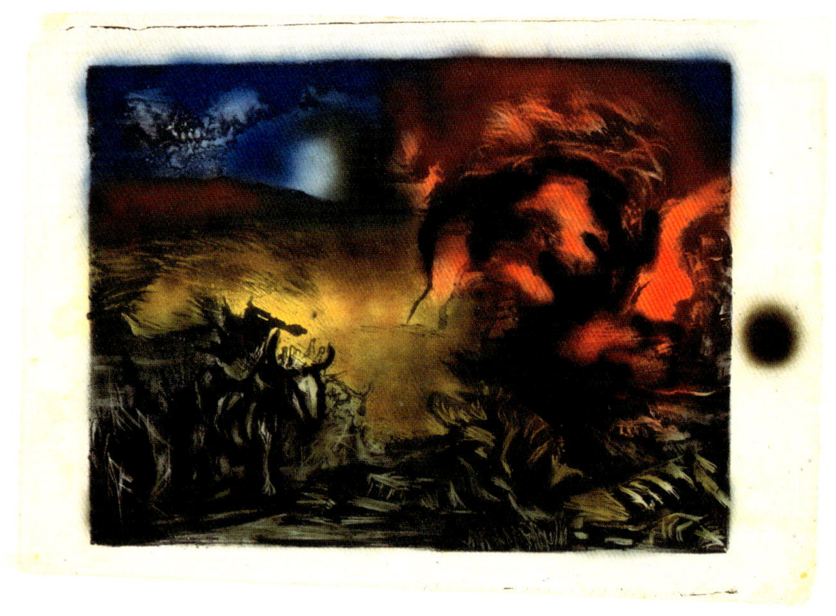

According to Axel Horn, another workshop "comrade," shortly after *Collective Suicide* was completed he and Mervin Jules observed Jackson's attempt to replicate this method by dripping paint onto a canvas placed flat on the floor.[70] That effort has not survived, but a Regionalist-themed lithograph done in 1936 or 1937 to which Pollock added lurid airbrushed color, and a more nonobjective composition of pigment squeezed onto cardboard made a few years later (which he once characterized as his "breakthrough picture"), are two extant indications of a continuing captivation with the spontaneous, nontraditional facture combinations introduced at Union Square (fig. 59).[71] As will be discussed, shortly after creating the latter Pollock took part in another brief experimental group project: joint painting sessions in the winter of 1942–43 at the New York studio of Chilean Surrealist Roberto Matta Echaurren.

Knowledge of Matta's approach to automatism undoubtedly supplied another important variable in Pollock's ability, by the time of his first solo exhibition in November 1943, to rechannel, as it were, his training with Siqueiros. Ideas on risk and method propounded in the late 1930s by the eccentric author, painter, and entrepreneur John Graham[72] were also seminal for helping engender the more intuitive stream-of-consciousness approach Pollock began to take in *Composition with Pouring II* and a few other works like it also exhibited at his debut.[73] In these, recalling Siqueiros, Pollock used improvisation with materials to promulgate content, but what he produced cast a distinctively different meaning.

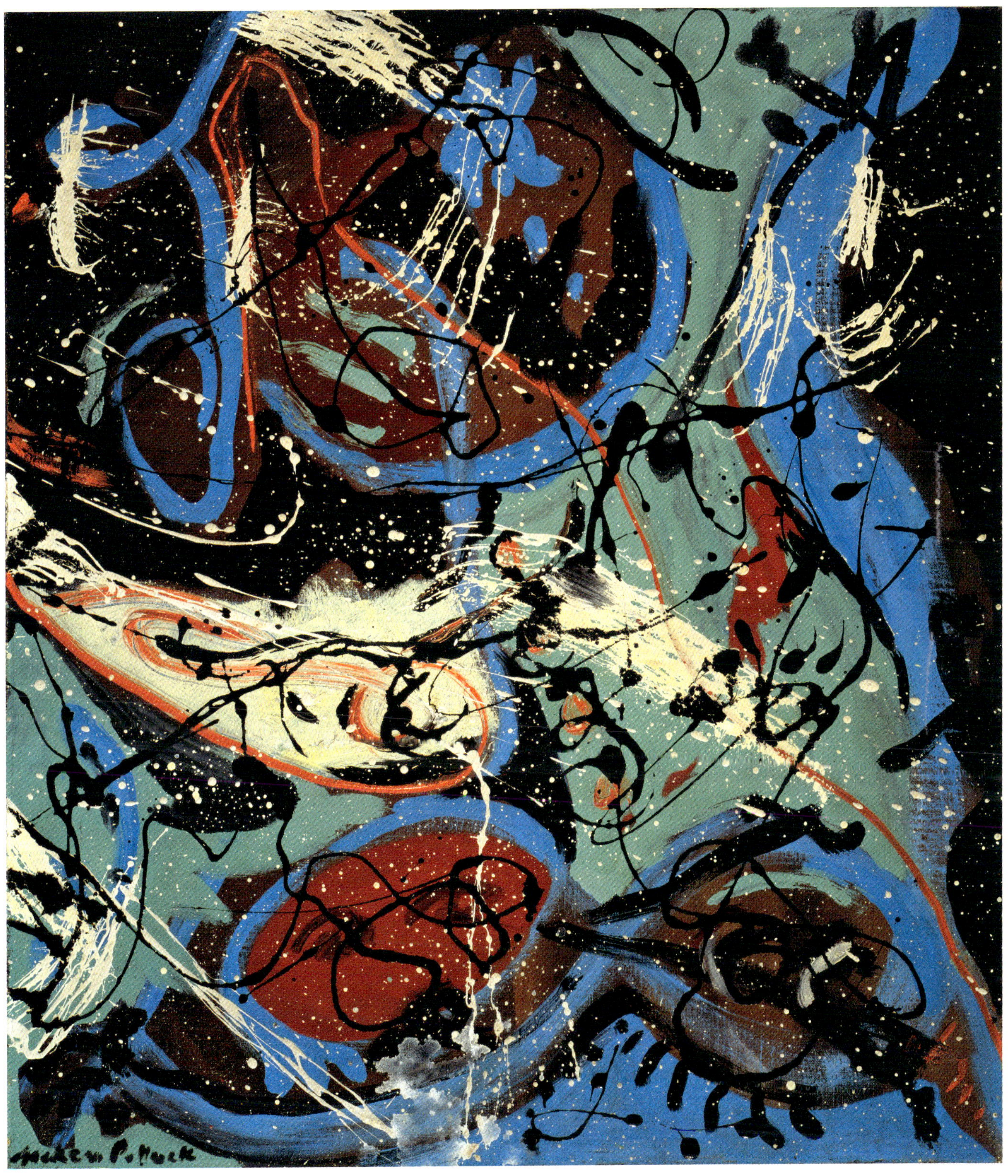

Jackson Pollock

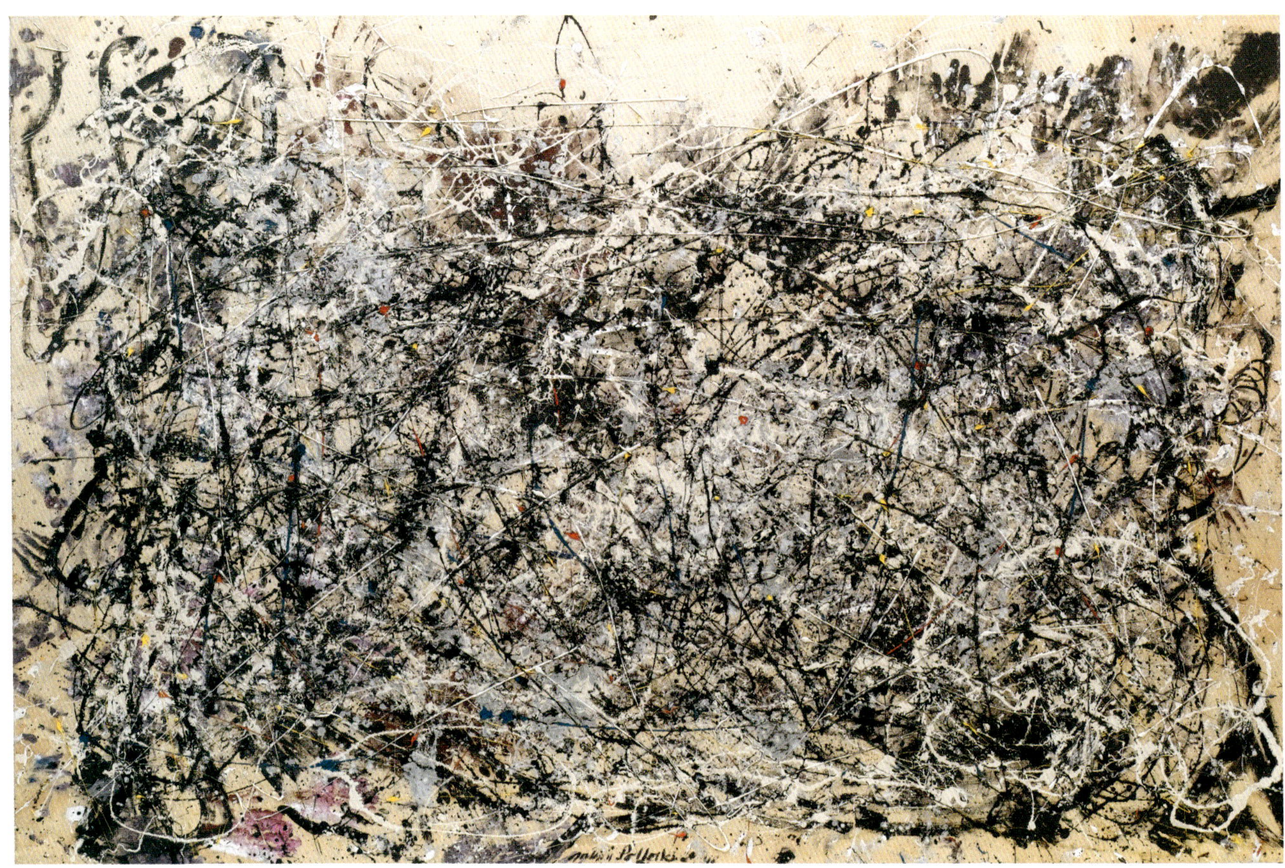

61 Jackson Pollock, *Number 1A, 1948*, 1948. Oil and enamel paint on canvas. The Museum of Modern Art, New York. © 2012 The Pollock-Krasner Foundation/ Artists Rights Society (ARS), New York.

Featuring his initials at upper left interwoven with two phalluses ejaculating pigment, *Composition with Pouring II* in effect constitutes Pollock's admission, or at least his deepening realization, of the inextricable extent to which his psychic, sexual, and painterly identities were intertwined (fig. 60).[74] In this work, with its more obvious drips and spatters, Pollock continued to ponder virility questions he had addressed more imagistically in such earlier paintings as *Woman* or *Naked Man with Knife*.[75] More vividly metaphorizing masculinity both *with* and *in* his process of painting, Pollock now began to demonstrate his growing ability, as Greenberg put it, to advance "beyond the stage where he needs to make his poetry explicit in ideographs."[76]

By 1949, when Pollock's latest exhibition opened at the Betty Parsons Gallery, his retrenchment from methods and imagery associated with the easel tradition—a move incipient six years earlier in *Composition with Pouring II*—was even more patently evident. In the close to mural-sized allover poured canvases initiated the previous year, his ability to release and register physical and psychological experience through pure painterly means had exponentially increased. Using methods that obviously recalled Siqueiros—

working on the floor, pouring pigment from a can, dripping it off sticks, and, as in *Number 1A, 1948*, sometimes imprinting his hand or foot[77]—these signature works demonstrated Pollock's astounding competence at achieving free-standing indexical effects Siqueiros would never have dreamed of generating without argumentation (fig. 61).[78] Converting technique and its calligraphic evidence into a primary and very visceral "means of arriving at a statement," he refocused both his own and the viewer's attention, highlighting causality (how a work has been created) as opposed to message or figuration. Responding, as Motherwell put it, with "his body-and-mind as a whole to the events of reality," Pollock found a way to literalize his "energy and motion," documenting his thoughts and actions in pictorial space.[79]

Although visual evidence exists to prove that Siqueiros also used his own body movements to mediate between concept and material fact, Namuth's splendid photographic images track the astounding, aesthetically transformative powers of Pollock's more autoplastic "cursive sweep" (compare figs. 45 and 62).[80] Differentiating himself from Benton, Pollock shared with and possibly derived from Siqueiros the notion that modern painters should not express their own place and time with forms and methods conceived in the past. Both he and Siqueiros desired, as Pollock once phrased it, to "experience [our] age in terms of painting—not an illustration of— (but the equivalent)."[81] Akin to his radical conversion of Benton's muscular action principles, however, Pollock's conclusions ultimately differed from Siqueiros with implications for himself and others who followed that turned out highly significant.

As John Berger realized, while as interested as the revolutionary Mexicans in monumentality and conquering large areas of visual space, Jackson Pollock's basic instincts also produced a more radical conviction, that a painter's best and truest surfaces were positioned internally. Demonstrating how social meaning can be powerfully expressed through the autographic, Pollock threw an ingenious bridge between the aims and accomplishments of the easel and mural traditions.[82] Despite their age and national differences, he and Siqueiros were simpatico indeed.[83] Transcending any such conventional categories as beauty and ugliness, David Alfaro Siqueiros's dream of an ideal art for the future defined dynamically and interactively was to be realized, but in a way he could never have envisioned.

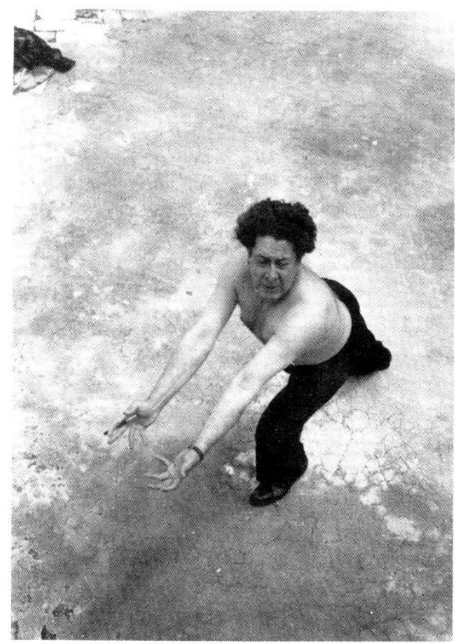

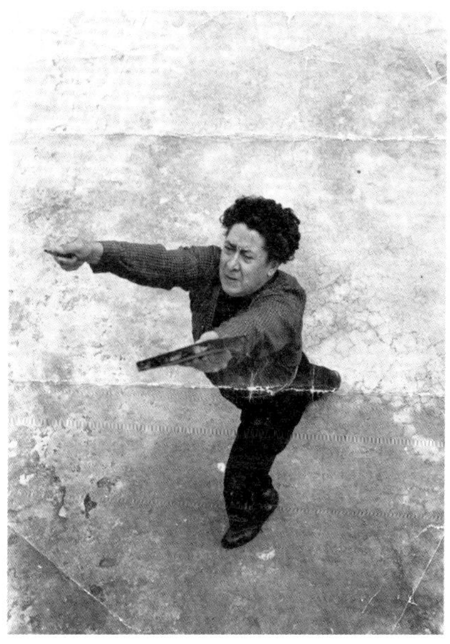

62 (a–b) David Alfaro Siqueiros posing for the figure of the student in his mural, *The People to the University, the University to the People*, 1952. Photographs in black and white. Photographer unknown. Courtesy of Sala de Arte Publico Siqueiros. © 2012 Artists Rights Society (ARS), New York / SOMAAP, Mexico City.

In February 1944, just a few months after his startling debut at Peggy Guggenheim's gallery Art of This Century, Jackson Pollock granted his first interview, set up as answers to a questionnaire in the West Coast–based *Arts and Architecture* magazine. Queried by an anonymous interviewer on whether he found it "important that many famous modern European artists were now living in this country," Pollock answered at first that Picasso and Miró, still abroad, remain "the two artists I admire most." Acknowledging, however, "the fact that good European moderns are now here is very important, for they bring with them an understanding of the problems of modern painting," he added, "I am particularly impressed with their concept of the source of art being the unconscious." [1]

While not specifying any of these "good European moderns" by name, Pollock was certainly referring to the sizable Surrealist contingent residing in New York, escapees from the Nazi repression of "degenerate" art. A baffling point that his first biographer would highlight, Surrealism was never cited as a critical influence in any of Pollock's early reviews, although the artist himself was clearly aware of his debt. [2] By 1989, Steven Naifeh and Gregory White Smith felt they could firmly identify Pollock's *Arts and Architecture* interlocutor as fellow painter Robert Motherwell, another young Art of This Century exhibitor (fig. 63). Jackson, these authors say, nervously "accepted" help from his more erudite friend in formulating answers to questions the latter had devised. [3]

If Motherwell was indeed the interviewer—Peggy Guggenheim's assistant Howard Putzel has also been credited, but without mention of any further instructional role—then discussion of the Surrealist exiles, and Pollock's positive response, should come as little surprise. [4] By 1944 Pollock's and Motherwell's understanding of the merits of Surrealism was having a significant effect on their approaches to painting. Both were familiar with Surrealist art and artists through affiliation with Guggenheim's gallery, a European

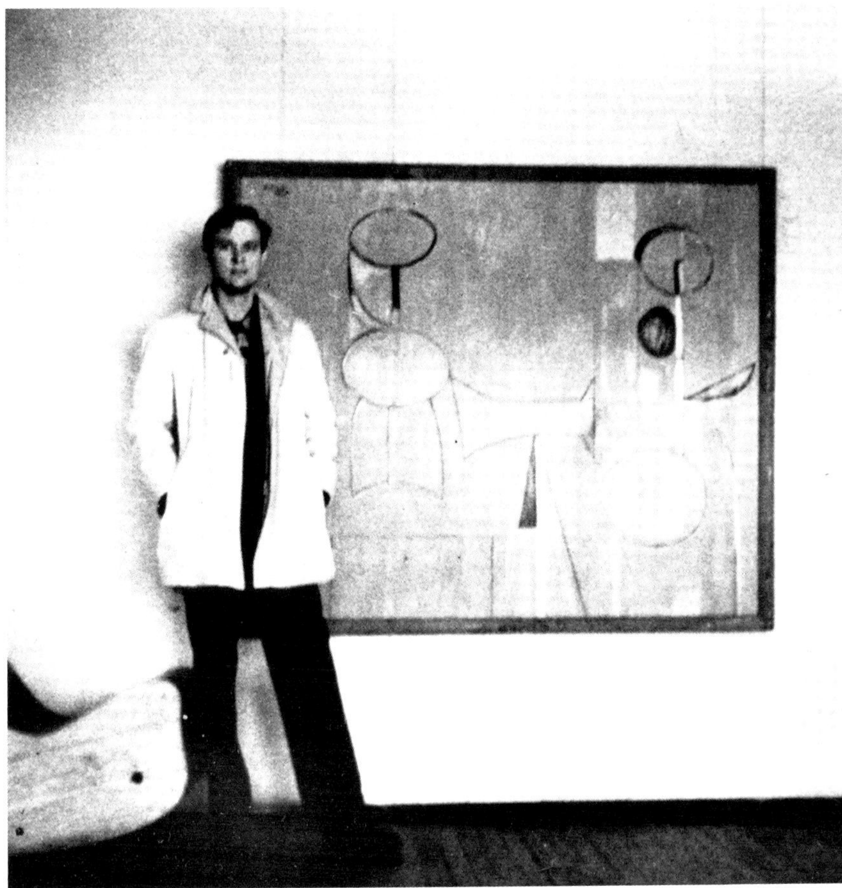

63 Robert Motherwell at his first one-man show, Peggy Guggenheim's Art of This Century Gallery, 1944. Art © Dedalus Foundation, Inc./Licensed by VAGA, New York, NY. Photographer unknown.

émigré exhibition venue and gathering place, and, in Pollock's case, also through his friendship with the Russian-born artist/entrepreneur John Graham. Graham's popular polemic *System and Dialectics of Art*, published in 1939, advocated a somewhat eccentric version of Surrealist ideas, including promotion of the unconscious as a vital source of creative inspiration.

Robert Motherwell's connections to Surrealism were even more direct. Stanford- and Harvard-educated in French literature and philosophy, through additional study at Columbia University with art historian Meyer Schapiro, he came into direct contact with Surrealists-in-exile Kurt Seligmann, Wolfgang Paalen, and Chilean wunderkind Roberto Sebastián Matta Echaurren, to whom he introduced Pollock. Motherwell liked to claim that he had received the equivalent of an in-depth "post-graduate" education in Surrealism under Paalen after traveling to Mexico in 1941 with Matta, Matta's wife, Anne Clark, and another artist, Barbara Reis. Paalen, with his wife, the painter and printmaker Alice Rahon, and their friend and patron photographer Eva Sulzer, had relocated near Mexico City, also to escape

Hitler. Remaining in Mexico longer than the others, Motherwell spent several months living close to Paalen in the Federal District suburb of San Angel. There he solidified his budding romantic liaison with a beautiful Mexican-born woman whose uncle had been a general in the time of Pancho Villa and there, in direct defiance of his father's wishes, Motherwell fully committed himself to painting.

Prologue

What we love best in the surrealist artists is not their Programme. The strength of Duchamp and Ernst has been their dada disrespect for traditional uses of the painter's medium, with its accompanying technical innovations. The strength of Arp, Masson, Miró and Picasso lies in the humanity of their formalism. Dalí long ago became reactionary; art has its traitors, too. [5]

— ROBERT MOTHERWELL, 1944

The same month that Motherwell's own first show opened at Art of This Century, his observations above appeared in the final number of *Dyn*, a widely read avant-garde journal published by Paalen in Mexico and imported to New York. Motherwell's text, "The Modern Painter's World," had been written for a conference panel held the previous summer at Mount Holyoke College. [6] In appraising this notable group of major European modernists he clearly considered himself to be articulating shared opinions and beliefs.

Since Robert Motherwell was not yet thirty and had been painting seriously for only the past three years, what credentials did he have for making this judgment? With the exception of short stints during the late 1920s and early '30s at the Otis Art Institute in Los Angeles and at San Francisco's California School of Fine Arts, as well as some also brief forays at *académies* in Paris, Motherwell had no real art school training. [7] Furthermore, in pursuing advanced humanities degrees at prestigious American universities, taking a European Grand Tour in 1935 with family, spending a year alone in France (1938–39, theoretically to write a thesis on Delacroix's journals), [8] and receiving a $50 per month allowance from his father, an executive at San Francisco's Wells Fargo Bank, he had gained no on-the-job training through the Works Progress Administration. [9] The government's Depression-era fine arts projects provided a defining experience for a great many Americans who would rise to prominence during the following decade; Motherwell was just becoming acquainted with some of these around the time he published "The Modern Painter's World."

After a short stretch teaching in Oregon in 1939, Motherwell made the momentous decision to not return to Harvard, where, prior to his sojourn in Paris, he had been immersed in studying philosophy. Although uninterested in pursuing his father's recommended law or business degree, graduate school of any kind fulfilled minimum family expectations, allowing him to enroll in art history at Columbia University. On the advice of musician Arthur Berger,[10] Motherwell chose as his advisor Meyer Schapiro, a respected medievalist and an avowed Marxist immersed in modernism as well—Schapiro's focus on the ethical and social implications of art was of considerable interest to the mildly rebellious Westerner.[11] As Motherwell would later admit (at least privately), Schapiro became the "most decisive person in my life."[12]

Well aware of Motherwell's affinity for French art and culture (especially his love of Symbolist poetry), Schapiro soon concluded that this would-be painter hounding him for advice might better profit from actual contact with noted European artists residing in their midst. By late 1940 he put Motherwell in touch with Kurt Seligmann, a Swiss émigré and the first of the Surrealists to escape to the United States. Schapiro and Seligmann (both Jewish) met by chance at the Museum of Modern Art and had formed an immediate bond. Before moving to New York, Seligmann, an ethnology enthusiast, had made two trips to North America, including stops in Los Angeles, Colorado, and Alaska. In British Columbia he communed with leaders of the Tsimshian tribe, an account of which appeared in spring 1939 in *Minotaure,* the Parisian Surrealist journal.[13] With the pretext of attending his own exhibition at Karl Nierendorf's Manhattan gallery, Kurt and his wife, Arlette, again traveled to the U.S. and simply never returned.

A side benefit of Seligmann's move across the Atlantic was the opportunity to teach, a necessity contrived to provide a steadier income in his new circumstance. Initially Seligmann accepted just a few private students at his studio in the Beaux-Arts Building at Fifth Avenue and Fortieth Street.[14] On Schapiro's recommendation, Motherwell somewhat unenthusiastically joined Barbara Reis and Monica Flaherty as an early pupil.[15] Monica was the daughter of experimental film producer Robert J. Flaherty, famous for such 1920s silent classics as *Nanook of the North*. Reis's parents had first met Kurt and Arlette at the 1939 New York World's Fair. Her father Bernard, an accountant, financial advisor, and collector, quickly became a patron of sorts to the newly arriving Surrealists, some of whom Seligmann helped to escape.[16] Several evenings a week her mother Becky Reis prepared food "in the French manner" so their recent friends would feel more at home. *VVV,* André Breton's Surrealist magazine-in-exile begun in 1942, was purportedly cooked up at the Reises' Thanksgiving table and could not have been produced without Bernard's support.[17]

In 1984, playwright and essayist Lionel Abel published a fascinating memoir, one chapter of which was dedicated to his wartime experiences with the Surrealists in New York. In this text, first put out a few years earlier in *Commentary* magazine, Abel provides a vivid firsthand idea of what the youthful Bob Motherwell was like. "I visited Meyer Schapiro one summer night in 1942," he writes, "and found him engaged in conversation with a slender, well set-up, quite handsome young man, with blond hair falling in pale, flat lines across a high forehead. This was Robert Motherwell, then only up to the prologemenon of what has been a brilliant career." Motherwell, he said, "followed some courses by Schapiro and had studied the aesthetics of the American philosopher David Prall, whom, during this evening, he frequently cited. Apparently blind to his own rather Saxon blondness, he stressed that evening the fact—to him, it seemed a fact—that Anglo-Saxon painters lack pictorial imagination." Sensing this young man's strong desire to overcome his WASP upbringing, upon discovering Motherwell's "deep" involvement with Chilean Surrealist Matta, Abel credits this opinion to the powerful draw of that burgeoning friendship.[18]

In view of Motherwell's obvious naïveté and somewhat disheveled appearance ("I can hardly remember any time," the writer recalled, "when he didn't have a little paint on his face or even the tip of his nose, and his shirt always hung out over his pants") Abel was astonished to find that this virtually unknown young artist was also in close touch with André Breton, the founder of Surrealism. They had met at Seligmann's studio, where Motherwell also first encountered Duchamp, Ernst, and Tanguy. Somewhat credulously, he appeared at Schapiro's that night to ask for recommendation of sources to read on the class struggle. He wanted to bone up for conversations with Breton, who was also a Marxist. Schapiro's response, "You can't just open a book . . . to learn about class you have to struggle yourself," led Motherwell to see "at once that he had been imperceptive" and blush. A decision was then made that he would take Abel along on his next meeting with the French poet.

By the time of this encounter at Schapiro's, Motherwell had actually already been to Mexico, gotten married, and at least begun several paintings presciently based on a Spanish theme. One of these would be featured in dealer and collector Sidney Janis's influential 1944 traveling exhibition *Abstract and Surrealist Art in America,* which was finishing its run at the Mortimer Brandt Galleries in New York. Motherwell's eloquent statement for Janis's catalogue indicates a further level of maturity by then in regard to Surrealism (fig. 64). *The Spanish Prison,* he wrote, "like all my works, consists of a dialectic between the conscious (straight lines, designed shapes, weighed color, abstract language) and the unconscious (soft lines, obscured shapes, *automatism*) resolved into a synthesis which differs as a whole from either. The hidden Spanish prisoner must represent the anxieties of modern life, the intense Spanish-Indian color, splendor of any life."[19] What had transpired in the intervening several years to produce this situation?

64 Robert Motherwell, *Spanish Prison, Window* (formerly *The Spanish Prison*), 1943–44. Oil on canvas. Mr. and Mrs. Meredith Long, Houston, Texas. Art © Dedalus Foundation, Inc./Licensed by VAGA, New York, NY.

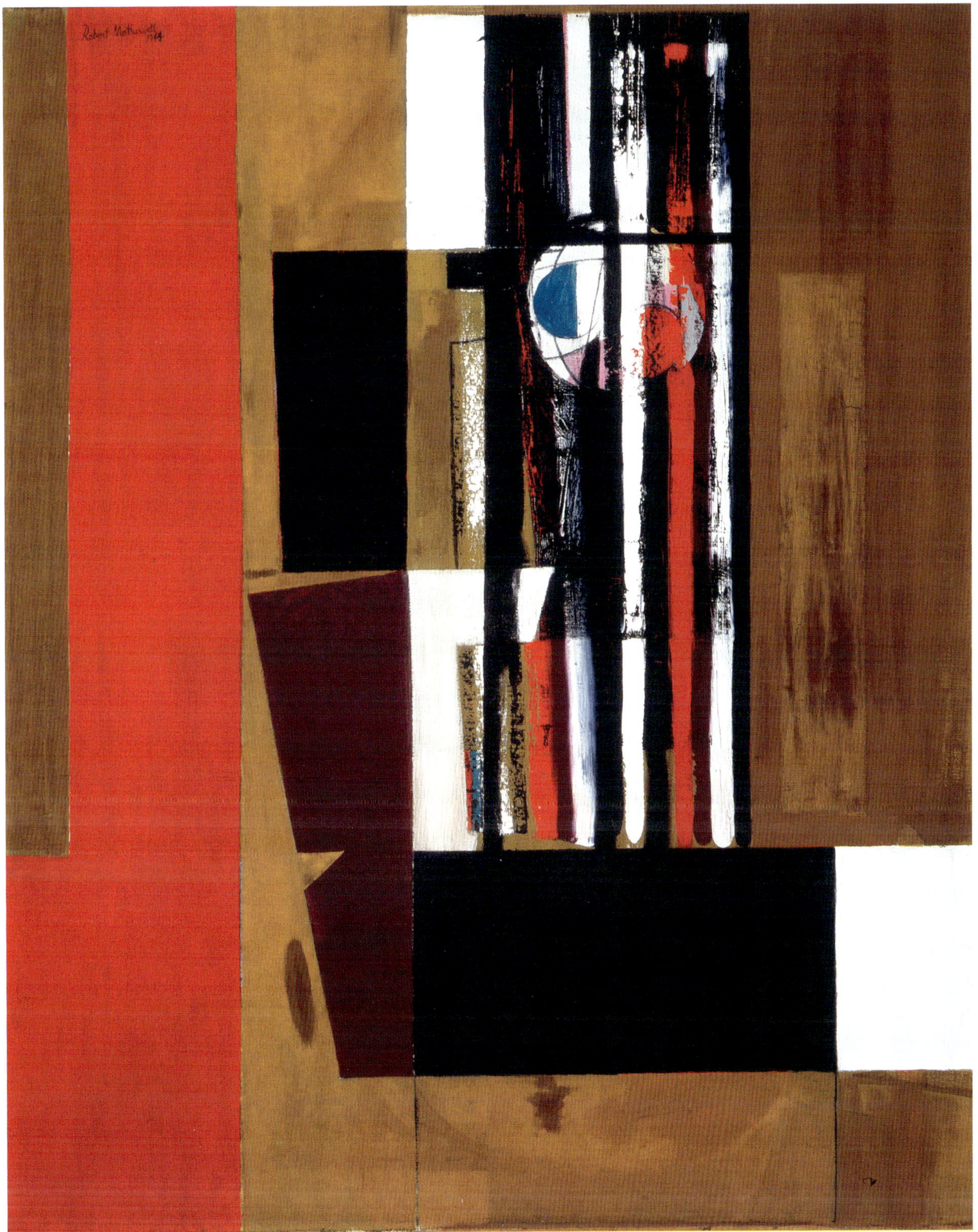

Robert Motherwell
1954

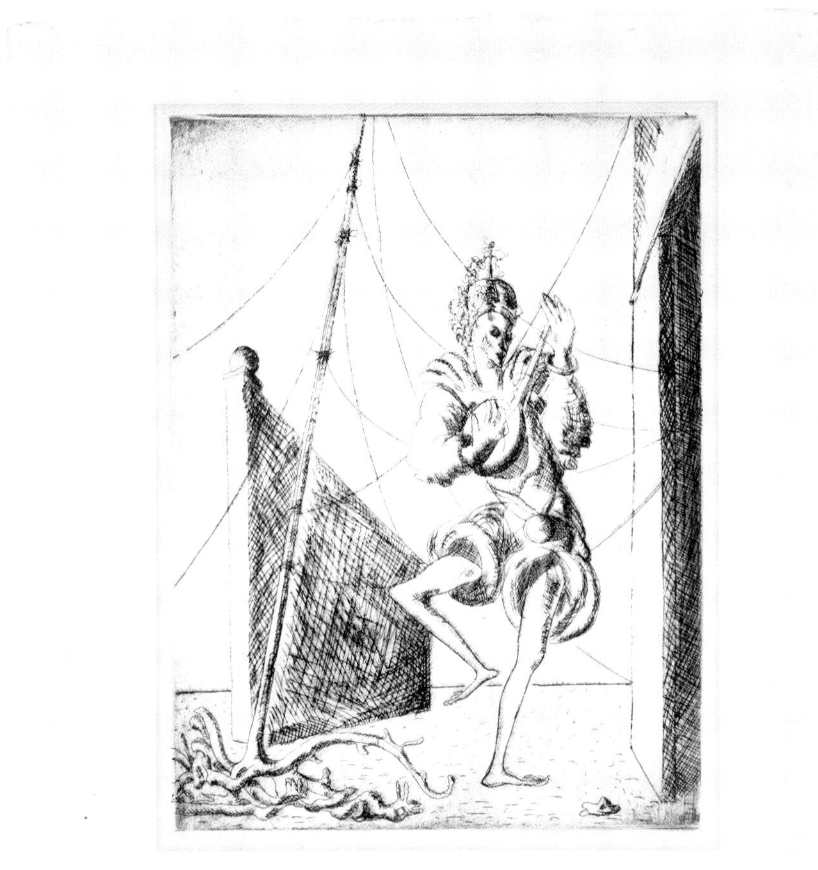

All of these events had actually been made possible by Motherwell's attendance at Kurt Seligmann's studio. His sessions there began in the spring of 1940, reconvening the following late winter and spring; exact dates and details of tuition and so forth are meticulously documented in Seligmann's archive.[20] By Motherwell's own admission, this experience, however reluctantly begun, also turned out to be seminal. The only surviving visual evidence of Motherwell's work at Seligmann's studio is apparently a peculiar 1940 etching with the unexpected subject of a skeletal figure in troubadour garb playing the mandolin (fig. 65). Its authenticity is unquestioned; one impression was lent to his Art of This Century debut by composer Livingston and pianist Virginia Gearhart, friends Motherwell had made in Paris.[21] Under Seligmann's tutelage he'd created a vaguely Watteauesque musician sporting a crown and an attenuated build somewhat analogous to that of his teacher's own "phantom" knight figures populating contemporaneous prints.[22] While Seligmann typically situated his weirdly constructed, puppet-like figures in strange outdoor landscapes (fig. 66), Motherwell placed his hollow-eyed string player within a shallow indoor setting, its most prominent feature a network of ropes draping downward from a tilted pole that magically sprouts from gnarled roots. Flanked as well by an architectural prop and what appears to be a darkened doorway, this ghostly musician, one skinny leg bent in an exaggerated dance, plays his tune on a Surrealist stage.

This corresponding effort notwithstanding, Motherwell always portrayed himself as unsympathetic to the illustrative and fantasist direction of Seligmann's signature works — he really had balked at Schapiro's suggestion that he study with such a "retrograde" artist. With just a bit of distance, however, a reevaluation apparently ensued.[23] Writing to the Seligmanns the following summer from Mexico, Bob exclaimed that he was now "all the time . . . very conscious of how much I have learned from Kurt." Not specifying art, state of mind, or some combination thereof, he admitted, in fact, "I never would have gotten out of my original muddle by myself," testifying to Seligmann's salutary role in the recent events of his life.[24]

Beyond teaching him how to design and pull prints, Seligmann seems, importantly, to have provided Motherwell a direct opportunity to acquire appreciation of the accomplishments of Joan Miró. Ostensibly on opposite sides of the Surrealist spectrum, Seligmann not only shared Miró's penchant for grotesque deformation, he took very seriously the originality

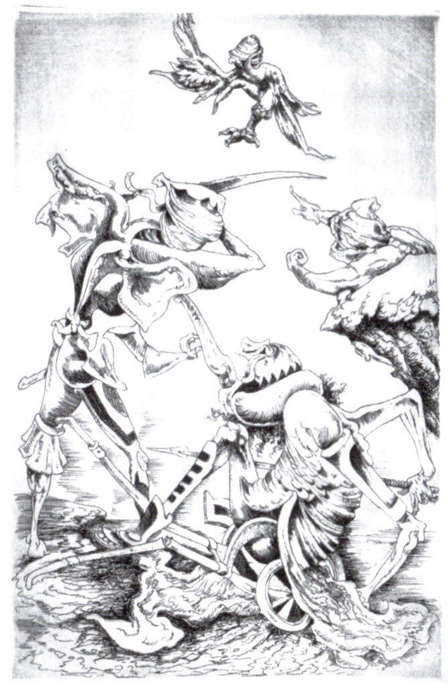

66 Kurt Seligmann, *The Slaying of Laius*, Plate 3 from *The Myth of Oedipus*, 1944. Etching on off-white wove paper, 22 13/16 x 15 1/2 in. (57.9 x 39.4 cm). University of Michigan Museum of Art. Museum purchase made possible by the Alfred E. Pernt Memorial Fund, in honor of Dr. of Technical Sciences Max H. J. Pernt and his wife Anna Pernt (née Mueller). © 2012 Orange County Citizens Foundation / Artists Rights Society (ARS), New York.

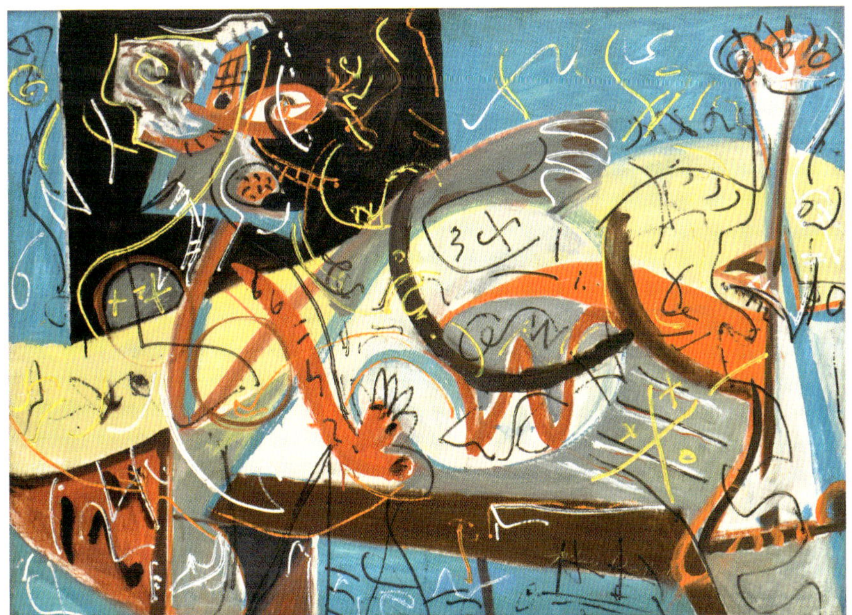

67 Jackson Pollock, *Stenographic Figure*, 1942. Oil on linen. The Museum of Modern Art, New York. Mr. and Mrs. Walter Bareiss Fund. © 2012 The Pollock-Krasner Foundation / Artists Rights Society (ARS), New York.

of the latter's abstract innovations.[25] Pollock's great admiration for Miró has already been cited. Around the time of the Museum of Modern Art's highly influential 1942 Miró retrospective, he painted *Stenographic Figure*, sending it shortly afterward to one of Peggy Guggenheim's younger artist salons (fig. 67). While obviously derived from his parallel "competition" with Picasso, Pollock indisputably incorporated into *Stenographic Figure* what one critic recognized as "curious reminiscences" of the Catálan Surrealist.[26] Motherwell's figure with mandolin produced two years earlier at Seligmann's had as yet no such affinities, resembling more closely the prancing skeletal musicians common in late medieval and early Renaissance Dance of Death compositions, a genre his teacher knew from Switzerland.[27]

During the following year in Mexico, however, Motherwell made an abrupt stylistic turn. Right after returning from this trip he began the synthesis of Picasso and Mondrian easily recognized in his own characterization of *Spanish Prison, Window*, as the work in Janis's show would soon be renamed. By the time Pollock began creating in the mode of *Stenographic Figure*, Motherwell was also thinking seriously about what he could learn from Miró. In his case, the exceptional access he was afforded through Seligmann to some of the most important refugee Surrealists paved an unswerving path toward more intense exploration.[28]

The Surrealist Adventure (Part One: New York Before Mexico)

Most people think of surrealism as the bizarre, the morbid, the upsetting, as a species of shock, in the sense that Saint-Beuve said to Baudelaire, "You have created a new shudder in poetry." But at the core of all true surrealist activity is one form or another of free association.[29]

— ROBERT MOTHERWELL, 1965

During the winter following his earliest sessions at Seligmann's, a friend from Stanford extended Motherwell an invitation that luckily he found hard to refuse. From late January through early March 1941, twenty-nine-year-old British painter and naval officer Gordon Onslow-Ford was scheduled to give four talks at the New School for Social Research on the topic of Surrealist painting, and the writer Jacqueline Johnson (who would presently become Onslow-Ford's wife) suggested to Motherwell that he join her at the first of these. Onslow-Ford's stated goal for the New School lecture series, subtitled "An Adventure into Human Consciousness," was a demonstration of the extent to which "far more than other modern artists the surrealists have adventured in tapping the unconscious psychic world."[30] His presentations

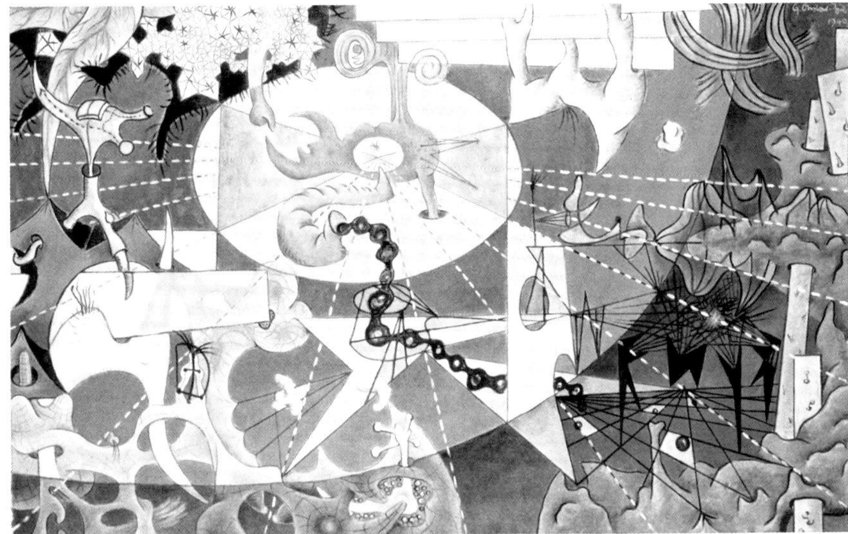

were to be accompanied by exhibitions organized by Howard Putzel. These were planned to feature original works, including a selection of Surrealist paintings "recently imported" by the speaker himself.[31] "I was slightly late and crept to the seat next to [Johnson]," Motherwell would recall about the night of January 22, 1941. "At a certain moment," he said, "during a brief lapse in the lecture, she pointed to the young man sitting next to her, and, to my astonishment, said he was a genius."[32] Thus were Motherwell and Matta introduced.

A few years before, Onslow-Ford (the grandson of a famous Victorian sculptor) had taken some of his own drawings evoking multidimensional space to Paris to show to André Breton.[33] As a result of this meeting, set up by Salvador Dalí, Breton decided to reinvigorate his movement with younger artists working on Surrealism's cusp, and he promptly invited Onslow-Ford, Matta, and Esteban Frances to join the official Surrealist group.[34] Matta, who was already married to an American, had worked as a draftsman for the architect Le Corbusier from 1935–37, but he had not found this vocation, recommended by his parents, fully satisfying. Stranded in London after studying housing projects in Russia, Matta began to "doodle" as a nervous outlet, and these doodles soon progressed into astounding crayon, graphite, and colored pencil drawings with imagery conversant to Onslow-Ford's spatial and scientific interests (fig. 68).[35] To produce a look that was partly fortuitous, Matta first rapidly sketched in soft gray lead, then switched to a pencil that changed colors as he worked (fig. 69). As Onslow-Ford characterized them, Matta's *graphismes* developed into "the most extraordinary landscapes full of maltreated nudes, strange architecture and vegetation."[36] Working together, the two took as their shared goal the enlargement of

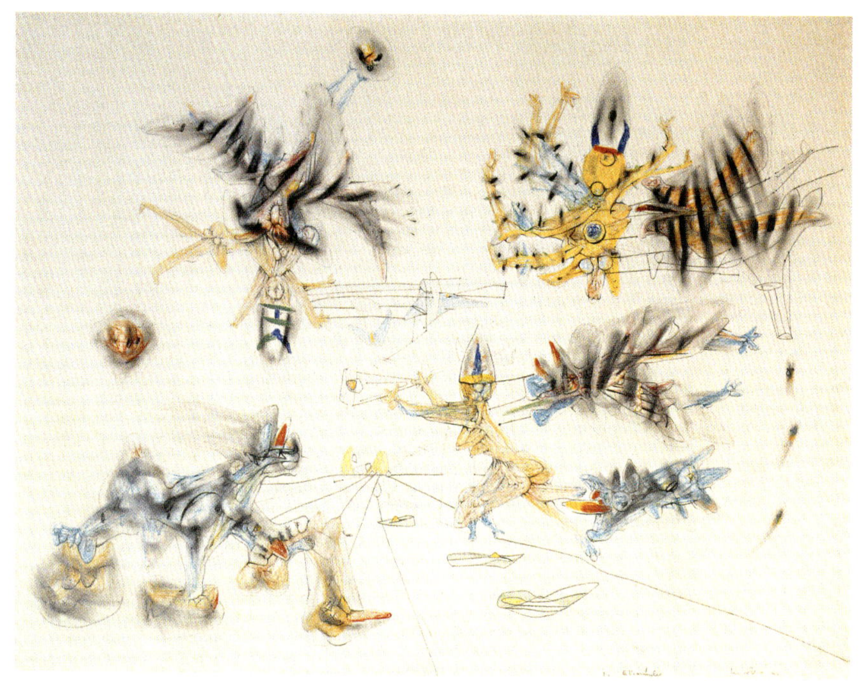

perception: "We wanted not to be limited by what we could see but to extend in time, to see through the mountains, to see the roots of a tree as it grows." "The first major discovery that Matta and I made," Onslow-Ford remembered, "was that when you work spontaneously you express reality. Intuitively we were both in possession of knowledge about the inner world." Describing a circumstance that would mirror Motherwell's a little later and a continent away, he also bragged, "Neither of us had been corrupted by art school."[37]

This lacuna was not to prove any impediment to success, for Matta in particular. Having "signed too many anti-Hitler and anti-Stalin papers not to be persecuted by the SS," he left Europe for the United States in October 1939. Soon after Matta's landing (on the same ship as Tanguy) his exceptional drawings were featured by New York gallerist Julien Levy in an exhibition with Pavel Tchelitchew and Walt Disney. Looking back, Matta characterized the scene upon his arrival as "very strange to me. There were—how would I say?—many artists who knew something about European art. But it was as if 'art' was something not in *Europe* but something *imported to America*. . . . Art was something rare or artificial instead of being the expression of a man."[38] He set his sights on rectifying this, an enterprise in which his friendship with Motherwell would figure prominently.[39]

Gordon Onslow-Ford began his own visit to the United States in June 1940, the same month the Germans marched into Paris. His trip was underwritten by the Society for the Preservation of European Culture, and he came at the invitation of American painter Kay Sage, who would soon marry Tanguy. Onslow-Ford's New School lectures, planned "quite frankly [as] a plunge into the unknown and the little explored," were approved by Breton, still stuck in Marseilles.[40] In the wake of the Museum of Modern Art's highly publicized *Fantastic Art, Dada and Surrealism* exhibition of 1936, Breton's movement was already under discussion in a variety of American media, but its treatment remained mostly quizzical or critical, even verging on satire.[41] As "a mental attitude and a method of investigation," Surrealism was still mostly misunderstood.[42] Motherwell had been curious enough to obtain Julien Levy's groundbreaking book on the topic even before arriving at Seligmann's studio; written for accessibility to American audiences, it was published the year of the Modern's big show.[43] But reading it had not yet contributed to a positive opinion.

While Motherwell attended only the first of Onslow-Ford's lectures, it is clear that what he heard there started him thinking.[44] In this talk Onslow-Ford (only three years older than Motherwell but seemingly much more advanced) counseled listeners that leading a more exciting life required greater self-knowledge. The best way to achieve this, he said, is to study one's own dreams. "The rational world of the waking state," Onslow-Ford pointed out, "is not the only measure of the reality in which we live. . . . You are constantly carrying within yourself a free world of images which will come to the surface, if you are ready to see them." Emphasizing how a painter "paints because he has to paint," Onslow-Ford recommended tapping into both the Freudian and Jungian (individual and collective) versions of the unconscious to find consequential subject matter. The latter, he said, had become especially critical in a world where "civilization is in an acute form of crisis."[45]

Whereas the average viewer likely considered Surrealist works little more than personal flights of fancy, Onslow-Ford advocated for art's social responsibility: "The Artist, though he may work by himself in his studio, is nevertheless very much under the influence of his surroundings, and, as one of the most sensitive members of society, he can be regarded as a psychological barometer, registering the desires and impulses of the community." Before launching an imaginative interpretation of Scuola Metafisica works by Surrealist forerunner Giorgio de Chirico, he reminded his audience of the real meaning of "the marvelous," a term liberally employed by the Surrealists to designate a revered and sought-after condition: "In the French language, the word '*merveilleux*' is used to describe that land or that state of spirit from which we receive revelations, from which we catch a glimpse of the true functioning of the universe and the part we play in it." He praised Matta's recent painting *Invasion of the Night* for providing "a glimpse of that

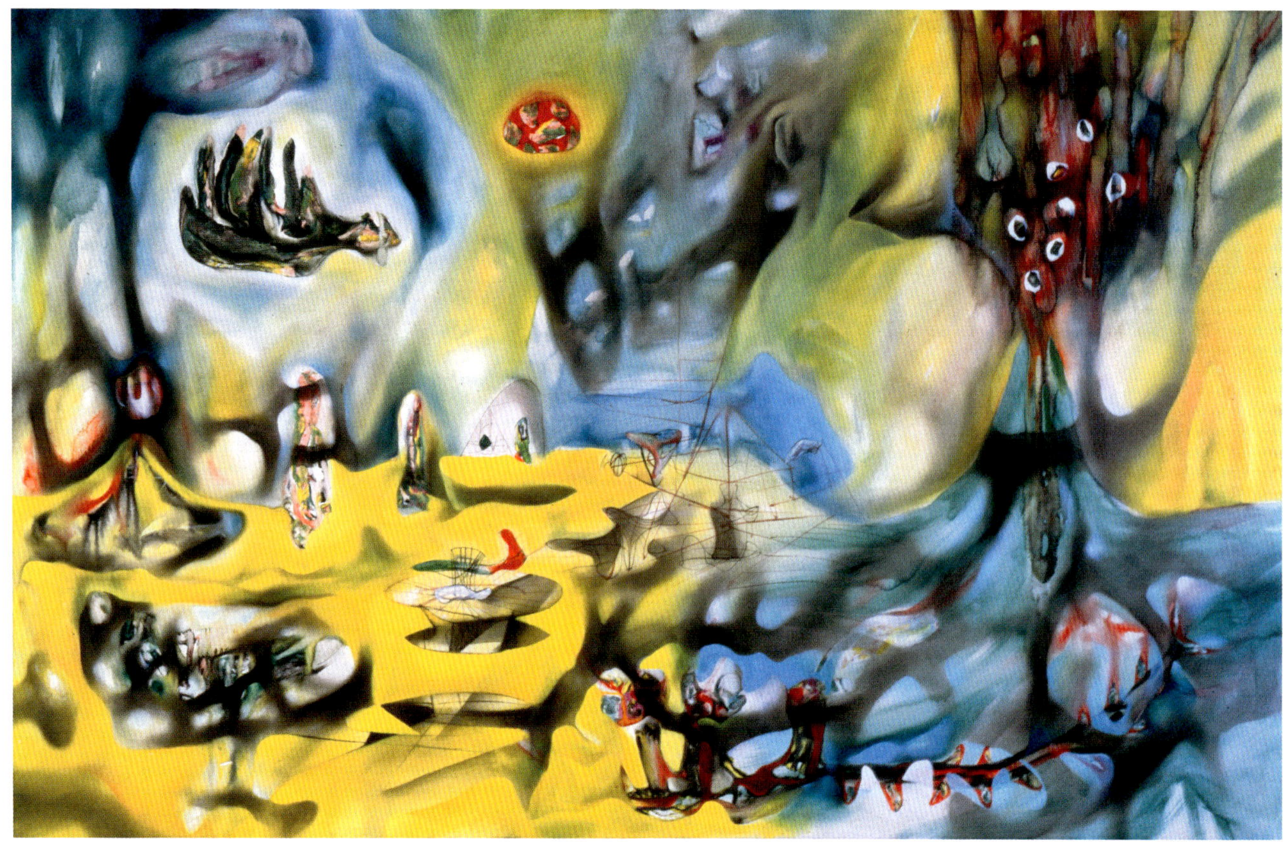

marvelous world that is perhaps buried in each of us; once we can become aware of it, it can lead to a fuller life" (fig. 70).[46]

Matta's fluid and spatially complex "psychic morphologies," of which *Invasion of the Night* was a primary example, Onslow-Ford designated as representing the future direction of painting.[47] As Jimmy Ernst, another admirer, explained, these ambiguous, semiautomatic landscapes seemed to represent "a step beyond Breton's Surrealism and, indeed, beyond the Freudian dream catalog. To some of us [Matta's works] seemed to say for the first time, 'Why not?' rather than, 'It has to be.'" As early as 1938, Matta had published his own call for aesthetic revolution, writing in *Minotaure,* "Let us overturn all the historical showpieces, with their styles and elegant ornamentation in order that there may escape the rays of dust out of which pyrotechnics can create space." "We need walls like damp cloths which assume odd shapes and complement our psychological fears," he proclaimed, sounding somewhat as if he were describing one of Dalí's notorious paranoiac-critical paintings.[48] Looking back, Matta recalled feeling then that "nothing would be *new,* only *old-new*—that is, until *we changed the game.*"[49]

Making Matta's acquaintance in 1941 was a self-proclaimed "cataclysmic" event for Robert Motherwell. "An electrifying personality," Matta, he said, was simply the "most energetic, enthusiastic, poetic, charming, brilliant young artist" he'd ever had the chance to meet. And Motherwell—who Matta recalled as "painting something like Chirico's horses" at the time—was not the only American to form such an extravagant opinion.[50] "Confidant, exuberant, and mercurial," Julien Levy colorfully wrote, Matta "burst on the New York scene as if he considered this country a sort of dark continent, his Africa, where he could trade dubious wares, charm the natives, and entertain scintillating disillusions. He was chock full of premature optimism and impatient disappointment; believing ardently in almost everything and in absolutely nothing, as he believed ardently and painfully in himself." The brash young Chilean simply appeared one day at Levy's gallery, producing the "explosive" portfolio of drawings that led to his first American presentation.[51]

Born in Santiago, Roberto Sebastián Matta Echaurren was actually of French and Catálan Spanish descent, and, like Motherwell, he came from a well-to-do upper-class family (fig. 71). Charismatic, flamboyantly Hispano-Catholic in temperament, and by all accounts a brilliant conversationalist, Matta came across as Motherwell's opposite—hence Abel's surprise at their friendship. By contrast, Motherwell felt he himself was "stiff, Protestant, clumsy, depressed, un-socialized." Nonetheless, and perhaps due in part to their shared experience of parental insistence on an uncongenial career, the two formed an instant bond.[52] Matta later said he was drawn to Motherwell's "theoretical bent," a turn of mind allowing the American to quickly comprehend the value of the Surrealist enterprise once it was better explained.[53] Matta described what this involved, citing Breton's 1924 definition, "SURREALISM, noun (masculine): pure psychic automatism by which one intends to express verbally, in writing or by any other method, the real functioning of the mind. Dictation of thought in absence of any control exercised by reason, and beyond aesthetic and moral pre-occupation."[54]

While no trace is left of any horse compositions like those Matta thought that he recalled, during the year before they met Motherwell had been laboring over a series of ink and watercolor landscapes, some of which are extant. In three examples painted in Oregon in 1939, he adopted the School of Paris style of artists like Georges Rouault and Raoul Dufy. Two of these landscapes present direct recollections from Motherwell's time in France, likely based on sketches made there. One portrays the Cathédrale Saint-Théodorit in Uzes, situated behind a high wall with prominent foreground trees; the other shows stacked buildings along the quay in La Tronche, a picturesque town near Grenoble where he briefly studied French.

Motherwell's third extant 1939 landscape, *Homage à Poussin,* differs

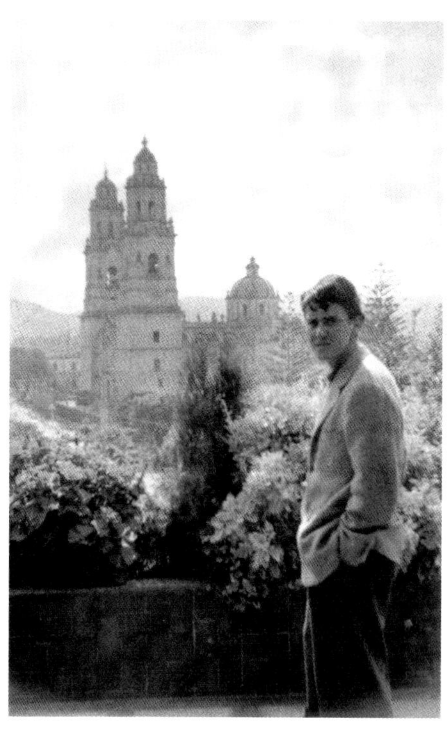

71 Matta in Taxco, 1941. Courtesy Jane Crawford.

slightly in its freehand interpretation of the classicizing style associated with Baroque artists Claude Lorraine and Nicolas Poussin, although here a light watercolor wash with ink outlines and added touches of gouache was likewise employed. In view of these plainly derivative recent efforts—Motherwell would recall them with distaste as attempts that "demonstrated how far his own execution lagged behind his knowledge and appreciation of great art"—Matta's ability to invest the outer world with qualities of the interior mind must have seemed stunning, to say the least.[55]

The Surrealist Adventure (Part Two: The Lure of Mexico)

In the second World War, Mexico played the part of . . . haven of refuge. . . . Thus, in our convulsed world, the Atlantic fulfills the former function of the Mediterranean. . . . To all these vanquished people Mexico offers liberty without restrictions.[56]

— VICTOR SERGE, 1947

Unlike Noguchi, Guston, or Pollock, Robert Motherwell had no direct contact with any of the revolutionary Mexican muralists (all three of whom, at various times, were resident in New York) nor was he attracted in any way to the aesthetic and/or ideological functions of their work. He does not mention attending the Museum of Modern Art's 1940 blockbuster, *Twenty Centuries of Mexican Art,* billed as the largest, most comprehensive exhibition on that subject to date. Motherwell seems indeed to have been completely uninterested in the fact (stated in an earlier MoMA catalogue) that Mexican mural painting was widely considered "the most important foreign influence upon our country's art" by 1933.[57]

Questioned later about why then had he traveled to Mexico in 1941, Motherwell admitted his decision had not been based on any interest in experiencing Mexican art, but rather on a desire to "remain close" to Matta, who desperately wanted to get out of New York that summer. Matta, as he explained, had by then "become temporarily and somewhat unwillingly, my mentor." Another reason he cited reflects Victor Serge's observation in *Horizon,* but with less urgent stress on the political ramifications so crucial for radical Europeans. "The War was on," Motherwell explained. "It was impossible to go to the Mediterranean, and Mexico was a substitute."[58]

Matta, his American wife, Anne Clark, Motherwell, and Barbara Reis set off on their voyage of discovery in June 1941. They were preceded in Mexico by Breton and his then-wife, Jacqueline Lamba, who'd spent much of 1938 in and around Mexico City. Breton's pretext was a French Foreign

Office cultural services mission, but he had personal agendas as well that were mostly fulfilled through contacts made for him by Diego Rivera. Breton spent quite a bit of time with Leon Trotsky, who was in hiding after his 1936 expulsion from the Soviet Union by Josef Stalin. At Trotsky's home in Coyoácan and on incognito travels to provincial towns and ancient ruins, the two men discussed the intersection of aesthetics and politics, conversations leading to a jointly issued manifesto on revolution and art.[59] Mexico's "palpable atmosphere" and "innate sense of poetry" were found to be spectacular beyond his wildest dreams by the so-called "Pope" of Surrealism. In 1947 German novelist Gustav Regler meditated on Mexico's attraction to European intellectuals and artists:

> I often wonder if it is due to the landscape. This wide swing of all horizons. This cruelly burnt earth which in its curves still shows the terror and the power of its volcanic beginnings. And add to this the cries coming out of the virgin woods with their naked trees; no leaves but lush blooms, children of impatience. Then that desert of four arid months and in its wake the voluptuous season of thunderstorms when thoughts sprout like gorgeous orchids in rank exuberance. A haunted country which seems nearer both to cold infinite space and to the fiery marrow of the earth, nearer than most of the countries on the planet.[60]

In light of what he considered the exotic, otherworldly, "convulsive" beauty of its topography, its innate mysticism, the "dynamism arising from its racial mixture," and its world-shattering politics, Breton somewhat superciliously proclaimed Mexico "the Surrealist place *par excellence*."[61] Upon his return to Paris, he organized *Mexique*, a group survey exhibition at the Galerie Renou et Colle, highlighting paintings by Frida Kahlo and photographs by Manuel Alvarez Bravo. He identified the works of these two artists as paradigmatic of a "native" brand of Surrealism, one in which the ultimate binaries are more fully integrated. "This power of conciliation of life and death," Breton wrote, "is no doubt Mexico's primary allure. In this sense, it deploys an inexhaustible register of sensations."

These assertions appeared in Breton's essay "Souvenir de Mexique," which took up the entire final issue of *Minotaure*, for which Rivera supplied an appropriate cover. While Breton had viewed Mexico as "mythic" ever since his childhood fascination with adventure novels set there, a letter he received from Guatemalan writer Luis Cardoza y Aragón, which extolled its visceral sensations, had thrilled him even more. "I feel Mexico's past life in my entrails," Aragón wrote, "the way I sometimes feel my entrails upon the sacrificial stone."[62] Illustrating his points in *Minotaure* with a range of examples of Mexican art, including remarkable images by Alvarez Bravo (in one of which, *Escala de escalas,* he pictures a factory for children's coffins), Breton praised the "contemporary wonders" of Mexico and its archaic culture, "the 'Surrealist' nature of which has allowed it to escape the desecrations of Western civilization." A part of the "entire mental landscape of Surrealism," Breton declared, "is manifestly delineated by Mexico."[63]

The following year, André Breton organized, with Wolfgang Paalen and Peruvian poet César Moro, an *Exposición Internacional del Surrealismo,* in which Pre-Hispanic, Native American, local, and European works were displayed together on the walls of Inés Amor's Galería de Arte Mexicano in Mexico City. Widely touted, with a catalogue published in both Spanish and English, this manifestation generated interest and controversy on two continents.[64] It is not known whether Motherwell had access to Breton's *Minotaure* essay (he was one of only a small group of Americans who could read it), but he had probably heard about this show before traveling to Mexico, since Onslow-Ford, Matta, and Seligmann all sent paintings. Motherwell was also likely aware in advance of his trip of Russian avant-garde filmmaker Sergei Eisenstein's film project *¡Qué viva México!* A short version, *Thunder over Mexico,* had been released in the United States, and Motherwell told British curator Bryan Robertson that he was pretty sure he'd seen it before they left.[65]

The journey leading Robert Motherwell to Mexico was actually planned by the Seligmanns for themselves; not quite certain they found New York totally sympathetic, the couple had begun actively considering relocation. In January 1941, Kurt wrote a note to Wolfgang Paalen in which he mentioned receiving a card onto which his friend added raindrops to Manhattan's sky. "I think you pass the days in a very different ambiance," he writes back, not the "gloomy climate" he and Arlette were forced to suffer farther north. Mexico, Seligmann wistfully observes, must truly seem the "Land of Cockaigne," where responsibilities vanish and pleasure reigns. He explains to Wolfgang that, while they would love to visit Mexico during the winter, because of teaching commitments his "hands and feet are tied" and they simply can't get away.[66] By late spring, the Seligmanns decided at last to book passage for Veracruz, now planning to take Motherwell and Barbara Reis along. But with the Germans entrenched in Paris, it soon became obvious that transferring funds from Europe would be complicated. The venture appearing too dangerous to contemplate, Matta and Anne took their place.[67]

The Surrealist Adventure (Part Three: "Thunder over Mexico")

*During my encounter with Mexico, it seemed to me to be, in all the variety
of its contradictions, a sort of outward projection of all those individual
lines and features which I carried and carry within me like a tangle
of complexes. Monumental simplicity and unrestrained Baroque (in each of
its aspects, Spanish and Aztec). . . . One was as dear to me as the other. . . .
Mexico—lyrical and tender, but also brutal!* [68]

— SERGEI EISENSTEIN, 1935

Not unlike Guston's letters to Harold Lehman, Robert Motherwell's earliest written communications from Mexico indicate a significant measure
of disappointment on his part in regard to what he had hoped to find. The
short version of Eisenstein's film, assuming Motherwell did see it first, would
likely have conjured an overly romantic, exoticized view of the Mexican
people, its landscape and culture that reality could never match. Eisenstein's
undertaking had been inspired by Rivera's historicizing murals (the two met
in 1927 in the Soviet Union) and by the ethnographic productions of Robert Flaherty, whose daughter was Motherwell's friend. Rivera's "profound"
influence predisposed the filmmaker's interest in all things Mexican, and
upon his arrival in December 1930 Eisenstein was "entirely captivated."
According to his biographer Marie Seton, his experiences there "moved
him more deeply than anything else in his life." [69]

Thunder over Mexico, a seventy-minute feature financed by leftist writer
Upton Sinclair and his wife, was compiled in Hollywood by Sol Lesser from
footage shot by Eisenstein's cameraman Edward Tisse. Based on "Maguey,"
one of the four "novels" intended to constitute *¡Qué viva México!* (and titled
after the country's ubiquitous spikey plant), some of Eisenstein's original
prologue was also included. This largely comprised dramatic shots of the
impassive profiles of indigenous "pure-blooded" Mexicans—Eisenstein
used no actors—juxtaposed against look-alike pre-Columbian stone gods
and towering ancient ruins. Establishing a direct visual link between the
nation's past and present, these magisterial images and their still, deep
shadows set an austere and tragic tone for a narrative of rape and murder
intended to encapsulate "the suffering of all Mexico." [70]

The principal points guiding Eisenstein's project—"that the ancient
Indian religion survived hidden behind the forms of Catholicism, and Mexican mythology sought to triumph over death by laughing at it"—were
stimulated by his reading of Anita Brenner's 1929 *Idols Behind Altars*, recommended by Rivera. [71] In it, Brenner wrote passionately of the Mexicans'
urgent need to create and its relation to their distinctive attitude toward

death. Nowhere as in Mexico, she said, is art as "organically a part of life, at one with national ends and longings."[72] While there is no firm indication that he too read *Idols Behind Altars* before, during, or after his own Mexican interlude, these are ideas with which Motherwell was clearly familiar.

Indeed, in 1965 Motherwell told Bryan Robertson that, upon returning from Mexico, his "constant companion" in New York had been another of Brenner's books, a compilation of photos of that country's revolution. Since *The Wind That Swept Mexico* was not published until 1943, he must have been referring to the aftermath of a second journey made that year with his Mexican wife. Meant to become another extended stay, this trip was cut short by his father's fatal illness. Motherwell's admitted preoccupation with images of violence and death featured in *The Wind That Swept Mexico,* many displaying rebel banditos with bullet belts and guns, and bodies lying in pools of blood on the streets, has played a deserved role in discussions of *Pancho Villa Dead and Alive,* arguably his earliest masterwork (see figs. 85 and 87). As Motherwell declared to Robertson (like Breton and Eisenstein before him), he had been "profoundly moved" and his imagination intensely stimulated by Mexico's "continual presence of sudden death."

Whatever he said about it later, Motherwell's originally more tentative thoughts about Mexican art and life are recorded for posterity in a set of plaintive letters sent to the Seligmanns in June and July 1941. Interestingly, before reaching Veracruz, on a stop in Havana, he, Reis, and the Mattas paid a visit to Afro-Cuban artist Wifredo Lam. Lam, part Chinese and a former protégé of Picasso's, had also been involved with the Surrealists in Paris. He was recently returned from a Vichy prison camp in Martinique, briefly interned alongside anthropologist Claude Lévi-Strauss as well as Breton and his family.[73] Lam and Motherwell would both be included in the celebrated exhibition *First Papers of Surrealism,* held in 1942 at New York's Whitelaw-Reid Mansion. While this Cuban encounter was rarely mentioned by Motherwell, there were to be some intersecting similarities between his and Lam's "personage" imagery developing around the time of this show.

In his first letter to Kurt and Arlette, begun on June 18, 1941, on stationery from the Hotel Regis in Mexico City, Motherwell recited a litany of complaints, foremost among which was the abominable food, made further indigestible due to the altitude of twenty-five hundred meters.[74] Describing his environs as "noisy and peculiar, very American in many respects and rather like Moscow (or so Barbara and Matta say) in others," Motherwell added more meaningfully, "The things that interest me the most, the conflict of the Indian with the black earth, and the passions which are sometimes expressed in the Catholic Church, are not to be found in Mexico City—I suppose naturally enough." "The difficulty," he lamented, "is where they might be found, if indeed they exist, the living conditions are so primitive, particularly in regard to sanitation and drinking water, that they are impossible for civilized people." Their group, as a result, had been looking into other living possibilities, including Cuernevaca ("a bit ritzy and society"), Taxco ("beautiful like Greco's View of Toledo but very Montparnasse"), and "San Miguel de something or other (where Tamayo's school is/is lovely but sweet and sugary—no guts.)" As "the lesser of the evils," Taxco was their eventual decision; but in a lengthy postscript Motherwell added on July 9, after their move, he decribes this town as "so dull there is nothing to do but work." Consequently, perhaps, he wrote, "I've radically changed the way I paint—much more flatly than I was—and I think perhaps I am on a track which will lead to some good things."[75]

The best part of Motherwell's letter, in addition to his retroactive praise for Seligmann's advice and teaching, is his account of witnessing a scene that could have come right out of *¡Qué viva México!* And, with one very important distinction, footage at the close of Eisenstein's prologue does somewhat approximate what Motherwell describes. Eisenstein's sequence, included in *Thunder over Mexico,* was reportedly inspired by Siqueiros's solemn 1924 fresco *Burial of a Worker,* located in the Colegio Chico; Motherwell's anecdote is more sadly reminiscent of Alvarez Bravo's *Escala de escalas,* whose melancholy message was admired by Breton. "One evening at dusk we were on the highway, and we came over the hill suddenly to a little Indian procession," Motherwell narrates. "They were wearing a flimsy white cloth of flowers in their hair, and carrying white candles which burnt brightly in the grey light like fire-flies; and in the center was a tiny white pine coffin covered with flowers. A couple of Indians were playing little tunes (like you hear at a carnival sometimes) on strange instruments; the whole funeral was like a child's conception: death of the young is so common here it is not very meaningful."[33] Such haunting episodes aside, Motherwell grumbles from his three-room studio in Taxco, that, while Reis and Matta seem to like it, he would not wish a summer in Mexico on his worst enemy.[76] Begging pardon for his recognizably bad humor, he claims that he would come home immediately if only he had the funds.[77]

As things turned out, the future evolved very differently from what this letter implies. When the Mattas and Barbara Reis returned to the United States in mid-September, Motherwell chose not to leave, remaining in Mexico until almost the very end of 1941. Two compelling reasons for this about-face developed by the end of summer. One was a chance to deepen his relationship with María Emilia Ferreira y Moyers, a young woman born in Mexico and raised in Los Angeles whom he'd met on the ship from New York, and the other an exceptional opportunity to work more closely with Wolfgang Paalen, the Austrian expatriate Surrealist. In his initial letter to Kurt and Arlette, Motherwell mentions having already met their friend,

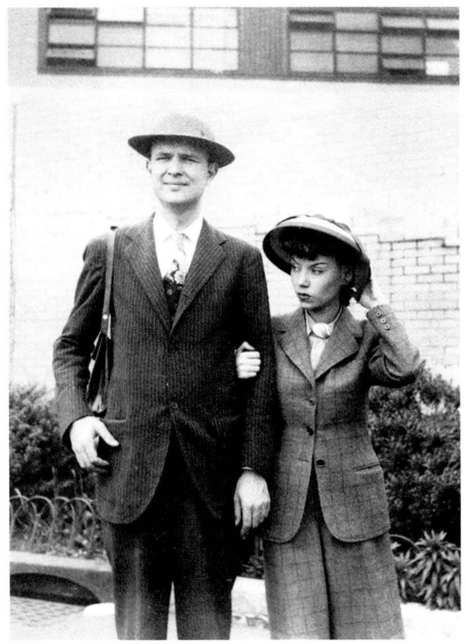

"whom I like very much." Reis notes in her correspondence to the Seligmanns that they'd seen the Paalens twice in Mexico City and "had a lovely time with them." "They have a charming home," she reports, "about 15 mins. [*sic*] from the center of the city. Naturally they wanted to know all about you both, what the New York news was." Motherwell's decision to stay behind was just about equally premised on romance and professional advancement.[78]

Much later María Runyon would narrate her own version of their story in a privately published memoir, *Mr. Motherwell's Ghost,* its title a reference to Robert's father. She states that she had been living in Manhattan for about a year before deciding to go visit family and, by happenstance, some friends coming to see her off on the ship knew Barbara Reis, who then introduced her to Motherwell. At that time, María recalled, something seemed to be missing from her life; when she "first saw Robert out of the corner of my eye, tall and fair, wearing a pork pie hat, watching the New York skyline," she did not realize initially that she'd found what she was seeking. The two married in Provincetown the following summer but would divorce in 1949 (fig. 72).[79] Motherwell always described his first wife as a beautiful actress, once elaborating that she had "sacrificed her screen test for the role of Maria in Hemingway's "For Whom the Bell Tolls" (ultimately played by Ingrid Bergman), to live with me."[80] But even then, his María aspired to be a writer—typing scripts for a playwright, she'd "sort of landed in acting school."

The major painting to survive Motherwell's 1941 Mexican sojourn is a canvas called *La Belle Mexicaine,* an expressionistic portrayal he not unexpectedly identified as a portrait of María (fig. 73). Motherwell scholar Robert Mattison dates *La Belle Mexicaine* to the very end of that first trip to Mexico, although at first glance the painting seems less advanced than other works the artist is known to have made there at that time. Its composition is obviously indebted to Velasquez's many versions of the *Infanta Margarita,* and stylistically it calls to mind Picasso's late 1930s and early '40s depictions of expressively distorted women. Motherwell could easily have seen such examples in books or in Manhattan galleries and museums; he may already have been familiar with *Girl with a Cock* of 1938 hanging in his friend Mary Callery's New York apartment. Mattison's judgment of the chronology of *La Belle Mexicaine* is based on its highly intuitive paint handling, with spontaneous dabs placed over automatist scribbles still visible as *pentimenti* on the figure's left side.[81] While he heard much on the merits of automatism at Onslow-Ford's New School lecture and learned even more about it from Matta before they left, not until that summer in Mexico did Motherwell feel confident enough to begin his own experiments.[82]

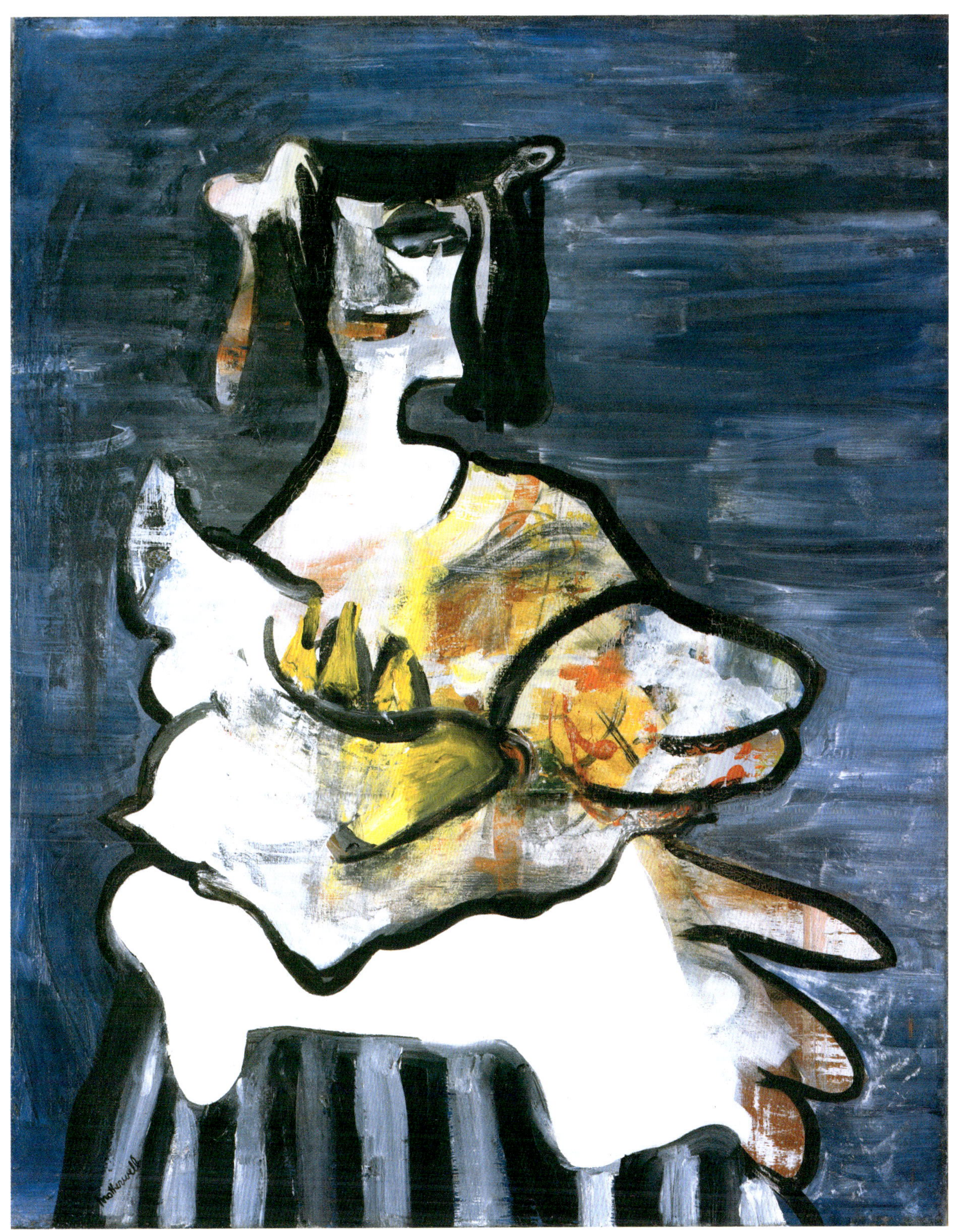

With the exception of *La Belle Mexicaine*, Motherwell's extant Mexican works were drawn in pen and ink, painted in tempera (like *The Red Sun* owned by his mother), or brushed in ink and watercolor on paper. Close examination of his artistic creations during those first months in Taxco indicates the extent to which he had dedicated this time to initiating a dialogue with Matta's latest innovations. Whereas Matta described himself as "very young and very brutal" in those days, "and very, how you say, strict, severe, against," at least throughout the period they were together in Mexico, Motherwell still viewed him as an optimistic and generous friend, and a "hypnotic proselytizer" of Surrealism.[83] By the time of their 1941 summer trip, Matta's "heir apparent" relationship with Breton and the other Surrealist émigrés had grown increasingly tense. Both he and Motherwell therefore stood to profit greatly from Mexico's relative isolation in regard to global and art world politics.

Well before embarking on their Mexican sojourn, Matta set himself a goal of finding new ways to express the psychological dimensions of simultaneity and four-dimensional non-Euclidean space. To comprehend the distinctive effects he began to devise along these lines, as Onslow-Ford explained, it would become necessary for a viewer to switch on "the cycloptic eye in the middle of the forehead to look inside yourself at the internal

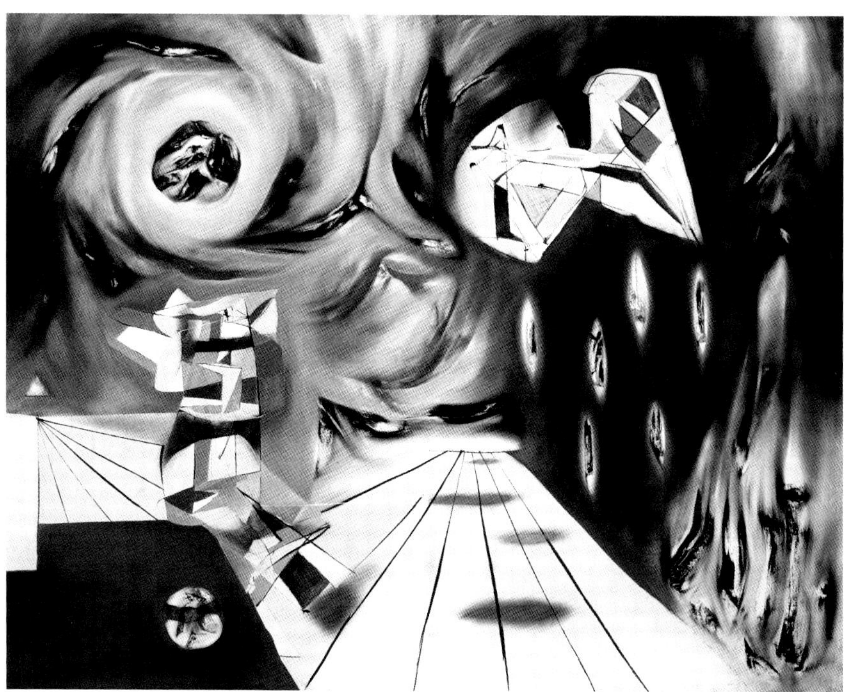

74 Matta, *The Initiation*, 1941. Collection of Patricia Phelps de Cisneros. © 2012 Artists Rights Society (ARS), New York / ADAGP, Paris.

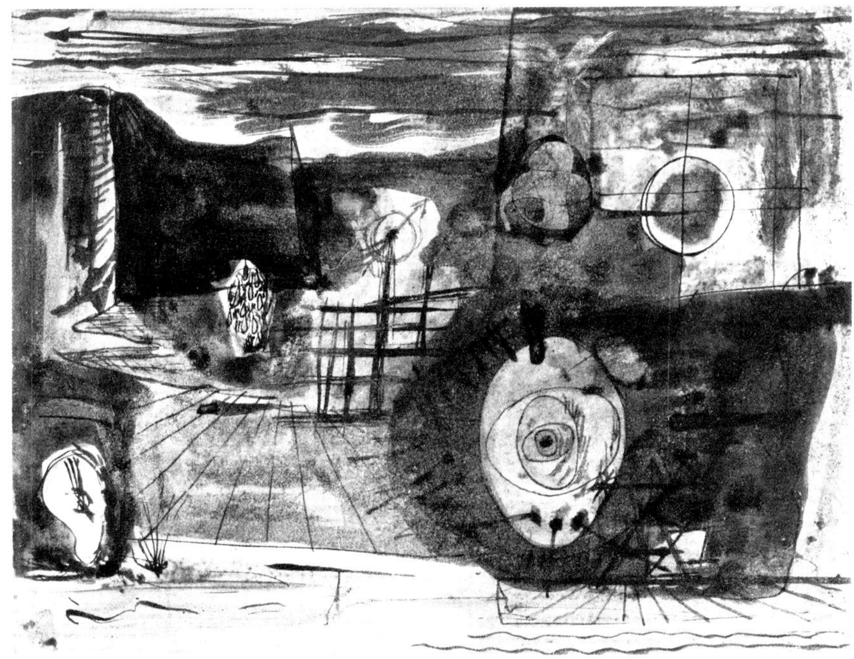

landscape." By the time he arrived in Taxco, Matta was working even harder to demonstrate pictorially the extent to which "the barriers dividing time into past, present and future must be broken down to give man a greater consciousness."[84] With this in mind, he began integrating linear orthogonals into an ambiguous cosmic ambience, often set aglow with microscopic forms (fig. 74). The experience of his Mexican surroundings, including the distinctive geology Regler described, as well as his viewing of the eruption of a volcano, only served to heighten Matta's desire for spectacle. The landscape of Mexico, as MoMA curator James Thrall Soby observed in 1947, taught Matta a more rhythmic relationship between earth and sky. Using "a labyrinth of diaphanous screens, tissue behind tissue, the light reflecting back and forth, through and between," working in Taxco helped to expand his apocalyptic capabilities.[85]

Motherwell's Mexican output includes several sketches inscribed "For Pajarito" (Matta's nickname for his wife, meaning "little bird"); two untitled automatic drawings featuring concentric patternization; and a more finished black-and-white example, *Landscape of the Inner Mind,* whose composition and title correspond with Matta's recipe (fig. 75).[86] There are also eleven exceptionally relevant drawings in his so-called *Mexican Sketchbook,* which Mattison titled after discovering it among Motherwell's papers. Comparing these to Matta's *graphismes,* which Motherwell greatly admired (he once described these drawings as "beautiful" and "roughly speaking, in the same

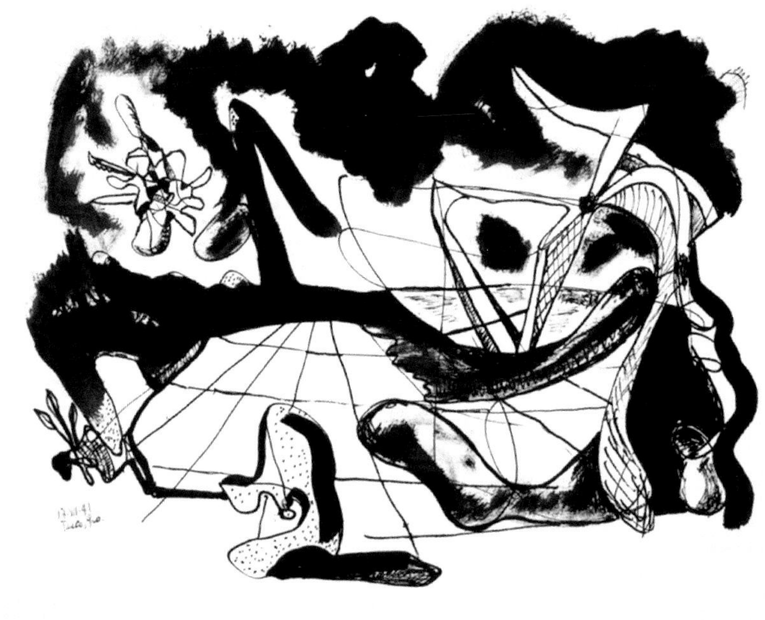

vein as Miró—very comic and very plastic") as well as to the Chilean's known Taxco paintings, can offer a rather precise set of clues to what skills Motherwell gained.[87] As noted by scholars already, a number of the most basic assumptions about image-making operative throughout Motherwell's career are already present in the *Mexican Sketchbook,* albeit in a form not yet refined. This being the case, Matta's formative role in his development— Motherwell called their Mexican summer together his "turning point"—can hardly be overstated.[88]

Robert Motherwell's Mexican oeuvre dates from July to the beginning of December 1941; he and María returned to the United States right before the Japanese bombed Pearl Harbor. That (in emulation of Picasso?) he inscribed Roman and Arabic numerals as a way to affix the day and month of completion on some of his Mexican drawings is very useful for tracking Motherwell's attempts to synthesize Matta's main tenets. Notations on pages 3 and 8 of *The Mexican Sketchbook,* for example, indicate these two compositions were worked on July 17 and 25, respectively. Based on such recorded dates, Motherwell used the sketchbook he brought from New York, first and for not more than two weeks. Many of its nine-by-eleven-inch pages, as well as *Landscape of the Inner Mind,* a nine-by-twelve sheet dated September 17, feature pictorial elements with recognizable reference points to Matta's concurrent imagery—"phenomenal," as Matta himself explained, in the sense that it was intended to represent "man inventing as nature invents."[89]

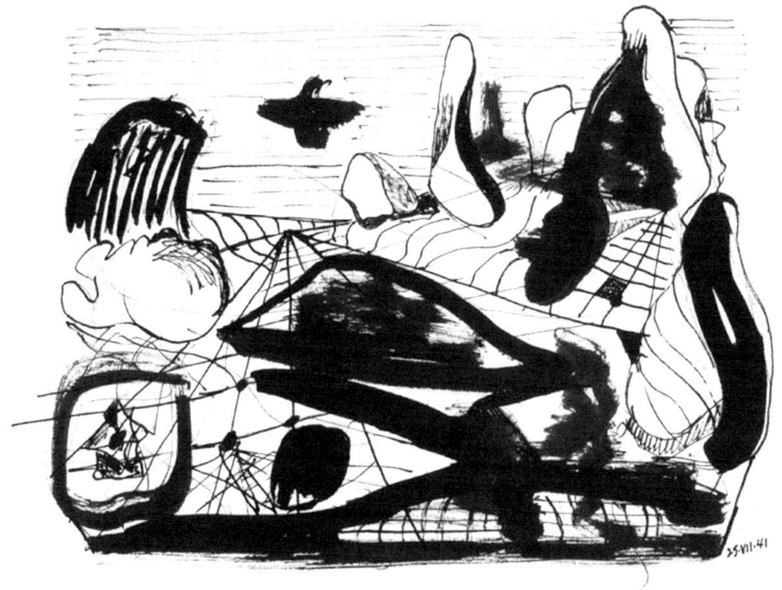

77 Robert Motherwell *Mexican Sketchbook, p, 9,* 1941. Ink on paper and watercolor on paper. The Museum of Modern Art, New York. Gift of the Artist. Art © Dedalus Foundation, Inc./Licensed by VAGA, New York, NY.

A number of Motherwell's Mexican works exhibit his concentrated effort to understand and emulate Matta's permutations of organic science and architectural perspective as a way to metaphorize psychic space.[90]

While far less polished and refined than Matta's attempts, many of the *Mexican Sketchbook* drawings highlight perceptibly related depth notations. Motherwell's grids are likewise reminiscent of de Chirico's haunted Italian piazzas and streets, as well as Matta and Onslow-Ford's adaptations of them, but his versions seem more scribbled and abstract than any of his prototypes. *Landscape of the Inner Mind,* with its recognizable column, gate, and recessive plaza is perhaps closest to imitating a metaphysical style. Akin to Matta's *The Initiation* and *Locus Solus,* two canvases he painted in Taxco, Motherwell sometimes juxtaposed gridded coordinates with a variety of imagined and realistic organisms. These—including a recognizable butterfly—might be ensnared or hovering, as in the ambience of a dream. Either uninterested or unable to reproduce in black and white Matta's vaporous atmosphere with its attendant erotic connotations, Motherwell did occasionally emphasize an ominous "sky" (fig. 76). Several sketchbook compositions suggest an actual horizon line; one in particular, dated July 25, conjures a local landscape complete with volcanic outcroppings, a lake, and a bird, its organic components united in Matta's graphic manner (fig. 77). As Mattison suggests, the latter was perhaps also inspired by Tanguy, whose May 1941 exhibition of "beingscapes" Motherwell could have seen before his trip

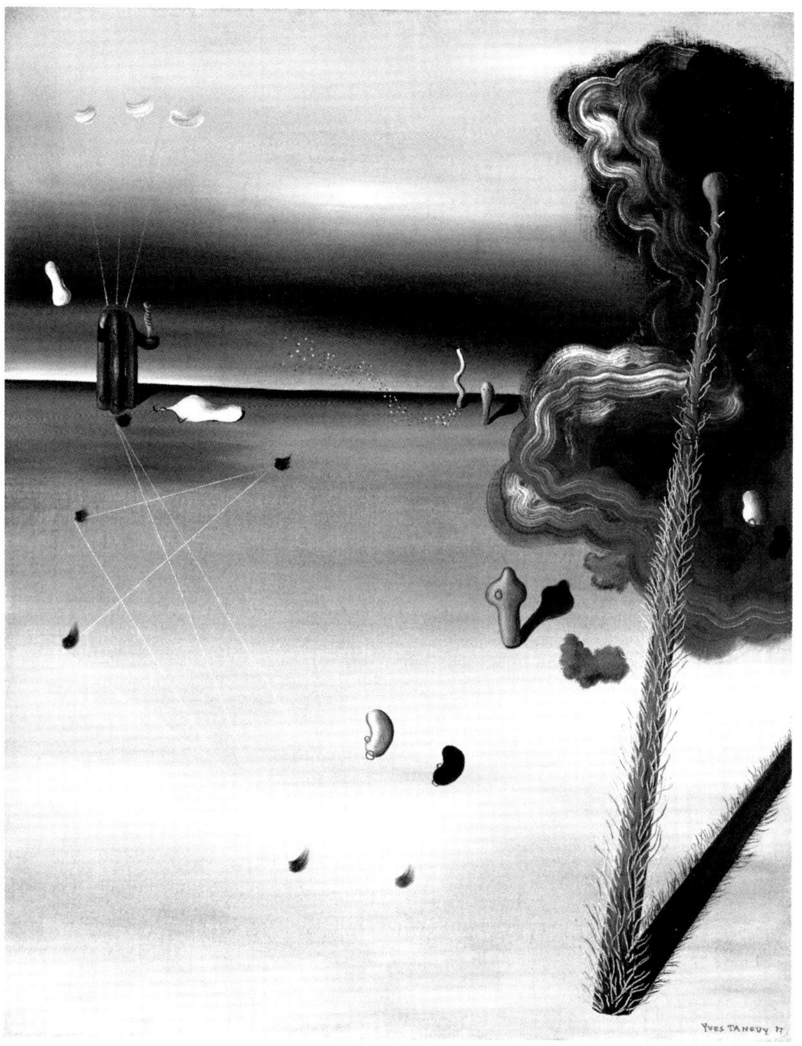

78 Yves Tanguy, *Mama, Papa Is Wounded!,* 1927. Oil on canvas. 36¼ x 28¾ in. (92.1 x 73 cm). The Museum of Modern Art, New York. © 2012 Estate of Yves Tanguy/Artists Rights Society (ARS), New York. Digital Image © The Museum of Modern Art/Licensed by SCALA/Art Resource, NY.

(fig. 78). Excepting a thinly washed, brightly colored rectangular composition with floating Arp-like shapes, other sketchbook pages appear to have been drawn before being inked; those with a less definitive focus seem the most spontaneous (fig. 79).

Interestingly, the two drawings Motherwell inscribed to Anne Clark (one is dated August 5, a month before she, her husband, and Reis left Mexico) go well beyond Matta's example by exhibiting a more nonfigurative style. Rapidly generated biomorphic imagery displayed calligraphically in the larger example (some of it birdlike) provides evidence that Motherwell had begun working to hone his own skills in the generation of improvisational imagery (fig. 80).[91] This direction was to improve dramatically under Paalen's watchful eye.

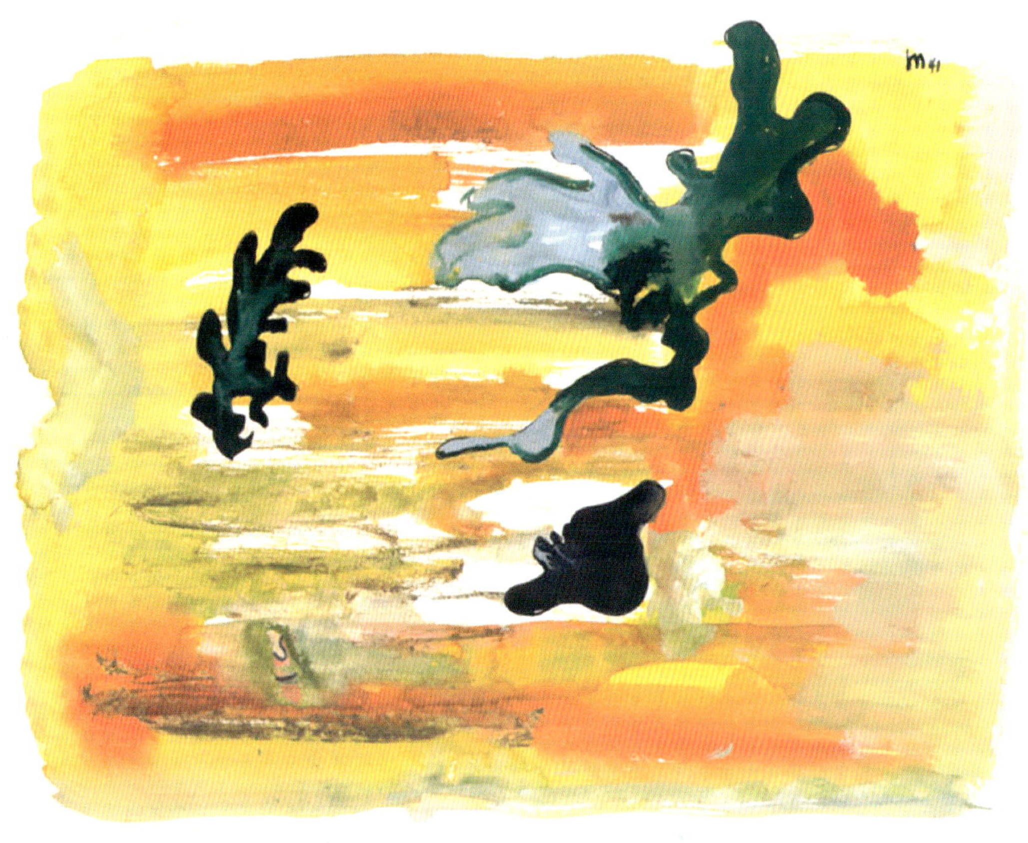

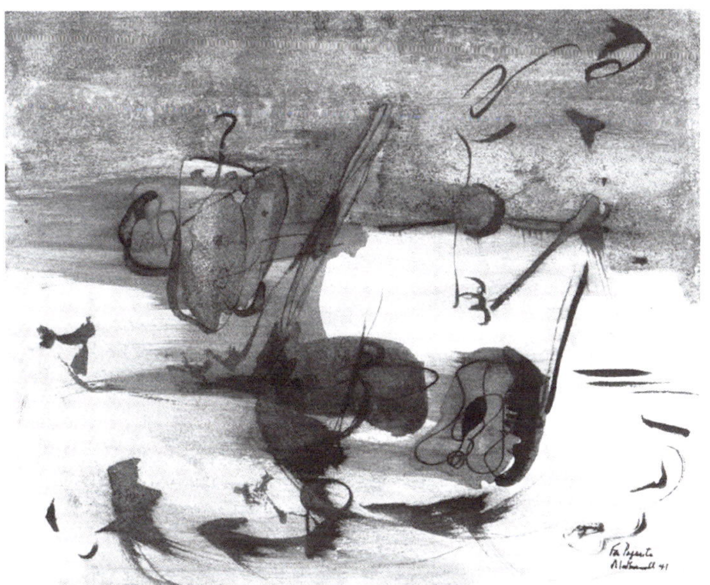

79 Robert Motherwell, *Mexican Sketchbook, p. 10*, 1941, Ink on paper and watercolor on paper. The Museum of Modern Art, New York. Gift of the Artist. Art © Dedalus Foundation, Inc./Licensed by VAGA, New York, NY.

80 Robert Motherwell, *For Pajarito*, 1941. Oil wash and ink on paperboard. Portland Museum of Art. Purchase from matching grants from the NEA and Casco Bank and Trust Co., 1981. Art © Dedalus Foundation, Inc./Licensed by VAGA, New York, NY.

Throughout his long career as a painter, collagist, and printmaker, Motherwell would remain convinced that one of modernism's overarching tasks was finding a "language that would be closer to the structure of the human mind." This core belief exemplifies the continuing impact of his youthful "association" with the Surrealists, as Sidney Janis described their unusual relationship.[92] A frequently quoted early statement, "The function of the artist is to express reality as *felt*," demonstrates the centrality of Matta's artistic philosophy in guiding the evolution of Motherwell's ideas on creativity. Articulated in "The Modern Painter's World," and published in 1944 in *Dyn*, this concept resonated equally with Wolfgang Paalen's beliefs. By the time Motherwell created *Landscape of the Inner Mind* he was well into the "post-graduate" phase of his Surrealist apprenticeship and under Paalen's more erudite influence.

After visiting Alaska, British Columbia, and the U.S. Pacific Northwest to collect artifacts for himself and the Musée de l'Homme in Paris, in September 1939 Paalen (who was half Jewish and unwilling to risk possible Nazi persecution) reluctantly resettled in a Mexico City suburb (fig. 81). He, Alice, and Eva took a house not far from the modernistic studios in San Angel that Juan O'Gorman had designed for Rivera and Kahlo. Working alongside Paalen in the fall of 1941 was to prove correspondingly stimulating although somewhat differently inflected, in comparison to the visual and intellectual experience Motherwell already had with Matta and Seligmann. The more introverted Paalen, a delicate man not particularly sympathetic to Matta's extravagance, would provide his education another significant series of benefits.

Interviewed in the late 1980s, Edward Renouf, an artist neighbor in San Angel's Via Obregón, distinctly recalled Bob Motherwell as frequenting Los Cedros y Begonias, the stimulating Paalen household.[93] Similarly to Abel, Renouf, a slightly older American painter, remembered Motherwell as "boyish and loquacious" with a "fertile imagination that easily overstepped historical fact" and recollected that he'd occupied much of his time at Los Cedros making copies of Miró, Picasso, and Braque. Motherwell's purpose in doing this, Renouf said, was "to give himself the feel of color and composition," and *La Belle Mexicaine* appears a likely result. Paalen, according to this neighbor, wanted Motherwell as both a disciple and a collaborator on *Dyn*, hoping in vain that he could help with its funding.[94]

While Motherwell turned down Paalen's offer of a permanent job as *Dyn*'s assistant editor (Renouf took the position, followed by Regler), he did agree to translate Paalen's "L'image nouvelle," written the prior summer. Along with another essay, which Paalen more provocatively titled "Farewell au Surréalisme" and published in French only, "The New Image" was to become a lead article in the inaugural number of *Dyn*.[95] At its outset (and strangely reminiscent of arguments advanced in favor of Pollock's early work) Paalen declared traditional notions of beauty and ugliness as "by no means necessary preconceptions for artistic creation."[96] Because photography can accurately reflect reality, he dismissed as reactionaries "those painters who today use exclusively this means of expression," a negative reference both to totalitarian-sponsored Social Realism and the more veristically inclined Surrealists. Needless to say, Paalen was especially critical of Dalí, denouncing as vulgar the Spaniard's "cross-image puzzles." Motherwell, as we have seen, would echo such critique.

Lauding automatism's ability "to sense unexpected images in aesthetically amorphous material," Paalen differentiated works produced automatically from mere subjective interpretation. He observed that to dream, in the widest sense of the word, is an automatist activity, but to relate one's dreams in an academic style is decidedly not. Breton, who supposedly almost "excommunicated" Motherwell for translating "The New Image,"[97] was likely to have been especially irritated by Paalen's key assertion: "The verbal flow of the poet and the kaleidoscopic flow of the painter, emancipated in automatism, are nothing but raw material—and it is the great merit of surrealism to have taught us that it is *this* (and not the exterior world) that is the true raw material of the poet and the painter." Emphasizing that "*the possible does not have to be justified by the known,*" Paalen provided a bulwark for his crucial belief (in contradistinction to Dalí, Breton, *and* Matta) that automatism could—and should—be used to trigger abstraction.

Anticipating the Abstract Expressionists, Wolfgang Paalen considered that a lack of recognizable subject matter did not in any way presume exclusion of significant themes: images, he said, have "the capacity to *project* a new realization which does *not* have to be referred to an object already existing." Maintaining that "the artist of our time can be authentic only when he creates new modes of seeing, only when he is original," Paalen also made an interesting corollary claim. "Significant artists of any period," he maintained, "have been more or less theoreticians." Both declarations could not have failed to stamp Motherwell's impressionable mind, and he would amplify these and other critical assertions of Paalen's in his own foundational essays, starting with "The Modern Painter's World."[98]

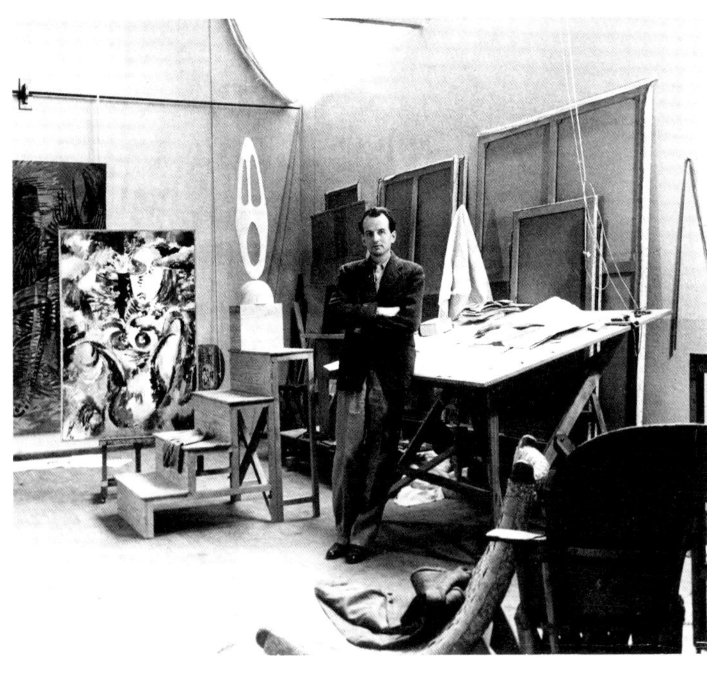

81 Wolfgang Paalen in his studio in San Angel, Mexico, 1945. Photo: Walter Reuter. Image courtesy of Andreas Neufert, Archiv Berlin.

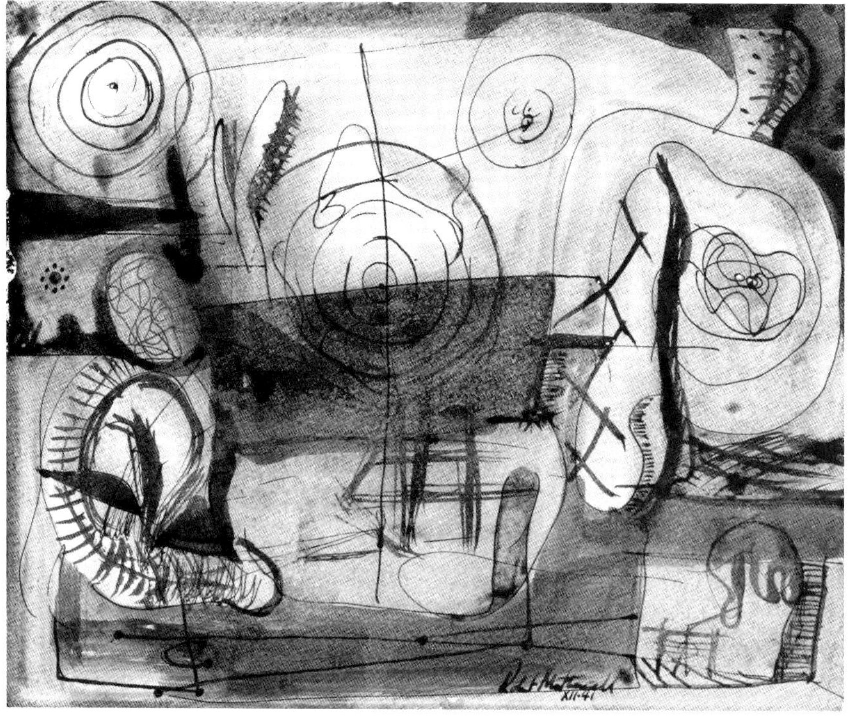

In 1945, as a measure of appreciation for Paalen's tutelage, Motherwell's first project as editor of the *Documents of Modern Art* series was to produce an anthology of the Austrian's writings that would be titled *Form and Sense*.[99] Another 1941 text included in this later volume found Paalen recording supplementary ideas about the nature of creativity likewise crucial for Motherwell. Completed in December, much or all of "Surprise and Inspiration," which was first printed in the summer 1942 second issue of *Dyn*, could have been conceptualized before Motherwell left for America. In it, Paalen advocated that "authentic artists must strive above all to *see*," stating they should not be concerned about appearing as "outcasts" from utilitarian values, a point to be reiterated with emphasis in Motherwell's writing.[100] Paalen commenced this discussion with an anecdote in which he recalled the effects of a lamp short-circuiting on his 1933 visit to Altamira's prehistoric caves. The result of its flashing off and on, he said, reconstructed for him the sense of surprise that primitive man must have felt when, out of the gloom, he saw in a sudden flash what he'd earlier drawn on the walls in brushstrokes "refulgent with genius." Reflecting philosophical discussions with his young American acolyte, Paalen quoted the pragmatist philosopher John Dewey ("To be set on fire by a thought or scene is to be inspired") in identifying the "surprise" of imagination as a central ingredient of all true creativity.

According to Breton's classic definition, Surrealism found its formal and ethical bases in the resolution of dream and reality, two seemingly antithetical states. Paalen's explanation that "*inspiration is the liberation of the torrent of imaginative association through the shock of surprise*" furnished a more nuanced psychological framework for the generative role of automatist technique. As might be expected, his thesis in "Surprise and Inspiration" (a phrase Peggy Guggenheim would borrow to retitle one of Motherwell's early '40s personage paintings; see fig. 98) stimulated Paalen to cite Sigmund Freud. Discussing Freud's theorization of the mechanics of dreamwork, Paalen took particular interest in the role assigned to condensation, a mind pursuit centered on bridge-building. Critical to understanding the function of "unconscious thought (the part of mental activity that takes place outside the focal points of consciousness)," the proclivities of condensation (also known as metaphor) are what help to differentiate imagination from thinking.

Whether or not he felt particularly sympathetic to Paalen's own art—once again, Motherwell maintained that he had not—viewing the transitional works he created in San Angel, it is difficult to altogether deny Paalen as a source for visual as well as intellectual exchange.[101] Motherwell inscribed the month of completion on two untitled automatist drawings from his Mexican period as "XII," indicating their creation at the tail end of his stay (fig. 82). While these works share some similarities with the smaller of the pair of sketches he had dedicated a few months earlier to Matta's wife, tightly delineated orthogonals no longer feature as prominently. In fact, Matta's gridding has been downplayed to the point where it has almost completely disappeared. Emphasizing space as more of a fluctuating allover field, with imagery pushed much closer to the forward plane, Motherwell placed greater emphasis on concentric circular motions. Despite claiming a "gentleman's agreement" with Paalen that involved never looking at his contemporaneous paintings—which would in any case have been somewhat difficult to fulfill, since, as Renouf confirmed, Motherwell often worked in Paalen's studio—the presence of spiraloid and nucleic shapes akin to those that Paalen featured at that time indicates a new set of models, more abstract than any Matta produced (fig. 83).[102] How this discovery played out back home will instigate discussion in the next and final chapters.

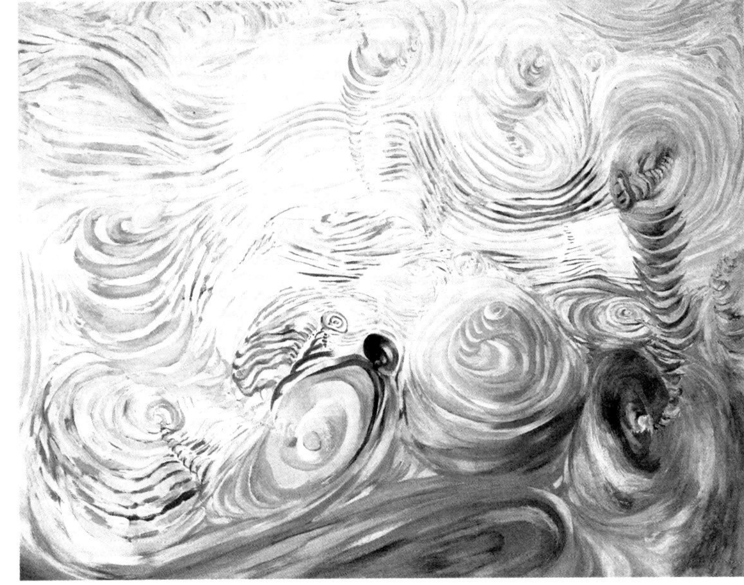

83 Wolfgang Paalen, *Espace libre, Space unbound,* 1941. Oil on canvas, 44⅞ x 57⅛ in. (114 x 145 cm). Collection of Lucid Art Foundation, Inverness, Calif. © Estate of Wolfgang Paalen and Eva Sulzer.

The differences in specific emphases and styles notwithstanding, New York School artists took their subjectivity as thematic in their work, a subjectivity they imagined as "interior." . . . The "subjects of the artist" were the artists as subjects.[1]

— MICHAEL LEJA, 1993

By the time that the National Gallery of Art in Washington, D.C., opened its long-awaited 1978 show *American Art at Mid-Century: The Subjects of the Artists,* a new crop of art historians was already hard at work countering its premise. The exhibition's contention, that meaning in works by major artists of the New York School derived primarily from direct confrontation with material processes, seemed for many younger scholars too closely indebted to Clement Greenberg's rigid recipe for medium purity, albeit flavored with rival critic Harold Rosenberg's existentialist "Action Painting" thesis thrown in for good measure.[2]

Rosenberg's Action Painter, defined in 1952 in his controversial *Art News* essay, "no longer approached his easel with an image in mind; he went up to it with material in his hand to do something to that other piece of material in front of him."[3] Disputing Greenberg's strictly formalist emphasis, Rosenberg accepted art making as a "moment" in the "adulterated mixture" of an artist's life. But his own focus on liberation from the tyranny of the object, while differently predicated than Greenberg's, resulted nonetheless in rejection of "self-recognition." "Since there is nothing to be 'communicated,'" Rosenberg explained, "a unique signature comes to seem the equivalent of a new plastic language. In a single stroke the painter exists as a Somebody—at least on a wall. That this Somebody is *not he* seems beside the point."[4]

Published a full decade after "The New Image" and "Surprise and Inspiration," Rosenberg's "The American Action Painters" diverged somewhat from Wolfgang Paalen's imbrication of the self and painting. Stimulated by primitive art's inherent abstraction, as well as by discoveries in quantum physics, Paalen had already begun to evolve a "post-Surrealist" philosophy by the time Robert Motherwell arrived on his doorstep. In choosing a name for his concept and its accompanying journal, he shortened the Greek phrase *tó dynaton,* meaning "that which is possible." Dynatic art was to exclude any kind of mysticism or metaphysics, aiming instead at a "plastic cosmogony, which means no longer a symbolization or interpretation but, through the specific means of art, a direct visualization of forces which move our body and mind."[5] Motherwell's unequivocal embrace of body-mind dualism would become central to his evolution.

It is not clear whether Rosenberg considered Motherwell an Action Painter; his paradigm was allegedly based on a composite of the working methods and artistic beliefs of Jackson Pollock, Willem de Kooning, and Franz Kline. But five years before his eponymous article appeared in *Art News,* Rosenberg had collaborated with Motherwell on a short-lived journal of their own. In a number of interesting ways — including its title, *Possibilities*[6] — their one-issue periodical comprised a sort of existentialist updating of Paalen's main ideas.[7] "This is a magazine," the two men wrote in winter 1947, "of artists and writers who 'practice' in their work their own experience without seeking to transcend it in academic, group or political formulas." Additional ideas that Motherwell and Rosenberg expressed in their joint editorial statement reprised some of Paalen's expressions. These include the convergence of energy into experience, avoidance of "the trap of politics," and the creative benefits of risk (also a Bretonian prescription).

Placing heavier stress on evidence than on theory, *Possibilities* featured statements by Pollock, William Baziotes, and David Smith, among other artists; an interview between Francis Lee and Joan Miró; and essays by writers ranging from Edgar Allan Poe to Paul Goodman, Lionel Abel, Richard Huelsenbeck, Edgar Varèse, and Rosenberg himself.[8] (Composer John Cage and architect Pierre Chareau were additional area editors.) While one informed observer described the publication as "very Motherwell," a reference, perhaps, to its tone of ambivalence, he contributed no text beyond the editors' statement and only one illustration.[9] The latter was an ink drawing made three years earlier, and whose title, he admitted, "may have been influenced by my association with Paalen and his enthusiasm for Northwest Indians."[10]

Motherwell's *The Indians* (fig. 84) appeared in *Possibilities* in juxtaposition with a short play by Lionel Abel, "The Bow and the Gun," featuring characters Chief Joseph, Toohulhotsote, and Buffalo Child Long Lance of the Nez Perce tribe, as well as Looking Glass, a "tall, powerfully built man with long blond hair," a half-breed with an odd but obviously significant name. Its plot involves trying to persuade an unwilling Looking Glass to

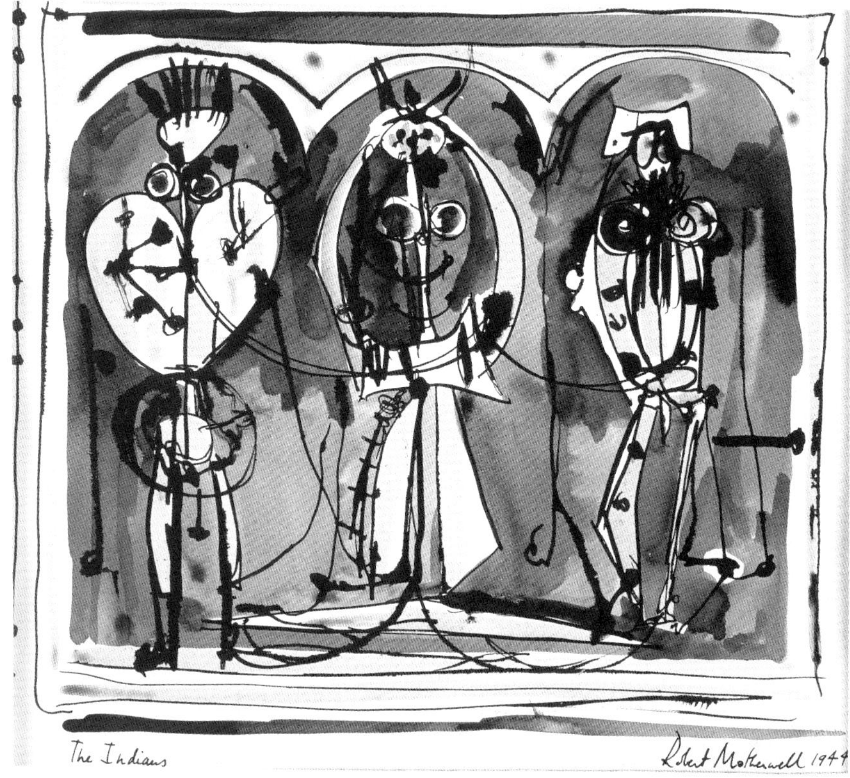

show the full-blooded Indians how to use a battered Gatling gun against white troopers en route for battle. When Looking Glass refuses, tossing the gun over a cliff because he believes in Indian ways, Chief Joseph, judging him a traitor, kills him with a traditional bow and arrow. While Motherwell's 1944 drawing does not directly illustrate this plot, its three abstracted figures stand side by side, like players on a stage, to face the picture plane. Each is framed by one roundel of a tripartite semicircular proscenium niche. Somewhat reminiscent of the print Motherwell made under Seligmann's tutelage, *The Indians* corresponds even more closely to *The Actors* also done in the early 1940s. In both, Motherwell connects a group of vaguely Miróesque figures at midpoint with a swinging horizontal line that suggests readiness to take a bow. The "Indian" at far right models a distinctly European black-dotted costume, with ruff and squared-off hat obviously borrowed from Harlequin and Pierrot, stock characters of the commedia dell'arte. While arrows pierce the heart-shaped torso of the faceless player at left, Motherwell provides no other discernible Native American attributes.[11]

Shown publicly three years earlier in his Art of This Century debut exhibition, *The Indians* had appeared on the walls of Peggy Guggenheim's gallery alongside several additional linked figural friezes. Some of these

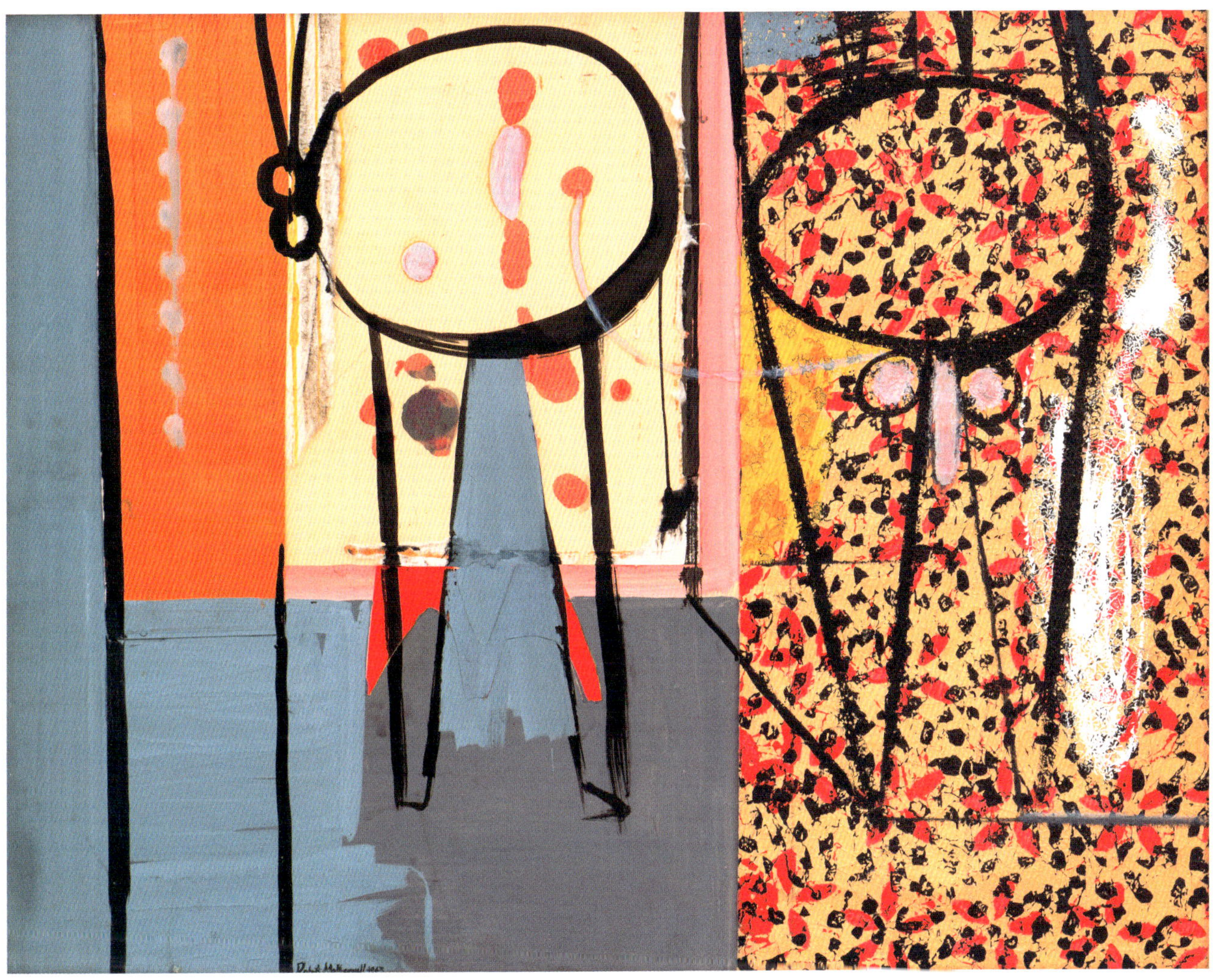

demonstrate more sinister implications corresponding to the subject matter of *Pancho Villa, Dead and Alive* (fig. 85). These drawings (whose disturbing connotations have been barely remarked) include *Two Personages Shot* and some with additional victims.[12] Underscoring their violent meaning, as in *Pancho Villa,* Motherwell included splotchy blots in all of these, approximating stains of blood (fig. 86). Anita Brenner documented a firing squad in *The Wind That Swept Mexico,* including as well another photograph picturing shooters at practice following a 1924 plot to murder Villa's enemy, Mexican president Álvaro Obregón. As we know, she also featured numerous photos of bodies on the ground in the aftermath of mass violence and street executions (fig. 87). Motherwell dedicated one version of *Three Personages Shot,* perhaps based on an image Brenner used of a man about to be executed seen

85 Robert Motherwell, *Pancho Villa, Dead and Alive,* 1943. Cut-and-pasted printed and painted papers, wood veneer, gouache, oil, and ink on board. The Museum of Modern Art, New York. Art © Dedalus Foundation, Inc. / Licensed by VAGA, New York, NY.

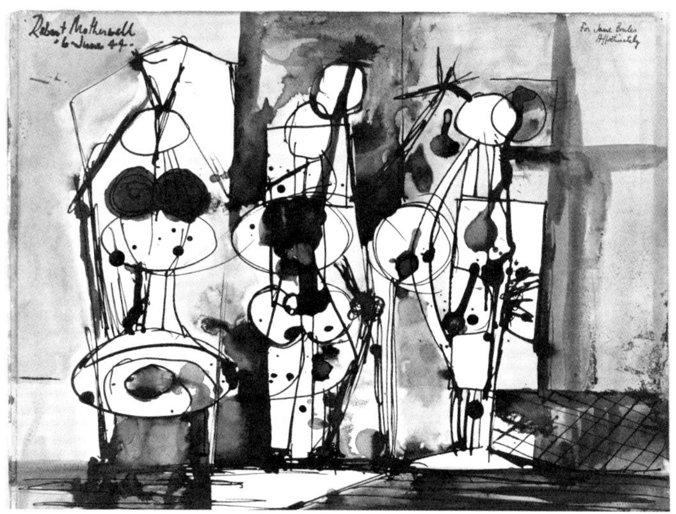

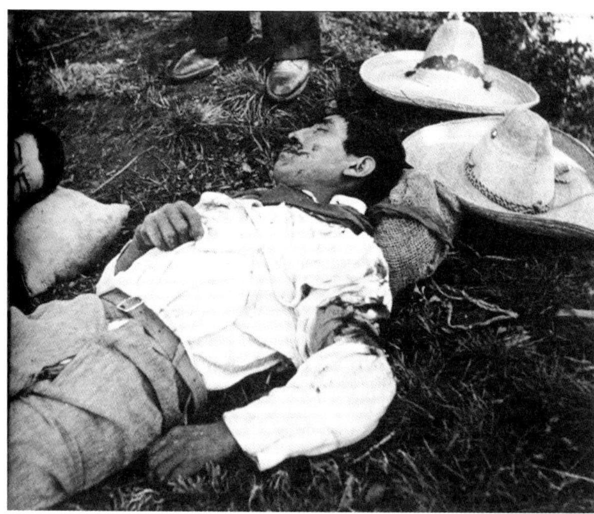

standing between two cardboard dummies against a pockmarked wall, to author and playwright Jane Bowles.[13] Jane and her famous writer husband, Paul, were friends of Motherwell's in Mexico, and she agreed to lend this drawing to his debut presentation. Proclaiming that "the Spaniards Picasso and Miró are especially loved, just as in the political sphere it is the Spanish Civil War and the Mexican efforts that strike our hearts," Motherwell clarified his enmeshed artistic and political sympathies in "The Modern Painter's World."[14]

Lionel Abel dedicated "The Bow and the Gun" to Freud and Jung's American translator Ralph Manheim and his wife, Mary, neighbors and friends of Jackson Pollock's. Its theme concerns the consequences, sometimes dire, of making political choices, as well as the moral implications of identity understood as "self-reflection."[15] Looking Glass—whose description and inclinations come awfully close to Abel's later characterization of a youthful Bob Motherwell—tries in vain to persuade Chief Joseph:

> *You reason like a white man. I am no traitor.*
> *If I wanted to be what I was*
> *before I was put in connection with life*
> *I would wear a cavalry cap*
> *over this head that remains fair*
> *(though I keep the oath*
> *you are ready to break*
> *and even force you to keep it).*
> *I would ride against you with the troopers.*
> *If not a Nez Perce,*

I would be with the white men who are not weak.
But I am your brother
and will fight beside you tomorrow
with bow and tomahawk
and ready sculpting knife,
not thinking whether to win or lose.

The chief's rueful words are the last to be spoken, "Let the young men say yes or no. I have seen too many of my people dead: the wrong dead: dead. Nothing is in order."[16]

Before his collaboration with Rosenberg on *Possibilities*, Motherwell, like Abel, played a brief editorial role on the staff of *VVV*, André Breton's exile magazine initiated in June 1942.[17] Two more issues followed, one a double number, the last published in early 1944 with a fearsome cover by Matta apposite to the world's currently more brutal situation.[18] Shortly after his return from Mexico, writing to physician and poet William Carlos Williams to solicit collaboration in choosing verse and prose for this journal, Motherwell was frank about his relationship to the Surrealists "against whom [at first] I had many philosophical prejudices." But, he soon realized that "they seemed to understand empirically . . . a solution to those problems of how to free the imagination in concrete terms, which are so baffling to an American."[19] Expressing belief in "the pursuit of increased *consciousness,* of consciousness of the *possibilities* inherent in *experiencing,*" Motherwell provided Williams a tantalizing foretaste of his own developing thesis.

Make, and in Making, Make Oneself

Faire, et en faisant, se faire.[20]

— PAUL VALÉRY (quoted by Lionel Abel)

Before their ideas began to diverge significantly, Breton had praised Paalen for his incarnation of a new "way of seeing," one that promoted "comprehension of what is *around* and *within* oneself."[21] Settling with María in Greenwich Village in late 1941, Motherwell seems to have pursued this kind of self-knowledge directly, aiming in the process to shed his fledgling status so strikingly described in Abel's memoir (and hers).[22] This was not to be so easy. Breton insisted on drafting Motherwell as a translator and go-between, asking him, for instance, to advise the Surrealist contingent about American grocery store equivalents for French cooking, and taking him to junk shops to assess the Surrealist quality of random objects.[23] At

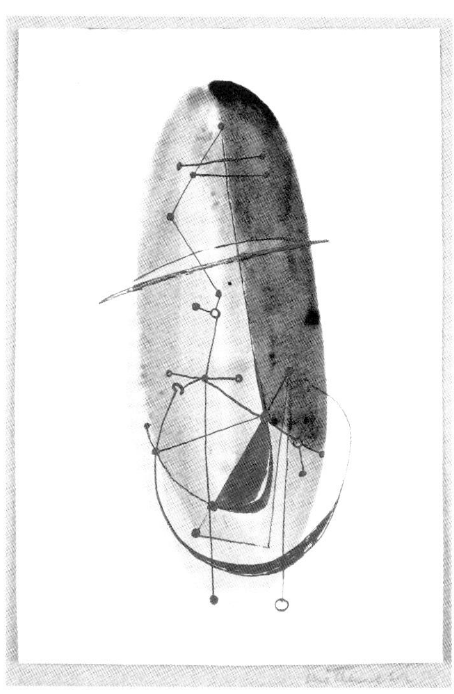

88 Robert Motherwell, *Yellow Abstract Composition*, 1942. Pen and ink and watercolor on paper. Tel Aviv Museum of Art Collection. Gift of Charles and Evelyn Kramer Collection, 1990. Art © Dedalus Foundation, Inc./Licensed by VAGA, New York, NY.

89 Robert Motherwell, *The Little Spanish Prison*, 1941-44. Oil on canvas. The Museum of Modern Art, New York. Gift of Renate Ponsold Motherwell. Art © Dedalus Foundation, Inc./Licensed by VAGA, New York, NY.

their first meeting, Abel noted Motherwell's "lack of ease in conversation." His speech was that "of a man not yet fully in touch with himself." While Abel somewhat misremembered the young painter's self-characterization as "inauthentic," stating it appeared as late as 1947 in *Possibilities*,[24] Motherwell did publicly expose his lingering insecurities in 1945. "The main thing is not to be frightened," he wrote in David Porter's catalogue for a show called *Painting Prophecy 1950:* "Or rather, since this is impossible, to act as if one is not." Thinking back, Motherwell would ascertain a vital motivating factor for Abstract Expressionism as its practitioners' need to counter feelings of "being nobody during the Depression." "It was a kind of desperation and acceptance that [we] never would be anybody" that propelled him and his peers to seek and find subsequent fame.[25]

Specifying more generally a little bit later in *Dyn* that "the artist's problem" had become finding something "*to identify with,*" after his return to New York, Motherwell made a consequential decision to widen his circle of aesthetic alliances. As seen in a group of abstract compositions devised in early 1942 for the *VVV Portfolio*, Miró took immediate precedence. To help fund the proposed Surrealist-in-exile magazine, Bernard Reis had suggested the creation of limited-edition portfolios for sale. Twenty were made, consisting mainly of prints pulled by a variety of artists at Seligmann's studio, but Motherwell and Matta chose to hand-create their own contributions. Using ink, watercolor, and gouache, Motherwell devised a set of pale vertical lozenges decorated with semi-abstract boat and pennant shapes (fig. 88). On the fence as yet about Mondrian's nonobjectivity (he considered Neo-Plastic paintings too dehumanized, rational, and not emotive enough, but judged them "great" nevertheless in *VVV*),[26] Miró's somewhat lighter-hearted approach seemed more palatable initially.[27]

By the time Motherwell completed his two *Spanish Prison* compositions—the version lent to Janis's show was followed by *The Little Spanish Prison*, a more abstract rendition (fig. 89)—his avant-garde ambitions had significantly increased. His statement for *Abstract and Surrealist Art in America* and early critical essay "The Modern Painter's World" reveal an artist still somewhat pessimistic about his relationship to society but more confident aesthetically.[28] Although these two paintings, begun in 1941 and finished three years later, both express an apprehensive theme, they signal as well a more deliberate attempt on Motherwell's part to take command of a wider variety of modernist material. While frequenting Peggy Guggenheim's gallery and apartment played a significant role in this advancement, repercussions from Motherwell's Mexican experience continued to factor into his transformation.

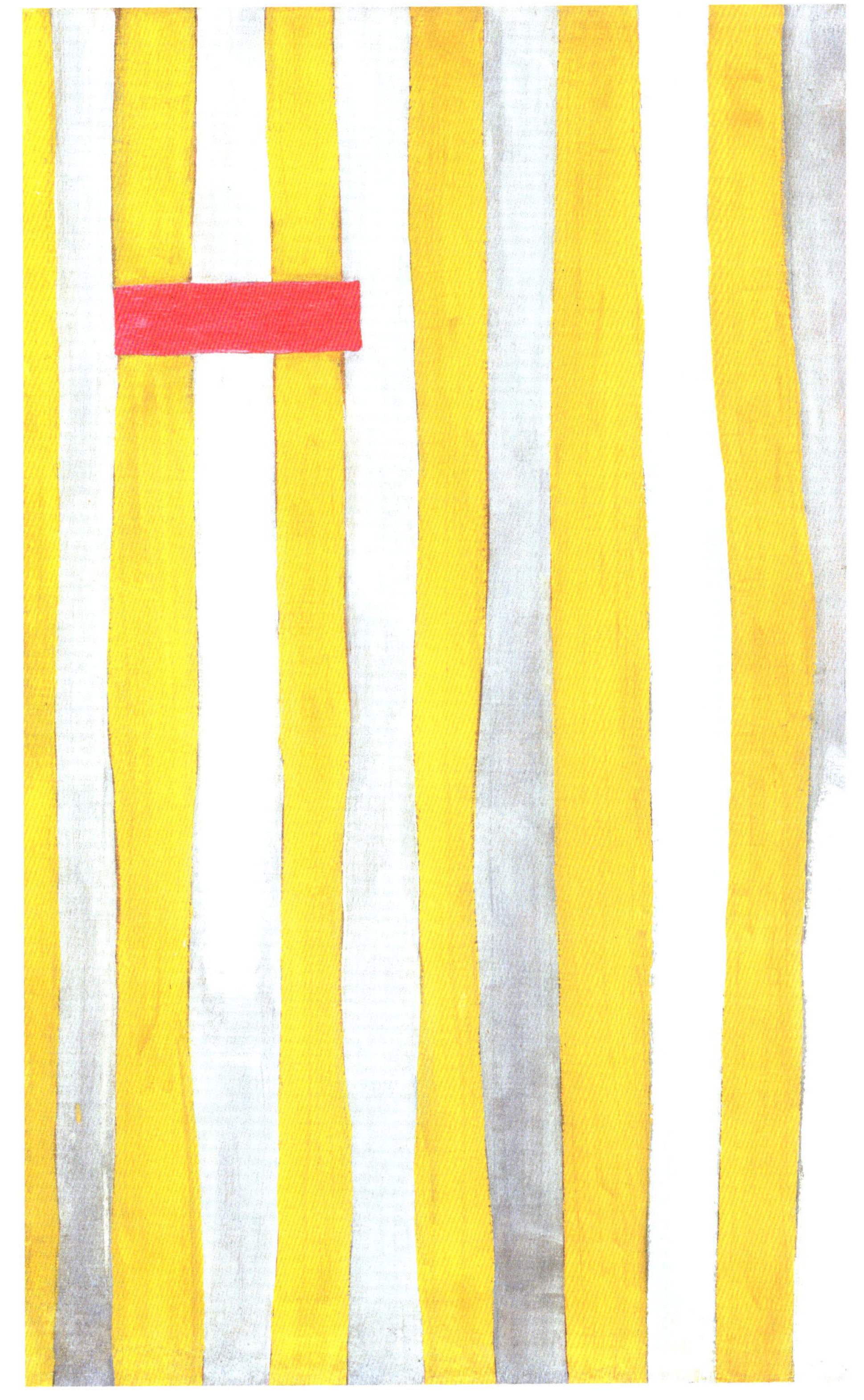

Remembrance of Coyoacán

Robert Motherwell's 1965 interview with Bryan Robertson includes many noteworthy admissions, but one in particular helps considerably to explain the unusual path of his early career. "For some reason I do not know," he confessed, "painting-wise I am often affected by places *after* I leave them. When I was in Oregon, I painted France; and as I remember, Mexico for a time became dominant in my painting after I returned to the U.S.A. It takes me a long time to absorb impressions of places." The particular benefits of this delayed reaction are abundantly evident in both the title and imagery of *Recuerdo de Coyoácan*, painted in 1942 (fig. 90).

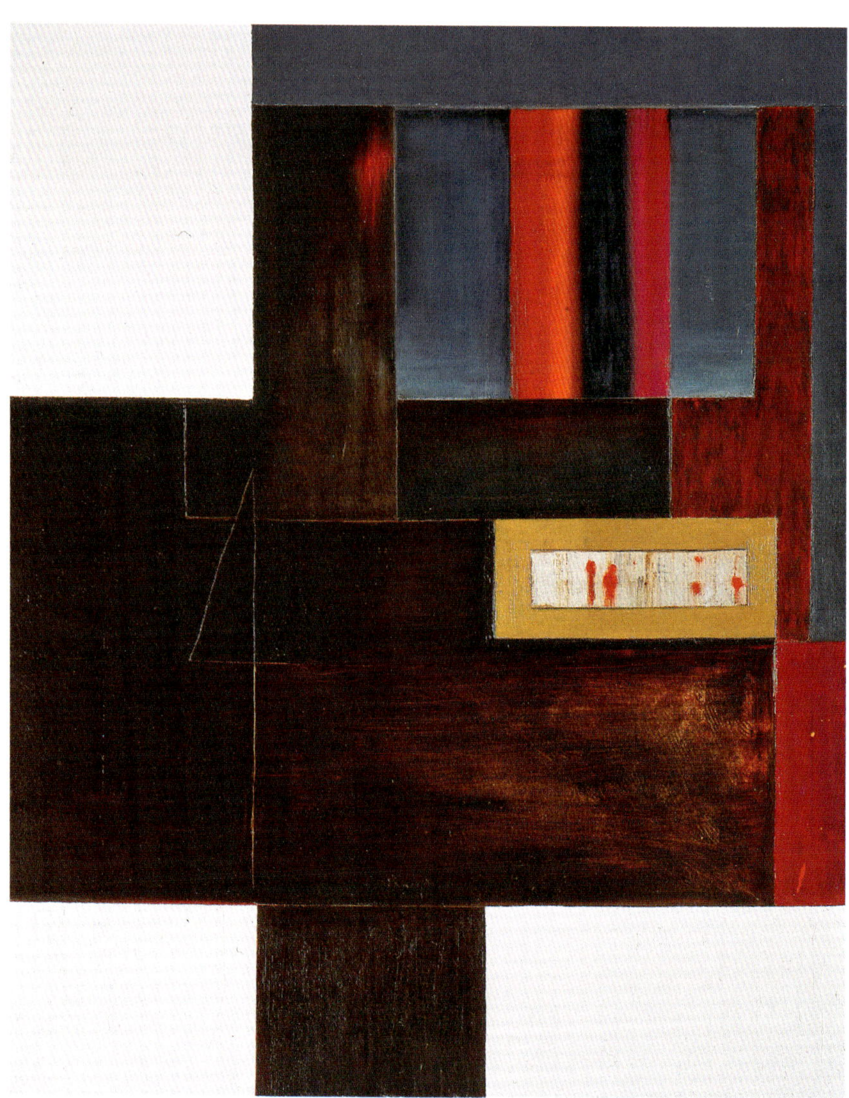

90   Robert Motherwell, *Recuerdo de Coyoácan*, 1941. Collection of Dedalus Foundation, New York. Art © Dedalus Foundation, Inc./Licensed by VAGA, New York, NY.

Seeing "more and better abstract pictures" at Peggy Guggenheim's was crucial in the months following Motherwell's return from his Mexican-based Surrealist immersion. At this time, he told Robertson, he started feeling the "full impact of Mondrian for the first time very deeply—I realize now I think much more than I was aware of then." This new enthusiasm fostered a fresh sense "that painting could be wholly expressive without 'literature' or expressionism." That being said, Motherwell also recalled his favorite picture at Peggy's as "the white Picasso which she told me Max Ernst [her then-husband] persuaded her to buy."[29] The impact of this 1928 work *L'Atelier* (The Studio), is patently evident in Motherwell's oeuvre; studying it, and another version of the same subject at the Museum of Modern Art helped him systematize his thoughts about the interaction of theme with format and design (fig. 91). Combined with structural lessons from Matisse (especially *Bathers by a River*, 1909–16, a large work also on local view) and his interest in Mexican folk traditions, these considerations would culminate in *Pancho Villa, Dead and Alive*.[30]

As Dore Ashton writes, pondering his Mexican experience during the war years in New York, Motherwell "revert[ed] to strong impressions of his first journey to an exotic place." One result was his conscious adoption of a "Latin-American" palette featuring blood reds, blacks, yellows, and magentas, in addition to blinding white; all are evident in *Recuerdo de Coyoácan*, along with deep turquoise, common in Mexican crafts and jewelry. Pertinent to his present and future artistic development, as Ashton noted, "Mexico revisited him in his imagination. Not only Mexico, but Spain as well, where he had never been."[31] *Recuerdo de Coyoácan* also drew upon European modernist sources, not only Picasso's *L'Atelier* but also Mondrian's *Composition No. 1: Composition with Red* of 1938–39, likewise owned by Guggenheim. Motherwell reconceptualized these stimuli in correlation with his own visual and psychological memories of that particular place.

Spanish Picture with Window, a related canvas signed and dated 1941, is apparently the first painting that Motherwell finished after returning from his extended Mexican trip (fig. 92). Presaging his *Open* series of the late 1960s, this work features a textured, chalky backdrop and a faintly delineated rectilinear vocabulary comprising thin horizontal and vertical lines made with a striping brush in imitation of the decoration on Mexican masks.

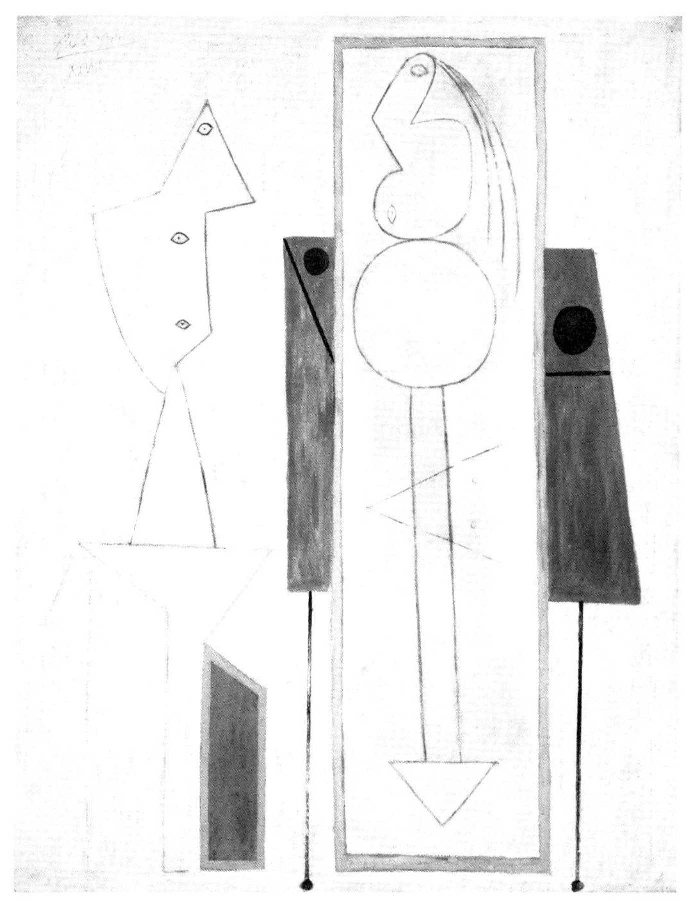

91 Pablo Picasso, *The Studio (L'Atelier),* 1928. Oil and black crayon on canvas, 63⅛ x 51⅛ in. (161 x 129.9 cm). The Solomon R. Guggenheim Foundation, Peggy Guggenheim Collection, Venice, 1976 (76.2553.3). © 2012 Estate of Pablo Picasso / Artists Rights Society (ARS), New York.

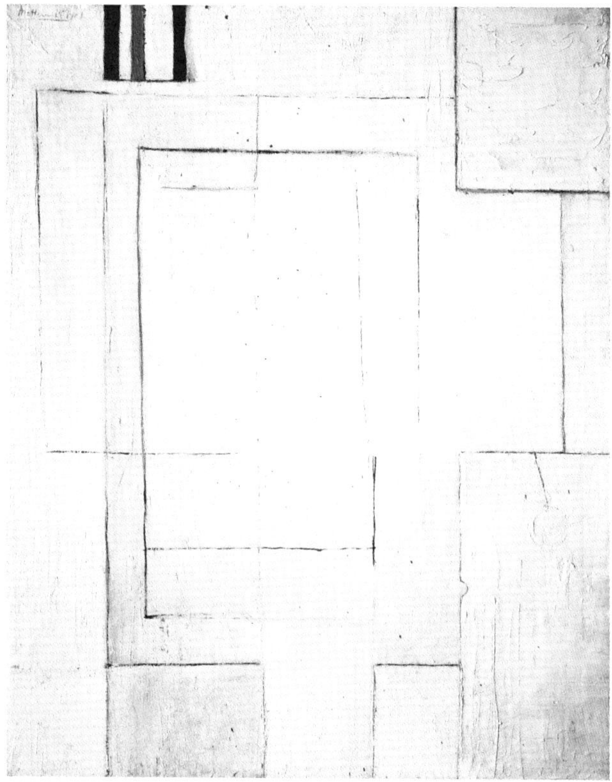

("When I came back to America at Christmastime," he recalled, "one day I looked at the masks again and thought now come on, go ahead, do something.")[32] Subtracting Picasso's figures, Motherwell also suggests in *Recuerdo de Coyoácan* the ubiquitous stucco walls in Mexico that he admired yet grew tired of being confined behind. He often complained about his and María's desolate living situation near Paalen's home in San Angel, not far from Coyoácan but too distant in those days for regular travel into Mexico City: "At night it was very dreary. Everything had high walls with broken glass bottles on the tops so intruders couldn't enter. We were almost in a kind of melancholic fortress at night and it really became too sad."[33]

Most of the hues employed in *Recuerdo de Coyoácan* Motherwell would use throughout his career, but in this early instance especially they reflect the strong interest he took in Mexican *art populaire*, an enthusiasm shared with Matta and Paalen. The latter decorated Los Cedros with local folk items in addition to world-class indigenous and precolonial artifacts; the former bought brightly colored piñatas and such in outdoor markets (including a life-sized animal used for processions), taking them back to New York to join his collection of tribal objects. Motherwell told Robertson that Matta used to say in those days, "North Americans have made the error of painting Indians. The thing to do is paint as though you *were* an Indian"—in other words, to emulate the simpler forms and high coloristic qualities common in folk art. "I think Mexico has the most beautiful of these kinds of objects, of any place," Motherwell described, citing in particular "skulls in spun sugar and *papier maché* bulls that are filled with fire crackers, *papier maché* masks of all kinds."[34] As noted, some of those masks exerted on him a very specific visual influence.

Recuerdo de Coyoácan presents a less rigidly geometric version of the horizontal/vertical hard-edge format of de Stijl that Motherwell overlaid on more unconstrained automatist markings, the same instinctual initial stratum he obscured in *La Belle Mexicaine*. Its stripes (seen on María's skirt as well) connect stylistically to *The Little Spanish Prison* and its variant, *Spanish Prison: Window,* the work in Janis's show.[35] At that time, he related to Robertson, "I began pictures automatically—the automatism consisting of dabs of paint scraped across the surface of the canvas with razors or sticks or spatulas—the kind that doctors stick down your throat—but then in my efforts to resolve a picture a great deal of the canvas would slowly be covered over with a more formal architectonic surface."[36] Motherwell had however phrased the roots of this technique somewhat more emotionally in 1947. "I begin painting with a series of mistakes," he noted in a Kootz gallery statement that year. "The painting comes out of the correction of mistakes by feeling. . . . My pictures have layers of mistakes buried in them—an X ray would disclose crimes—layers of consciousness, of willing."[37]

Unlike *Recuerdo de Coyoácan*, both *Spanish Prison* pictures and a work he called *The Spanish Jailer's Wife* were included in Motherwell's November 1944 Art of This Century solo exhibition. *Recuerdo* exhibits points of convergence with each of these, and also with two contemporaneous untitled abstract paintings and *Figure with Rectangular Window*, all created soon after Motherwell returned home but not all represented at his debut. Four of the seven oil paintings featured at Art of This Century displayed some kind of Mexican connection and, in addition to *Pancho Villa, Dead and Alive* in the collage category, a significant number of Motherwell's "Colored Drawings" involved Mexican subject matter as well. In the latter group, two versions of *Three Personages Shot* (dated June 6 and June 12, 1944), as well as *Two Personages Shot, The Spanish Flying Machine,* and *Zapata Imprisoned* were among the forty-eight total works on view.[38] Of interest, none of these Mexican (or even any Surrealist) links were remarked by contemporary reviewers; Greenberg mentions Motherwell's debt to Picasso alone.[39]

Many decades hence Robert Motherwell would categorize the "overall feeling" of *Recuerdo de Coyoácan* as anxiety, styling its mood and resolution of pictorial problems in direct opposition to Mondrian's principles of harmony and equilibrium, and considerably subjectivizing its apparent objectivity. *Recuerdo*'s flat, ochre-outlined horizontal "window," a device appearing roughly mid-canvas in a number of concurrent early '40s paintings,[40] discloses the blood stains he associated with Mexico's brutalist identity, a trait in opposition to (although, as Breton and Sergei Eisenstein declared so eloquently, coexistent with) its astounding light effects and sun-drenched beauty. Motherwell admired the latter even more in retrospect, rhapsodizing to Robertson about the "natural mode of a sunlit country: a white plaster wall, with matte bright colors on it, and hovering around it, the blackness of intense black shadows. A sense of painting profoundly atavistic."[41]

But he had seemingly found the former more in sync with mounting wartime tensions, described alternately as "grey or black anxiety, anguish, dread, *angst*." According to Motherwell, "The sense of possible death of European humanism was as palpable in New York's air during the early '40s as the death of one's father or mother—a collective nausea from fear, not of one's own death, but of one's lives and beliefs."[42] He ordained the red splotches and splashes glimpsed in *Recuerdo de Coyoácan* as "all the confusion I could stand in the painting," probably a reference to its synthesis of opposing styles, automatism (spontaneity), and geometry (structure). His gut fascination with the effects and paraphernalia of violence (bandages and the like) is also, however, effectively signified.[43]

In a random notation scrawled one day across a file cover, Motherwell let slip an important admission. "My mind," he inscribed at some unknown time, "is as black as the backgrounds in my paintings."[44] *Recuerdo de Coyoácan*'s blocky, darkly colored interlocking shapes, superimposed over automatist scribblings and barely perceptible stripes, take on a roughly cruciform shape, their ponderousness ostensibly an added initial gambit in Motherwell's quest to literalize his internal "black abyss."[45] A frequently cited declaration about his Mexican experience summarizes the imperative role that his short stay there played in helping devise the right visual imagery to define his lifelong mental state. Perhaps in part due to suffering severe childhood asthma (his mother believed he would not make it past age twenty-one), Motherwell freely admitted to Robertson, "All my life, I've been obsessed with death." Marking himself "profoundly moved by the continual presence of sudden death in Mexico (I've never seen a race of people so heedless of life)!" he enumerated the elements of Mexico's cult of *el muerte* that "seized" his imagination:

> The presence everywhere of death iconography: coffins, black glass enclosed horse carriages, sigao skulls, figures of death, corpses of priests in glass cages, lurid popular wood-cuts, Posada (he is staggering the way Verdi is: the people really find their voice in a man like that) and many other things, women in black, cyprus trees in their cemeteries, burning candles, black edged death notices and death announcements, calling cards . . . all of this contrasted with bright sunlight, white garbed peasants, blue skies, orange trees and everything you associate with life.

"For years afterwards," Motherwell confirmed, "spattered blood appeared in my pictures—red paint."[46]

Painters' Objects

Prior to the appearance in *Dyn* of "The Modern Painter's World" and shortly after completion of *Pancho Villa, Dead and Alive*—certainly the most accomplished early expression of his morbid fascinations—Motherwell published another foundational essay, this time in the Marxist journal *Partisan Review*. Remarking in this text called "Painters' Objects," that the "poverty" of modern existence had given rise to a circumstance where "art is more interesting than life," Motherwell quotes Picasso: "That to search means nothing in painting: *To find is the thing.*" He cites with added emphasis Breton's aphorism, "*Experience is bound to utility and guarded by common-sense.*" Both of these statements are background to an examination of the relevance of nonobjectivity in light of contemporary events. Here Motherwell notes with interest Mondrian's recent turn toward a more expressive transformation of analytic art in *Broadway Boogie-Woogie*. "Though its appearance is torn away, and only the structure bared," for "the first time a subject is present," he (somewhat inaccurately) explains. Motherwell also lauds sculptor Alexander Calder's adaptation of Neo-Plasticism to movement, while the "various devices for finding pleasure" that the Surrealists invented in Paris before the war—"spiritual games, private explorations, public provocations, sensory objects, and all the rest"—are subject to critique. "In the hard and conventional English-speaking world [i.e., New York] the devices simply could not work," he writes. "Here it was the surrealists who were transformed."[47]

Although continuing to evaluate the work of "mature men" as best, Motherwell's ruminations in "Painters' Objects" also take a turn toward opportunities for those, like himself, whose careers were just beginning. While not articulated specifically as such, shared aspirations seem evident in his assessment of the importance of Jackson Pollock's fall 1943 Art of This Century debut, a year before his own. Based on the "extraordinary gifts" revealed in this show, including a color sense that is "remarkably fine, never exploited beyond its proper role" and a sense of surface that is "equally good," it is here that Motherwell pronounces Pollock "one of the younger generation's chances."[48] Describing painting as a "medium in which the mind can actualize itself" in "The Modern Painter's World" (which was actually written first), Motherwell indicates the value he placed on the lessons of Surrealism, but in an alternate assertion in that essay—that painting, like music, can "become its own content"—he comes out on the side of abstraction as well. The stakes for both are raised in "Painter's Objects," in which Motherwell identifies Pollock's "principal problem" as discovery of his own "true *subject*," remarking with great prescience that its resolution "must grow out of the process of his painting itself."

These judgments clearly presuppose close acquaintance with Pollock's most recent canvases, such as *The She-Wolf, Male and Female, Moon Woman Cuts the Circle*, and *Guardians of the Secret*, works initially not so well appreciated but now considered catalytic. Motherwell's perceptive remarks on process as meaning were likely provoked by noticing that the drips and spatters Pollock observed and participated in making at the Siqueiros Workshop in 1936 had begun to resurface in a newer, more directed guise. While such automatic markings were still minor aspects—we already know what was to come—their incorporation by Pollock during the year prior to his first show was critical in helping him engender a mytho-poetic iconography closely connected to his search for a personal and artistic identity.[49]

In a state of turmoil tied to his recalcitrant "fear of the 'Terrible Mother'" and fueled by alcoholism, Pollock had begun consulting Jungian therapists and had endured a four-month psychiatric hospital stay in 1938. By 1941 he was working with Violet de Laszlo toward reconciliation of his animus and anima (Jung's terms for a person's male and female sides), a personality deficit that Dr. Joseph Henderson had previously identified as dire. Both of his therapists well understood that art was Pollock's only real expressive outlet.[50]

Although relevant to his therapeutic quest for individuation, the imagery and technique Pollock used in *Male and Female* also correlate with experiences he and Motherwell were sharing, the roots of which extended back to the latter's Mexican stay (fig. 93). The two young painters had been brought together by William Baziotes, one of the first American artists Motherwell met (through Matta) upon his return to New York. On the surface, each man's background and disposition seemed very different, although Motherwell had his own issues with a vain and cruel mother who beat him severely as a child.[51] Without question, both Pollock and Motherwell were reacting to similar aesthetic stimuli in 1942. *Male and Female,* indeed, had also been inspired in part by Picasso's series on the subject of himself and a model in his atelier. Whereas Motherwell's opening attempts to assimilate Peggy Guggenheim's version involved omitting its abstract figures, Pollock's fixation on gender differentiation, and the first example of his reliance on phallic spatter to help express its contrast, constituted *Male and Female*'s primary subject. As we've seen, Motherwell's slightly later shift toward figuration would display a very different species of obsession.

Despite observations to the contrary made in "Painter's Objects," in Pollock's case (and considering his admitted propensity for the slow burn, perhaps Motherwell's as well) this genre of subject matter was influenced by their participation in the current vogue for playing Surrealist games. During the summer of 1942 in Provincetown, Motherwell engaged with Matta, Max Ernst, and others in making Cadavres Exquises, poems or drawings in which each person adds a section, folds the paper so the next one can't see the words or sketch by the previous participant, and passes it on until the page is complete. That fall, he and María began indulging this pastime with Pollock, Lee Krasner, Baziotes and his wife, Ethel, and others, in order to create joint artistic and poetic statements. According to Steven Naifeh and Gregory White Smith, venues for this activity included the apartment of Matta, whose idea they say it was, Francis Lee's loft, and the Motherwells' flat on Eighth Street (Ethel Baziotes recalled the last circumstance only). Wherever they were made, none of these collective efforts have survived,

93 Jackson Pollock, *Male and Female,* 1942–43. Oil on canvas. 6 ft., 1¼ x 4 ft., 15⁄16 in. (186.1 x 124.3 cm). Philadelphia Museum of Art. Gift of Mr. and Mrs. H. Gates Lloyd, 1974 (1974-232-1). Image courtesy The Philadelphia Museum of Art / Art Resource, NY. © 2012 The Pollock-Krasner Foundation / Artists Rights Society (ARS), New York.

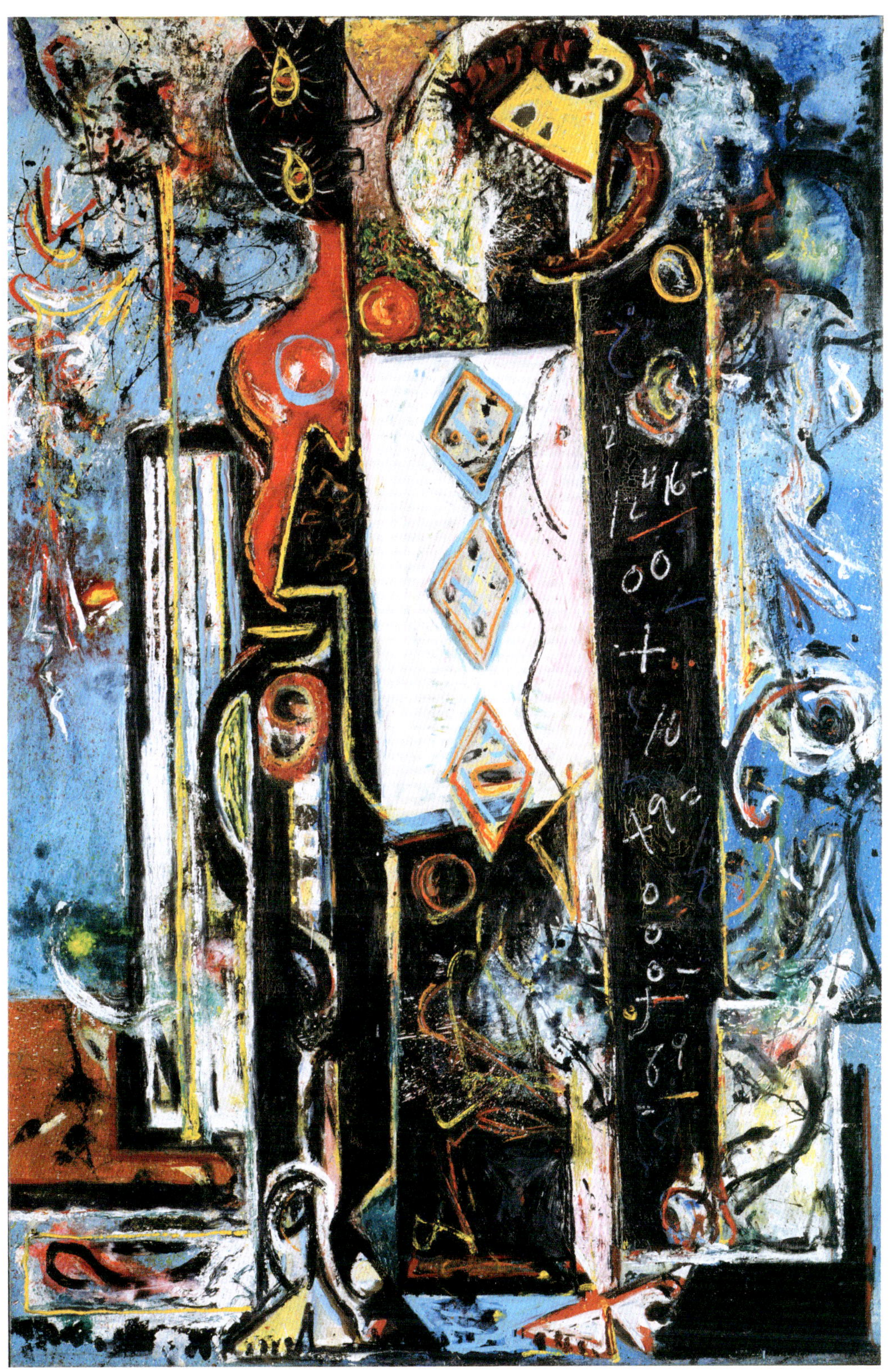

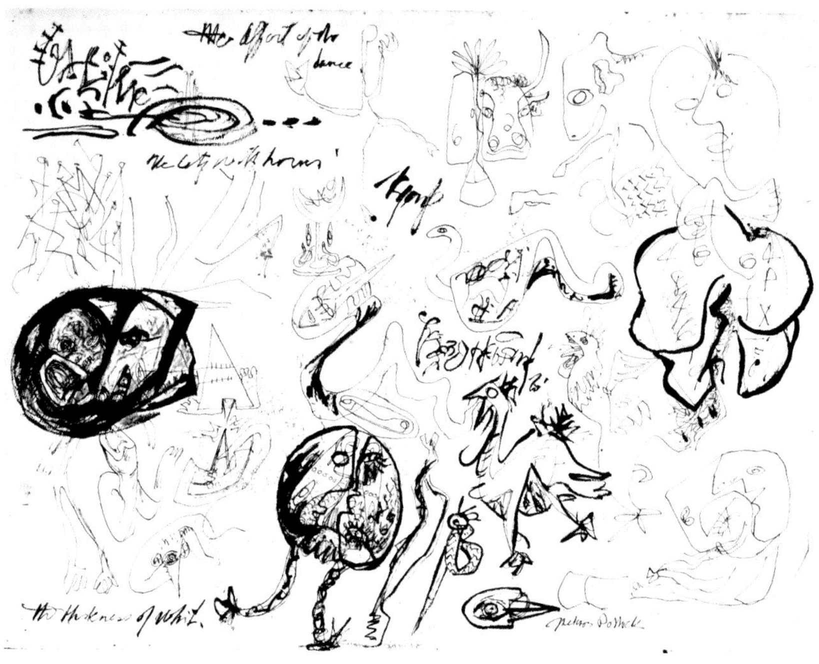

although several of Pollock's 1942–43 drawings introject a comparable form of word and image free association (fig. 94).[52]

By the time she and Pollock took part in such group parlor games, Krasner said, the couple had already been playing "Male and Female," their name for the Cadavre Exquis variation in which sketching parts of the body replaced linking unrelated words. This diversion had been introduced as a Surrealist activity by Gordon Onslow-Ford in conjunction with his New School lectures. Following the Surrealist example, no stylistic rules governing realism or abstraction were enforced, only an overall intent "to locate a common meeting of the psyches." Much better educated than the others, Motherwell was the most "fluent" speaker, but Pollock delighted in interpreting masculine/feminine dichotomies using terminology borrowed from his analysts.[53]

In 1950, despite Surrealism's manifest unpopularity by then, Motherwell cautioned art critic Thomas B. Hess not to "underestimate the influence of the Surrealist state of mind on the young American painters in those days [the war years] or that through them we had our first understanding of automatism as a technique."[54] October 1942 saw him contributing (perhaps somewhat perversely) a fully abstract painting to *First Papers of Surrealism,* the flamboyant Surrealist manifestation commencing one week prior to Peggy Guggenheim's New York gallery opening. Although also invited to submit, Pollock declined to join a group activity. Baziotes agreed; he and Motherwell were thrilled by their better placement at the Whitelaw-Reid

Mansion than more famous artists, albeit crisscrossed by Duchamp's disorienting installation employing five miles of tangled string.[55] Added to his initial role in the preparations for *VVV,* this opportunity—unthinkable a mere two years earlier, when his European friends had all exhibited in Mexico—indicated substantial progress toward Motherwell's desired repositioning.

"A sense of painting profoundly atavistic"

Interestingly, Motherwell and Matta's now infamous falling-out was engendered by the former's agreement to proselytize for the latter's vision of automatism among the aspiring avant-garde. This task could have been only partially successful at best; most of the artists Motherwell visited in New York were already practicing automatic techniques—for many it had been a surreptitious WPA practice—and a number were openly disdainful of the version he at first consented to advocate. Confessing that he had for some time been too reliant on Matta "to make a map for him," by 1944 Motherwell disclosed to Baziotes that he only now understood a need to "see the whole terrain."[56] Initially in league with Matta in a plan to show up Breton and the other émigrés through a counter manifestation spearheaded by younger American artists, during the late fall of 1942 Motherwell managed to marshal Pollock, Baziotes, and two other painters, Peter Busa and Gerome Kamrowski, to attend group tutorials.

Abstract Expressionist scholars have by now thoroughly parsed the Americans' equivocal reactions to these meetings (without wives), held sporadically early in the following year at Matta's studio. Mostly skeptical of Matta's occult interests, including his belief in *personnages transparents* and simultaneous worlds, they were resentful of his dogmatic attitudes, toward which Pollock's disaffection was quickest and most obvious. As David Rubin points out, Matta believed, in contradistinction to the Americans, that automatism "might be more fruitful than it had been for the Surrealists if it were directed."[57] His lesson plans, aimed at "attacking a vocabulary" together, required coordinated response to structured themes, including natural elements (recall Matta's enthrallment with the Mexican volcano, which he considered "the best image of my body"),[58] Ernst's concept of the "blind swimmer," life and death, or the hours of the day.

A related subject, gender binarism, was also promoted for group study but Matta's approach to it was found unappealing by the others. Matta expected representations of the concept of male and female to "keep a degree of reference to reality, and a sense of the possibility of the deep space in the picture. It couldn't be all explosion, you know."[59] More accepting than Breton of Jung's atavistic notion of a collective unconscious, an idea admired by his "pupils," Matta had no tolerance for what he termed the New Yorkers' propensity for "magazine painting," their tendency to incorporate formal advancements by famous European artists based on studying reproductions in journals and books. In any case, rebellion against his directives was virtually instantaneous—the study group lasted at most six sessions.[60] "The Americans did not understand what I meant by conception," Matta later complained, "they only wanted to manipulate color."[61]

The formerly close Matta and Motherwell were at loggerheads almost instantly in conjunction with this project.[62] While previously in awe of the expatriate Surrealists, by the time he wrote "The Modern Painter's World" (and perhaps inspired by Paalen) Motherwell had become fairly eloquent in his critique of their overreliance on the individual unconscious, and capable of articulating a new desire among his peers, unshared by Matta, to nuance "pure" automatism with formal advancements. A major tendency of Surrealism, which Motherwell explicated in "The Modern Painter's World," was described as their desire to "renounce the conscious ego altogether, to abandon the social and the biological, the super-ego and the id." For the Surrealists, he wrote poetically, "Everything in the conscious world is held to be contaminating, "as when the hero in search of the fabulous princess in the Celtic fairy tale, must never permit himself to be touched, whether by a leaf, an insect, or anything from the external world, as he flies through the forests on his magic horse. If he were touched by the world, his quest would immediately come to a disastrous end."

Delineating the Surrealists' Freudian conception of the journey into the unconscious as "some such hero's task," and their version of automatism as a "dark forest through which this path runs," Motherwell now chose to demur. Asserting that the unconscious "cannot be directed" in ways that the Surrealists imagine, he explains that actually "it presents none of the possible choices which, when taken, constitute any expression's form." Consequently, "to give oneself over completely to the unconscious is to become a slave." Somewhat more in line with Paalen's dynatic thinking, and even more synchronous with ideas percolating among his newly made younger artist friends, Motherwell proposes an alternate version of automatism, one that he says is "very little a question of the unconscious." It is rather a "plastic weapon" with which to invent new forms.[63] Matta's objections were instant, since he firmly believed "the action of the imagination is more valid than the action of the arm." However, as Rosenberg's *Art News* article demonstrates, the prioritizing of process was to become a hallmark of the new avant-garde (although not its only content). Automatism, Motherwell would observe, became the "first modern theory of creating that was introduced into America early enough to allow American artists to be equally adventurous or even more adventurous than their European counterparts."[64]

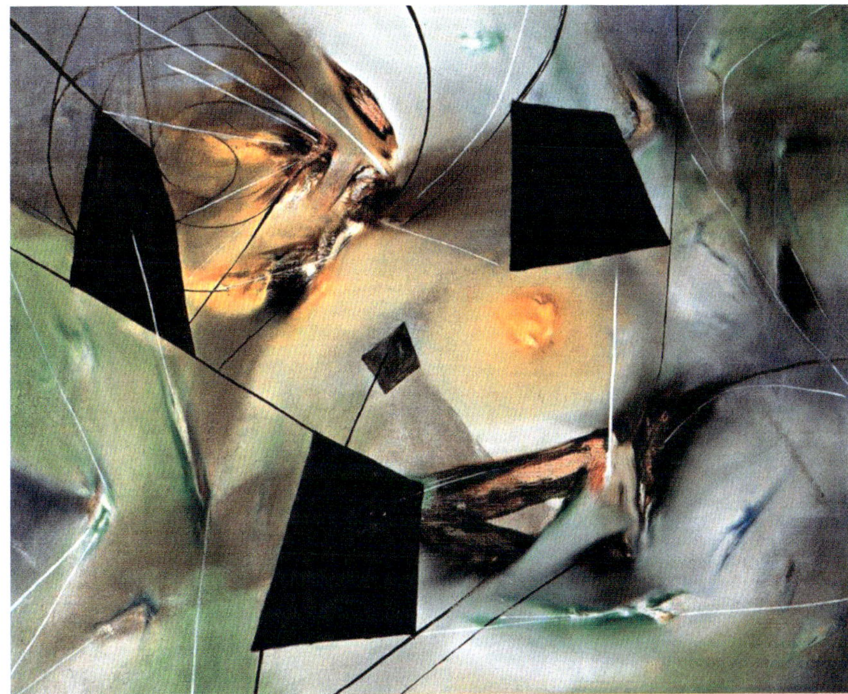

Not quite totally rejecting Surrealism's automatic approach and retaining Matta's focus on finding new ways to symbolize "images of man," Jackson Pollock nevertheless took important steps toward greater aesthetic and personal self-definition in producing *Male and Female*. Admittedly stimulated by the European émigrés' presence in New York, by the time he painted this work, like Motherwell, Pollock's "idea of the role of the imagination" had begun to differ somewhat.[65] Aided by D'Arcy Wentworth Thompson's popular book *On Growth and Form*, he began to redirect Matta's use of organic principles of transformation to suggest psychic process in ways that were less static.[66] As Busa said, he began aiming "to represent a whole chain of events in his unconscious which is very much like believing in something as a primitive might."[67]

Pollock's more spontaneous approach to paint handling is evident in certain key areas of *Male and Female*, stimulated in part by Matta's example but transformed through divergent inflection. Despite his own increasingly supra-realistic inclinations and reliance on sketches, when preaching to the Americans Matta encouraged risk taking; he recommended working with paint as if it were a free agent, to minimize conscious control and eliminate as much as possible any direct contact of the brush. In order, as Breton put it, to "express in the most concrete language the process of the reaction of the psychic on the physical," Matta would himself sometimes also take a

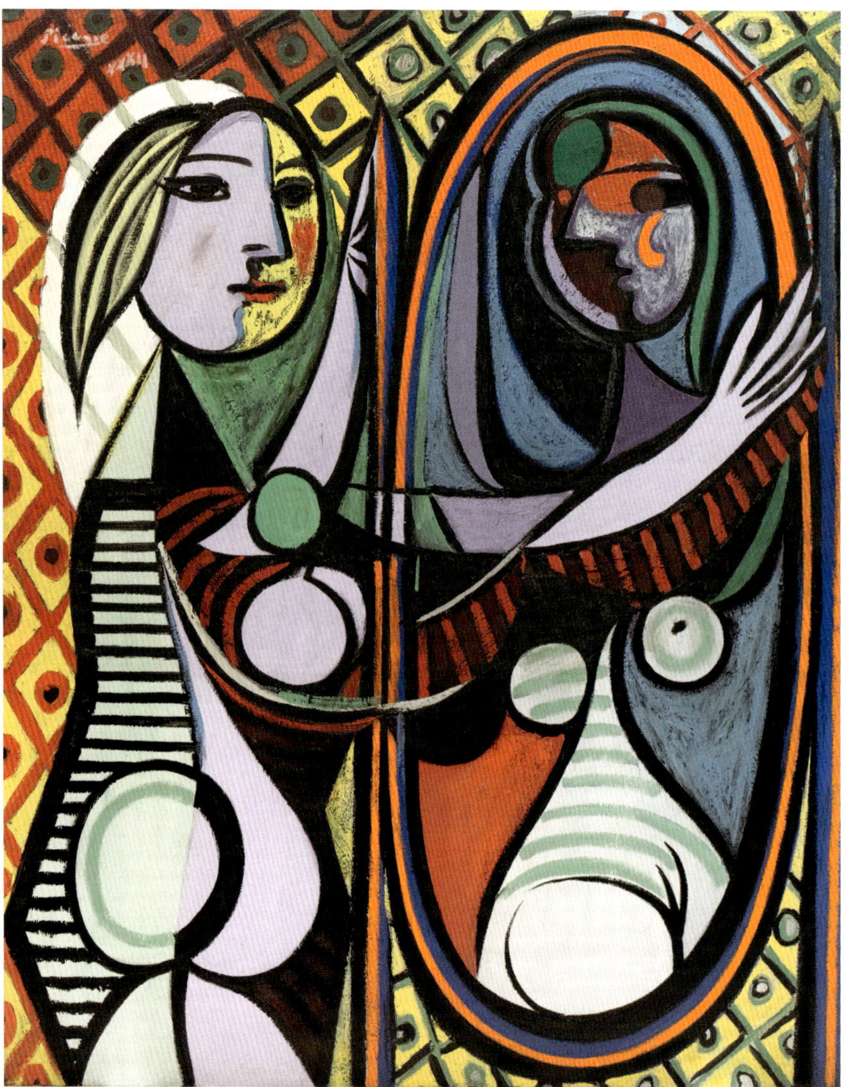

more painterly approach, spreading color with sopping rags, allowing it to smear and clot, or scraping it thinly to animate an unexpected "convulsive" image in areas of his composition (fig. 95). "The wonderful thing about Matta's stimulus," Busa said, "was his grasp of the morphology [forming powers] of paint."[68]

Without a doubt, as Noguchi realized, David Alfaro Siqueiros had also encouraged artists working with him at Union Square in 1936 to employ atypical technologies and use pigment and other materials in more uninhibited ways; putting out to pasture "the stick with hairs on its end" was a primary workshop goal. Several of his WPA colleagues, Busa among them, remembered that Pollock continued intermittently to squeeze paint directly from the tube long after Siqueiros left to fight in Spain.[69] According to Gerome Kamrowski, about a year before their experience with Matta, Baziotes (who definitely attended Onslow-Ford's lectures) argued with Pollock over whether those experiments at Union Square could be considered truly automatic. Refusing to believe that such an important Surrealist innovation might have been "upstaged" by the Mexican, Baziotes suggested they make an automatist painting with Kamrowski on a canvas "that wasn't going well" in order to prove his point. The resulting document might be considered one of the very first to qualify as "more emotional and more violent in appearance than geometric abstraction . . . but more abstract than any expressionism that had been seen in New York."[70]

As a variety of scholars have already discussed, *Male and Female* is not the only early '40s work where Pollock recalled Matta's thematic suggestions. Some of his topics, rejected during the study group, were also featured in various drawings of this period, a 1943 canvas Pollock originally called *Male and Female in Search of a Symbol* (but shortened to *Search for a Symbol*) and a series of paintings with night- and moon-related themes continuing through 1946. Both of the canvases originally titled in reference to gender dichotomy include facing figural pictographs, reminiscent of Picasso and Miró, respectively. While differentiated sexually, as Frank O'Hara remarked of the second example, Pollock's boy/girl figures in each also reflect each other's characteristics: "They are not double-images in the routine Surrealist sense, but have a multiplicity of attitudes."[71] A large white rectangle located midway between the two flanking totemic personages in *Male and Female* acts to divert the female's hourglass form onto her counterpart seen at right ejaculating beneath. One of her breasts seems to float above this area, an obvious visual reference (like the central diamond shapes) to *Girl Before a Mirror,* Picasso's 1932 Surrealist masterwork at the Museum of Modern Art (fig. 96). Pollock's flirty-eyed "girl" coyly observes her own projected characteristics, but now thrown onto her opposite.

In line with Pollock's well-known psychological confusion, additional cues in *Male and Female* might also encourage a reverse gender interpretation. Amalgamating Freudian and Jungian symbolization to post-Cubist formal innovations, Pollock in this work manages to retain the allusive eroticism familiar from Matta's paintings just before, during, and right after Mexico. Whereas Motherwell had so far left his own automatic markings visible only as pentimenti, in a final surge of spontaneity Pollock dripped and spattered around *Male and Female*'s upper borders and in the place where maleness is defined, putting a newer agenda in place.

A Hero's Task

Although well acquainted with the collages of Braque and Picasso, and with Ernst's recombination of existing pictorial images into disturbingly discordant narrations, neither Pollock nor Motherwell had ever attempted this medium prior to Peggy Guggenheim's invitation to enter her 1943 collage international. While the Surrealists' attraction to the "marvelous" led to a search for fortuitous avenues to engender form (decalcomania, frottage, fumage, etc.), collage, a Cubist invention, mostly privileged careful rearrangement of existing materials, a different route to destabilize and destandardize meaning. Pollock's untitled entry has not survived, but *The Joy of Living*, Motherwell's offering to Guggenheim's spring 1943 collage show, was acquired by Saidie May and given to the Baltimore Museum of Art in advance of his 1944 debut (fig. 97).

In this initial attempt at what would become a lifelong pursuit, Motherwell cut and tore ten disparate fragments of three kinds of paper previously spotted with ink or paint; the lowermost sections pasted onto *The Joy of Living* exhibit those telltale red blots he would use more frequently in the months to come.[72] Apparently unwilling as yet to venture too far afield compositionally, some of the incongruent sections in *The Joy of Living* are loosely united by linear or painted perspectival elements familiar from both Matta's *Inscapes* and his own *Mexican Sketchbook*. As Greenberg noticed, areas of layered ground in *The Joy of Living*, which were created in ink, oil paint, and crayon on various types of board and paper, seem "smokily" painted. Perhaps an oblique war-era allusion, this effect is given credence by a pasted fragment at upper right of a military combat map cut out of a magazine or newspaper. Motherwell and Pollock apparently essayed their first collages together; working somewhat more audaciously, Pollock burned one of his attempts with a match, intending the scorched areas to function as part of his composition.[73] Adopting a title somewhat ironically borrowed from Matisse, Motherwell substituted for Pollock's physical violence a mood that is disquieting and ill-at-ease.[74]

In many ways, *Pancho Villa, Dead and Alive* can be considered Motherwell's dyadic counterpart to the erotic content and structure of *Male and Female*. In it he reconfigured Pollock's initial ferocity in executing collage by converting disjunctivity and the ripping of paper into signs of his own preoccupation with the connection of heroism to violence. As Motherwell would later confirm, his collage practice tended toward the autobiographic, and his earliest attempts in this medium reflect a particularly troubled wartime psyche. The tearing methods he used to create these works, "made during some of the most tormented and exhausted years of my life," Motherwell designated as "equivalent to murdering, symbolically."[75]

97 Robert Motherwell, *The Joy of Living*, 1943. Collage of construction paper, mulberry paper, fabric, and printed map with tempera, ink, crayon, oil, and graphite, 43½ x 33⅝ in. (110.5 x 85.4 cm). The Baltimore Museum of Art. Bequest of Saidie A. May (BMA 1951.344). Art © Dedalus Foundation, Inc./Licensed by VAGA, New York, NY.

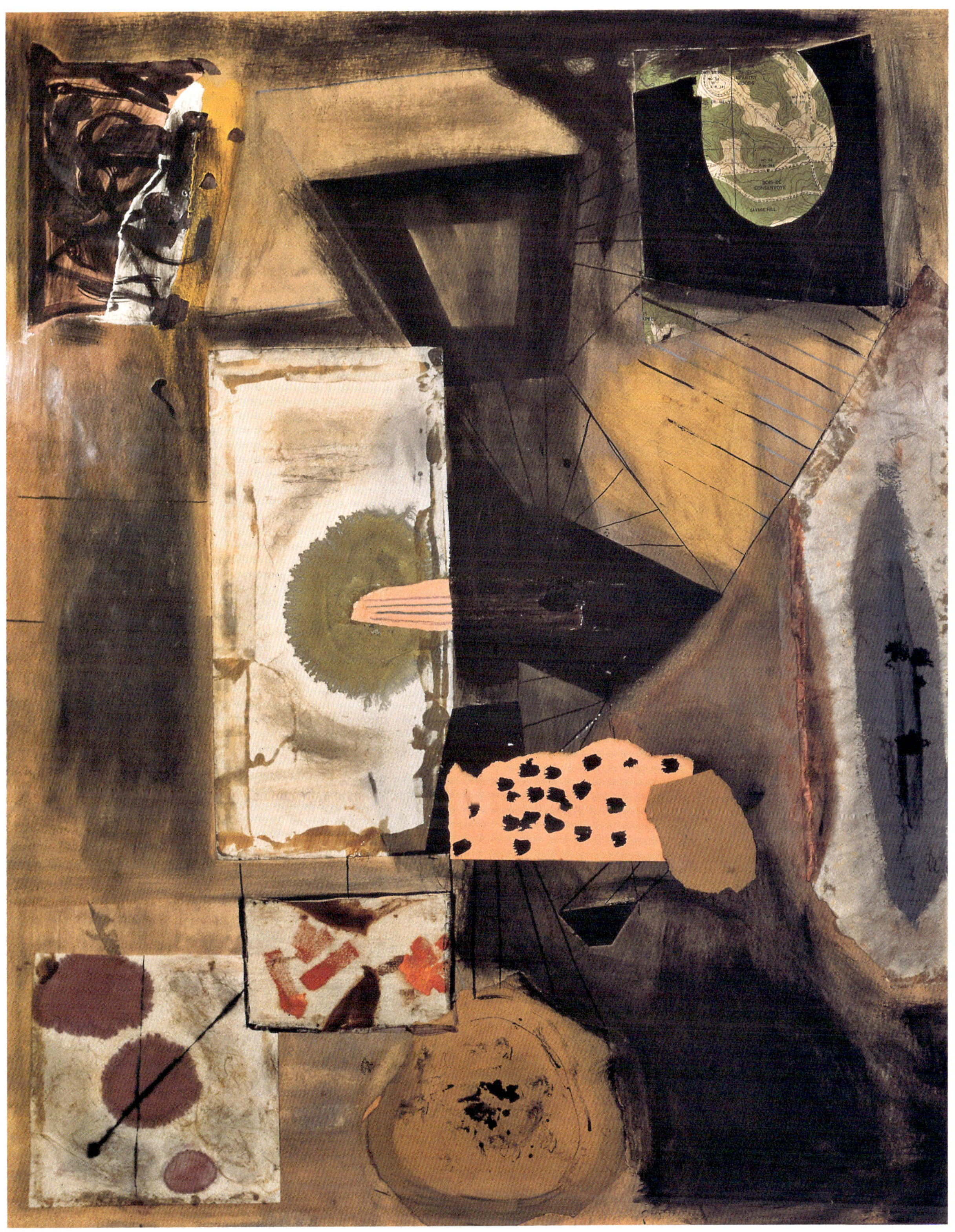

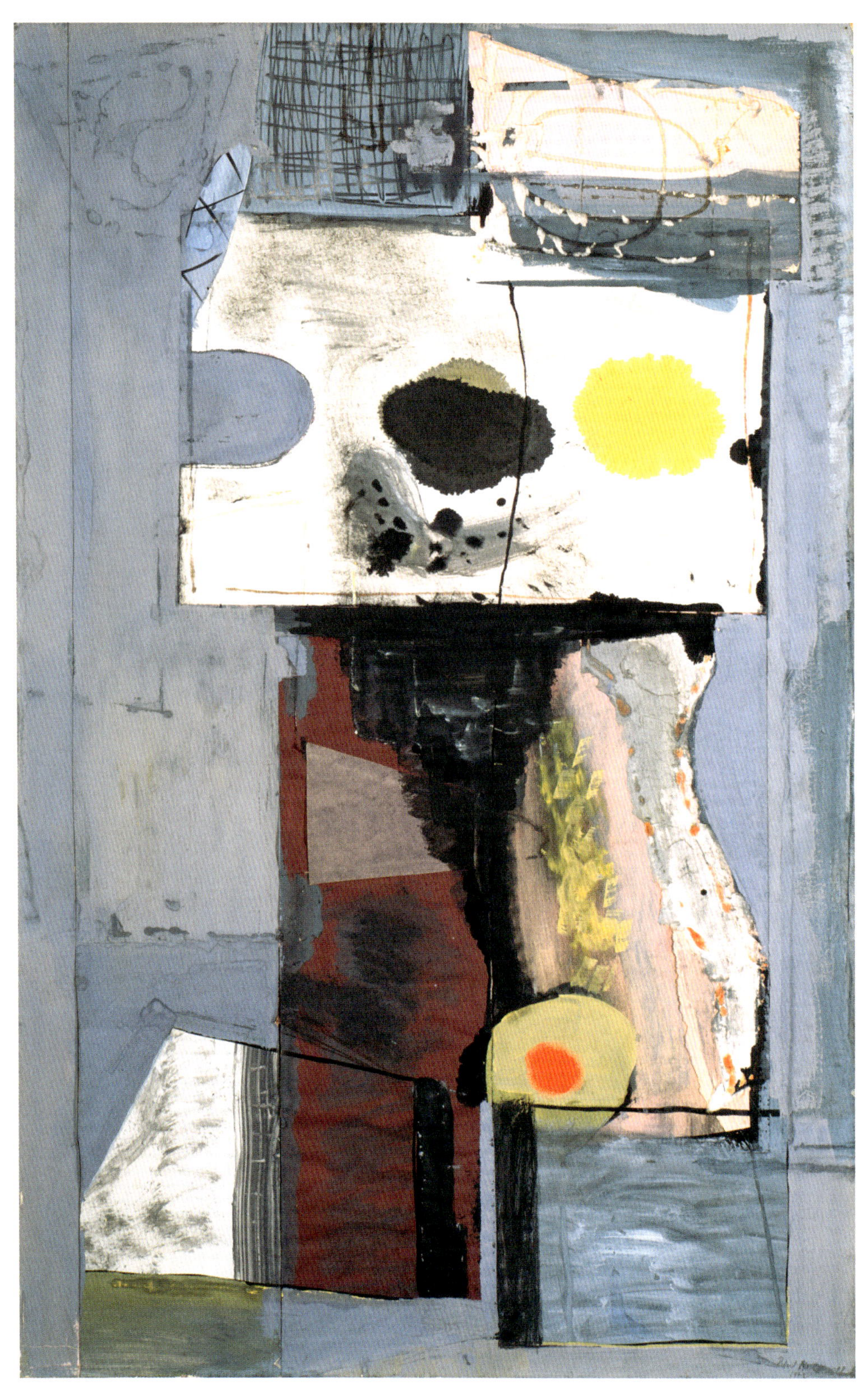

Helpful in advancing an alternate version of the Hegelian World Historical Figure—Siqueiros was Pollock's prototype—the story of Mexican revolutionary Pancho Villa, connected as it was to his wife's family history, provided Motherwell a ready-made paradigm for reflecting on current events.[76] Adopting Villa as both surrogate self and substitute "Other" helped him begin to "feel his own presence" in the global arena. In making *Pancho Villa, Dead and Alive,* Motherwell would amplify the mournful mood suggested in both *The Joy of Living* and a counterpart, another collage Peggy Guggenheim confusingly renamed *Surprise and Inspiration* (fig. 98). This work has had many titles, providing it with a history somewhat resonant in itself. Simply designated *Collage* when it was reproduced in *Form and Sense,* it is now known as *Personage (Autoportrait).* Upon its completion, Motherwell had, however, explained to Meyer Schapiro that he was intending to call it *Wounded Personage.*[77] Wounds, as we should have figured out by now, had become Motherwell's perfect vehicle to signify his "psychic tensions."[78]

The second iteration of Peggy Guggenheim's Spring Salon for Young Artists prompted Clement Greenberg to pronounce *Pancho Villa, Dead and Alive* "perhaps the most interesting work present."[79] Writing his May 1944 art column for *The Nation,* Greenberg did not mention that, in executing it, Motherwell appears to have inflected Picasso and Matisse by reference to Posada. José Guadalupe Posada, admired by some of the other artists in this study as well, was apparently the only Mexican artist whose work exerted any attraction for Motherwell. He is still widely considered Mexico's most beloved and truly national artist, and even Los Tres Grandes shared this opinion.[80] The humorously barbed cartoons that Posada drew in the late nineteenth and earlier twentieth century encapsulated growing opposition to Porfirio Díaz's oppressive regime, and seemed to foreshadow the upheaval

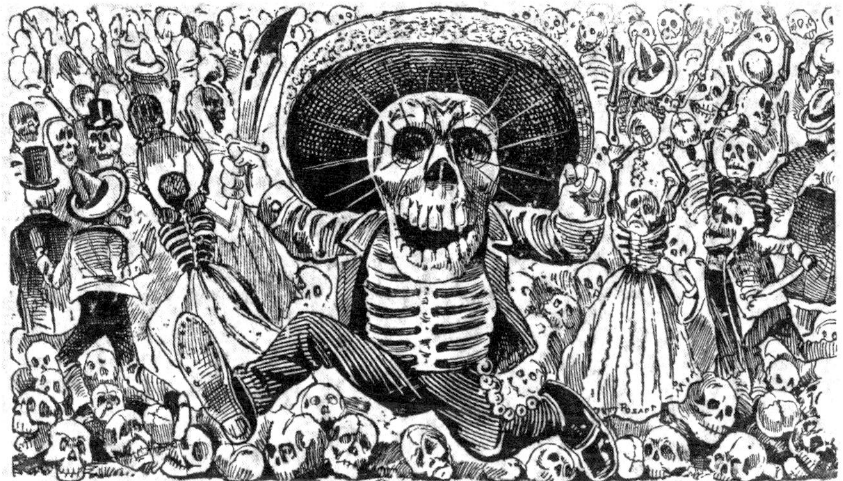

99 José Guadalupe Posada, *La calavera oaxaqueña (The Oaxaca calavera).* One print on white fabric, relief etching. Library of Congress Prints and Photographs Division, Washington, DC.

to come. Posada's broadsides, hawked on streets throughout Mexico, commemorated disasters, crimes, and miracles, glorifying rebels and bandits. As Noguchi also knew, Posada made frequent use of Mexico's ubiquitous *calaveras,* skeletons sometimes depicted in ways not unlike Seligmann's European late medieval models (fig. 99). His fliers were typically printed on cheap paper in garish colors, the kind that Motherwell told Robertson he'd liked so much in Mexico: "magenta, bright lemon yellow, lime green, indigo, vermilion, orange, shocking pink, deep ultramarine blue, black and white, and purple, lots of purple, and nobody else uses it, (no metallic color, which I detest), beautiful intense greens."[81]

Not surprisingly, the firing squad, a form of punishment common in the Díaz regime, was a topic frequently subjected to Posada's biting satire. Sometimes criminals, but often perpetrators of political unrest (especially the so-called Zapatistas), were publicly executed during that era. In a well-known example whose targets are unidentified, one victim lies lifeless on the ground while another still barely alive, his mouth open and eyes turned upward, falls down next to him. Although Posada, who died in 1913, could not have represented the martyred rebel Pancho Villa, killed in 1924, the guerilla *jefe* Emiliano Zapata provided him an obvious model, and, as in *Collision Between a Trolley and a Hearse,* corpses encased in coffins are a common element in his art. Motherwell's mistaken remembrance that Brenner had included the image of a bullet-ridden, blood-spattered corpse of Villa in *The Wind That Swept Mexico* has been corrected by scholars, but there are abundant other sources, such as commemorative postcards, from which he could have gotten this idea.

As Ann Gibson points out, automatism and collage share a similar aim: the circumvention of logic and narrative sequence.[82] In a variety of ways, both technical and conceptual, Pollock's *Male and Female* and Motherwell's *Pancho Villa, Dead and Alive* illustrate the combined powerful effect of these interrelated methods of contingency. In the latter, temporal confusion has replaced gender dysfunction—you can't be dead first and alive second, and why is the "alive" Villa, delineated on the German Christmas wrapping paper side, the one who is enclosed by a coffin? Like Pollock's "female," the "dead" Villa at left, his torso marked by spots that bled through after the removal of a piece of Japanese rice paper covered with red paint, lacks evident phallic activity. In each artwork this is a key delineator of meaning in terms of both presence and absence. Motherwell could have seen Joris Ivens's 1937 film *The Spanish Earth,* narrated by John Dos Passos and Ernest Hemingway, in which the head and arms are blown off the body of a bookkeeper shot by rebels, pruning his corpse in a similar manner.[83] And it should not be forgotten that Motherwell's father, with whom he had a contentious, unsatisfying relationship, died the year he made this collage, as

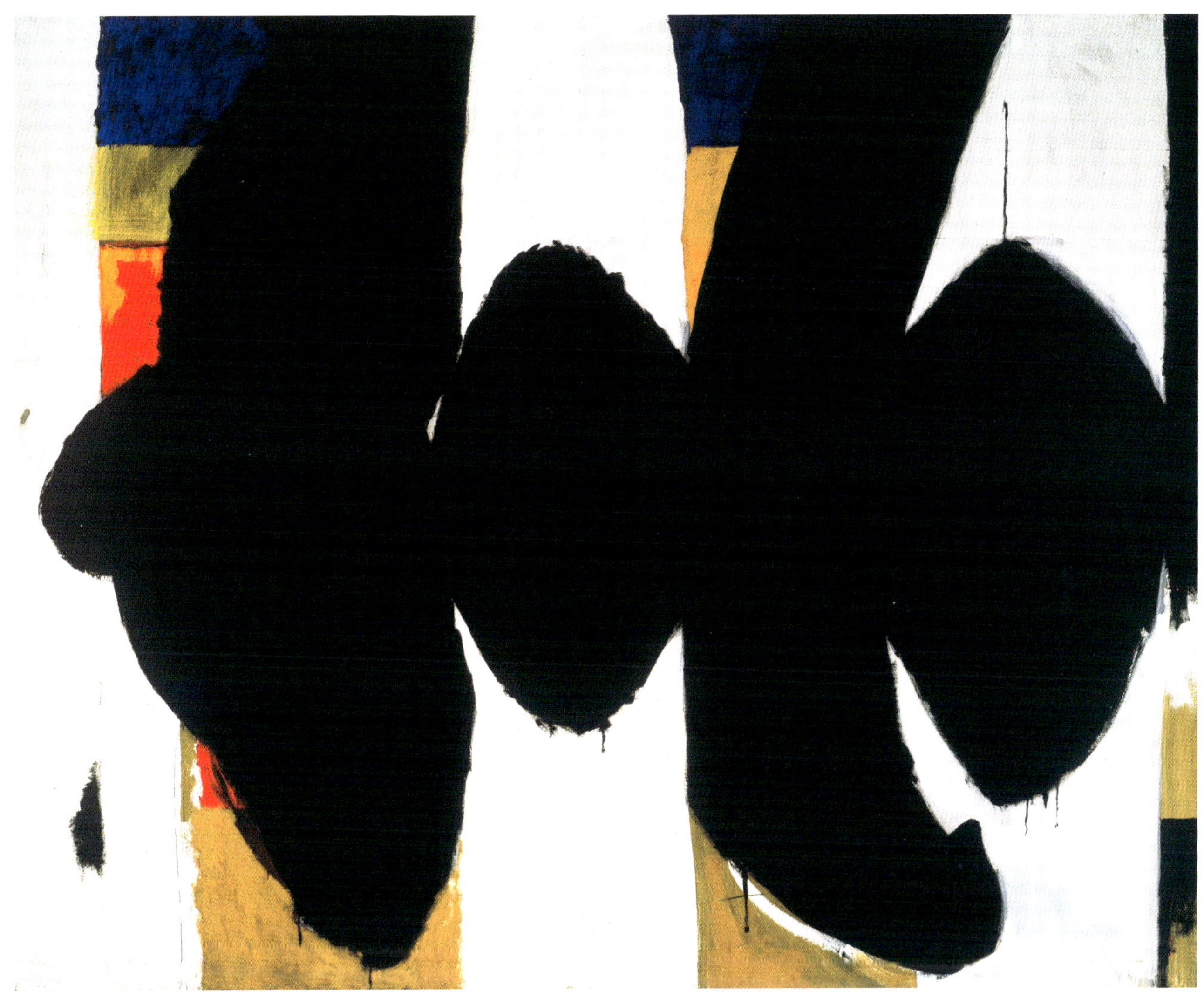

100 Robert Motherwell, *Elegy to the Spanish Republic No. 34*, 1953–54. Oil on canvas, support 80 x 100 in. (203.2 x 254 cm). Albright-Knox Art Gallery, Buffalo, NY. Gift of Seymour H. Knox, Jr., 1957. Albright-Knox Art Gallery / Art Resource, NY. Art © Dedalus Foundation, Inc. / Licensed by VAGA, New York, NY.

well as a related painting, *Personage*. Squared-off black outlines in *Personage* were identified by Motherwell as a schematic coffin, a fact, he said, that "few people notice."[84]

There is little question of direct iconographic, thematic, and stylistic links between *Pancho Villa, Dead and Alive* and Motherwell's most characteristic and longest-running series, his *Elegies to the Spanish Republic*. In these, the memory of revered Spanish bullfighter Ignacio Sánchez Mejías, gored in the ring on August 13, 1934, "at five in the afternoon," seemingly supplanted Villa as Motherwell's male heroic lead (fig. 100). Based on a "Llanto por Ignacio Sánchez Mejías," composed by the poet and playwright Federico García Lorca, Matta's friend who would be brutally assassinated by fascists, the repeated schematic elements comprising Motherwell's *Elegies* first surfaced in a 1948 pen-and-ink illustration for a poem by Harold Rosenberg (see fig. 107). Rosenberg's poem and Motherwell's drawing were meant for the never-published second issue of *Possibilities*.

In March 1943, Motherwell's wife, María, played a part in *The Wind Remains*, an opera performed at the Museum of Modern Art with a libretto by Paul Bowles that was based on one of Lorca's plays; Motherwell painted the first major *Elegy* in 1949, the year María left him. He greatly admired Lorca's ritualistic expression of grief, a reaction so different from what he experienced in his repressed upbringing, and he initiated a forty-year attempt to construct evocative, comparatively visual correlatives to tragedy that was completed only by his own death in 1991.[85] Much starker, rawer, and far more sexually explicit than any previous works, Motherwell's *Elegies to the Spanish Republic* (especially the earliest ones) concretize violence by distilling it through synecdoche. Pancho Villa's "alive" pink penis and testicles propagate into brutal upright slabs that squeeze (or trap like prison bars, a personally meaningful trope) the ovoid forms of Villa's combination torso/head. Molding their "expressive core" out of a context of helplessness and private desperation, Motherwell deeply personalized the Abstract Expressionists' universalizing principle of "simple expression of the complex thought."[86]

If he wasn't exactly an "action painter" like Jackson Pollock, was Robert Motherwell a "mythmaker" in the sense of his other colleagues Mark Rothko, Adolph Gottlieb, and Barnett Newman, all of whom reinvestigated archetypes and ancient motivations in their initial works, or were his own favored hero tales too contemporary? In terms of addressing both the diversity and unity of what he and his peers were doing, Motherwell expressed his opinion that Abstract Automatism would have been a better name for their movement than Abstract Expressionism. A number of scholars have signaled belief that the earlier paintings of the New York School (a name Motherwell coined) had discrete characteristics; some designate this developmental period Abstract Surrealism.[1]

William Baziotes pretty much remained an Abstract Surrealist throughout his life as a painter; Pollock and Motherwell certainly did not. Irving Sandler's inclusion of Motherwell as a final entry in the section on Color Field Painting in his pioneering history of Abstract Expressionism, *The Triumph of American Painting*, appears a bit like an afterthought.[2] Did Motherwell's Mexican affinities play a role in precluding his firm inclusion into any accepted category? Extrapolating to a larger spectrum, is it possible to recognize the Mexican-related experiences of Motherwell, Pollock, Philip Guston, and Isamu Noguchi as setting all four artists somewhat apart from concurrent New York developments?

As the Whitney Museum of American Art's 1978 exhibition *Abstract Expressionism: The Formative Years* fully clarified, neglecting to study late 1930s and early '40s painting and sculpture by those considered the movement's major practitioners had been a mistake. Introducing that show, directors Tom Armstrong and Thomas W. Leavitt (head of Cornell University's museum, a cosponsor) explained that gathering works from this period turned out to be a "revelation," one indicating the impressive extent to which Americans "searching for new subject matter within an abstract format" had reevaluated European aesthetics. "The early paintings explain the later ones," Robert Hobbs wrote in his lead essay. "They provide the key to interpreting the significant content that preoccupied the Abstract Expressionists."[3] By now it should be evident that for all four main protagonists in this book European modernism was not their only crucial resource. In every sense of the word, Mexico played catalytic roles, acting as spur, facilitator, and medium. In varying but essential ways, reverberations from the contacts that Noguchi, Guston, Pollock, and Motherwell made with Mexican artists and/or experiences in Mexico would have critical long-term implications for each.

As Martica Sawin correctly notes, the genesis of Abstract Expressionism, while written about brilliantly, has often been imperfectly understood. Ann Gibson elaborated this point, explaining as one of its main causes the "eviction of artists' personal histories from the historical development of the meaning of the art they produced," a legacy of Clement Greenberg's influential criticism. Gibson's *Abstract Expressionism: Other Politics* (1997) is one of numerous studies taking a more definite turn toward examination of aspects of the movement "intimately related to the identity of the artist."[4] Such re-vision, continued here, involves asking questions, in the words of David Anfam, that "interrupt or contradict" the received story, addressing in particular what these artists appear *not* to engage—at least not to prior interpreters.[5] As a result, narrative, theoretically suppressed to better achieve originality and express the universal, has reemerged as a more definitively active component of Abstract Expressionism. And its links both to the artists' own personal histories and to the "specificities of immediate cultural influence" were not simply operative in early or more transitional works, nor only characteristic of minor players. "What makes any definition of a movement in art dubious," Harold Rosenberg wrote in "The American Action Painters," "is that it never fits the deepest artists in the movement—certainly not as well as, if successful, it does the others. Yet without the definition something essential in those best is bound to be missed." "The attempt to define," he explained, "is like a game in which you cannot possibly reach the goal from the starting point but can only close in on it by picking up each time from where the last play landed."[6] Such an approach is not altogether amiss in more generally recalibrating American modernist complexity.

As Anfam expounds, scrutinizing what stands before and after the phase typically regarded as decisive, Abstract Expressionism appears less clear-cut, becoming indeed "powerfully problematized by what it seeks to exclude, by its framing edges and a play of contradictions." On the one hand, despite Motherwell's and Rosenberg's articulated directive in *Possibilities* to "avoid the trap of politics," the movement's putative depoliticization seems more than ever to lack force of evidence; turning inward for subject matter in the 1940s did not at all preclude inspiration imbued with temporal specificity. "I believe all art to be historical," Motherwell confirmed in 1950. "There is no such thing as an eternal art that transcends a specific historical period." The will of their age, defined by the Depression, the rise of fascism and the advent of World War II instantiated a "psychology of crisis" that commanded collective attention.[7]

Consecutively, it appears that many artists (ours included) found varying possibilities — not excluding abstraction — for linking internationalism and a concern with self. In this, Wolfgang Paalen again proved a model, and not just for Motherwell; the artist Fritz Bultman explicitly recalled to Pollock's biographers that "it was Paalen who started it all." Ad Reinhardt's 1952 *PM* newspaper cartoon *How to Look at a Cubist Painting* (fig. 101) encapsulates the coexistent inward and outward subjective potentialities of abstraction to which Paalen

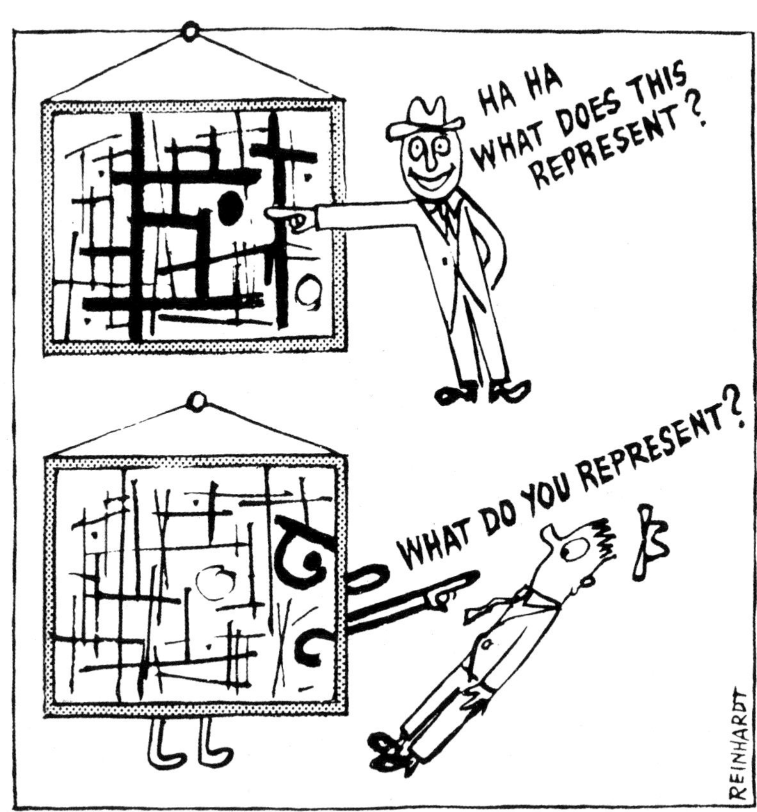

101 Ad Reinhardt, *How to look at a Cubist Painting*, c. 1946, detail. Ad Reinhardt papers, Archives of American Art, Smithsonian Institution. © 2012 Estate of Ad Reinhardt / Artists Rights Society (ARS), New York.

alluded in his introduction to *Form and Sense*. Here Paalen wrote, "There is no true work of art without a deep meaningfulness — but meaningfulness need not mean straightforward intelligibility. Why should works of art be easy to understand in a world in which nothing is easy to understand? Paintings no longer *represent;* it is no longer the task of art to answer naïve questions. Today it has become the role of the painting to look at the spectator and ask him: what do *you* represent?"[8] Of course, as he well knew, an artwork's first viewer is its maker. "Nothing as drastic an innovation as abstract art could have come into existence," Motherwell confirmed, "save as the consequence of a most profound, relentless unquenchable need."[9]

Noguchi and Pollock

It is interesting that, at some point along their various routes to authenticity, each of the artists under consideration in this study in one way or another made a commitment to epic form. Whereas all four saw somewhat selectively what Mexico and Mexican art had to offer on this journey, its effect on their affinity for the grand over the intimate (the latter a hallmark of French painting) was to prove transformative. While Noguchi's and Guston's attraction to scale and daring spatial effects along the lines of Mexican muralism (fig. 102) seemingly peaked in the mid-1930s, its attendant allegorical connotations were to find new life, in either a different guise or a later phase. Scholars might disagree on whether Noguchi was, strictly speaking, an Abstract Expressionist, but his collaboration with Martha Graham of interest here shares many important (and heroizing) characteristics, as well as aiding and abetting the dancer's own self-mythologizing and her Surrealist penchant to "adventure into the hallucinatory landscape of the mind."[10] As an example of the psychological nuance their dialogue produced, Noguchi described the flaming nimbus he created for Graham to wear like a dress in *Cave of the Heart* as "perhaps a neurological tree that depicts how the heart is spiked forever when one has committed oneself to jealousy" (see fig. 20). In designing for the stage Noguchi found it possible "to realize in a hypothetical way those projections of the imagination into environmental space which are denied us in actuality. . . . Theater is a ceremonial; the performance is a rite."[11]

As we know, even before conceiving his Mercado Abelardo L. Rodríguez relief in Mexico City, Noguchi's spare setting for Martha Graham's *Frontier* revolutionized a new perspective of space (see fig. 9). Neil Printz reminds us of its audacity: "It is as if Noguchi envisioned *Frontier* as a great lung, and Graham's body as a column of air, that levitated and collapsed within its chamber." In subsequent works for her company Noguchi would restate in a new, more dynamic medium some of *History as Seen from Mexico*'s more emotionally charged, space-permeating effects.[12] In many cases, equally interested "in getting a certain plasticity of form, like something alive," his designs would play an increasingly active role in the production; Printz cites *Seraphic Dialogue* (1955), the set itself appearing to work in tandem with the dancers, falling and rising on stage (fig. 103).[13]

Noguchi explained the milieu that he provided for *Seraphic Dialogue,* a piece based on the exaltation of Joan of Arc, in clearly epic terms: "I depicted her life as a cathedral that fills her consciousness. A transparent edifice of brass tubing was shaped to resemble this. The whole structure was held in suspension by wire cables throughout along with adjacent structures that created a kind of piazza. There was a long sword with which [Martha] dances." For the Ballet Russe de Monte Carlo's 1944 production of *The Bells,* based on Edgar Allan Poe's haunting poem and danced by Ruth Page, he had previously constructed a set with less complicated marionette principles. As he described it, "a church steeple full of bells rises to the full height of the stage. Made of wood and also articulated, it crashes down in a pile at the end."[14] Noguchi portrayed St. Michael's movable gates in *Seraphic Dialogue* as operating "like the womb"— Graham surely knew that

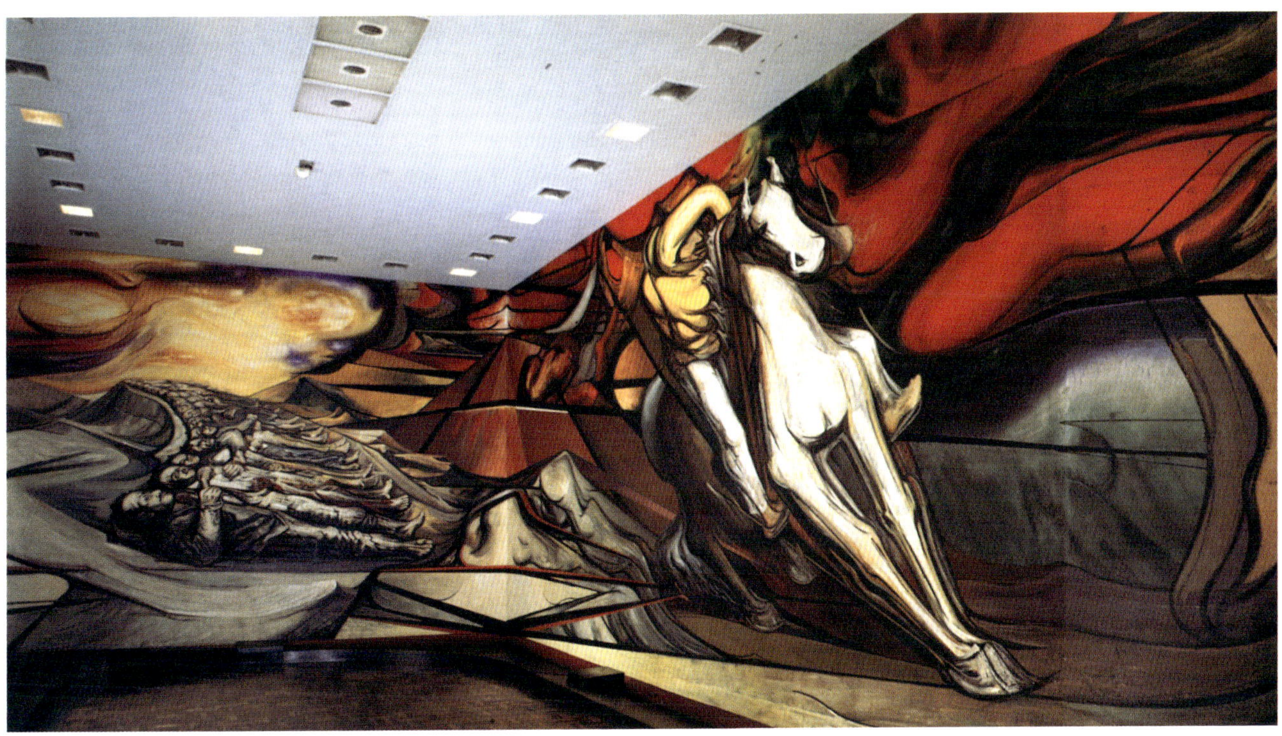

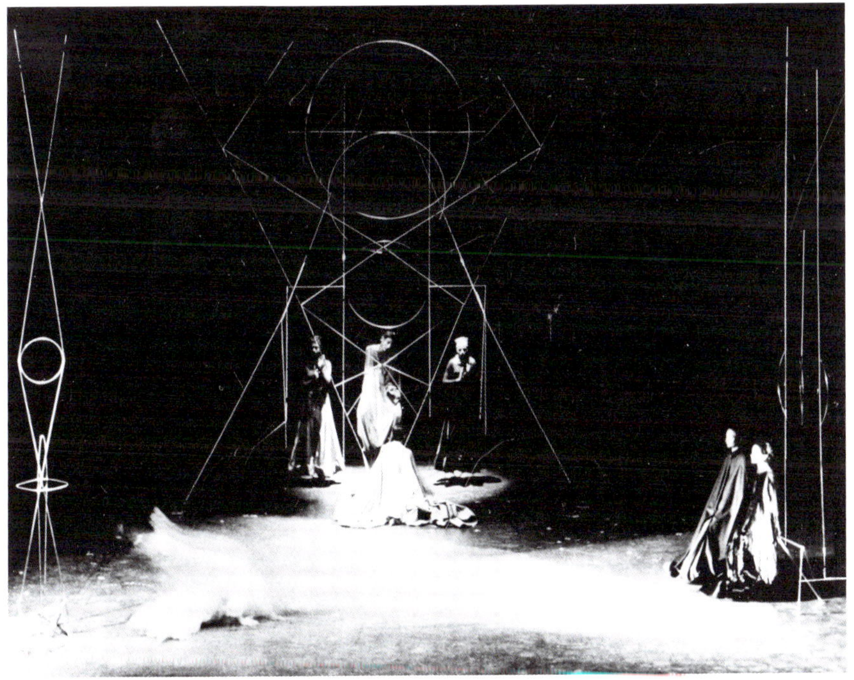

102 David Alfaro Siqueiros. *From the Dictatorship of Porfirio Díaz to the Revolution – The Martyrs and Mounted Revolutionary*, 1957–65. Hall of the Revolution, detail of left-hand section, National History Museum, Chapultepec Castle, Mexico City. © 2012 Artists Rights Society (ARS), New York/SOMAAP, Mexico City.

103 *Seraphic Dialogue*, 1955. Choreographed by Martha Graham. Set designed by Isamu Noguchi. Costumes by Martha Graham. Music composed by Norman Dello Joio. © 2012 The Isamu Noguchi Foundation and Garden Museum, New York/Artists Rights Society (ARS), New York.

she could refer this metaphor equally well to the female psyche.[15] Noguchi demanded that his sets be active and indispensable "characters" in the over-all drama, never merely decorative backdrops.[16] Even those more abstractly conceived so potently defined and dramatized the total field, or volume, of performance that the dancers' "every movement takes on an added value by its automatic justification of the design."[17] Graham brilliantly modified her own body to both occupy and act upon the spaces left for her.

In the instances of Pollock and Motherwell, the epic was reanimated by focusing it through an automatist lens, a situation inducing innovative conceptual, psychic, and physical responses to various painting problems.[18] Although recognition of self might be considered an "uncalculated result" rather than an intended outcome of Abstract Expressionism's open-end-edness (especially toward process), Motherwell's admission that "all of my pictures are slices out of a continuum whose duration is my whole life" spells out what this book strives to demonstrate: that may not have been the entirety of the case.[19]

Whereas Motherwell was impelled from the start toward abstraction, Pollock began more figuratively, flirting with representation at least at the initial level, even during 1947–50, when he was making his signature all-over poured paintings, and circling more conclusively back in this direction briefly from 1951–53. "I've had a period of drawing on canvas in black—with some of my early images coming thru," he wrote to his friends and patrons Alfonso Ossorio and Ted Dragon in June 1951, adding, "Think the non-objectivists will find them disturbing—and the kids who think it simple to splash a Pollock out."[20] In works Pollock had recently begun painting in serial fashion, using black enamel on rolls of unprimed canvas, more gestural and disturbingly rendered reworkings of identifiable configurations from the past had started to re-emerge. These included recurrences from his flirtation with Orozco, such as disembodied eyes and dismembered human limbs, the detritus of ritual violence. A number of images of this period represent exaggeratedly seated females reminiscent of the main character in his phan-tasmagorical family reformulation created during the early '30s (see fig. 55).

In perhaps the climax of this style, *Portrait and a Dream* of 1953 (Pol-lock painted this work in oil, not enamel, and included color on one side), a large head is juxtaposed with several other figures who are seemingly engaged in a savage and distinctly erotic conflagration to its left (fig. 104). Referring to the ostensibly calm and stoic face at right, the artist remarked to his doctor and her husband, "That's a portrait of me, can't you see it?" further claiming it as a representation of himself when he was "not sober."[21] The tense feeling of containment exuded by this "portrait" contrasts with Pollock's more expressionistically conceived "dream," which he told his wife reprised the dark side of the moon. Pollock's grafting of an upturned

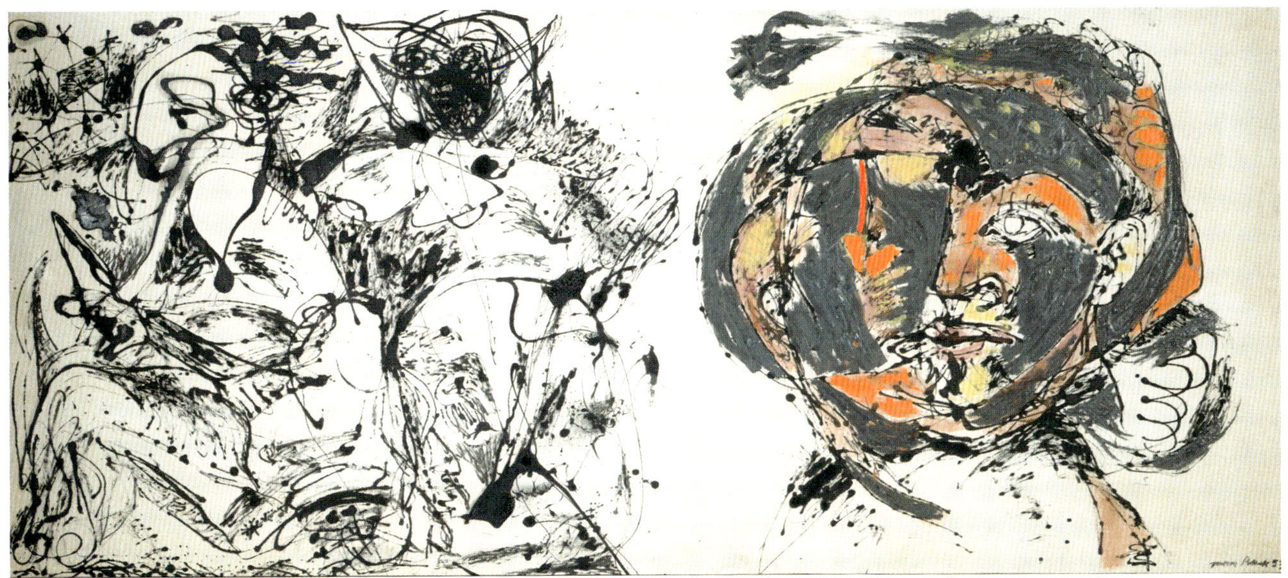

crescent onto the blackened face of the centrally distorted female suggests a reappearance of symbolic associations of the Moon Woman with which he had been fixated around the time he painted *Male and Female*.[22] Gibson, discussing the "rhetoric" of Abstract Expressionism, associates some of its later works, including *Portrait and a Dream,* with a resurgence of allegory in the movement's end phase.[23] Supposedly outmoded, allegory had been rejected by the 1940s New York avant-garde because it smacked too much of the storytelling approach Thomas Hart Benton and his Regionalist compatriots had taken, as did many Social Realists in the previous decade.

But allegory, by definition, simply implies that an image can speak of something other than what it appears to represent, typically adding a value that implicates moral significance. While the Abstract Expressionists apparently preferred the ambiguity of more personally developed symbols over allegory's doubling of meaning and inherent didacticism, as Gibson points out, pastiche is an inherently allegorical approach that many sometimes chose to use. The juxtapositions at work in collage qualify as allegorical but in a different way from Benton or Orozco's narratives, one that allows for more open-endedness. Contrasting moods and modes of expression as seen in *Portrait and a Dream* is one way to approach the dialogic potentiality of pastiche; the actual bringing together of commonly recognized items for disparate purposes that is the basis of collage provides another allegorical avenue, as does purposeful inclusion of the palimpsest, described by Craig Owens as the "paradigm" of an allegorical work.[24]

While Pollock was apparently not as interested in collage as his wife,

104 Jackson Pollock, *Portrait and a Dream,* 1953. Oil on canvas, 58 ½ x 134 ¾ in. (148.6 x 342.3 cm). Dallas Museum of Art. Gift of Mr. and Mrs. Algur H. Meadows and the Meadows Foundation, Incorporated. © 2012 The Pollock-Krasner Foundation/ Artists Rights Society (ARS), New York.

Lee Krasner, or Robert Motherwell, he did learn from and apply its juxtapositional methodology in initiating his allover paintings. In *Full Fathom Five,* one of the earliest dripped compositions Pollock created after moving from Manhattan to The Springs, he seemingly discarded his decade-long preoccupation with mythic and primitivist iconography, initializing the procedure of converting his energies to process-based abstraction (fig. 105). Greenberg's claim that, by early 1947, Pollock had finally developed "beyond the stage where he needs to make his poetry explicit in ideographs" has already been noted. This, the critic opined, allowed the painter to devise a style whose "very abstractness and absence of assignable definition" could now project a "more reverberating meaning."[25]

Asked in a 1969 interview with B. H. Friedman to comment on her husband's 1951–53 poured enamel compositions, Krasner made specific reference to his mid-to-late '30s (often Mexican-related) drawings:

> For me, all of Jackson's work grows from this period; I see no more sharp breaks, but rather a continuing development of the same themes and obsessions. . . .There's one other advantage I had: I saw his paintings evolve. Many of them, many of the most abstract, began with more or less recognizable imagery—heads, parts of the body, fantastic creatures. Once I asked Jackson why he didn't stop the painting when a given image was exposed. *He said, "I choose to veil the imagery."* Well, that was that painting. With the black-and-whites he chose mostly to expose the imagery. I can't say why. I wonder if he could have.[26]

Five years before Krasner's observations to Friedman, the editor and critic Thomas Hess had already made a suggestion (then considered heretical) that Pollock always incorporated buried representations, even in his so-called "classic" abstractions of 1949–50. Pollock had articulated a fundamental strategy for these in the statement he wrote for *Possibilities* that was published at precisely the time he was beginning to "re-enter" and revise outmoded conformations. Because "the painting has a life of its own," he had "no fears about making changes, destroying the image, etc.," he explained.[27]

To cite one example of this, the delicate and lacy poured loops of multicolored paint that Pollock mixed with gravel and applied over brushed aluminum in *Galaxy,* a work closely related to *Full Fathom Five,* almost but not quite cancel out a year-old image called *The Little King.* Resulting pentimenti create a situation not unlike Motherwell's early 1940s practice of leaving a first layer of markings visible in small "windows" and using these as reference points against which to react. Compelling indications support the notion that, by 1947, if Pollock did not have at hand a prior depictive

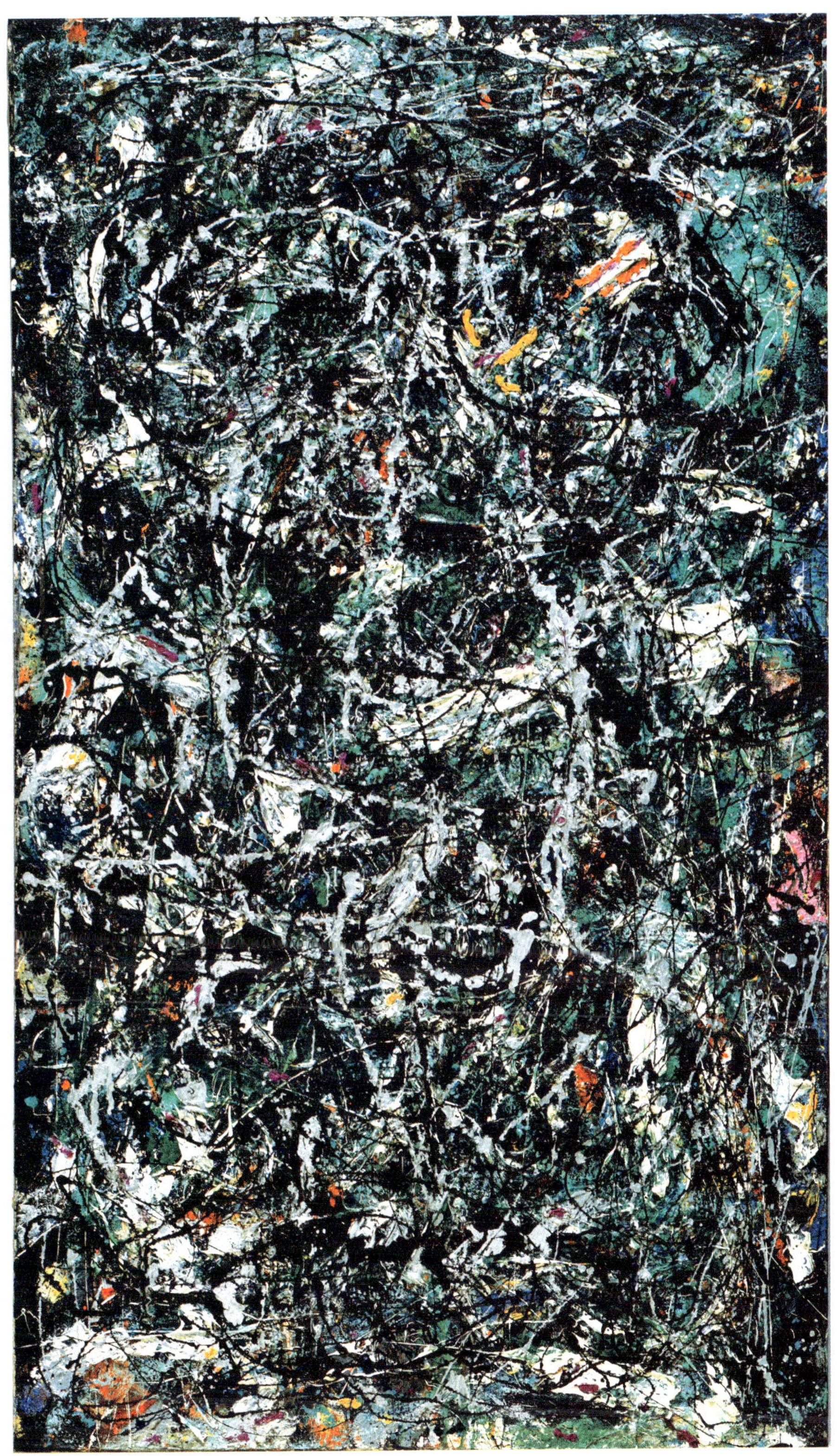

configuration he was willing (or needed psychologically) to obliterate, he would simply generate a new one and cover it up.[28]

An uncharacteristically vertical work not originally praised by Greenberg, *Full Fathom Five* has since occasioned intense discussion, not only because of its admirable evocation of natural phenomena but also as a result of its unusual facture and multiple levels of contextual resonance, including Shakespeare's *The Tempest* and James Joyce's *Ulysses*.[29] In addition to the small pebbles he mixed around the same time into *Galaxy* and *Sea Change* (all works named by Ralph Manheim) Pollock affixed a wide variety of other objects to *Full Fathom Five,* including nails, tacks, buttons, pennies, two keys, combs, torn cigarettes, matches, a dead bee, and paint tube tops, interspersing them amid thickly interwoven skeins of oil and industrial paint. Akin to the rayograms his friend Herbert Matter was producing in the early 1940s (photographs Pollock surely knew) the items embedded in *Full Fathom Five,* while not obtrusive in the final design, manage to retain a certain individuality despite their transformation. Indeed, forensic evidence indicates that, very like Motherwell, Pollock actually kept these buried elements in mind throughout his execution of the work. X-rays not only expose a full-length human form created with highly leaded pigment submerged into this painting, they also indicate that, far from erasing its presence, the pieces of studio rubbish (as well as some of Pollock's final touches of paint) were "placed in direct response to and elaboration of this shape."[30] Positioning of the implanted phallic key designates the body's gender as identical to the painter's.

Pollock's assemblage technique in *Full Fathom Five* not only evokes his favorite poet Dylan Thomas's dialectical process of "image-breeding,"[31] the hybrid approach he assumed equates in significant ways with the cardinal premises of Joyce's celebrated *bricolage* writing style, predicated on "allover" juxtaposition of wide-ranging citations and the imaginative recombination of unrelated terms. While formally uneducated, as Ossorio (a Harvard graduate) confirmed, Jackson Pollock was nonetheless "very much in tune with Joyce's idea that one word could mean many and even contradictory things."[32] Producing a visual equivalent of Joycean wordplay in *Full Fathom Five,* he moved allegory's reinterpretive capacity well beyond the masking or "veiling" of previous imagery that leaving pentimenti signified. In future, only the painting on glass that Pollock made for Hans Namuth's color film shot in 1950 would prominently feature actual foreign objects—in this case, string, stones, agates, marbles, and bits of colored glass and wire lathe mesh—but he forgot none of this in the course of improvising his signature works. In addition to almost approaching mural-size, their facture exemplifies larger meaning, finalizing production of his primary aim, "not an illustration, but the equivalent."[33]

Motherwell and Guston

*Guston, Pollock and I were . . . all reared in California—if there is a
"California School," which I doubt, it never acknowledges the three of us—
the three of us filled with self-torment and . . . anxiety.*[34]

— ROBERT MOTHERWELL, 1957

Although much smaller in scale than Noguchi's and Guston's Mexican
murals, and even diminutive-seeming in comparison to Pollock's classic
poured works or his own *Elegies to the Spanish Republic*, by celebrating the
feats of a legendary or traditional hero Motherwell's *Pancho Villa, Dead
and Alive* demonstrates a prime characteristic commonly associated with
the epic. It is by equating persons and actions of a narrative with extrinsic
meanings that an epic composition, whether visual or literary (Homer's
Iliad and *Odyssey* being the fundamental models), generally aims to evoke
social, moral, religious, or political significance. But Motherwell's *Elegies*
are not simply differentiated from *Pancho Villa* by their greater dimensions
(fig. 106). Rather, as Gregory Gilbert explains, a much bolder move away
from narrative without discarding allegory's rhetorical intent is also operative
in producing their epic effect. Continuing to explore in a more extravagant
and recognizably anguished format the kind of tragic meaning expressed
more modestly (and ironically) in *Joy of Living,* when hypothesizing this
important series Motherwell also chose the option of pastiche. He did not,
however, use it exactly the same way as in collage. Whether consciously or
not, in creating the *Elegies to the Spanish Republic,* Motherwell conflated
condensation and displacement, the two mental actions providing a basis
for the most powerful figures of speech.[35]

Reinterpreting the vertical/ovoid oppositions of Pancho Villa's stick-
figure body into concurrently metaphoric and metonymic shapes, Motherwell replaced Pollock's tension between "control and uncontrol" (a tension
causing his webs to read as a signifier for the disunity of modern life) with a
different psychocultural dynamic, fragmentation.[36] In 1959 Eugene Goosen
described Motherwell's abstract *Elegy* format as an objective correlative
firmly rooted in Surrealist practice. The artist's despair over the lost cause of
democracy in mid-1930s fascist-controlled Spain, the critic said, mirrored in
microcosm the larger chaos of human life, its virtues and violence sexually
expressed. To nail down his point, Goosen provided an evocative, and memorably provocative, interpretation of Motherwell's signature shapes. In creating
the *Elegies to the Spanish Republic,* Motherwell, he wrote, "uses the Spanish
theme as a metaphor of a metaphor, a distillation from the second alembic.
The huge ovarian forms hang in heavy precariousness between broad male

uprights, or perhaps it is the phallus and *cojones* of the sacrificial bull hung on the whitewashed wall. Or drops of blood, congealed, lodged as a ripe plum in a pipe, waiting as if commitment was its own irremedial doom."[37]

Such a redolent trope, some believe, can trigger the *Elegy* shapes to function like literary protagonists, "highly developed pictorial actors [that] acquire further nuances with each new painting in a series," and Motherwell deftly employed color (or its absence) to enhance his imagery's resultant "blunt force."[38] Whereas Pollock's primary focus was on the expressiveness of line, for Motherwell the austere "non-being/being" polarity of black and white became a crucial analogic agent. By sometimes adding ragged areas or spots usually of ochre or red, (shades he associated with California and Mexico—representing the former's arid land and the latter's ferocious destiny) he further invigorated many *Elegy* compositions, both structurally and in terms of associative meaning.

While generally endorsing Baudelaire's concept of symbolic correspondence, Motherwell believed that color should always to be tied to sensations in reality. As he explained in 1946, "The 'pure' red of which certain abstractionists speak does not exist. Any red is rooted in blood, glass, wine, hunters' caps, and a thousand other concrete phenomena. Otherwise we should have no feeling toward red or its relations, and it would be useless as an artistic element."[39] Black, Motherwell said, "perhaps above all colors except its traditional polarity, white—is imbued with associations that strengthen the primary metaphor: the work of art as an expression of human experience." "This is not to say," he continued "that black in the painting necessarily nor directly symbolizes things or ideas such as Death, or a shadow, or melancholy, specifically, but rather that it carries with it into the new context the history of its meanings, a litany of associations by which it is eternally complicated. As vague as the dawn of creation itself but nonetheless as incontestable, layers of thought, points of sensation—especially and exclusively evoked by the color black—load this color as no other in the spectrum."[40]

Speaking on the occasion of an exhibition organized in 1980 to demonstrate his preoccupation with this (non)color, Motherwell predictably remarked, "In Hispanic countries, you see Black everywhere." "I tend to think of black much more as 'thingness,'" he added, "like a piece of coal, a piece of paper, a black dress, or a black shadow which you might see in Mexico in the summer." "Most artists," he explained elsewhere, "draw a form and then color it, and I so to speak, take a piece of color and form it."[41] As these and other such statements indicate, color played an extremely active role in realizing the artist's epic and allegorical proclivities.

Allegory is typically defined as presentation of a story with two meanings, one literal and one symbolic. As already suggested, their more universalizing structural and rhetorical implications notwithstanding, the origins of

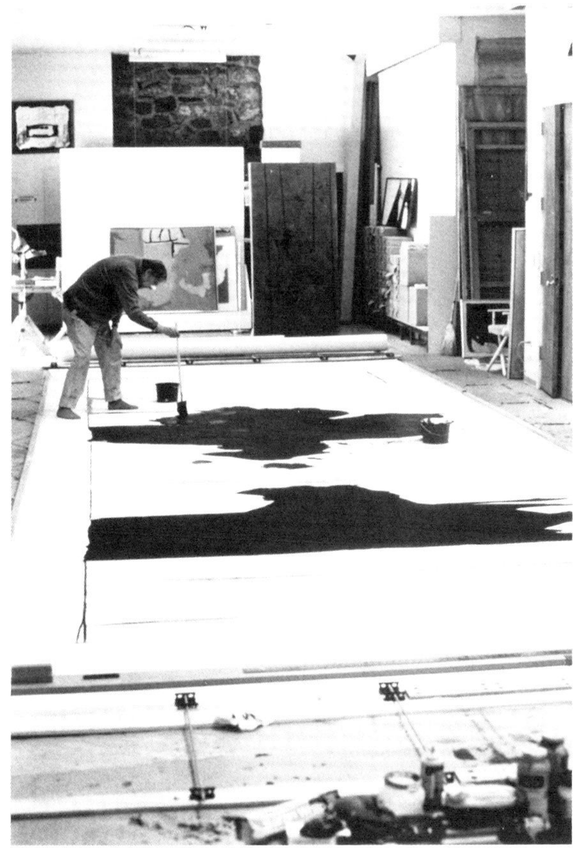

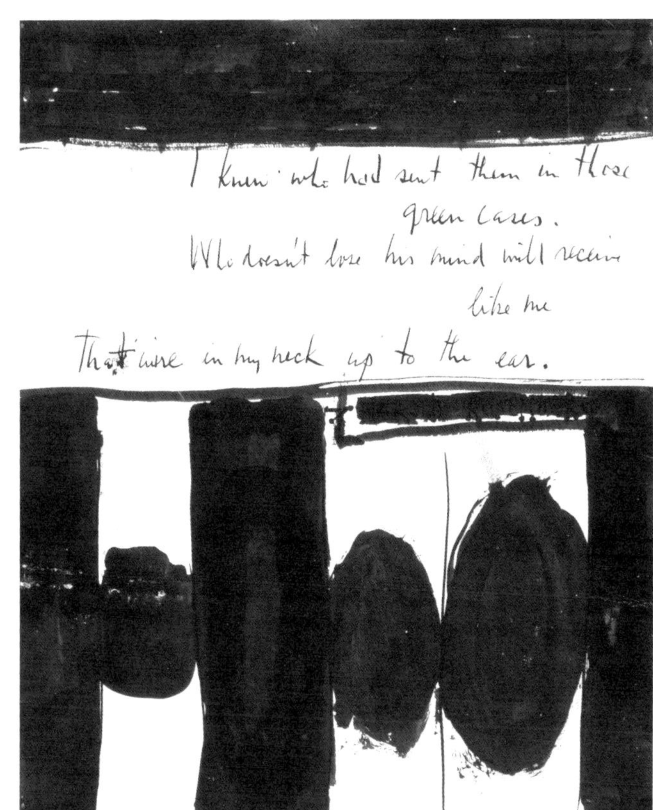

Motherwell's *Elegies to the Spanish Republic* can also be located in the artist's individual psyche. The first major iteration on canvas of what would become his Elegies' standard binary upright/oval motif appeared in a 1949 composition Motherwell called *At Five in the Afternoon*. This title indicates its basis in contemplation of Federico García Lorca's haunting funeral dirge, but, as we know, the first sketch made for this subject the prior year had actually been intended for a never-realized second issue of *Possibilities* (fig. 107).[42] Producing an ink sketch in 1948 meant for collocation with Harold Rosenberg's poem "A Bird for Every Bird" coincided with Motherwell's depressive, even suicidal thoughts after María's decision to leave their marriage; he very pointedly included on it the inscription, "Who doesn't lose his mind will receive like me / That wire in my neck up to the ear," wounding lines from Rosenberg's second stanza.[43]

While he understood the "Spanish sense of death" mostly from Lorca's verse, Motherwell explained this motif and mood as stemming from other sources as well: the very first he named was "my Mexican wife." After María's defection with (he said) another man he experienced feelings of "abandon-

106 Robert Motherwell painting the *Reconciliation Elegy*, 1978. National Gallery of Art, Washington, DC. Art © Dedalus Foundation, Inc. / Licensed by VAGA, New York, NY.

107 Robert Motherwell, *Ink Sketch, Elegy to the Spanish Republic, No. 1*, 1948. The Museum of Modern Art, New York. Gift of the Artist. Art © Dedalus Foundation, Inc. / Licensed by VAGA, New York, NY.

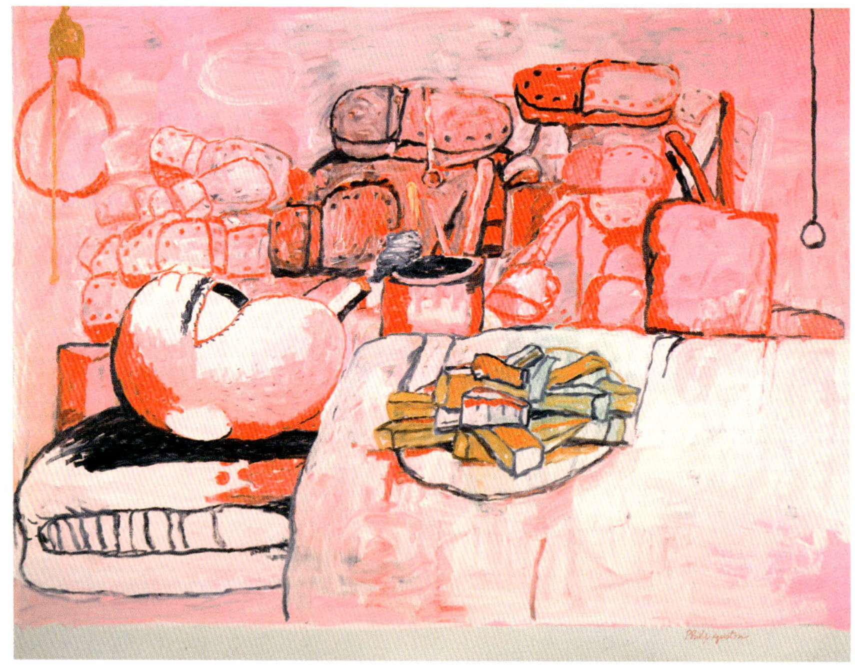

108 Philip Guston, *Painting, Smoking, Eating,* 1973. Oil on canvas. Collection Stedelijk Museum, Amsterdam. Courtesy of McKee Gallery. © Estate of Philip Guston.

ment, desperation and helplessness" so intense that childhood vulnerabilities occasioned by the harsh and withholding actions of his mother came back to haunt him.[44] Motherwell's notably ambiguous 1963 assertion, "*The Spanish Elegies* are not 'political.' But my private insistence that a terrible death happened that should not be forgot,"[45] undoubtedly also implicates a crushing alternative to the heroic.

Philip Guston presents yet a different picture. As we know, long after his and Reuben Kadish's truly epic Mexican mural experience, Guston garnered high repute as a prominent member of the New York School by producing nonobjective and often deliriously lyrical Abstract Impressionist easel works (see fig. 40). But in the uncertain U.S. political climate of 1969, "bored and disgusted by the skills that had gained him renown," he did a sudden about-face, making what appeared an unexpected retrenchment to the figurative. Including an apparent recommitment to allegory, in comparison to what he had collaborated to produce in Morelia, this new style was both strikingly similar and totally divergent.[46] In keeping with an accompanying reemergence of the urgency to reacknowledge his roots, Guston began thinking of himself as a "tortured Talmudist."[47] By choosing this term he likened his renewed fascination with narrative meaning to the centuries-old fixation of rabbinic scholars on continuous reinterpretation of the Torah—scrolls of which sometimes made an appearance in Guston's later paintings. "From 1967–69," Guston wrote, "I painted like mad. The pictures came so fast I had to make memos to myself, at a table drinking coffee. '*Paint them.*' I felt like a movie director. Like opening a Pandora's box, and all those images came out."[48]

Training a "gimlet eye" (in Dore Ashton's words) on what he and his late-in-life friend, the much younger novelist Philip Roth, liked to call the "crapola" of modern life, Guston's new pre-occupations were not with compulsive editorial reshaping of the morality tales of the Hebrew Bible like a real Talmudist, but with his own bad habits, the junk in his home and studio—to which he gave an inflection very different from Cub-ism or Pop art—as well as with his own and his wife's deteriorating bodies and the flotsam and jetsam of the streets.[49] (We should never forget his father's fate.)[50] Beginning in 1969, Guston's newly crude, raw urban style seemed to many a purposeful attempt to travesty Abstract Expressionism's grand ambitions (fig. 108). Literary critics have analogized Roth's equally vulgar writing style to Jewish stand-up comedy skits specializing in travesty, most particularly the manic improvisational performance known as the "spritz" where perform-ers "spray" forth a continuous, typically self-involved torrent at the audi-ence—pretty much the way Guston represented himself in *Painter's Forms* in 1972 (fig. 109). He explained this new pictorial modus operandi in terms of imaginative displacement. "You're painting a shoe," Guston recounted to poet Bill Berkson, "you start painting the sole and it turns into a moon; you start painting the moon and it turns into a piece of bread."[51]

The spritz, begun on the burlesque and vaudeville stage and carried to its ultimate form in the 1950s and '60s by Mort Sahl and Lenny Bruce, is typically a bad-mannered monologue, often insulting, usually dark in mood, and generally narcissistic in the extreme. While it constitutes a singular, somewhat more aggressive manifestation of characteristic Jewish humor—memorably defined by Freud as a coping mechanism designed to mitigate the psychological disconnection of being "chosen" by God and despised by society[52]—the spritz also shares a number of characteristics with the gentler self-mocking irony of all those schlemiels in the stories of Sholom Aleichem and other popular immigrant literature. Guston, Ashton affirms, was clearly "interested in the logic of farce, of burlesque, of slapstick," and his own hypercritical late work draws on the same deep well of insecurities as these tales of his parents' generation.

Another of Guston's acknowledged interests in the popular Depression-

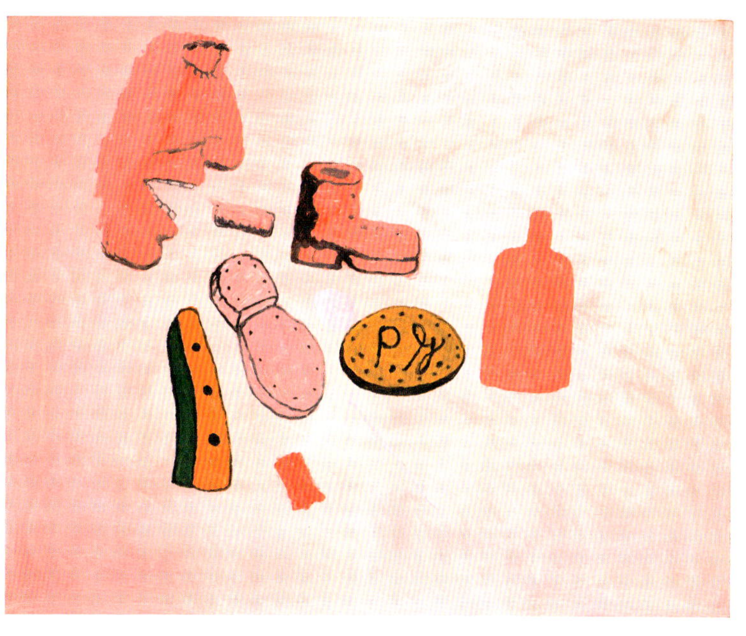

109 Philip Guston, *Painter's Forms*, 1972. Oil on panel. Courtesy of McKee Gallery. © Estate of Philip Guston.

era comic strip "Krazy Kat," may very well be related. It likely stemmed at least in some measure from creator George Herriman's liberal and hilarious use, although he was not Jewish, of nonsensical sounding mangled Yiddish. Such fractured elocutions typically came out of the mouth of Krazy Kat's nemesis Ignatz, a very untimid mouse. In almost every episode Ignatz hurls a brick at Krazy, who repeatedly chooses to misunderstand these missiles as manifestations of love.[53] Such willful acts of misrecognition no doubt struck Guston[54] (pun intended) as a laughable permutation of the fascination he and Roth shared with pondering the "what if?"—a quintessentially Jewish equation.[55]

Musing on *what if* he himself were hidden behind a white hood and what it would feel like "to be evil" and "to plan, to plot," as he painted his "Ku Klux Komix" (*Time*'s tart moniker for the works exhibited at Marlborough in 1970), Guston proved just as engrossed as Krazy Kat with alternate meanings and possibilities, and the positing of what he called a "substitute world."[56] Reminiscing about their unusual relationship, Philip Roth remarked that the "brooding, brainy" man he came to know, whose white hair and by now bulky torso was reminiscent of an Old Guard Israeli politician, seemed "full of the doubts and uncertainties that can beset an artist of consequence in middle age." "Although painting monopolized his personal despair and his seismic moodiness to make the intense anxiety of being himself something even he could sometimes laugh at," Roth explained, "it never neutralized the nightmares entirely."[57]

Adopting a back-and-forth dialogue similar to skits in the repertoire of an argumentative Borscht Belt comic (see also Woody Allen's various alter egos, such as Alvy Singer, or more recently Borat, Sacha Baron Cohen's alternate persona as a sly fool), after his so-called "silly" Klan canvases (seen in fig. 24) ran their course, the paintings Guston now said he simply *had* to make often still induce a nervous hilarity. Speaking of a whole series painted of smokers smoking, Guston mused over the notion of laughter: "When I show these, people laugh and I always wonder what laughter is. I suppose Baudelaire's definition is still valid, it's the collision of two contrary feelings." This, of course, also sounds like a methodology intimately related to allegory. That his viewers might burst out laughing at the sight of these pictures was, Guston said, "exactly what I want and expect."[58]

Antiheroic in any traditional sense, Guston's late paintings locate the (often tragic) universal embedded in the quirks of his own lugubrious personality. "Being a painter," he admitted, "has to do with self-involvement. I know the result, the by-product are paintings. But I think my curiosity and boredom and just plain wanting to know what to do with my life leads me to an area of preoccupation with my evolution as a human being." Discussing the ethics of risk with the critic Gene Baro, Motherwell reiterated his belief that "every artist's problem is to invent himself." "No wonder," he said on this occasion, "the artist is constantly placing and displacing, relating and rupturing relations."[59] Likewise pondering the "moral problem" of identity and the concomitant burden of individualism, by designating himself in effect the butt of his very own Jewish joke, Guston chose a far less grandiose route than Motherwell for its exploration. In a similar situation, Alexander Portnoy, Roth's most infamous alter-ego, bitterly "complained," but embracing its reflexive consequences pushed Guston toward a unique and presciently postmodern route to rewriting the past for needs of the present.[60]

Mexico and American Modernism

I have come to Mexico to get a new idea of man.[61]

— ANTONIN ARTAUD, 1945

Would the careers of Isamu Noguchi, Philip Guston, Jackson Pollock, or Robert Motherwell have developed the way they did without their connections in and to Mexico? I strongly argue that they would not, and that links in and to Mexico played a critical role in the psychic and artistic maturity of these four major mid-twentieth-century American modernists associated with Abstract Expressionism. Previous authors, including myself, have analyzed Mexican impact on some of these artists individually, but here I have taken a broader and more synthetic approach. Uninterested in picturesque depictions of the enchantment of Old Mexico, a preoccupation of many predecessors on trips or extended stays south of the border, or patronizing co-option of Mexican originality like André Breton, these artists, I have argued, were not simply aesthetic tourists on the way to crafting their own originality. Each, in his own particular way, took full advantage of border-crossing's liminal status as a way to crossbreed and ultimately validate modernism.

It is has been declared that the major Mexican muralists (for the most part) found a relatively congenial atmosphere in the United States during the 1930s and early '40s; in the cases of Noguchi, Guston, and Motherwell the reverse was also true, with of course similar reservations. Excepting David Alfaro Siqueiros and Diego Rivera for brief periods, none of these artists were exactly in exile, but even short stints of displacement had a profound impact on both groups, conceptually, iconographically, and embedded in material process. Meeting up with Mexican artists in the United States offered Pollock an analogous opportunity to test the potential of aesthetic hybridization. This study brings to the forefront a somewhat different cast of characters from ones intent on privileging American painting's European roots. Picasso, for example, looms less overwhelmingly from its perspective; in comparison, Orozco, Rivera, and especially Siqueiros, as well as Kadish, Matta, Paalen, and even Breton or the Greenwood sisters and Seligmann, take up a more prominent place. Allowing Mexico more standing in the story brings to the foreground issues of ethnicity, marginality, inter- and intra-subjectivity, and social and political conscience, highlighting especially the interface between a concern with publicly significant meanings and the search for personal identity. It also provides a slightly different vantage point from which to assess Surrealism's impact on Abstract Expressionism, as well as a more nuanced way to understand, as Noguchi put it, the "humanly meaningful" goals of mid-century abstraction.[62]

Although this version of modernism's heroic American phase might suggest a contradiction to the notion of its originality, the achievements of Abstract Expressionism were not made in isolation; rather, they were an affirmation of newly important internationalist values. Octavio Paz, Mexico's foremost twentieth-century intellectual, wrote memorably in *The Labyrinth of Solitude* that "to be oneself is always to become that other person who is one's real self, that hidden promise or possibility."[63] It should be evident that the notion of "possibility" became something of a leitmotif for art in an era climbing out of the devastation of two world wars and the atomic bomb. Interaction with Mexico and Mexican art during this key period played an essential role in helping four talented American creative minds to actuate their own authenticity.

1 | Body Si(gh)ting

1. Dore Ashton, *Noguchi: East and West* (Berkeley: University of California Press, 1992), 64–66; Masayo Duus, *The Life of Isamu Noguchi: Journey Without Borders* (Princeton: Princeton University Press, 2004), 153–58. Noguchi discusses Frida (whom he met through Miguel Covarrubias's wife) in a 1987 Mexican Televisa interview: "I'm sure she was loved by all Mexico the same as I loved her." Circa 1936 he wrote, "Dearest my most lovable Frida": "That I see the light sometimes proves that I will come back to you one day grown up and more understanding and more worthy of you should you by then still care for Isamu." Amy Wolf, *On Becoming an Artist: Isamu Noguchi and His Contemporaries, 1922–1960* (Long Island City, N.Y.: Isamu Noguchi Foundation and Garden Museum, 2010), 70; hereafter INFGM.

2. Greenwood sisters' Mexican work: James Oles, "The Mexican Murals of Marion and Grace Greenwood," *Out of Context: American Artists Abroad,* Laura Felleman Fattal and Carol Salus, eds. (Westport, Conn.: Praeger, 2004), 113–34 (Mercado murals: 121–28) and "Walls to Paint On: American Muralists in Mexico, 1933–1936," Ph.D. diss., Yale University, 1995.

3. Olivier Debroise, "Action Art: David Alfaro Siqueiros and the Artistic and Ideological Strategies of the 1930s," *Portrait of a Decade: David Alfaro Siqueiros, 1940–1940* (Mexico City: Museo Nacional de Arte, Instituto Nacional de Bellas Artes, 1997), explains that Anita Brenner coined the term Los Tres Grandes in 1932.

4. Duus, *Life of Isamu Noguchi,* 154.

5. Arthur Millier, "East-West Races Join to Produce Art Prodigy," *Los Angeles Times,* March 19, 1933, A-4. In "Famous Sculptor Returns to This City of His Birth: Isamu Noguchi Pauses in His Search for a 'Community' to Model Portraits and Design a Swim Pool," *Los Angeles Times,* September 1, 1935, A9, Millier writes that Noguchi is not a typical portrait sculptor. "He likes to model from interesting people because divination and creation are his twin passions. External likenesses interest him little. In a portrait he makes the life that flows through a person mold the clay. His just completed head of Helen Gahagan, who sat to him here, is an example. Even in unsympathetic plaster, this head seems to be floating forward on invisible wings of spirit. . . . [His portraits] . . . are not imitation people in the flesh. They are haunting memories of experiences."

6. Nancy Grove, *Isamu Noguchi Portrait Sculpture* (Washington, D.C.: Smithsonian Institution Press for the National Portrait Gallery, 1989): Orozco, 62–63; Greenwood, 48–49; Gahagan, 90–91.

7. John Crosse, "Richard Neutra and the California Art Club: A Pathway to the Von Sternberg and Murphy Commissions," http://socalarchhistory.blogspot.com, posted May 16, 2011. Noguchi car-pooled to the Texas border with poet e. e. cummings and fashion model/photographer Marion Morehouse.

8. Noguchi Interview, January 16, 1987, Camino Réal, Mexico City; Videotape, INFGM.

9. Arthur Millier, "Mexican Art Ferment Stirring in LA," *Los Angeles Times,* May 22, 1932, B13.

10. Murphy mural: Laurance P. Hurlburt, *The Mexican Muralists in the United States* (Albuquerque: University of New Mexico Press, 1989), 213–16.

11. Elizabeth Fuentes Rojas, "El Abelardo Rodríguez: Un Mercado del Pueblo y Para El Pueblo," *Crónicas: El Muralismo, Producto de la Revolución Mexicana, en América, Seminario de investigación,* no. 5–6 (September 1999–August 2000), 17–24; hereafter *Crónicas,* no. 5–6.

12. James Oles, "Noguchi in Mexico: International Themes for a Working-Class Market," *American Art* 15 (Summer 2001), 10–32; Oles and Karen Cordero Reiman, *South of the Border: Mexico in the American Imagination, 1914–1947* (Washington, D.C.: Smithsonian Institution Press, 1993).

13. Oles, *Out of Context,* 123. Noguchi lived in Mexico City with the Greenwoods in the Calle Columbia, except when holed up in a secret apartment with Kahlo.

14. Brancusi's studio as a "laboratory for distilling basic shapes":

"Famous Sculptor Returns," A9. See also Bruce Altshuler, *Isamu Noguchi: Early Abstraction* (New York: Whitney Museum of American Art, 1994).

15. Her Morelia mural's creation: Dorothy Seckler, "Tape-recorded Interview with Marion Greenwood at Woodstock, New York," January 31, 1964; http://archivesofamericanart.si.edu/oralhist/greenw64.htm. Its topic is described as "the Tarascan Indian as an ancient race, and the way they live now." Oles, "Walls to Paint On," 122–23: Marion met Gustavo Corona, rector, University of San Nicolas Hidalgo, Morelia, at a dinner party in Mexico City, May 1933. In a letter to Josephine Herbst, October 26, 1933, Marion writes that Corona "feels like Sforza, and wants to get a lot of painters here including Rivera to cover the walls of Morelia and thus go down in history as a patron of the arts." *Out of Context*, 117. As will be seen, Philip Guston writes home similarly.

16. Marion Greenwood to Josephine Herbst, June 8, 1933; Oles, "Walls to Paint On," 138. Jack Star-Hunt, "Brooklyn Girls Delight Mexico with 8 Murals," *New York Herald Tribune*, March 4, 1934. Marion's composition "is praised by Mexican critics for its originality and fidelity to the physical traits of the Mexican Tarascans. The work reveals a deep sympathy with the burdens and struggles of the oppressed native races." In Morelia, Grace "aims at portraying the pitiless struggle of the workers in the Machine Age."

17. Avis Berman, *Rebels on Eighth Street: Juliana Force and the Whitney Museum of American Art* (New York: Atheneum, 1990), 346–48. These include *Monument to Ben Franklin*, *Monument to the Plow*, and *Play Mountain*, all 1933. Artist's comments: *The Isamu Noguchi Garden Museum* (New York: INFGM and Harry N. Abrams, 1987), 144–45.

18. Untitled, unsigned review, *New Yorker*, February 9, 1935, 47.

19. Born Paul Higgins Stevenson in Salt Lake City, 1907, Pablo O'Higgins immigrated to Mexico in 1924, joining the Communist Party. He assisted Rivera at the National School of Agriculture, Chapingo, and the Ministry of Education, Mexico City. In 1937, O'Higgins cofounded the Taller de Gráfica Popular, a print collective.

20. On the Mercado Abelardo L. Rodríguez, see Carlos Mérida, *Frescoes in Rodríguez Market by Various Artists: An Interpretive Guide with 16 Reproductions* (Mexico City: Frances Toor Studios, 1937) and various articles in *Crónicas*, no. 5–6. Mérida, a Guatemalan painter, founded the Union of Workers, Technicians, Painters, and Sculptors with Rivera, Orozco, and Siqueiros.

21. "What's the Matter with Sculpture?" *Art Front* 3, no. 16 (September–October 1936), 14.

22. Marion Greenwood recalled Noguchi's use of an ax, Seckler Interview.

23. "I agreed to do it for the same price that the muralists were getting, so much a square meter. Which wasn't very much, I forget what it was." Interview with Isamu Noguchi Conducted by Paul Cummings at the Artist's Studio, Long Island City, New York, November 7, 1973, AAA. Noguchi states that he went to New York to raise money, although it is unclear how that was possible. Apparently he did not have to submit to Antonio Mediz Bolio, Mexico City government's head of culture, who was supervisor of political content of preliminary sketches while Rivera oversaw visual content. Nor was he required to get an official work permit. Oles, *Out of Context*, 123, and "Walls to Paint On," 385; Esther Acevedo, "Dos muralismos en el mercado," *Plural* 121 (October 1981), 47. Noguchi's payment: "Walls to Paint On," 399; Julio de la Fuente, "Insistimos en nustro programa de reinvindicaciones en el arte," *Frente a Frente*, no. 5 (August 1936), 19.

24. Ailes Gilmour in Graham Company, 1929–33: Marian Horosko, *Martha Graham: The Evolution of Her Dance Theory and Training* (Gainesville: University Press of Florida, 2002), 8.

25. "Cement: Noguchi's Polychrome Relief Achieves a Powerful Effect," *New Masses*, September 15, 1936, 10.

26. "What's the Matter with Sculpture?" 13–14.

27. Noguchi Interview, January 16, 1987, Camino Réal, Mexico City; Videotape, INFGM.

28. Isamu Noguchi, *A Sculptor's World* (New York: Harper and Row, 1968), 22. "Walls to Paint On," 368–69, n. 157. Irene Herner, *Siqueiros from Paradise to Utopia* (Mexico City: Ministry of Culture of the City of Mexico, 2010), 192: "The influence of Siqueiros can first be felt in [Noguchi's] sculpture *Lynched Figure*, where a Black martyr, whose synthesizing image is shaped like a crucifix made from distortions, resembles the Christ in *América Tropical*."

29. *New Yorker*, February 9, 1935, 47.

30. L[aurie] E[glington], "Noguchi—Marie Harriman Gallery," *Art News* 33 (February 2, 1935), 8.

31. "Aesthetic opportunism": M. M., "Art Commentary on Lynching: Arthur U. Newton Galleries," *Art News* 33 (February 23, 1935), 13.

32. See Marlene Park, "Lynching and Antilynching: Art and Politics in the 1930s," *Prospects* 18 (1993), 311–65; Margaret Rose Vendryes, "Hanging on Their Walls: *An Art Commentary on Lynching*, the Forgotten 1935 Exhibition," *Race-Consciousness: African-American Studies for the New Century*, Judith Jackson Fossett and Jeffrey A. Tucker, eds. (New York: New York University Press, 199), 10–39; Helen Langa, "Two Antilynching Art Exhibitions: Politicized Viewpoints, Racial Perspectives, Gendered Constraints," *American Art* 13 (Spring 1999), 10–39.

33. Now lost work, illustrated in "Cooperation in Philadelphia," *American Magazine of Art* 27 (November 1934), 613.

34. Bruce Altshuler, *Isamu Noguchi* (New York: Abbeville, 1994), 29, quoting Henry McBride, "Attractions in the Galleries," *New York Sun*, February 2, 1935, 37; Amy Lyford, "Noguchi, Sculptural Abstraction, and the Politics of Japanese-American Internment," *Art Bulletin* 85 (March 2003), 137–51; Dora Apel, *Imagery of Lynching: Black Men, White Women, and the Mob* (New Brunswick, N.J.: Rutgers University Press, 2004), 92–96.

35. "Lynching as a Japanese Sculptor Sees It," *Christian Century: A Journal of Religion*, February 13, 1935, 196–97. Although this review is generally positive (*Death* is said to "hit the mark" in its intensification of emotional response), the unidentified author ends with an equivocal racial comment: "And besides, it is bitter but wholesome medicine for us to see what features of American life a Japanese artist considers important enough to perpetuate in bronze. Frightfully ruthless people, those Japanese! Think of their cruelty in Manchukuo and Shanghai!" The writer seems unaware Noguchi was American born.

36. James W. Lane, "Current Exhibitions," *Parnassus* 7 (March 1935), 22; Dora Apel and Shawn Michelle Smith, *Lynching Photographs* (Berkeley: University of California Press, 2007), 52. *Death* in Marie Harriman Gallery brochure: "A Lynching (Made after a photograph in the I. L. D.)," meaning the magazine *International Labor Defense*.

37. Oles, "Walls to Paint On," 368. Both were completed in Woodstock, New York, where Noguchi went to nurse his wounds after his PWAP debacle. Abstracted head of a laboring mother (the only extant segment of *Birth*): INFGM collection.

38. Lyford, "Noguchi, Sculptural Abstraction, and the Politics of Japanese-American Internment," 139.

39. Apel, *Imagery of Lynching*, 94. L[aurie] E[glington], "Noguchi—Marie Harriman Gallery," 8, criticized "the impact of artificially engendered activity upon the high tension wires of our modern intellect."

40. Noguchi wrote: "That settled it! If what could be taken seriously as art precluded a search beyond the accepted purposes and dimensions, what was I to do? I wanted widening horizons and a way of art to seek for myself. I determined to have no further truck with either galleries or critics." *Sculptor's World*, 23.

41. Graham, interview, *Santa Barbara News*, October 2, 1920; Ernestine Stodelle, *Deep Song: The Dance Story of Martha Graham* (New York: Schirmer, 1984), 32.

42. "[Itō] had a studio in the John Murray Anderson studio building, the dance studio building. He had a dance class there, and so did Martha Graham. I think I met Martha Graham there": Cummings interview, AAA. Ailes's 1928 introduction: Robert Tracy, "Noguchi: Collaborating with Graham," *Ballet Review* 13 (Winter 1986), 9, or meeting through Leonie Gilmour in 1929: Grove, *Portrait Sculpture*, 46.

43. Tobi Tobias, Interview with Isamu Noguchi, Long Island City, N.Y., 1979; typescript, New York Public Library of the Performing Arts [hereafter NYPLPA], MGZMT 3–558, 1. Noguchi said in regard to Graham's request for a set for her composition *Frontier:* "That she asked me was no doubt due to our friendship and to my familiarity with the development of the modern dance, which I had watched since its inception in her own work." *Sculptor's World*, 23.

44. Tracy, "Collaborating with Graham," 9; Neil Printz, "'A Nearer Function than that of the Eye': Noguchi, Graham and the Physicality of the Dance," *Noguchi and Graham: Selected Works for Dance* (Long Island City, N.Y.: INFGM, 2004), 48.

45. Graham's comment: "From Collaboration, a Strange Beauty," *New York Times*, January 8, 1989, section 2, 6. Noguchi's: Tracy, "Collaborating with Graham," 9. See also Grove, *Portrait Sculpture,* 46–47; Patricia Richmond, "Gender and the Forms of Modernism: Dancers and Painters," Ph.D. diss., Case Western Reserve University, 2003, 278–79.

46. Richmond, "Dancers and Painters," 272, cites Agnes De Mille, *Martha: The Life and Work of Martha Graham* (New York: Random House, 1991), 13: "Her face was arresting: long, Oriental, with dead-white skin and a scarlet mouth, and eyes that seemed to protrude slightly but in fact did not—dark, all-absorbing, all-expressive, glowing with golden lights. Her regard was usually downcast or hooded. Martha's skull-like head with its deep-set eyes, the gaunt cheeks, the very visible teeth, and the long, well-defined jaw looked to me even then like a death's head—until one considered the eyes. And one returned to them again and again. Her eyes flashed light."

47. Isamu Noguchi, "Tribute to Martha Graham," typescript of ceremony, November 20, 1973, Library and Museum of the Performing Arts, New York, 5; NYPLPA: MGZMT 7–537. "Pronounced bony structure": Tobias interview, NYPLPA, 6.

48. Horst was Graham's musical director, advisor, promoter, and (before she married Erick Hawkins), her lover for almost two decades: Janet Mansfield Soares, *Louis Horst, Musician in a Dancer's World* (Durham: Duke University Press, 1992). Horst introduced Graham to philosophy (Nietzsche's opposition of the Apollonian and Dionysian) and to German Expressionist art and dance (Mary Wigman). Richmond, "Dancers and Painters," 254–56; Anna Kisselgoff, "Dance View: Reflections on Martha Graham's Revolution," *New York Times*, May 29, 1988.

49. Graham, *Blood Memory* (New York: Washington Square, 1991), 143–44:

> In March 1932 I was granted the first fellowship given to a dancer by the John Simon Guggenheim Foundation, which offered me the opportunity go to Europe and study with the German dancer Mary Wigman but I said no. I didn't want to go to Europe without something American so I chose Mexico as a compromise. . . . I was in Mexico during the agrarian revolution. Men wore very short white pants, white tops and big hats. They rode in the streets in a wild fashion on any pony they could get. Guns were constantly being fired, but nobody cared enough about my presence to shoot in my direction. I remember climbing to the top of the pyramids. It was so striking going up those steps and arriving at the top to be absorbed in a very hallowed place. I raised my hands high above my head and was enthralled by the wind and the sun, the height. A great deal of what I do today is not only American Indian but also Mexican Indian. It is not that I tried to be either a Mexican or an Indian, but to gain ability to

identify myself with a culture that wasn't mine. One begins to realize that all human beings are the same. Mexican photos: Russell Freedman, *Martha Graham: A Dancer's Life* (New York: Clarion, 1998), 71.

50. Graham on *Dark Meadow:* "I seem to feel in the first part—the opening—a memory of standing in the wind on the top of the Mexican pyramid—And then to remember the descent afterwards—There was an awareness up there of ancient rites — sacrifices — sufferings — prayers — but enduring through all—the sun, the wind, the rain—." *The Notebooks of Martha Graham* (New York: Harcourt Brace Jovanovich, 1973), 190. Gilmour: Horosko, *Martha Graham: The Evolution of Her Dance Theory and Training,* 22. Noguchi also describes *Dark Meadow* as "my homage to Mexico": *Sculptor's World,* 126. He told Robert Tracy, "In 1936 I was in Mexico. My first large work was a wall in Mexico. So I was greatly attached to that country, as was Martha. *Dark Meadow* is not specifically Mexican, though. It's more primitive and in the realm of myth." "Collaborating with Graham," 11.

51. De Mille, *Martha: The Life and Work of Martha Graham,* 184–85.

52. Noguchi on *Frontier:* "A rope running from the two top corners of the proscenium to the floor rear center of the stage, bisected the three-dimensional void of stage space. This seemed to throw the entire volume of air over the heads of the audience. At the rear convergence was a small section of log fence, to start from and to return to. The white ropes created a curious ennobling—of an outburst into space and, at the same time, of the public's inrush toward infinity." *Sculptor's World,* 125. The idea came to him at a party at art dealer Julien Levy's: "Thinking of the volume of the stage, the stage volume—not the stage space—but the whole mass of air, that cubic piece of air. Suddenly I had this flash, what it is I wanted to do. It was to bisect that volume of air." Tobias interview, NYPLPA, 11–12.

53. Tobias interview, NYPLPA, 13; Printz, "A Nearer Function," 50. Ailes on Graham's early dances: "The public was not used to the starkness and simplicity of the movement in her work. It was not 'pretty' and contained none of the conventions of ballet. It was a complete break from tradition. People unused to the bare bones of dance were often repelled. I loved it! There, it seemed, was truth." Horosko, *Martha Graham: The Evolution of Her Dance Theory and Training,* 21–22.

54. Quote: Stodelle, *Deep Song,* 154. Noguchi on *Frontier,* "Tribute to Martha Graham," NYPLPA, 7: "I think . . . because of my Japanese background there is a good deal of unconscious, sort of regard for the kind of simple but significant, not pointed directly but obliquely, such as exists in the Noh theatre, suggestive and essential." Graham, in Soares, *Louis Horst,* 121: "The dance *Frontier* came from our discussion of the hold, as an American, the frontier has always had for me as a symbol of a journey into the unknown. Traveling to California by train, the tracks were to me a reiteration of that frontier. When at last I asked Isamu for an image of those endless tracks for my dance, he brought to me the set for *Frontier*—the tracks now the endless ropes into the future."

55. Ernestine Stodelle, "Before Yesterday: The First Decade of Modern Dance, Martha Graham," *Dance Observer* 48 (January 1962), 7.

56. Tracy, "Collaborating with Graham," 10.

57. Noguchi, "Tribute to Martha Graham," NYPLPA, 6. "I would say that in regard to my sets too, [Martha] so absorbed them completely that I could not claim that they were mine. I mean they were hers. They were part of her anatomy, so to speak. She could use them in ways that I could not even imagine. I just merely, you know, tried to become a part of her as she talked to me. I sort of blended and melded with her somehow. And we were one, and it was a kind of mutual involvement, if you will, which [you] might say is the real gist of collaboration."

58. Printz, "Nearer Function," 50. Noguchi in Stodelle, *Deep Song,* 153: "I felt that I was an extension of Martha and that she was an extension of me." Also Elizabeth Forsyth Harris, "Sculptural Theatre: Isamu Noguchi's Sets for Martha Graham," Ph.D. diss., University of Virginia, 2000.

59. O'Donnell in Robert Tracy, *Goddess: Martha Graham's Dancers Remember* (New York: Limelight, 1997), 31. Late 1920s and '30s dance reviews: Merle Armitage, ed., *Martha Graham: The Early Years* (New York: Da Capo, 1978).

60. Additional images: Gerald Ackerman, "Photography and the Dance: Soichi Sunami and Martha Graham," *Ballet Review* 12 (Summer 1984), 32–66. Richmond, "Dancers and Painters," 284–85, describes comedienne Fannie Brice's parody by Ira Gershwin, "Modernistic Moe," making fun of Graham's seriousness, presented in the 1936 Ziegfield Follies.

61. Tracy, *Goddess:* Maslow, 48; Dudley, 55. Maslow on Graham's principles: Horosko, *Martha Graham: The Evolution of Her Dance Theory and Training,* 50–53; O'Donnell in same, 57–63. Also Alice Helpern, "Martha Graham's Early Technique and Dances: The 1930s, a Panel Discussion," Part 2, *Choreography and Dance* 5 (1999), 7–32.

62. "Martha Graham Speaks," *The Medium of Dance,* Walter Sorell, ed., *Dance Observer* 29 (April 1963), 53.

63. Horosko, *Martha Graham: The Evolution of Her Dance Theory and Training,* 232. Also Henriette Bannerman, "An Overview of the Development of Martha Graham's Movement System (1926–1991)," *Dance Research* 17 (Winter 1999), 9–39.

64. Richmond, "Dancers and Painters," 251–52. Graham: Horosko, *Martha Graham: The Evolution of Her Dance Theory and Training,* 235 (Graham's emphasis). Don McDonagle, "A Conversation with Gertrude Shurr," *Ballet Review,* no. 4 (1973), 12; also Horosko, 33–43.

65. Blanche Evan, "From a Dancer's Notebook," Part 2, *New Theatre* (April 1936), 31.

66. Printz, "Nearer Function," 53.

67. "Humanistic sculpture": Gay Morris, "Review, *Isamu Nogu-*

chi: Essays and Conversations (1994)," *Dance View* 12 (Spring 1995), 35. Noguchi, "Tribute to Martha Graham," NYPLPA, 6–7: "Anyway, my interest was to see how sculpture might be in the hypothetical space of theater as a living part of human relationships, you see. . . . And, I mean, she gave the flesh and I gave, maybe another sort of spatial sense, so that altogether it made a theater."

68. Edna Ocko, "Martha Graham—Dances in Two Worlds," *New Theatre* 2 (July 1935), 26; Stacey Prickett, "Reviewing on the Left: The Dance Criticism of Edna Ocko," *Of, By and For the People: Dancing on the Left in the 1930s*, Lynn Garafola, ed., *Studies in Dance History* 5 (Spring 1994), 85.

69. Nell Anyon [Nadia Chilkovsky], "What *Is* the New Dance Group?" unidentified brochure (1st annual recital?), c. 1933, 3. Miriam Blecher Scrapbook: see n. 73 below. Also Anyon, "The Tasks of the Revolutionary Dance," *New Theatre* (September–October 1933), 21; Mark Franko, *Dancing Modernism/ Performing Politics* (Bloomington: Indiana University Press, 1995), 113–15.

70. On poet Yonejirō Noguchi's relationship with Leonie Gilmour, Isamu's 1904 birth in California, and early upbringing in Japan, see Ashton, *Noguchi: East and West*, and Duus, *Life of Isamu Noguchi*. Duus, 64–66: Ailes's birth in January 1912 (her father, likely one of Leonie's Japanese students); Ailes as Celtic version of Alice, from a 1920 poem, *Beauty's a Flower* by Moira O'Neill [Agnes Shakespeare Higginson]: "Youth's for an hour, an' the taste o' life is sweet/Ailes was a girl that stepped on two bare feet/In all my days I never seen the one as fair as she/I'd have lost my life for Ailes, an' she never cared for me."

71. Elizabeth Cooper, "Tamiris and the Federal Dance Theatre, 1936–1939: Socially Relevant Dance Amidst the Policies and Politics of the New Deal Era," *Dance Research Journal* 29 (Autumn 1997), 23–48. Photos including Ailes: American Theater Collection, Special Collections and Archives, Fenwick Library, George Mason University, Fairfax, Va. Ailes seen performing in "Pickin' Off de Cotton," *How Long Brethren?:* Pauline Tish, "Remembering Helen Tamiris," *Dance Chronicle* 17, no. 3 (1994), 349.

72. Elizabeth Skrip [Edna Ocko], "World of the Dance: All-Day Dance League Festival," *Daily Worker*, June 13, 1935; Prickett, "Reviewing on the Left," 84. *Lynch* is described as a "pictorial but unclear social comment."

73. Edna Ocko, "New Dance Group," *New Theatre* 1, no. 10 (November 1934), 28. See Franko, *Dancing Modernism/Performing Politics;* Stacey Prickett, "Dance and the Workers' Struggle," *Dance Research* 8 (Spring 1990), 47–61; Ellen Graff, *Stepping Left: Dance and Politics in New York City, 1928–1942* (Durham: Duke University Press, 1997). Basis for discussion: clippings from scrapbooks of New Dance Group founder and director Miriam Blecher, access facilitated by Abigail Rasminsky, author of "Dancing with the Dead," *Nextbook Reader*, no. 5 (Fall 2007), 17–18. Permission from Judy Sklar Rasminsky, Zachary Sklar, and Daniel Sklar.

74. Ocko, "New Dance Group," 28; "New Dance League's Three Years End with Tomorrow's Recital," newspaper unknown, April 24, 1937, Blecher Scrapbook. "Dance of Death" by Bill Matons's Experimental Unit is singled out for praise. Review of leftist dance subjects: Stacey Prickett, "'The People': Issues of Identity within the Revolutionary Dance," Garafola, *Studies in Dance History*, 14–22.

75. John Martin, "The Dance: To the N. D. L. [New Dance League]: An Open Letter on the Occasion of the Annual League Conference," *New York Times*, June 16, 1935, Blecher Scrapbook. A dance benefit for the *Daily Worker*, February 17, 1935, sold out Radio City's Center Theater for the first time. Horst's belief: Soares, *Louis Horst*, 65, 67. According to Franko, *Dancing Modernism/Performing Politics*, 25, the 1930s was a decade of cultural centrality for dance, and the imprint of radicalism on dance was more seminal than for any other art.

76. Likely reference to such Graham works as *Ceremonials*, 1932. Jean Bolan, "2,000 Witness First Workers' Dance League Recital," newspaper and date unknown [probably late December 1934], 5, Blecher Scrapbook. Paul Douglas, states Graham "will be remembered as the greatest dance exponent of the last stages of capitalism struggling in its final agonies to salvage something out of its chaotic and dying torment." "Modern Dance Forms," *New Theatre* 2 (November 1935), 26–27: Franko, *Dancing Modernism/Performing Politics*, 140.

77. Edna Ocko, "Martha Graham—Dances in Two Worlds," *New Theatre* 2 (July 1935), 26–27: Prickett, "Reviewing on the Left," 85–87. Ocko argues that Graham must decide between abstract and socially conscious approaches. Earlier, more forceful pleas to Graham to "open her eyes and mind to the world as it is today" and interpret that for us: Ocko, "The Dance Season in Review," *Workers Theatre* 5 (July–August 1933), "Whither Martha Graham," *New Theatre* 3 (April 1934), 7: Prickett, "Reviewing on the Left," 67–70. Graham's own roots went back to the Mayflower. Her background was very different from that of most revolutionary dancers, many of whom came from (often Jewish) immigrant families. While such ethnic and class disparity likely contributed to Graham's disinclination to deemphasize the individual in favor of the group, some of her dancers could and did bridge both worlds. Ellen Graff, "Dancing Red: Art and Politics," in Garafola, *Studies in Dance History*, 6–7.

78. Simon Hall, "Workers Dance Movement Makes Great Strides Forward," newspaper and date unknown [November 193?], Blecher Scrapbook. Hall notes some of these dances as "over-heavy and unmitigatingly somber." Critique of revolutionary dance as "Communist choreography": E[manuel] E[isenberg], "Dancers Depict Proletarian Ills," *New York World Telegram*, June 4, 1934, Blecher Scrapbook. See also Franko, *Dancing Modernism/Performing Politics*, 115–19, 129–33. Dudley's inspiration: Graff interview, New York, January 7, 1992, in "Dancing Red," 11, n. 8. Graham: "Propaganda

is one subject I will not allow to be discussed in my studio": "We Visit Martha Graham," *Dynamics*, May 5, 1934, Martha Graham Clippings, 8, NYPLPA.

79. Anyon, "What Is the New Dance Group? 3. Mitchell, "Capitalism Is Tottering," *New York World-Telegram*, December 18, 1934.

80. Ocko, "Dances in Two Worlds," in Prickett, "Reviewing on the Left," 87. Regarding Graham's technical tours de force, Ocko complains, "the worker is mystified, irked by non-comprehension."

81. Fliers for two of these programs in Blecher's scrapbook give dates (January 15, October 4) but omit the year. On the latter, Ailes Gilmour is identified as "Guest Artist" dancing with Matons in *American Rhapsody*, set to poetry by Kenneth Fearing and music by Alexander Scriabin.

82. Lynne Connor, "'What the Modern Dance Should Be': Socialist Agendas in the Modern Dance, 1931–38," *Crucibles of Crisis: Performing Social Change*, Janelle Reinelt, ed. (Ann Arbor: University of Michigan Press, 1996), 231–48; Wilma Salisbury, "Anti-war Message from 1936 Rings True," *Cleveland Plain Dealer*, November 4, 2003.

83. Noguchi, "Cement," 10.

84. Noguchi, Cummings interview, AAA: "After all, for one with a background like myself, the question of identity is very uncertain. And I think it's only in art that it was ever possible for me to find any identity at all." Narration of mural: Noguchi, *Sculptor's World* and "What's the Matter with Sculpture?"

85. Noguchi, Cummings interview, AAA; Interview, January 16, 1987, Camino Réal, Mexico City; Videotape, INFGM; Noguchi, *Sculptor's World*, 118. "Do what I pleased": *Sculptor's World*, 23.

86. Describing his friend as "in a continuous state of dialectic activity," Noguchi was probably not surprised by Fuller's outsized telegram. Isamu Noguchi, "A reminiscence of four decades," "The World of Buckminster Fuller," *Architectural Forum* 136 (January–February 1972), 59: "Sometime [after meeting Fuller] I got an old laundry room on top of a building on Madison Avenue and Twenty-ninth Street with windows all around it. By then under Bucky's sway I painted the whole place silver, top, bottom, and sides, to the effect that one was almost blinded by the lack of shadows. There I made his portrait head in chrome-plated bronze, also form without shadow." Fuller bust: Grove, *Portrait Sculpture*, 42–43.

87. Noguchi, *Sculptor's World*, 23.

88. Mérida, *Frescoes in Rodríguez Market*, n.p.

89. Sarcastic meaning of Rivera's microbes: Hurlburt, *Mexican Muralists in the United States*, 163. Noguchi's amoebic forms perhaps resonate more closely with Guadarrama's Mercado panel, *El Atardecer (Sunset)*. See Adrián Soto Villafaña, "Ramón Alva Guadarrama: Las Esquinas Estridentes," *Crónicas*, no. 5–6, 64. *Sunset* also pictures an in utero fetus.

90. On *Birth*: Nancy Grove and Diane Botnick, *The Sculpture of Isamu Noguchi, 1924–1979: A Catalogue* (New York: Garland, 1980), 23; Nancy Grove, *Isamu Noguchi: A Study of the Sculpture* (New York: Garland, 1985), 24.

91. *Las obras de José Guadalupe Posada, grabador mexicano*, introduction by Diego Rivera; Frances Toor, Paul O'Higgins, Blas Vanegas Arroyo, eds. (Mexico, Mexican folkways, 1930); Carl O. Schniewind and Hugh L. Edwards, *Posada: Printmaker to the Mexican People*, text by Fernando Gamboa (Chicago: Art Institute of Chicago, 1944).

92. Grace includes a foundry foreman counting ingots, Marion an accountant counting bundles of sugar cane. Oles, *Out of Context*, 126.

93. Maricela González Cruz Manjarrez, "Isamu Noguchi en el Mercado Abelardo Rodríguez," *Crónicas*, no. 5–6, 92–93, complains that the market's painted murals lack a sense of expressive unity, that themes are not integrated and quality is uneven. Rivera's influence is reflected without his uniform quality. Manjarrez critiques the Mexican painters' elemental coloring and drawing, disproportionate figures, poor use of spatial elements, and cluttered horror vacui designs without clarity, praising the Greenwood sisters and O'Higgins more highly. Rivera's influence: Esther Acevedo de Iturriaga, "Diego en el Mercado Abelardo," *Uno más uno*, August 14, 1981.

94. Noguchi, "What's the Matter with Sculpture?" 13–14. Oles, in "Walls to Paint On," 376, n. 176, and "Noguchi in Mexico," 32, n. 15, takes exception to Noguchi's recollection that he "carved a wall" and "chopped deeply" into brick. Siqueiros's employment of Portland cement and industrial tools in L.A.: see Chapter 3.

95. Author's conversation with Irene Herner, Mexico City, July 26, 2002.

96. Mérida, *Frescoes in Rodríguez Market*, n.p.

97. Seen, for example, on December 23, 1934, in group recital, Workers' Dance League, New York's Town Hall, where *We Remember (Parnas)* was performed by the New Dance Group. It would be interesting to know if Noguchi attended this performance, at which the Theatre Union Dance Group reprised its *Anti-War Cycle* of the previous year. Mary Jo Shelley, "Workers' Dance League," *Dance Observer* 2 (January 1935), 4–5.

98. Dane Rudhyar, "Art and Propaganda," *Dance Observer* 3 (December 1936), 109, 113, delineates the difference between "art with vital content" and propaganda. Both make use of "emotion-rousing big words or dramatic situations." O'Higgins, letter to Marion Greenwood, June 12, 1934, recommends that she regard everyday problems of the Mexican proletariat and "get immediate demands up on the walls with as little allegory as possible." *Crónicas*, no. 5–6, 170.

99. Oles, "Noguchi in Mexico," 24, and "Walls to Paint On," 391: "awakening labor" used to paraphrase Noguchi. Olmec parallel: conversation with Herner, July 26, 2002. Graham believed that the body "must always be in a state of listening."

100. Noguchi, Interview, January 16, 1987, Camino Réal, Mexico City; Videotape, INFGM, where "study of space" describes *Frontier*.

101. O'Higgins to Marion Greenwood: "The only suggestion I have about the projects is to *relate* them to *Mexico.* . . . Emphasize local conditions, actual struggle, & present day reality of exploitation, misery & social retrogression." *Crónicas,* no. 5–6, 170.

102. *Sketches from Chronicle: Dances Before Catastrophe (Spectre—1914, Masque), Dances After Catastrophe (Steps in the Street, Tragic Holiday— In Memoriam), Prelude to Action.* Premiere: December 20, 1936.

103. Mérida critiqued Noguchi's mural: "While this decoration is a very interesting experiment, the results are more a form of modern advertising than a work of art." Noguchi, *Sculptor's World,* 23. Here Noguchi called the mural *History Mexico,* different wording from *Art Front* and *New Masses.*

104. *Modern Migration of the Spirit,* Baker Library, Dartmouth College, 1932–34. Orozco also painted engineering girders and other factory-related forms in *Modern Industrial Man* and *Man Released from the Mechanistic to the Creative Life.* Jacquelynn Baas, "*The Epic of American Civilization:* The Mural at Dartmouth College (1932–34)," *José Clemente Orozco in the United States, 1927–1934,* Renato González Mello and Diane Miliotes, eds. (New York: Norton and Hood Museum of Art, Dartmouth College, 2002), 142–85.

105. Jane Dudley, "The Mass Dance," *New Theatre* (December 1934), 17–18.

106. Noguchi, *Sculptor's World,* 21.

107. Quoted in "Noguchi the Sculptor; Acclaimed for Stage Settings and Designs for Ballet," *Art Voices from Around the World* (December 1962), 20–21.

108. Noguchi Cummings interview, AAA.

2 | Envisioning History

1. The mural, begun in August 1934, was completed by January 21, 1935, when the artists signed the visitors' book and departed; author's interview with Arq. Eugenio Mercado López, then-director of the Museo Regional Michoacano de Morelia (its current name), Morelia, Mexico, May 28, 1998. Handwritten data, Reuben Kadish Papers, Archives of American Art, Smithsonian Institution (hereafter AAA) confirms these dates and indicates the total cost of materials as $60 (210 pesos). Mercado López relates that Lic. Antonio Arriaga, 1940s head of the museum, ordered the mural covered with coarse cotton cloth mounted on a frame and painted in order to gain wall space for anthropological and historical exhibits, and to protect the mural from destruction by radical religious groups, such as the Cristeros. He conjectures that the museum was unable to obtain from the archbishop a huge eighteenth-century painting depicting an important event in local religious history, *El traslado de las monjas dominicas a su nuovo convento,* until this mural was removed from view. Mercado López, "*La Inquisicion:* Un mural del Museo Regional Michoacano de Morelia, Michoacán, México," July 2001 (unpublished manuscript); revised for *Acento: Seminario de la Cultura, La Voz de Michoacán,* year 11, no. 584, May 12, 2004, 2–5. Photographs of the patio before the mural's rediscovery in 1973 by workers fixing a humidity problem show what appears to be a flat white wall. Tests on the fresco performed in 2005 by conservators Maura Kelly and Krystal Saltmeyer indicate that whitewash was applied in at least in some areas. Author's interview with David McKee, New York, June 9, 2005.

2. "On a Mexican Wall," *Time,* April 1, 1935, 46, 48. All quotations identified as from *Time* are in this article.

3. In addition to Anita Brenner, *Idols Behind Altars* (New York: Payson and Clarke, 1929) and Octavio Paz, *The Labyrinth of Solitude: Life and Thought in Mexico,* Lysander Kamp, trans. (New York: Grove, 1961), see Wallace Thompson, *The Mexican Mind: A Study of National Psychology* (Boston: Little, Brown, 1922); Samuel Ramos, *Profile of Man and Culture in Mexico,* Peter G. Earle, trans. (Austin: University of Texas Press, 1963); Roger Bartra, *The Cage of Melancholy: Identity and Metamorphosis in the Mexican Character* (New Brunswick, N.J.: Rutgers University Press, 1992).

4. Langsner to Kadish, letter of March 30, 1938, Kadish Papers, AAA. Information on Langsner: obituary, *Los Angeles Times,* October 2, 1967; biographical statements, Jules Langsner Papers, AAA and http://www.aaa.si.edu/collections/jules-langsner-papers-9117/more.

5. Fletcher Martin, "Retrospective Notes About My Friendship with Philip," typescript, Dore Ashton Papers, AAA, calls them "angry young men."

6. Reuben's family background: Frank Kadish, *In Search of Samuel Kadish: A Genealogical Journey* (Phoenix: Privately published, c. 1999), 3–5. Born Samuel Schuster, May 15, 1885, their father was raised in Kovno, now Lithuania. Although Frank maintains that his family did not flee direct persecution, implications are incorporated into the Morelia mural of Samuel's association with the General Jewish Worker's Union (or Bund), "part of the nascent Marxist movement in Russia."

7. Phillip Goldstein was born June 27, 1913. See Musa Mayer, *Night Studio: A Memoir of Philip Guston by His Daughter* (New York: Alfred A. Knopf, 1988). Purportedly at Guston's behest, Dore Ashton in *Yes, But. . . : A Cultural Study of Philip Guston* (New York: Viking, 1976) never states that his birth name was Goldstein or that his parents were Jewish, although she mentions friends, including Kadish, "whose father had fled persecution after the Russian Revolution of 1905." Ashton writes vaguely, "Like most first-generation children, they fled the aroma of their parents' alien cultures, which faded into the background but were never entirely banished" (12). She comments, regarding Kafka, that "as remote as his experience was from the culture of Prague, Guston could identify with the Jewish artist working in an alien environment" (56). Given the Goldstein family's date of emigration, rumors of the affair in Odessa seem implausible.

8. Apparently referencing his father, Guston commented on

Joseph Brodsky's statement, "When a Russian refuses consolation, it means that things are bad, it means that there really is no consolation. . . .Without consolation, one can live only on love, memory and culture": "I feel such identity with this—I feel this is what my paintings are about in a way." Ashton, *Yes, But . . .* 177–78. As implied below in the concluding chapter, Guston's late paintings of piled-up refuse seem, at least in part, to reference Lieb Goldstein's fate.

9. Author's interview with Reuben Kadish, New York, May 2, 1979. Letters Guston sent to Kadish as late as 1937 are signed "Phill."

10. Post-Surrealism: Susan Ehrlich, ed., *Pacific Dreams: Currents of Surrealism and Fantasy in California Art, 1934–1957* (Los Angeles: UCLA at the Armand Hammer Museum of Art and Cultural Center, 1995); Michael Duncan, ed., *Post Surrealism* (Pasadena: Pasadena Museum of California Art, 2003). Guston and Kadish's relationship with Feitelson was somewhat equivocal because he was a right-wing ideologue who delivered weekly red-baiting speeches over the airwaves during the Depression. While admiring their mentor's works and aesthetic acumen, they did not endorse his reactionary politics. Feitelson stopped including them in Post-Surrealist exhibitions because of their leftist leanings. A letter from Morelia dated December 11, 1934, indicates respect nevertheless: "After having seen the works of the so called masters of the 'Mexican Renaissance' and met and spoken to the very masters themselves, we can evaluate your value to painting with clearer heads than ever before. In true earnestness we say that you are the master over them all. Of course we knew this before, but now we have a surer right to speak, for we have seen and are able to judge with more competent equipment." Lorser Feitelson Papers, AAA; Diane Degasis Moran, "The Painting of Lorser Feitelson," Ph.D. diss., University of Virginia, 1979, 112. Arthur Millier, "Time Magazine Errs," *Los Angeles Times*, April 7, 1935, indicates that Guston and Kadish protested "sneering remarks devoted to Feitelson" in *Time*.

11. According to painter Stephen Greene, after he and Guston watched films about the concentration camps at the University of Iowa, "much of our talk was about the holocaust and how to allegorize it." Ashton, *Yes, But . . .* 74. Literary enthusiasms: Dore Ashton, "Parallel Worlds: Guston as Reader," in Michael Auping, ed., *Philip Guston Retrospective* (New York: Thames and Hudson in association with Modern Art Museum of Fort Worth, 2003), 83–91.

12. William Corbett, *Philip Guston's Late Work: A Memoir* (Cambridge, Mass.: Zoland, 1994), 45. On his late works: "The Jewishness he masked in naming himself Guston is one such old and intimate presence he pulled up from the deepening well of his imagination" (64). Corbett verifies: "Guston often characterized himself as a victim, willingly at the mercy of images that came from the blue as he painted through the night" (56). Babel: authors' comments, Harold Bloom, ed., *Modern Critical Views: Isaac Babel* (New York: Chelsea House, 1987).

13. First quote: Mark Stevens, "A Talk with Philip Guston," *New Republic* 182, March 15, 1980, 26. Second: Renee McKee, ed., "Philip Guston Talking," transcript, March 1978 lecture, University of Minnesota, *Philip Guston Paintings, 1969–1980* (London: Whitechapel Art Gallery, 1982), 52.

14. Daniel Bell, "Reflections on Jewish Identity," *Commentary* 31 (1961), 471, 476. Motives in rejecting Goldstein name: Mayer, *Night Studio*, 21–24, 228–29; Corbett, *Guston's Late Work*, 60–61.

15. Los Angeles in 1920s and '30s: Carey McWilliams, *Southern California: An Island on the Land* (Santa Barbara: Peregrine Smith, 1973). Articles decrying West Coast aberrant right-wing behaviors: Herbert Klein and Carey McWilliams, "Cold Terror in California," *Nation* 161 (July 24, 1935), 97–98; Lillian Symes, "California, There She Stands!" *Harper's* 170 (February 1935), 366. Symes: "It was like this, I imagine in Rome in 1922, in Berlin in 1932."

16. This would have predated better-known New York shows mentioned in Chapter 1. Destruction of "a dozen or more" Hollywood John Reed Club panels: Grace Clements, "A Letter from the West," *Art Front* 2 (February 1936), 2.

17. Oral History Interview with Harold Lehman Conducted by Stephen Polcari, March 28, 1997, AAA, http://www.aaa.si.edu/collections/interviews/oral-history-interview-harold-lehman-12894: "We had at our disposal this shed [behind the home of Angelica Arénal who would later become Siqueiros's wife], which we used for the fresco paintings. . . . The frescoes and the frames were about four by six feet . . . they were done in cement, and they were very heavy. Each painting was hardly able to be lifted. We learned how to construct these things up to the finished surface of the fresco paintings. And we painted these things in a group—we each had our own sets of the paint—but we painted them together along the wall. We would line one up after another. And each of us had a subject to paint, in fact we had two subjects to paint. One was the exploitation of labor by capital in America, and the other was the persecution of the Blacks, or at that time whom [*sic*] we called the Negro in America: those two subjects. So we each painted frescoes on each one of those subjects. I did too."

18. While the frescos for *Negro America* were in preparation, circumventing NAACP efforts, the Communist Party's International Labor Defense Committee convinced top New York litigator Samuel Liebowitz to take up the cause of the Scottsboro Boys. Despite startling new evidence of innocence presented in their second trial, the prosecution successfully appealed to the jury not to allow "Jew money" from the North to influence Alabama justice. See James Goodman, *Stories of Scottsboro* (New York: Vintage, 1994). Since they were crusaders for social equality (many Jewish and some, like Kadish, emulating radicalized fathers), the Hollywood John Reed Club collaborators would likely have identified with and cheered on Liebowitz's efforts.

19. Photographs of some *Negro America* murals: Kadish Papers,

AAA. In James Oles, "Walls to Paint On: American Muralists in Mexico, 1933–1936," Ph.D. diss., Yale University, 1995, 326, n. 35, the author states, "No concrete evidence of Kadish's participation [in this show] has been documented." Most of the photos in Kadish's Papers are, however, identified by artist, including his own lynched black man hanging from a tree pictured with a bent white-robed figure (see fig. 30). Luis Arénal depicted an African-American and a white man in overalls, striding arm in arm. The artist showing a black "boy" set aflame is not identified. For Lehman's shackled African-American man kneeling before two columns, see *Analogy: Labor-Capital:* Laurance P. Hurlburt, *The Mexican Muralists in the United States* (Albuquerque: University of New Mexico Press, 1989), 216. Murray Hantman, *Free the Scottsboro Boys: International Literature* 3 (March 1935), 107. Its picture after the raid and Guston's damaged panel: "Where Vandals Wrecked Paintings," *Los Angeles Illustrated Daily News*, February 13, 1933 (see fig. 31). Another Los Angeles newspaper article appearing on July 15, 1933, relates some details of the suit brought against the city for $5,200 on behalf of the John Reed Club and the "Bloc of Painters" artists' organization. Hantman's damaged mural is illustrated, as is another captioned, "This picture of a convict tied around an iron post was brought to court to indicate how the painting appeared before it was damaged by raiders, according to the plaintiffs. Harry Buchanan testified that he hid behind a curtain and watched. He declared that raiders took art works and hurled them in a pile on the floor." I thank Irene Herner for access to this dated but otherwise unidentified article discovered by Luis Garza.

20. Langsner's quote: letter to Kadish, March 30, 1938, Kadish Papers, AAA.

21. Kadish, interviewed June 1991, in Oles, "Walls to Paint On," 330.

22. Lehman, Oral History Interview:

> I still have a card, a linoleum card done by Arenal, which he announces the Bloc of Painters Exhibit. The first exhibit at the John Reed Club, but that's a little ahead. We did these frescoes, and were now planning to exhibit them, and it was arranged that it would be exhibited at the John Reed Club in Hollywood. A truck came and took them up to the location, and this was on a Friday. The exhibit was supposed to start on a Saturday. Friday night I get a phone call, it might have been Kadish. I get a phone call, and the voice says "Harold, don't bother to come to John Reed tomorrow, there won't be any exhibit." "Why?" I ask. "Because they're all destroyed. The frescoes have been destroyed by the Red Squad." Sure enough, I went up to see and there they were laying all over the floor.

23. "Decidedly 'Red'": Arthur Millier, "Brushstrokes," *Los Angeles Times,* February 10, 1935, Part II, 10. Kadish stated that, on another occasion, "The papers wrote about us, saying we were 'misguided individuals committing themselves to Commu-

nism'": Jeffrey Potter, *To a Violent Grave: An Oral Biography of Jackson Pollock* (New York: G. P. Putnam's Sons, 1985): 49. Lehman, Oral History Interview:

> So we sued the Red Squad, the Police, for this action, and they took the thing to court. And we had one among us in our group, an older fellow who had come from New York. He was appointed spokesman for us, because he was mature, and he had a coat, a regular suit, so he could appear as a witness, and make a nice impression; he was an artist. So they put him on the stand, and the opposing lawyers, the ones for the police, started to accuse him. He had photographs of all the frescoes. So this independent lawyer had the photos in his hand and would present them one after the other to our witness saying, "How much is this fresco worth?" The witness would give a price, and he would go on to a second and a third, until he got through all twelve, he got through all of them. When he got through with the photos, he wouldn't lay them aside on the table, he simply put them underneath the pile. Now, he got to the end, but the first one came up again, and he presented them all over again to our witness, and "How much is this fresco worth?" Our witness now gives a different sum. Whereas the first time, he said the painting was worth three-hundred dollars, this time he would say five-hundred dollars. "Oh?" said the defense lawyer, "I thought it was worth only three-hundred dollars, that's what you said a moment ago, and it was in the transcript. He was demolished as an expert witness and the case was thrown at [*sic*]. And what was the judgment of the court? It was a judge and no jury. And the judge said that he dismissed the case because he felt that these frescoes were destroyed by parties unknown, possibly the artists themselves for the publicity. That was the verdict.

24. Guston's Stanley Rose exhibition was positively reviewed by Arthur Millier in "Two Pairs of Painters and Some Singles Offer Shows," *Los Angeles Times*, September 17, 1933, sec. II, 5, Ferdinand Perret Papers, AAA: "Goldstein is precociously clever. After experimenting with bold distortions of the figure—jazzing Michelangelo so to speak—he paints his large picture of three Ku Klux Klan members preparing to do 'justice.' Not a face is shown, nor any victim; but by strong arrangement of forms, lines and tones and a gravely beautiful color scheme, he builds a dignified picture which expresses the menace of mob justice more convincingly than many printed pages could do. His architectural details aid the ominous feel of this interesting painting." Medieval inquisition hat: Guston, handwritten note, June 1973, Ashton Papers, AAA.

25. Herman Baron, unpublished "History of the A.C.A. Gallery," A.C.A. Gallery Papers, AAA. The Klan and Jews: Bram Dijkstra, *American Expressionism: Art and Social Change, 1920–1950* (New York: Abrams for the Columbus Museum of Art, 2003), 138.

26. Arthur Millier, *Los Angeles Times*, September 18, 1932, Part III, 16: "A third fresco by Siqueiros is now in progress, this time in the auditorium of the John Reed Club in Hollywood. The four walls are to be covered by a mural symbolic of the cultural role of the Club. . . . The work will be done, as with Chouinard and the Plaza Art Center, by a class of students working with the Mexican." *Time* states that one of the Morelia artists (i.e.,Kadish) "had helped Siqueiros finish a fine fresco in the Workers' Cultural Center in Los Angeles two years before," a probable reference to the Reed Club auditorium mural, not the Workers' Alliance Center mural discussed below. Oles states that Kadish recalled images of the Klan in this composition.

27. Steven M. Gelber, "The Irony of San Francisco's 'Commie Art': An Artistic and Political Appraisal," *City of San Francisco* 10 (February 4, 1976), 37: California New Deal art was generally productive of "patriotic, nationalist, economically conservative images that based an unreal present on an artificial past." The only published discussion of L.A. Workers' Alliance Center fresco is Millier's negative review, "Communists Incited to Stir Up Trouble Through Artists' Propaganda-Paintings," *Los Angeles Times*, August 26, 1934, Part II, 1, 3. Oles, "Walls to Paint On," 332, n. 54, cites confusion over Kadish's references to this project, incorrectly surmised as references to the aborted John Reed Club Scottsboro protest exhibition planned for the prior year. Millier critiqued *Negro America* frescos as Communist propaganda: "No matter how brilliant such work may sometimes be, its merit as art is no justification for its preservation." An October 4, 1934, letter from Mexico includes Guston's tart instructions to Harold Lehman, "I have plans for killing Millier when I get to L.A. So leave him alone. I want the pleasure of shooting him." Ashton and Kadish Papers, AAA.

28. Guston's comments on Rivera: letter to Lehman, July 14, 1934 (Ashton and Kadish Papers, AAA). Getting to Mexico in a jalopy (Kadish to Ashton, March 9, 1973): Ashton, *Yes, But . . .* 30–31. Experiences in Mexico prior to Morelia: Oles, "Walls to Paint On," 335–36. Kadish told Ashton of "a little trouble" at the end of their stay: "Called up before governor [Benigno Serrato]. We came back to L.A." He told Oles they had to leave because of Langsner's amorous dalliance with a Mexican official's wife.

29. See Chapter 1, n. 15. "Modern Florence": Guston, letter to Lehman, July 14, 1934. He writes of Mexico, "Here a painter is judged only by his political content, the other things (plastique, comp[osition?] etc.) is not secondary, but unimportant! Some country." "To make a long story short, Rivera told us about some available walls in a smaller city called Morelia in state of Michoacan (look it up, you dope!). It is a lovely old city centered around the university." Guston writes, October 4, 1934, that Orozco visited Morelia and liked their fresco: "It was quite a shock to meet him—so diff[erent] than one would expect him to be." Ashton and Kadish Papers, AAA. Oles discusses Ludins's ill-fated mural in Morelia: "Walls to Paint On," 118–92; Ludins's useful memoir: "Painting Murals in Michoacán," *Mexican Life* 11 (May 1935), 22–23.

30. Marjorie Becker, *Setting the Virgin on Fire: Lázaro Cárdenas, Michoacán Peasants, and the Redemption of the Mexican Revolution* (Berkeley: University of California Press, 1995).

31. In a letter of October 4, 1934, Guston explains to Lehman that the mural will be half completed in two or three more plasterings, noting that he and Kadish are making other paintings on the side to earn money. He had sold one to the local president of the PNR (a political party), and he had recently finished a portrait of a local magistrate: "Just a huge head four feet high. Plenty of fat on this boy, too." Kadish did a portrait of a "local playboy"; Guston adds, "We must live." Guston later identified his sitter as Manuel Moreno Sanchez, a local judge and friend of Gustavo Corona's, also editor of a poetry magazine to which Guston contributed (see fig. 33). He writes to Kadish, October 13, 1964: "I'm sure it's the same Manuel Moreno Sanchez—just think if he becomes 'el Presidente' we can say we used to go a whoring with the President of Mexico! Remember that huge 6' portrait head I painted": Kadish Papers, AAA. Oles, "Walls to Paint On," 340–41, postulates the portrait may have been a commission for the state Supreme Court, although its Botero-like style is not in keeping with official portrait conventions. I thank Musa Mayer for access in Guston's papers to a photograph of this painting, whereabouts unknown. Guston also mentions to Lehman that he gave a large canvas to Corona "that constitutes my '*obras hasta ahora.*'" In his files is a photo of a work depicting two masked actors with musical instruments, one dressed as harlequin, identified in Guston's handwriting, "In the Collection of Sr. Lic. Gustavo Corona. Rio de la Piedad #214 Interiór 14. Mexico D.F."

32. Benjamin Molina, "El Fresco de Kadish y Goldstein," *La Atalaya*, Año 1, February 16, 1935. I thank Mercado López and David McKee for access to all three installments of this article and Jay Landau for translation assistance. Mercado López on Molina's possible role as assistant: Author's interview, May 1998; Mercado López, "*La Inquisición,*" 4. Based on his name, Molina may have been Jewish.

33. Undated letter, Sande McCoy to Kadish, likely refers to this element of the mural: "The kinesthetic problem you are working on is an interesting one—more mural painters might do well to consider things of that nature when attacking a wall." This was probably written before October 4, 1934; on that date, Guston tells Lehman, "Sandy [*sic*] wrote us from New York and says nobody there is doing the kind of stuff all of us are doing." Kadish Papers, AAA.

34. Guston's letter describing polyangularity, July 14, 1924; its description of Siqueiros's *Plastic Exercise*: Ashton, *Yes, But . . .* 31–32. Guston: "Let me tell you how stunning this is. Siqueiros did everything with an air gun. The painting in itself may be full of shit, but he's experimenting with kinetics! . . . This is truly an innovation. But he waves his hand and merely considers it a plastic exercise!" Irene Herner, *Siqueiros from Para-*

dise to Utopia (Mexico City, 2010), 275. Their bound female figure to the right of the hurtling giant was likely inspired by the heavy plasticity of Siqueiros's *Proletarian Victim*, a 1933 portable mural.

35. A handwritten diagram, labeled "Detail from Mural in Museo Michoacana, Morelia, Mich. Mexico 1934," was sent by the artists to Los Angeles photographer Floyd Faxon, along with an in situ photograph showing the next section over. This shows the three men depicted on ladders eventually located above the hurtling giant. It appears partially finished, with the next figure over blocked in. Their diagram indicates that so far only the lamentation scene above the balcony was complete. Inscription: "This photo is from the middle top section—the other section will be ready next week. The part painted is about 16' high. Thus the figures are about twelve feet or twice life size." Other in situ photographs indicate that both ends were painted prior to the middle. Kadish Papers, AAA.

36. Which artist was responsible for what sections remains in question. In later years, as in *Time*, both professed not to recall. (After the 1930s, Guston did not publicly acknowledge his participation until Ashton's biography in 1976.) Comparison with their jointly created, but less polemical mural *The Physical Growth of Man*, painted August 15, 1935, to July 24, 1936, under Federal Art Project sponsorship, for the library of the Jewish Consumptive and Expatients Relief Association's Los Angeles Sanitorium and Expatients Home (now the City of Hope National Medical Center, Duarte, California), and with other works, each made separately both immediately before and after Mexico, can provide important clues. For example, the upper right figures in Morelia carrying Communist symbols exhibit the more generalized forms characteristic of Kadish, while the deeply shaded and muscular pietà figure and hurtling man represent Guston's more typical style. A photo of Guston posing on a scaffold next to the hooded priest with dagger and book seems to confirm his responsibility for the Klan-related figures. Oles asked Ashton and Francis V. O'Connor for their opinions. Both leaned toward Kadish as responsible for structure, technique, and overall design, with Guston the probable primary initiator of specific iconographical concepts, and I concur. "Walls to Paint on," 343–44. Nat Goldstein's death from gangrene: Mayer, *Night Studio*, 17.

37. *Time* concludes its negative critique of Feitelson's impact on the Morelia mural thus: "Fortunately, Reuben Kadish and Phillip Goldstein took nothing but their technique from New Classicist Feitelson." But the artists told Arthur Millier ("Time Magazine Errs"): "*Time* ignored 'the culminating panel of our fresco, done in this very New Classicist manner.'" Kadish writing to Feitelson, December 11, 1934, requests "some material on composition as applied to sur-realism" in order to "introduce one section painted along sur-realist concepts" (Feitelson Papers, AAA). Langsner would write a Post-Surrealist manifesto for the group's second exhibition at the Stanley Rose Bookshop, May 1935.

38. Guston to Lehman, July 14, 1934: "We are getting a huge staircase [*sic*] in the Museum here to paint, and the wall has excellent problems, the only disadvantage is that there is much saltpeter in the walls." A c. 1936 letter from Guston to Kadish confirms damage to this area as almost immediate; their friend Doris Rosenthal had just visited Morelia and described the saltpeter as "very bad mostly on the lower left of the fresco." Kadish Papers, AAA.

39. Mercado López incorrectly surmises that the tacked-up cartoon shows indigenous people being burned on the feet by Catholic priests. Although it is unknown who copied the cartoon, Kadish probably painted the fallen colossal head. Ralph Stackpole, "Reuben Kadish," *California Arts and Architecture* 58 (April 1941), 21, remarks that Kadish had "some delight in the busted heads of Greek statues, appearing often crushed and shattered."

40. See the exhibition catalogue *Medieval Justice: The Trial of the Jews of Trent* (New York: Yeshiva University Museum, 1989); R. Po-Chia Hsia, *Trent 1475: Stories of a Ritual Murder Trial* (New Haven: Yale University Press in cooperation with Yeshiva University Library, 1992); "Blood Libel": *The Encyclopedia Judaica* (Jerusalem: Keter, 1972), 4: 1120–31. Kunne's woodcut images: Eric Zafran, "The Iconography of AntiSemitism: A Study of the Representation of the Jews in the Visual Arts of Europe, 1400–1600," Ph.D. diss., Institute of Fine Arts, New York University, 1973; Lamberto Donati, *L'inizio della stampa a Trento ed il Beato Simone* (Trent: Collana Edizioni del Centro Culturale, 1968); Dana Katz, *The Jew in the Art of the Italian Renaissance* (Philadelphia: University of Pennsylvania Press, 2008); David S. Areford, *The Viewer and the Printed Image in Late Medieval Europe* (Farnham, U.K.: Ashgate, 2010).

41. Michoacán trial of Gonzalo Gómez: Richard E. Greenleaf, *The Mexican Inquisition of the Sixteenth Century* (Albuquerque: University of New Mexico Press, 1969), 45–73.

42. Donati describes Scene 11 of Kunne's folio: "Seven Jews, accused for the death of Simon, were convicted by the court and were to be burned alive. The scene represents the execution. In the presence of three magistrates, they have been placed on wooden supports under which an executioner lights the fire. Moses, an old man of eighty years, died during the trial, but was also subjected to torture" (trans. Michael Morford). The only book illustrating Scene 11 of Kunne's 1475 Trent series published before 1934 and therefore Guston and Kadish's probable source: Georg Hermann Theodor Liebe, *Das Judentum in der deutschen Vergangenheit* (Leipzig: E. Diederichs, 1903). Hooded monks rooting out Jewish heretics: Jeremy Cohen, *The Friars and the Jews: The Evolution of Medieval Anti-Judaism* (Ithaca: Cornell University Press, 1982).

43. Guston, August 25, 1974, letter, Ashton Papers, AAA; Mayer, *Night Studio*, 12.

44. It is unclear whether Langsner provided *Time*'s title, *The Workers' Struggle for Liberty*, or if it was inferred from his

description. Langsner's role as PR flack: interview with Kadish in Oles, "Walls to Paint On." Although *The Struggle Against War and Fascism* is used in *South of the Border: Mexico in the American Imagination, 1914–1947* (Washington, D.C.: Smithsonian Institution Press, 1993), 198–201, Oles suggests the artists adopted this title retroactively in response to the Popular Front, stating in "Walls to Paint On" that he prefers *Time*'s title. Millier, in "Brushstrokes," employs *The Struggle Against Terrorism*. Mexican title: Mercado López, *Acento*, 2–5. The preferred Mexican title, *La Inquisicion*, correlates with *Time*'s description of the iconography where "Medieval" and "Modern Inquisition" are terms used to narrate the fresco's range. "Finding Aid to the Kadish Papers, AAA" incorrectly refers to the mural as *The Triumph of Good over Evil.*

45. *A Dissertation on Alchemy*, San Francisco State College Science Hall, painted December 15, 1936, to August 15, 1937: Stackpole, "Reuben Kadish," 20–21; data in Kadish Papers, AAA. Duarte joint mural: Francis V. O'Connor, "Philip Guston and Political Humanism," *Art and Architecture in the Service of Politics*, Henry A. Millon and Linda Nochlin, eds. (Cambridge, Mass.: MIT Press, 1978), 340–54; Susanne Muchnic, "The Shock of the Old," *Los Angeles Times*, June 7, 1998.

46. Alain Finkielkraut, *Le juif imaginaire* (Paris: Editions du Seuil, 1980), translated by Kevin O'Neill and David Suchoff as *The Imaginary Jew* (Lincoln: University of Nebraska Press, 1994), 7–8. As Guston and Kadish did in Morelia, Finkielkraut expressed his distinctly Jewish dilemma with a Christian signifier of pain and redemption, writing, "The calvary of my people gave my life a prestige and a beauty that I would have been unable to discover in its own unfolding." Christ's crucifixion adopted by Jewish artists: Ziva Amishai-Maisels, "The Jewish Jesus," *Journal of Jewish Art* 9 (1982), 84–104.

47. Morton Feldman, "Philip Guston: The Last Painter," *Art News Annual XXXI 1966* (October 1965), 99; emphasis added.

48. Ross Feld, *Guston in Time: Remembering Philip Guston* (New York: Counterpoint, 2003), 83.

49. Whether Guston's late works are "figurative": Robert Slifkin, "Philip Guston's Return to Figuration and the '1930s Renaissance' of the 1960s," *Art Bulletin* 92 (June 2011), 220–42.

50. Remark to Feld, September 1978 letter: "Guston in Time," *Arts Magazine* 63 (November 1988), 43; Guston's emphasis retained. Leon Trotsky was born Lev Davidovich Brunshtein; Vladimir Ilyich Lenin was one-eighth Jewish, a fact suppressed by the Bolsheviks.

51. Marianne Hirsch, *Family Frames: Photography, Narrative, and Postmemory* (Cambridge, Mass.: Harvard University Press, 1997), 22–23. Discussing children of Holocaust survivors, Hirsch states, "Postmemory characterizes the experience of those who grow up dominated by narratives that preceded their birth, whose own belated stories are . . . shaped by traumatic events that can neither be understood nor recreated." As a result, past and present "disturbingly intersect." Although in 1934–35 Guston and Kadish could not have known the extent of Nazi Jewish persecution, their parents' experience with pogroms was a rehearsal for the Final Solution. Guston's later fixation with the concentration camps (n. 11) confirms his deep feelings about World War II genocide of the Jews. Piled-up shoes and limbs in many of Guston's late paintings have been interpreted in a Holocaust context as well as a reference to his father's vocation as a rag seller.

3 | Reinventing Muralism

1. Author's interview with Lee Krasner, New York, July 18, 1979. Krasner's Trotskyite sympathies and friendship with anti-Stalinist critic Clement Greenberg played a role in her antipathy to Siqueiros. Also, the Mexicans were considered "the enemy" at the Hans Hofmann School of Fine Arts, where she had studied.

2. The extent of Pollock's political commitment has never been verified. In addition to attending Communist Party meetings with Guston, while working on the WPA he and his brother Sande signed a petition to have the Communist Party put on the ballot in New York, an action they instantly regretted. A 1944 postcard to Herbert and Mercedes Matter in Los Angeles does seem to confirm Jackson's leftist sympathies: "I have a brother at 901 E Hyde Park, Inglewood. If you're able to get around look him up, and I'll tell him to do the same—he's a swell guy and politically left—I feel he supports me in that direction." Collection of Alex Matter, courtesy Mark Borghi. In "Orozco and Pollock: Epic Transfigurations," *American Art* (Summer 1992), 40, Stephen Polcari characterizes Pollock's politics as "at best of the parlor and not the activist variety." See also Michael Leja's introduction to *American Letters, 1927–1947: Jackson Pollock and Family* (Cambridge: Polity, 2011), xvi–xxiv.

3. B. H. Friedman, *Jackson Pollock: Energy Made Visible* (New York: McGraw-Hill, 1972), 29.

4. Praising Pollock as not "afraid to look ugly," Greenberg opined, "all profoundly original art looks ugly at first." "Art: Review of Exhibitions of Mondrian, Kandinsky, and Pollock," *Nation*, April 7, 1945. The following year Greenberg commented that "in the course of time, this ugliness will become a new standard of beauty": "Review of Exhibitions of the American Abstract Artists, Jacques Lipchitz, and Jackson Pollock," *Nation*, April 13, 1946. See John O'Brian, *Clement Greenberg: Collected Essays and Criticism* (Chicago: University of Chicago Press, 1986), 2: 17, 74. "'American-Type' Painting," *Partisan Review* 22 (Spring 1955), O'Brian, *Collected Essays*, 3: 225. Greenberg on Pollock: Caroline A. Jones, *Eyesight Alone: Clement Greenberg's Modernism and the Bureaucratization of the Senses* (Chicago: University of Chicago Press, 2005), 205–302; on Siqueiros, 225–26.

5. See elsewhere in endnotes for authors giving this topic attention, especially Francis V. O'Connor, Stephen Polcari, Robert

Storr, and contributors to *Siqueiros/Pollock; Pollock/Siqueiros*, a catalogue published by the Städtische Kunsthalle, Düsseldorf (1995) for an exhibition organized by Jürgen Harten. The latter is responsible for piquing my interest in the Mexican impact on American artists.

6. Irene Herner, *Siqueiros from Paradise to Utopia* (Mexico City: Ministry of Culture of the City of Mexico, 2010). Also Peter Wollen, "Männerkunst: Siqueiros und Pollock," *Siqueiros/Pollock; Pollock/Siqueiros*, Jürgen Harten, ed. (Düsseldorf: Städtische Kunsthalle and DuMont Buchverlag, 1995), 2: 55–66.

7. Stephen Polcari, "Review: Siqueiros and Pollock, Düsseldorf," *Burlington Magazine* 138 (April 1996), 274.

8. Selden Rodman, *Conversations with Artists* (New York: Devin-Adair, 1957), 82.

9. Ann Gibson, "The Rhetoric of Abstract Expressionism," *Abstract Expressionism: The Critical Developments*, Michael Auping, ed. (Buffalo, N.Y.: Albright-Knox Art Gallery, and New York: Abrams), 71.

10. Lawrence Alloway, *Paintings, Drawings, and Watercolours from the Collection of Lee Krasner Pollock* (London: Marlborough Fine Art, 1961), n.p., entry 17.

11. Reuben Kadish, letter to author, March 22, 1987: "As you know Jackson worked with Benton on the New School murals. Orozco was also on a mural job at the school—by this time there was a very decided interest in the Mexican mural movement in the U.S.—While Rivera was on the fringe and Siqueiros was known but mostly via Anita Brenner—Orozco was the most admired and heralded figure among the artists—Jackson was often enthusiastic but reserved—but did go way overboard on the 'Prometheus' at Pomona College—and it sure does show in his painting as he began to make the bridge from Benton into his own idiom. There was more than one painting and many drawings that show that stamp—No question. Orozco was a major influence."

12. Comparative discussion: Polcari, "Epic Transfigurations," 36–57; Ellen G. Landau, *Jackson Pollock* (New York: Abrams, 1989), 47–56. Orozco's North American murals: Laurance P. Hurlburt, *The Mexican Muralists in the United States* (Albuquerque: University of New Mexico Press, 1989), 13–87; Marjorie L. Harth, ed., *José Clemente Orozco: Prometheus* (Claremont, Calif.: Pomona College Museum of Art, 2001); Alejandro Anreus, *Orozco in Gringoland: The Years in New York* (Albuquerque: University of New Mexico Press, 2001); Anna Indych-López, *Muralism Without Walls: Rivera, Orozco, and Siqueiros in the United States, 1927–1940* (Pittsburgh: University of Pittsburgh Press, 2009); *Men of Fire: José Clemente Orozco and Jackson Pollock* (Hanover, N.H.: Hood Museum of Art, Dartmouth College, and University Press of New England, 2012).

13. Guarding murals with guns: Wollen, "Männerkunst," 56; Steven Naifeh and Gregory White Smith, *Jackson Pollock: An American Saga* (New York: Clarkson N. Potter, 1989),

302: Pollock and Siqueiros scuffled under the table the night before his departure for Spain. Each was "silently attempting to choke the other into unconsciousness. Jack in a wild exhilarated effort and Siqueiros in a desperate attempt to save himself." See Axel Horn, "Jackson Pollock: The Hollow and the Bump," *Carleton Miscellany* 7 (Summer 1966), 87.

14. Friedman, *Jackson Pollock: Energy Made Visible;* Naifeh and Smith, *Jackson Pollock: An American Saga;* and Jeffrey Potter, *To a Violent Grave: An Oral Biography of Jackson Pollock* (New York: G. P. Putnam's Sons, 1985; hereafter *TVG*) discuss his Dr. Jekyll/Mr. Hyde personality, meek when sober and violent when drunk.

15. Naifeh and Smith, *Jackson Pollock: An American Saga*, 219, quoting Kadish. Pollock was apparently less impressed when he visited L.A. in 1932, saw the Chouinard School mural, and first met Siqueiros.

16. "Conservation of *América Tropical* by David Alfaro Siqueiros: A Joint Project of the Getty Conservation Institute and El Pueblo de Los Angeles Historical Monument: Project Fact Sheet," 1. Siqueiros called *Il Duco:* a play on Benito Mussolini's title *Il Duce* and the brand of industrial paint Siqueiros favored.

17. Shared high school experience of Pollock and Guston: Landau, *Pollock*, 24–25; Deborah Solomon, *Jackson Pollock: A Biography* (New York: Simon and Schuster, 1987), 37–43; Dore Ashton, *Yes, But . . . A Critical Study of Philip Guston* (Berkeley: University of California Press, 1976), 13–14. Their expulsion: Naifeh and Smith, *Jackson Pollock: An American Saga*, 134–36. Kadish comments: Potter, *TVG*, 49; Naifeh and Smith, 219.

18. Robert Storr, "A Piece of the Action," *Jackson Pollock: New Approaches*, Pepe Karmel, ed. (New York: Museum of Modern Art, 1999), 34–35. His endnotes indicate that Storr had access to an earlier version of this chapter: Ellen G. Landau, "Jackson Pollock und die Mexikaner," *Pollock/Siqueiros*, 2: 38–54. Storr notes correctly that underestimating the impact of Mexican art on Pollock was crucial to the shared agenda of Clement Greenberg, William Rubin (MoMA's former director of painting and sculpture), and Pollock's widow. Rubin's "Jackson Pollock and the Modern Tradition," *Artforum* 5 (February–May 1967) compares Pollock's classic poured pictures with Impressionism, Cubism, and Surrealism. He omits the impact of Siqueiros and Benton (the latter a main topic of heated exchange in *Artforum* with Francis V. O'Connor).

19. John Berger, *New Statesman* (London), November 22, 1956. Quoted in Francis V. O'Connor, *Jackson Pollock* (New York: Museum of Modern Art, 1967), 77.

20. Francis V. O'Connor and Eugene Victor Thaw, *Jackson Pollock: A Catalogue Raisonné of Paintings, Drawings and Other Works* (New Haven: Yale University Press, 1978), 4: 238; hereafter *JPCR*.

21. Benton was featured on the cover of *Time* magazine, December 24, 1934, in conjunction with an article by Alexander Eliot, "The U.S. Scene," helping to catapult the Regionalists (him-

self, Grant Wood, and John Steuart Curry) to national fame. Henry Adams, *Tom and Jack: The Intertwined Lives of Thomas Hart Benton and Jackson Pollock* (New York: Bloomsbury, 2009), 194–95.

22. Thomas Hart Benton, "The Mechanics of Form Organization in Painting, Part IV," *The Arts* 10 (February 1927), 95–96.

23. Personal and artistic relationship of Pollock and Benton: Adams, *Tom and Jack;* Naifeh and Smith, *Jackson Pollock: An American Saga;* Landau, *Pollock,* chapter 2; Stephen Polcari, "Jackson Pollock and Thomas Hart Benton" *Arts Magazine* 53 (March 1979), 120–24.

24. Greenberg: "Art: Review of Exhibitions of Jean Dubuffet and Jackson Pollock," *Nation,* February 1, 1947, *Collected Writings,* 2: 125. He states, "Pollock points a way beyond the easel, beyond the mobile, framed picture, to the mural, perhaps–or perhaps not. I cannot tell."

25. Hans Namuth, "Photographing Pollock," *Pollock Painting,* Barbara Rose, ed. (New York: Agrinde, 1980), n.p. Early publication of these photographs: Robert Goodnough, "Pollock Paints a Picture," *Art News* 50 (May 1951), 32–38; Hans Namuth, "Jackson Pollock," *Portfolio: The Annual of the Graphic Arts* (Cincinnati, 1951).

26. Horn, "The Hollow and the Bump," 86–87: "Spurred on by Siqueiros, whose energy and torrential flow of ideas stimulated us all to a high pitch of activity, everything became material for our investigation. . . . What emerged was an endless variety of accidental effects."

27. Harold Rosenberg, "The American Action Painters," *Art News* 51 (December 1952), 22–23, 48–50. See Chapter 5 for further discussion.

28. Asked in 1943 about the Surrealist émigrés in New York, Pollock answered, "I am particularly impressed with their concept of the source of art being the unconscious." This must have surprised his comrades from Siqueiros's 1936 experimental workshop. As Harold Lehman recalled, "To talk about Surrealism and the unconscious [was] absolutely diametrically opposed to everything Siqueiros stood for." Irene Herner and Jack Seligson, videotaped interview with Lehman, New Jersey, December 9, 1994.

29. Another theory holds that Pollock's true originality was based on an urge toward desublimation. Rather than marking transcendence, his was a more violent process of *bassesse,* or lowering, "going *beneath* the figure into the terrain of formlessness," a concept originated by Surrealist Georges Bataille. Rosalind Krauss, *The Optical Unconscious* (Cambridge, Mass.: MIT Press, 1993), 244, 276, 284.

30. Allan Kaprow, *Assemblages, Environments, and Happenings* (New York: Abrams, 1966), 10.

31. José Clemente Orozco, "New World, New Races, and New Art," *Creative Art* 4 (January 1929), 46.

32. Thomas Hart Benton, *An American in Art: A Professional and Technical Autobiography* (Lawrence: University Press of Kansas, 1973), 61. Benton qualified his praise of the Mexican school as "in spite of the Marxist dogmas, to the propagation of which so much of its work was devoted," adding that the "Mexican concern with publicly significant meanings and with the pageant of Mexican national life corresponded perfectly with what I had in mind for art in the United States." Orozco was the least Marxist of Los Tres Grandes.

33. Letter from Charles to Jackson Pollock, October 1929, recommending *Creative Art's* January 1929 article on Rivera and *The Arts* (October 1927) on Orozco. Jackson obtained the Rivera issue: letter to Charles and Frank, October 22, 1929. *American Letters,* 14, 16.

34. Solomon, *Jackson Pollock: A Biography,* 42–43.

35. Letter to Charles and Frank, October 22, 1929. *American Letters,* 16.

36. Will Barnet, telephone conversation with Alejandro Anreus, October 17, 1995; Anreus, *Orozco in Gringoland,* 35; Orozco's affiliation with Alma Reed and Delphic Studios, 21–46. Reed and Orozco were also romantically involved.

37. In *Siqueiros/Pollock,* 1: 154–55, *Composition with Donkey Head,* c. 1938–41 (*JPCR* 61) is compared to Orozco's panel, *Science, Labor, Art,* painted at the New School, 1930–31. The "transitions in an almost cubistic articulation of the surface at the right and left border" of Pollock's painting are described as similar to those in Orozco's panel.

38. E. S., "Orozco Blitzpaints Modern Museum Mural," *PM,* July 9, 1940, 20.

39. Alma Reed, "Orozco and Mexican Painting," *Creative Art* 9 (September 1931), 199–207. See Landau, *Pollock,* 47–48.

40. Dr. Joseph L. Henderson, "How a Disturbed Genius Talked to His Analyst with Art," *Medical World News,* February 5, 1971, 18–28; Landau, *Pollock,* chapter 3.

41. Hilton Kramer, "The Jackson Pollock Myth I," *The Age of the Avant-Garde: An Art Chronicle of 1956–1972* (New York: Farrar, Straus and Giroux, 1973), 335–38. Kramer did not mean this positively.

42. Naifeh and Smith, *Jackson Pollock: An American Saga,* 281. Their source: Ashton, *Yes, But . . .* 34, who presumably obtained her information from Guston.

43. Jackson wrote to Charles and Frank, October 22, 1929: "I became acquainted with Rivera's work through a number of Communist meetings I attended after being ousted from school last year. He has a painting in the Museum now. Perhaps you have seen it, Dia de Flores. I found the Creative Art January 1929 on Rivera. I certainly admire his work." *American Letters,* 16. By contrast, as we have seen, letters from Guston to Lehman indicate that he and Kadish, after seeing Rivera's murals in Mexican City, were less than impressed. Rivera's *Dia de Flores (Flower Day)* of 1925 is the type of work Siqueiros denigrated as "Mexican curious": "Diego Rivera, pintor 'Mexican curious,'" Taxco, 1931; Special Collections, Centro Nacional de las Artes, Mexico City; Herner, *Paradise to Utopia,* 115–23.

44. Robert Motherwell, "Jackson Pollock: An Artists' Symposium, Part I," *Art News* 66 (April 1967), 66.

45. Friedman, *Jackson Pollock: Energy Made Visible*, 29; Potter, *TVG*, 49. Sande wrote Charles in early 1939 that he had seen photos of Orozco's Guadalajara frescoes (probably at Delphic Studios): "Christ, what a brutal, powerful piece of painting. I think it would be safe to say that he is the only really vital, living painter." *American Letters*, 154. Pollock painted a circular Limoges porcelain bowl in enamels c. 1939 (*JPCR* 925) with a composition reflecting Orozco's *Man of Fire* mural, Instituto Cultural Cabañas in Guadalajara, 1938–39.

46. Naifeh and Smith, *Jackson Pollock: An American Saga*, 298. Busa recalled that Jackson kept a large reproduction of *Prometheus* prominently displayed in his studio in New York. Sculptor Tony Smith, a much later friend, reported to James Valliere in August 1965, "One time I asked [Jackson] what he thought was the greatest work of art in North America. He thought for a few minutes, then said, 'the Orozco fresco at Pomona College.'" Smith stated that Jackson remained "quite aware" of the Mexicans and "would allude to Mexico and the Southwest with a knowledge that struck me as Romantic." Valliere interviews, Pollock-Krasner House and Study Center, East Hampton, N.Y.

47. Harth, *José Clemente Orozco*, includes detailed discussion of this mural by a variety of art historians. See also "Orozco's Stylistic Evolution" in *An Artist in Art*, Jean Charlot, ed. (Honolulu: University Press of Hawaii, 1972); and *José Clemente Orozco in the United States, 1927–1934*, Renato González Mello and Diane Miliotes, eds. (Hanover, N.H., and New York: Hood Museum of Art and Norton, 2002).

48. Lisa Mintz Messenger, "Pollock Studies the Mexican Muralists and the Surrealists: Sketchbook III," *The Sketchbooks of Jackson Pollock* (New York: Metropolitan Museum of Art, 1998), 61–84. Trip to New Hampshire: Naifeh and Smith, *Jackson Pollock: An American Saga*, 298; Sarah G. Powers, "Introduction," *Men of Fire*, xi–xii.

49. Herner, *Paradise to Utopia*, 238, argues Pollock's reliance on Siqueiros for iconographic cues in *Head with Polygons*, c. 1938–41 (*JPCR* 66), postulating the geometric overlay in this work as Pollock's attempt to re-create effects in Siqueiros's diagrammatic mural *Plastic Exercise* that influenced Guston and Kadish. It is possible that the latter two showed images or described *Plastic Exercise* to Pollock later in New York.

50. Provenance: *JPCR*, 1: 46. Some scholars, including O'Connor (telephone conversation with author, December 30, 1987) suggest that this is a self-portrait, lending further credence to its interpretation as a matricide. As Guston was driven to inject the sad fates of his father and brother into *The Struggle Against Terrorism*, Pollock may have been motivated to personalize a universal theme. On *Naked Man with Knife* (*JPCR* 60) and both studies (*JPCR* 558 and 939): *Siqueiros/Pollock*, 1: 160–63. Storr, "A Piece of the Action," 56, also discusses these and points out that some aspects of Orozco's *Barricade* are reprised in *Black and White Painting III*, c. 1951 (*JPCR* 332).

51. Norman Bryson (referencing Jacques Derrida), *Tradition and Desire: From David to Delacroix* (Cambridge, Eng.: Cambridge University Press, 1984), 24.

52. Polcari, "Orozco and Pollock," 48–49 (reprinted in *Men of Fire*,9), explains that the central character in *Woman*, "old and wizened, with pendulous breasts and bright earrings, may have been inspired by Orozco's prints of prostitutes." Pollock, he states, approaches the Mexican's "caricaturish qualities": "In composition, *Woman* resembles Orozco's *Prometheus* and other works featuring a large figure surrounded by the masses of humanity." Polcari reads the central figure as "surrounded by several bald figures, mostly women, who seem to be of all ages." His differing analysis continues: "*Woman* has inspired many interpretations. If the woman is perceived as Pollock's image of a mordant Orozco prostitute, the work is a social critique. Or the woman may represent the life cycle, from nurturing woman to 'old hag.' The painting may also reflect the nurturing but fatal quality of a giant female force, in which case it may be a more troubled restatement of the mother nursing her child in *Two Landscapes with Figures* (1934–38, private collection), as well as an anticipation of the mythic theme explored in *She-Wolf* (1943, The Museum of Modern Art, New York)."

53. For instance, Gorky wrote about Lady Shushanik to his sister Vartoosh, November 2, 1946: "Mother's thoughts were so correct. So valid for so many things in life and especially nature. . . . She was the most aesthetically appreciative, the most poetically incisive master I have encountered in all my life. . . . Mother was a poetess of aesthetics. Mother was queen of the aesthetic domain." Karlen Mooradian, *The Many Worlds of Arshile Gorky* (Chicago: Gilgamesh, 1980), 309–10.

54. By contrast to Gorky, Sande wrote Charles in October 1941 that "part of [Jackson's] trouble (perhaps a large part) lies in his childhood relationships with his Mother in particular and family in general," adding that "it would be extremely trying and might be disastrous for him to see her at this time." *American Letters*, 178. A "source close to Henderson" (perhaps Henderson himself?) observed that it was obvious when Pollock talked that "there was a hell of a mother problem." Regarding LeRoy Pollock, Frank said, "Mother had him pretty well throttled," describing their father by middle-age as a "beaten man" (Potter, *TVG*, 21, 25–26.) Despite his young age, Jack seems to have understood his father's situation and become terrified that Stella would also siphon his manhood away. These feelings were later generalized to other women.

55. There is no access to records indicating whether any of the Mexican's prostitute pictures were on view at Delphic Studios around the time that Pollock painted *Woman*. He must have known Reed's article, "Orozco and Mexican Painting," *Creative Art* 9 (September 1931), 199–207.

56. The core of Bloom's widely discussed study *The Anxiety of Influence: A Theory of Poetry* (London: Oxford University Press, 1973) is his contention that misprision—the reading or understanding of the work of another which retains its

terms, but means them in another sense—provided a critical basis for modernist creativity. See Jonathan Weinberg, "Pollock and Picasso: The Rivalry and the Escape," *Arts Magazine* 61 (Summer 1987), 42–48. Bloom's hermeneutic is a valuable tool for measuring Pollock's emulation of Orozco, a rehearsal for his efforts to revise the "ratio of domination" between Picasso and himself.

57. Motherwell, in Potter, *TVG*, 99.

58. Sande is not mentioned among members of this class, "California Group Studies Fresco Technique with Siqueiros," *Art Digest* 7 (August 1932), 13. This article illustrates Siqueiros's Chouinard School mural, destroyed soon after completion, and quotes observations by Arthur Millier, art critic of the *Los Angeles Times:* "Siqueiros creates the most powerful forms that have yet come to us from [the] Mexican revolt. The effect of them is overwhelming. The paintings are dark and unframed. The massive forms and heads look out of an aura of black. The first impression is of brutality and dankness, of a complete absence of any 'charm'—that pleasant manipulation of pigment which means so much to the English and Americans. There is present, however, something else—that brooding sense of tragedy which exists where, century after century, the people of a race have repeated the same movements and gestures until the individual counts for little amid the long procession of types and gestures." In Potter, *TVG*, 49, Kadish recalls, "I had a car out there and carted Siqueiros around. Sande got acquainted with him that way and became the contact for Jack when Siqueiros became established in New York." Kadish states of the Mexican, "I was happy to do anything for him."

59. Title for this section: Horn, "The Hollow and the Bump," 86, cited in Storr, "Piece of the Action," 52: "The Mexicans . . . provided us with a direction away from the parochialism in which most of us had been caught. Being mural-minded, or wall-eyed as someone once said, Jack . . . was deeply stirred by the Mexican artists' ability to combine social revolutionary themes with a widespread public usage of their talents to create a new artistic language. . . . The possibilities inherent in the experimentation at the Siqueiros workshop offered [Pollock] a way out of his lack of technical facility."

60. Herner, *Paradise to Utopia*, 235, considers that Pollock condensed elements by Orozco and Siqueiros in *Bird:* "At the top center, Pollock recreated the eye of the eagle that appears in Siqueiros' mural; below it, the most dynamic area in *América Tropical* and Orozco's *Prometeo*. [W]here the waist of the crucified man in Siqueiros' painting seems to be surrounded by a concentric movement, Pollock painted two concentric circles. In addition, he also included the bird's wings and abstracted concentric forms inspired by the realist images of pre-Columbian sculptures that Siqueiros had painted on either side of the cross."

61. Pollock probably never viewed *América Tropical* in situ. Nevertheless, as Kadish states, "There is also no question about his knowing the work—he knew the wall. . . . But Jackson did not work on it or any other L.A. mural": Kadish 1987 letter to the author, 2–3. Photographs of *América Tropical* were exhibited at Delphic Studios in 1934. Kadish: Pollock "attended many museum shows—and no doubt with his interest saw most of what went on in N.Y. re the Mexicans." Shifra Goldman, "Siqueiros and Three Early Murals in Los Angeles," *Art Journal* 33 (Summer 1974), 327, n. 26, relates that Siqueiros mentioned Pollock's having been in L.A. in the summer of 1932. But Jackson writes to Sande, March 25, 1933, "The experience with Siqueiros must have been great—am anxious to see the job," suggesting he had no contact with *América Tropical* the previous year: *American Letters,* 46. See also Potter, *TVG*, 52; Naifeh and Smith, *Jackson Pollock: An American Saga*, 284–90.

62. Siqueiros believed that "in the visual arts material elements have a generic aesthetic expressive value stemming from them, blood of their blood. . . . The development of modern visual art production is based on this reality": 1934 document typed on letterhead from Hotel Albert, New York, Getty Research Institute. Irene Herner, "Siqueiros and Surrealism?" *Journal of Surrealism and the Americas* 1, nos. 1–2 (2009), 111.

63. Harold Lehman, "For an Artists Union Workshop," *Art Front* (October 1937) and David Alfaro Siqueiros, "How to Paint a Mural" (Ediciones Mexicanas, 1951), Jean Charlot, *The Mexican Mural Renaissance* (New Haven: Yale University Press, 1963), 117. Siqueiros explained that, in the U.S., he "faced unexpected physical realities which led me to conclude that all the techniques and methodologies of contemporary pictorial production are archaic and thus anachronistic. I learned that the process of pictorial technique, and of technique in general, is the fundamental premise of all transcendental artistic production. I learned that tools and artistic production processes had a generic value which fertilized artistic expression." Herner, *Paradise to Utopia,* 144.

64. David Alfaro Siqueiros, April 9, 1936, letter to María Asúnsolo, New York: *Palabras de Siqueiros,* Raquel Tibol and Ruth Solís, eds. (Mexico City: Fonda de Cultura Económica, 1996), 131–32; Herner, "Siqueiros and Surrealism?" 115.

65. Charles Pollock on the impact of Siqueiros workshop: letter to O'Connor, November 10, 1966: "I have always thought it to have been a key experience in Jackson's development. Amongst other things, the whole ambience was an antidote to regionalism; but it was so far-fetched and outlandish in the circumstance that in the end it only served to make social contact, whether provincial or revolutionary, a meaningless term for him. Nevertheless, the violation of accepted craft procedures and certain felicities of accidental effect, scale, must have stuck in his mind to be recalled." Francis V. O'Connor, "The Genesis of Jackson Pollock: 1912 to 1943," *Artforum* 5 (May 1967), 23, n. 9. Kadish on Siqueiros, "It didn't matter whether he was talking about peanuts or politics. Everything was explosive": Naifeh and Smith, *Jackson Pollock: An American Saga*, 285.

66. Siqueiros, June 9, 1936, letter to Blanca Luz Brum, *Palabras de Siqueiros;* quoted in Herner, "Siqueiros and Surrealism?" 113. In a 1960 lecture at the Central University of Caracas, Siqueiros recalled of his New York workshop period, "In our search for techniques we made prime use in our paintings of the artistic accident, which in our search for new forms we transformed into figurative art with an intensive realist purpose." David Alfaro Siqueiros, *Art and Revolution,* Sylvia Calles, trans. (London: Laurence and Wishart, 1975), 219. I am indebted to Christopher Fulton for sharing with me several obscure photographs of Siqueiros Experimental Workshop members creating a parade float for Independence Day, 1936. In one of these, fig. 57, the man at left wearing a hat appears to be Pollock. Fulton found these images in "Siqueiros Experimental Workshop: Técnica y creación al servicio de las Masas," *Nueva Cultura* 3 (March 1937), n.p.

67. Details and analysis of work at Union Square: Hurlburt, *Mexican Muralists in the United States,* 220–31; Herner, "Siqueiros and Surrealism?" 110–14, and *Paradise to Utopia,* 164–84. Horn, "Hollow and the Bump," 86: "Of course, we used all of these devices to enhance paintings with literary content. No-one thought of them as ends in themselves. The genesis of Pollock's mature art began to be discernible only when he began to exploit these techniques as final statement." Lehman's recollections: *Paradise to Utopia,* 168.

68. Oral History Interview with Harold Lehman Conducted by Stephen Polcari, March 28, 1997, AAA, http://www.aaa.si.edu/collections/interviews/oral-history-interview-harold-lehman-12894:

> [At the Siqueiros Workshop we used] automotive lacquers . . . The first thing we did is punctured holes [in the can] lid, punctured holes in all of them, and then we started dribbling the paint onto big 8 x 12 feet plywood panels on the floor. First we had to put a ground coat on, and that was done just by painting it on . . . and then we started dribbling the colors . . . because we wanted to see how it behaved when we poured thinner on it. Siqueiros had already had the experience of using some of the stuff and he saw the possibilities through the pouring thing that what happened is that thinner would dissolve the paint, and as it dissolved the paint would create completely new structures, forms, that would take on shapes that were recognizable: realistic shapes. . . . It then periforated [*sic*] onto all the work that we turned out at the shop as well. And Pollock was in on that, he saw that, he did that. There's no question that that is where he got the whole idea of dripping paint.

69. Siqueiros described generation of *The Birth of Fascism,* a work related to *Collective Suicide,* in an April 6, 1936, letter to María Asunsolo. Its political meaning analyzed: Hurlburt, *Mexican Muralists in the United States,* 224–25; Herner, *Paradise to Utopia,* 169–80. Herner writes that in such 1936 paintings,

"Siqueiros did not just portray war, he also managed to formally produce war-like explosions." Lehman states, "One person would pour a color, another person would pour a color, then a third would come along with a thinner. The thinner is what would activate the paint. We wouldn't get to let the paint dry. [That would make it] spread mixing with all the other colors. . . . And create an entire structure, specific structure of forms and colors. . . . We'd pick out forms from the abstraction" (AAA Oral History Interview).

70. Naifeh and Smith, *Jackson Pollock: An American Saga,* 287, authors' interview with Axel Horn.

71. *Landscape with Steer,* c. 1936–1937 (*JPCR* 1065 [P9]) and *Untitled,* c. 1942 (*JPCR* 952): *JPCR* 4: 139, 35. Pollock's comment: remarks to *JPCR* 952, given to Clement Greenberg as a 1956 wedding present. Pollock remembered splitting this work in two to smuggle it out of WPA headquarters. Mervin Jules (Potter, *TVG,* 52) recalled that, during late 1930s, Pollock sometimes experimented with Siqueiros's techniques: "Pollock would work at our studio occasionally—no one worked that way—and we all watched him. To prepare a canvas, he would put it on the floor and spatter it—that was the underpainting, spatter and drip—then let it lie there while he looked at it. Images began to appear for him. It was a stimulation, and he believed Michelangelo, who said he saw forms in clouds and such. Everything an artist sees becomes part of his visceral bank—exists in the subconscious. When the need arises, it comes forward. The underpainting would be dry when Pollock began to work, so it didn't show."

72. See Marcia Epstein Allenstuck, *John Graham's System and Dialetics of Art* (Baltimore: Johns Hopkins University Press, 1971) for Graham's ideas. Perhaps Pollock picked up more readily on Graham's espousal of risk, accident, and automatic *écriture* because of experiences at the Siqueiros workshop.

73. These include *Composition with Pouring I* (*JPCR* 92) and *Water Birds* (*JPCR* 93). Those two and *Composition with Pouring II* (*JPCR* 94) were probably among the five untitled paintings listed in his debut catalogue brochure. "Remarks," *JPCR,* 1: 85.

74. The open-topped initial "P" appears to be "capped" with a defecating animal figure; Matta's comment that Pollock was "anal-erotic about paint" might be applicable to reading this curious ideograph. "Concerning the Beginnings of the New York School: 1939–1943, An Interview with Peter Busa and Matta conducted by Sidney Simon in Minneapolis in December 1966," *Art International* 4 (Summer 1967), 20.

75. For example, *JPCR* 635, a 1941–42 drawing where the male partner of a rather inelegant embracing couple watches with apparent consternation as a (his?) phallus flies away. Landau, *Pollock,* 112.

76. Greenberg, "Art," *Nation,* February 1, 1947, O'Brian, *Collected Writings,* 2: 125. In Landau, *Pollock,* 149, I inaccurately included a description of this painting as completely nonobjective. I am indebted to the late artist Ray Johnson, who suggested to me the deeper meaning of its phallic imagery in 1990.

77. At least one float made at the Siqueiros workshop included handprints, as seen in Pollock's *Number 1A, 1948,* but he may have also been influenced by the similar, more recent practice of his close friend, photographer Herbert Matter. See Ellen G. Landau, "Action/Re-Action: The Artistic Friendship of Herbert Matter and Jackson Pollock," *Pollock Matters* (Boston: McMullen Museum of Art, Boston College, 2007), 31.

78. Herner ("Siqueiros and Surrealism?" 118) cites Rosenberg's concept of the action painter who "has ceased to be a contemplative artist in order to become an action hero, that is, a hero of virtual action, since he engaged in psychological battles using artistic spaces as his battlefield." She quotes Wollen, "Männerkunst," 55–56: "This new hero in existentialist thinking would be an angst-ridden solitary creator, whose personal conflicts would be worked out in the act of painting—in a battle which in many ways could only be self-punitive." See Chapters 5 and 6 below.

79. Motherwell's emphasis on body-and-mind duality: "The Modern Painters World," *Dyn* 6 (1944), 9–14; discussion below in Chapters 4 and 5. In an undated notation, Pollock listed his desire for total control, states of order, organic intensity, energy and motion made visible, memories arrested in space, human needs and motives, acceptance. *JPCR*,4: 253.

80. Photographs of Siqueiros striking poses during the 1950s to model for his Mexico City National Autonomous University mosaic reliefs, *El pueblo a la Universidad, la Universidad al pueblo,* indicate how closely he relied on his own actions to generate significant form (see fig. 62a–b). Additional examples: Irene Herner, "Ciudad Universita Segunda Etapa del Muralismo," *Siqueiros: el lugar de la utopia* (Mexico City: Instituto Nacional de Bellas Artes SAPS, 1994), figs. 168–75. Cursive sweep: Jim Fasanelli, quoted by Namuth, "Photographing Pollock," n.p.

81. *JPCR,* 4: 253.

82. Polcari, "Siqueiros and Pollock, Düsseldorf," 275: "Because he was a fantastic realist, Siqueiros was more influential and more parallel to Pollock than has hitherto been acknowledged. Siqueiros and Pollock are both chimerical artists of epic struggle and transformation. The former by using public spaces to paint transforming propaganda; the latter by creating private psychologized ritual art for public and personal benefit."

83. Herner, *Paradise to Utopia,* 187. Kadish commented to Naifeh and Smith, *Jackson Pollock: An American Saga,* 285, that Pollock and Siqueiros "had a great rapport. . . . They seemed to reflect each other in a strange way. Each felt the other's intensity. When you put them in the same room, they really bounced off each other."

4 | Motherwell, Mexico, and Surrealism Revised

1. "Jackson Pollock: A Questionnaire," *Arts and Architecture* 61 (February 1944), 14.

2. Clement Greenberg, in "Review of Exhibitions of Marc Chagall, Lyonel Feininger, and Jackson Pollock," *Nation,* November 27, 1943, mentions Miró as an influence without identifying him as Surrealist. John O'Brian, *Clement Greenberg: Collected Essays and Criticism,*1: 1939–44 (Chicago: University of Chicago Press, 1986), 166.

3. B. H. Friedman, *Jackson Pollock: Energy Made Visible* (New York: McGraw-Hill, 1972), 62. Steven Naifeh and Gregory White Smith, *Jackson Pollock: An American Saga* (New York: Clarkson N. Potter, 1989), 472.

4. As I cited in *Jackson Pollock* (New York: Abrams, 1989), 103, Lee Krasner thought that Howard Putzel, Peggy Guggenheim's assistant, helped Pollock with the interview. Motherwell's identification is more credible, I now think.

5. "The Modern Painter's World," *Dyn* 1, no. 6 (November 1944); Stephanie Terenzio, ed., *The Collected Writings of Robert Motherwell* (New York: Oxford University Press, 1992), 34.

6. Originally titled "The Place of the Spiritual in a World of Property," this text was presented as a lecture in August 1944 in "Arts Plastique," a session organized by French Surrealist André Masson at Mount Holyoke College's "Pontigny en Amérique" program cosponsored by the École Libre des Hautes Études. Terenzio, *Collected Writings,* 27, 35, n. 1–2.

7. Discussing his privileged, yet troubled childhood (his mother was schizophrenic and his father authoritarian), Motherwell said (describing kindergarten): "I still remember a blackboard, where every day in colored chalk the teacher would do the weather in Miro-esque. You know, the sun, a round circle with rays. Blue rain, against the ray. The green strokes of the grass. And she looked at me one day and said, Bobby I don't think you like singing and dancing very much. Would you rather paint while everybody else is singing and dancing? And I said, Would I? And painted and painted and painted." Motherwell was eleven the summer he went to Otis. He later drew at Moran Prep School in Atascadero, copying Old Masters and Cézanne from the *Encyclopedia Britannica.* James E. B. Breslin, "Robert Motherwell: From WASPism to Modernism," *Threepenny Review* no. 61 (Spring 1995), 24–25.

8. Motherwell spent much of his Paris time painting, studying briefly at the Académie Julien with Jean Souverbie: "He used to give his students composition problems with a woman and child. All the students made monumental paintings on that theme. I painted a woman in bed, in the manner of Pascin." Michael Ragon, *Vingt-cinq ans d'art vivant: Chronique vécue de l'art contemporain, de l'abstraction au pop art, 1944–1969* (Paris: Casterman, 1969, 309–15; Robert Motherwell, *The Writings of Motherwell,* Dore Ashton and Joan Banach, eds. (Berkeley: University of California Press, 2007), 238. Motherwell observed Picasso in cafés, "adoring" him and Matisse

by this time. He had a solo exhibition in 1939 at the Raymond Duncan Gallery on the Rue de Seine, described as seen by few and "best forgotten."

9. Additional biographical details: *Oral History Interview with Robert Motherwell, 1971 November 24–1974 May 1, Archives of American Art, Smithsonian Institution,* conducted by Paul Cummings in Greenwich, Connecticut: http://www.aaa.si.edu/collections/oralhistories/transcripts/mother71.htm. Recounting again the anecdote in n. 7, Motherwell states this allowed him to grasp at a young age, "that forms are symbolic, that it didn't have to look like rain but that blue lines for rain were even more beautiful than an actual photograph of the rain, and so on. And I determined on the spot that somehow I would learn to do that."

10. Meeting Arthur Berger in Oregon: "Concerning the Beginnings of the New York School: 1939–1943; An Interview with Robert Motherwell Conducted by Sidney Simon in New York in January 1967," *Art International* 2 (Summer 1967), 20; hereafter Simon, "Motherwell Interview." Elsewhere, he states they'd met in Paris.

11. See David Craven, "Aesthetics as Ethics in the Writings of Robert Motherwell and Meyer Schapiro," *Archives of American Art Journal* 36, no. 1 (1996), 25–32; Thomas B. Hess, "Sketch for a Portrait of the Art Historian among Artists," *Social Research* 45 (Spring 1978), 6–7.

12. Motherwell wrote to Schapiro, April 30, 1987:

> What I really want to say point-blank is that *you*, who probably do not know it, have been the most decisive person in my life. Without having been told about your existence, it never would have occurred to me to move to New York, and given that extraordinary decade of New York in the 1940s, if I had not done so, obviously my life and my work would have been wholly different.—I cannot even imagine what it would have been otherwise. Cambridge is no place for a painter and California in 1941 was not the right place either.—I still remember words of wisdom from you while I naively intruded on your privacy. When I finally understood the intrusion, I stopped, probably because your presence and mind are so overwhelming that I felt extremely vulnerable at a time when my confidence was not very strong, and I was faced with so many personal dilemmas. . . . Anyway, thanks for *being*. And I hope it goes on indefinitely in good health.

Dedalus Foundation, New York, Folder VI.142.

13. "*Entretien* avec un Tsimshian," *Minotaure*, no. 12–13 (Spring 1939): 66–69. See Martica Sawin, *Surrealism in Exile and the Beginnings of the New York School* (Cambridge, Mass.: MIT Press, 1995), 24–26.

14. "Eleven Europeans in America," *Bulletin of the Museum of Modern Art* 13, nos. 3–4 (1946), 12. Seligmann describes gratification from several "most promising young Americans": "In my association with them, I have enjoyed the stimulus of discussion and an atmosphere of sensitive effort which is a full reward in itself aside from all the personal promise it affords."

15. When Schapiro suggested study with Seligmann, Motherwell protested that he hated Surrealism. Schapiro countered that he was an intellectual and had shared interests with the Surrealists: "They were the last generation inheriting the tradition of symbolist poetry." Sawin, *Surrealism in Exile,* 72.

16. Sawin, *Surrealism in Exile,* 70: "Seligmann, because of his Swiss nationality, was able to get funds transferred to U.S. banks during the war years. Thus, while most of his fellow refugees had no means of support other than through the sale of art, he was in a position to afford both a New York apartment and a farmhouse in the country, to buy an etching press and paper of the finest quality, amass a collection of rare books on magic, and help his stranded friends in a variety of ways. Although their style was not lavish, the Seligmanns were at least free of the gnawing financial anxieties that were a fact of life for many refugees."

17. H. H. Arnason, "On Motherwell and His Early Work," *Art International* 10 (January 1966), 21. Paul Cummings, recorded interview with Bernard (and Rebecca) Reis, New York, June 31, 1976, typescript 20–39, AAA.

18. Lionel Abel, "The Surrealists in New York," *Commentary* 72 (October, 1981), 44–45. "After that encounter at Schapiro's," he states, "I saw a lot of Motherwell."

19. Sidney Janis, *Abstract and Surrealist Art in America* (New York: Reynal and Hitchcock, 1944), 65. Whereas Janis named Pollock a "Surrealist" and Motherwell an abstractionist, acknowledging his "association" with the French surrealists from 1940 to 1942 Janis agreed to Motherwell's claimed hybridity, even writing that his artist's statement raised a larger issue involving the two directions' possible "compatibility." "The schism between the factions," Janis concludes, "is not as insurmountable as their members believe."

20. A tuition slip from Seligmann's Papers is illustrated in Sawin, *Surrealism in Exile,* 71. Sawin: Seligmann's lessons "had a curious beginning as well as a momentous consequence."

21. Siri Engberg and Joan Banach, *Robert Motherwell: The Complete Prints, 1940–1991: Catalogue Raisonné* (New York: Hudson Hills, 2003), CR 1, 62. The authors were aware of *Figure with Mandoline,* from its listing in Motherwell's first solo exhibition, but no impressions were known at time of publication. Several, including the Gearharts', have since come to light. E-mail, December 14, 2010, Katy Rogers, Project Manager, *The Catalogue Raisonné of Paintings and Collages by Robert Motherwell,* and conversation with Rogers, New York, March 24, 2011.

22. "Spotlight on: Seligmann," *Art News* 45 (December 1946), 41, 57.

23. Motherwell told Mattison that "his contact with Seligmann involved primarily watching studio life rather than formal instruction in art," claiming he "disliked Seligmann's meticulously defined and explicit Surrealist drawings of creatures with machine and monster body parts, though he said that

he did appreciate 'a few more geometric etchings after which I made several drawings, now lost.'" Apparently no mention was made of *Figure with Mandoline*. Robert Mattison, "The Art of Robert Motherwell during the 1940s," Ph.D. diss., Princeton University, 1985, 39; hereafter "Art of Motherwell."

24. Robert Motherwell, letter to Kurt and Arlette Seligmann, Hotel Regis, Avenida Juarez 77, Mexico D.F., June 18, 1941; July 9 addendum starting p. 3. Kurt Seligmann Papers, Yale Collection of American Literature, Accession number 1997 1204b, Beinecke Rare Book and Manuscript Library, Yale University.

25. Arnason, "Early Work," 21. Arnason states that *Dog Barking at the Moon* (1926) at MoMA was the only work by Miró that Motherwell saw before entering Seligmann's studio, "to which he did not react in any positive way." Owned by the Philadelphia Museum of Art, perhaps it was on loan in New York.

26. Robert Coates, *New Yorker*, May 29, 1943, 49: "In Jackson Pollock's abstract 'Painting,' [*Stenographic Figure*] with its curious reminiscences of both Matisse and Miró, we have a real discovery."

27. James Johnson Sweeney, Durlacher Brothers gallery brochure, "Paintings by Kurt Seligmann," c. 1944, Bernard J. Reis Papers, 1934–1979, AAA: Seligmann "embodies a re-emergence of the spirit which gave the art of his Swiss fatherland its national individuality in the sixteenth century. . . . we find the fixed iconography of Manuel Deutsch and Graf's mediaeval fantasies translated into the free forms of unconscious association of the young romantic artists of today." King Death wearing a crown as popular in fifteenth-sixteenth century Northern European art: Elina Gertsman, *The Dance of Death in the Middle Ages: Image Text Performance* (Belgium and New York: Brepols Pub., 2010), 166–67.

28. Motherwell told Barbara Catoir, "I think that of all contemporary *living* artists, my work (different as it is) finds the most sympathy for Miró in one way and Tápies in another. It is curious that they are both Spanish. But I grew up in California, and took up the vocation of painting in Mexico, both of which have landscapes similar to Spain." "The artist as a 'Walking Eye': Fragen an Robert Motherwell," *Bruckmanns Pantheon* 38 (1980), 284.

29. "Interview with Bryan Robertson, Addenda, 1965," Terenzio, *Collected Writings*, 140; hereafter "Robertson Addenda."

30. *Bulletin from the New School for Social Research*, Winter 1941; Martica Sawin, *Gordon Onslow Ford: Paintings and Works on Paper, 1939–1951* (New York: Francis M. Naumann Fine Art, 2010), 55. Lecture dates and topics: January 22: "Giorgio de Chirico, the child of dreams"; February 5: "Max Ernst: the creative forces of evil," "Joan Miró, the primitive in the subhuman"; February 19: "Magritte, the poetry of the object," "Tanguy, the internal landscape"; March 5: "Adventures in surrealist painting during the last four years: Delvaux, Brauner, Paalen, Hayter, Seligmann, Matta, Onslow-Ford, Esteban Frances."

31. According to Putzel's list (Onslow-Ford Archives, Lucid Art Foundation) Onslow-Ford lent two of his own paintings, works by de Chirico (3), Tanguy (2), Max Ernst (2), Esteban Frances (2), Henry Moore, Victor Brauner and Paul Delvaux (1 each). Sawin, *Onslow Ford*, 19, n. 15.

32. Motherwell, "Letter to Ted Lindberg, October 19, 1988; Terenzio, *Collected Writings*, 290. Motherwell describes Onslow-Ford as "fanatically devoted to and influenced by Matta": Katy Rogers, "To Transform the World: Matta and Motherwell in New York and Mexico," *Nexus New York: Latin/American Artists in the Modern Metropolis*, Deborah Cullen ed. (New York: El Museo de Barrio and Yale University Press, 2009), 184. Matta recalled meeting Schapiro, Abel, Pollock, Baziotes, Frances Lee, Edison Price, Gerome Kamrowski, Arshile Gorky, Motherwell, and Frederick Kiesler at Onslow-Ford's lectures. (It is doubtful that Pollock actually attended.) Germana Ferrari, *Entretiens morphologiques; Notebook No. 1, 1936–1944* (London: Sistan, 1987), 200; Rogers, "To Transform the World," 194, n. 4.

33. This started when Matta met Frederico García Lorca through relatives in Spain. Lorca gave Matta a letter of introduction to Dalí who provided entrée to Breton. (Sawin, *Surrealism in Exile*, 32.) Matta's connection may have led to Motherwell's interest in Lorca's poetry, the basis for his *Elegies to the Spanish Republic*. See Chapter 5 and Conclusion.

34. Onslow-Ford expressed gratitude to Breton, "for admitting me to the house, telling me about the family tree, showing me the way to the jungles and deserts of automatism which seem no less exhaustible to me now than in 1938 when I had my first visions of the transparent, interpenetrating worlds of the mind." Gustav Regler, "Four European Painters in Mexico," *Horizon* 16 (August 1947), 100.

35. Sidney Janis, "European Artists Come to New York," *Decision* 2 (November–December 1941), 92.

36. Gordon Onslow-Ford, *Towards a New Subject in Painting* (San Francisco: San Francisco Museum of Art, 1948), 11; Dickran Tashjian, *A Boatload of Madmen: Surrealism and the American Avant-Garde, 1920–1950* (New York: Thames and Hudson, 1995), 186. According to Tashjian, Matta and Onslow-Ford met in a Parisian boardinghouse, 1937. See also Elizabeth A. T. Smith and Colette Darnall, "'Crushed Jewels, Air, Even Laughter': Matta in the 1940s," *Matta in America: Paintings and Drawings of the 1940s* (Museums of Contemporary Art, Chicago and Los Angeles, 2001), 10–31.

37. Sawin, *Onslow Ford*, 8, conversations with the artist, Inverness, California, March 1985. Before Germany invaded Poland in 1939, Matta and Onslow-Ford shared a summer chateau near the Swiss border with other artists, including Esteban Frances, also interested in non-Euclidean spaces and multiple vanishing points. These three, Sawin comments, "might well have been perceived as the nucleus of a new school in painting had not the war intervened." Breton described them as "the future of Surrealism" in *Minotaure* (10, 19 n. 11).

38. "Concerning the Beginnings of the New York School: 1939–

1943; An Interview with Peter Busa and Matta conducted by Sidney Simon in Minneapolis in December 1966," *Art International* 11 (Summer 1967), 17; hereafter Simon, "Busa/ Matta Interview."

39. Onslow-Ford: "I was the responsive audience that Matta needed so that he could make discoveries through spontaneous talk. We both learned from what he said." "Notes on Matta and Painting (1937–1941)," Ferrari, *Entretiens morphologiques*, 23. Rogers, "To Transform the World," 185, comments that later, "It was the same with Motherwell."

40. "Into the Unknown," *Art Digest* 15 (February 1, 1941), 29.

41. For example, "Modern Museum a Psychopathic Ward as Surrealism has its Day," *Art Digest* 11 (December 15, 1936), 5–6; S. Putnam, "Marxism and Surrealism," *Art Front* 21 (March 1937), 10; Klaus Mann, "Surrealist Circus," *American Mercury* 56 (February 1943), 174–81. Mann describes Surrealism as "Nazoid": irresponsible, mystic, cunning, anti-art, anti-civilization.

42. See Irving Sandler, "Dada, Surrealism and Their Heritage, 2: The Surrealist Emigrés in New York," *Artforum* 6 (May 1968), 25–31.

43. Prior to MoMA's more comprehensive show, Levy helped organize the first U.S. Surrealist exhibition, "Newer Super-Realism," Wadsworth Atheneum, Hartford, Connecticut, 1931. Breton was not involved, and Levy felt free "to present a paraphrase which would offer Surrealism in the language of the new world rather than a translation of the rhetoric of the old" (Tashjian, *A Boatload of Madmen*, 42). Sawin, *Surrealism in Exile*, 78: "For the American public the term Surrealism was synonymous with the name Dalí."

44. Motherwell told Lindberg, "As I remember, the lecture was a very good one, intelligent, clear, and filled with an enthusiasm that bordered on Onslow-Ford's sense of an ultimate revelation," adding, "I do not remember a face to face conversation with Onslow-Ford alone. His fanaticism about surrealism representing human redemption, in the midst of that impoverished and desperate scene, would have turned me off." Terenzio, *Collected Writings*, 290.

45. Quotes: Onslow-Ford, "First Lecture, January 22, 1941: Introduction," Sawin, *Onslow Ford*, 56–67. Sawin: "He did not exactly follow the prepared text when he spoke, but used it to clarify in advance what he was going to say." She includes verbatim transcription of longhand notes for lectures 1 and 4; notes for lectures 2–3 are unlocated, except excerpt on Tanguy. Assuming Onslow-Ford followed the script, his final talk would have ended, "I think I can speak for all my friends when I say that we are completely confident in our work and slowly but surely with the collaboration of the young Americans we hope to make a vital contribution to the transformation of the world" (71).

46. "First Lecture, January 22, 1941"; "Fourth Lecture, March 5, 1941," Sawin, *Onslow Ford*, 57, 70.

47. Matta used this term in Max Kozloff, "An Interview with

Matta—These things were like rain catching up with a man who is running," *Artforum* 4 (September 1965), 23. Sometimes he used "psychological morphologies" interchangeably.

48. Matta Echaurren, "Mathématique sensible—Architecture du temps," *Minotaure*, no. 11 (1938), 43; James Thrall Soby, "Matta Echaurren," *Magazine of Art* 40 (March 1947), 102. Soby: This theory "owes much to Dalí's interest in a malleable architecture, based on Freudian suitability to human needs, but it is nonetheless an interesting forecast of the direction Matta's painting would take."

49. Jimmy Ernst, *A Not-So-Still Life* (New York: St. Martin's, 1984), 196. Matta's quote: Simon, "Busa/Matta Interview," 17. Matta's pre-1941 work: Smith and Darnall, "Crushed Jewels, Air, Even Laughter," 10–31; William Rubin, "Matta," *Museum of Modern Art Bulletin* 25, no. 1 (1957), 3–35; Elisabeth Haglund, "The Morphologies of Matta," *Aris*, no. 2 (1969), 9–32; Irene Clurman, *Surrealism and the Painting of Matta and Magritte*, Stanford Honors Essay in Humanities, Number 14 (Palo Alto: Stanford University Press, 1970).

50. Motherwell on Matta: "Letter to Lindberg," Terenzio, *Collected Writings*, 290; Simon, "Motherwell Interview," 21. Matta quote: Kozloff, "Interview with Matta," 23.

51. Julien Levy, *Memoirs of an Art Gallery* (New York: G. P. Putnam and Sons, 1977), 247. Matta, he said, was "easily the most fertile and the most untrustworthy of the younger Surrealists."

52. Motherwell's self-description: "Robertson Addenda," Terenzio, *Collected Writings*, 144. "[Matta] was sociable and even frivolous. I seemed joyless to him and that one word is better than all the others. Matta was filled with enthusiasm. There was a streak of sybarite, of Chanel, of Catholic decadence, fascinated by the idea of sin, which seemed incomprehensible to a young American." Motherwell's first wife, María, recalled Matta saying, "You know, Bob, it takes tremendous courage to disobey your parents. You'll feel like an outlaw, but you'll gain strength as you become your own authority. Timidity has no place in art." María Runyon, "Mr. Motherwell's Ghost," typescript, 41. See n. 79.

53. Matta, letter to Mattison, September 24, 1979, "Art of Motherwell," 43.

54. André Breton, "Manifesto of Surrealism," *Manifestos of Surrealism*, Richard Seaver and Helen R. Lane, trans. (Ann Arbor: University of Michigan Press, 1969), 26. Motherwell told Mattison he learned of Breton's manifesto and definition from Matta in early 1941.

55. Distaste: Arnason, "Early Work," 20. Although these three extant examples were made in Oregon (conversation with Katy Rogers, New York, March 24, 2011), "brightly painted self-portraits and attempts at modernized versions of idyllic, imaginary landscapes, in the manner of Poussin *cum* Dufy" are described as what Motherwell exhibited at Duncan's gallery in Paris. See n. 8. The present volume went to press before publication of Motherwell's catalogue raisonné. More information on these works and images of them are included in the latter.

56. Victor Serge, "Letter from Mexico," *Horizon* 15 (January 1947), 63–64.

57. Holger Cahill, *American Sources of Modern Art* (New York: Museum of Modern Art, 1933), 18.

58. "Robertson Addenda," Terenzio, *Collected Writings*, 144. "Negatively speaking, I did not want to go back West for the summer. I had finally escaped my family! I was beginning to put down roots, of a fairly pliable kind, but in great anxiety, with fear and trembling."

59. "Toward a Free Revolutionary Art," Dwight McDonald trans., *Partisan Review* 6, no. 1 (Fall 1938). See Sawin, *Surrealism in Exile*, 19–23; Mark Polizzotti, *Revolution of the Mind: The Life of André Breton* (Boston: Black Widow, 2009), 407–19; Luis Mario Schneider, *México y el surrealismo 1925–1950* (Mexico City: Arte and Libros, 1978); Robin Adèle Greeley, "For an Independent Revolutionary Art: Breton, Trotsky and Cárdenas's Mexico," *Surrealism, Politics and Culture*, Raymond Spiteri and Donald LaCoss, eds. (Burlington, Vt.: Ashgate, 2003), 204–25. The manifesto was signed by Breton and Rivera to protect Trotsky. As Sawin points out, the tenets of Marxism and Surrealism uneasily canceled each other out. Trotsky was "apprehensive over Breton's interest in the '*au-delà*.'"

60. Regler, "Four European Painters," 90.

61. Breton in a May 1938 lecture, National Autonomous University, Mexico City: "The Transformation of Modern Art and Surrealism." This was repeated in *Universidad de México*, June 29, 1938, reprinted as "Diálogo de André Breton con Rafael Heliodoro Valle," *Los Surrealistas en Mexico* (Mexico City: INBA, Museo Nacional de Arte, SEP, 1986), 102–6; English excerpts in "*Recurring Utopia:* Conversation with André Breton," *México en el Surrealismo: los visitantes fugaces, Artes de México*, no. 63 (January 2003), 80, Harry Porter, trans. Mexican response to Breton: Schneider, *Mexico y el Surrealismo*. Other resources: José Pierre, "*Artistic Utopia:* A Volcanic Aftertaste (André Breton and Mexican Art)," *México en el Surrealismo*, no. 63, 75–78; Amy Winter, "Wolfgang Paalen and the American Avant-Garde of the 1940s," Ph.D. diss., CUNY Graduate Center, New York, 1995, 416–32; Courtney Gilbert, "'The (New) World in the Time of the Surrealists': European Surrealists and Their Mexican Contemporaries," Ph.D. diss., University of Chicago, 2001.

62. Eugène Louis Gabriel Ferry de Bellemare: *Costal l'Indien: Scènes de la guerre de l'indépendance du Mexique* (1852); *Scènes de la vie sauvage au Mexique* (1879). Luis Cardoza y Aragón, response to Breton's request for an overview of Mexican art in preparation for his trip, *El Nacional* 15, no. 2654, year VIII, second era, September 19, 1936. Prior to Breton's visit, Aragón welcomed to Mexico French playwright Antonin Artaud, whose Theatre of Cruelty was admired by the Surrealists. See Artaud's comment on Mexico in concluding chapter.

63. All quotes: "Souvenir de Mexique," *Minotaure*, nos. 12–13 (1939); André Breton, *Surrealism and Painting*, Simon Watson, trans. (New York: Icon/Harper and Row, 1972), 141–

44. Breton (again) somewhat reductively coupled Mexico's "anachronism and the will of anticipation," writing in a patronizing manner, "Everything that makes Mexico remain behind the times gives value to all that it is capable of accomplishing."

64. Critical controversy over this show: Luis M. Castaneda, "Surrealism and National Identity in Mexico: Changing Perceptions, 1940–1968," *Journal of Surrealism and the Americas* 3, nos. 1–2 (2009), 9–29; Gilbert, "'(New) World in the Time of the Surrealists,'" 225–40.

65. "Robertson Addenda," Terenzio, *Collected Writings*, 146. Motherwell mentions his passionate interest in the Mexican Revolution, the impact of Brenner's book (discussed below) "and Eisenstein's movie, *Thunder over Mexico*, for example, which I think I saw before I went to Mexico. That makes me think there is something very different about being a 20th Century man: we are the first people who've ever lived, who have seen all the places beforehand in the movies! Photography makes one recognize things or places, but the movies give one a sense of having *been* there."

66. Letter from Seligmann to Paalen, New York, January 27, 1941, Seligmann Papers, Accession number 1997 1204b (this author's translation).

67. Seligmann wrote to Reis in Mexico City on June 26, 1941, "Nous avons grande envie de vous rejoinder mais hélas, hélas, les choses se compliquent de plus en plus avec les événements et les nouvelles lois qui en découlent. Ainsi j'étais très content de ne pas être parti précipitamment pour des raisons que je vous expliquerai à votre retour. Pour un étranger la vie aux États-Unis commence à se compliquer. Heureusement j'ai Bernard toujours prêt à donner des consuls utiles." Seligmann Papers, Accession number 1997 1204b.

68. Inga Karetnikova and Leo Steinmetz, *Mexico According to Eisenstein* (Albuquerque: University of New Mexico Press, 1991), 155–56.

69. Eisenstein arrived with a letter of introduction from Flaherty and stayed fourteen months. Debacle surrounding *¡Que Viva Mexico!* Peter B. High, "A Mexican Tragedy: The Mutilation of a Cinematic Masterpiece," http://www.lang.nagoya-u.ac.jp/ sosha/4/high.pdf. Flaherty's role and quotes: Ernest Lindgren, "Introduction," *¡Que Viva Mexico!* (New York: Arno, 1972), 9. See also Harry M. Geduld and Ronald Gottesman, *Sergei Eisenstein and Upton Sinclair: The Making and Unmaking of ¡Que Viva Mexico!* (Bloomington: Indiana University Press, 1970).

70. Although Eisenstein gave permission, he hated *Thunder over Mexico*. M. H., *New York Times*, "In Old Mexico," September 23, 1933, states that its tale was violent and sadistic, but with "flashes of compelling beauty." See also High, "Mexican Tragedy," 94, 101–2; Lindgren, "Introduction," *¡Que Viva Mexico!* 10–11; Joanne Hershfeld, "Paradise Regained: Sergei Eisenstein's *¡Que Viva Mexico!* as Ethnography," *Documenting the Documentary: Close Readings of Documentary Film and Video*, Barry Keith Grant and Jeanette Sloniowski, eds. (Detroit: Wayne State University Press, 1998), 55–69.

71. Principle points: High, "Mexican Tragedy," 97–98. Eisenstein's recollections of Mexico and impressions of Rivera: Karetnikova and Steinmetz, *Mexico According to Eisenstein*, 155–67.

72. Anita Brenner, *Idols Behind Altars* (New York: Payson and Clarke, 1929), 26, 31–32.

73. Breton and Lam's internment: Sawin, *Surrealism in Exile*, 136–7; Polizzotti, *Revolution of the Mind*, 445–49.

74. Motherwell to Kurt and Arlette Seligmann, June 18, 1941, with July 9 addendum. All subsequent quotes from the same letter unless otherwise indicated. Seligmann Papers, Accession number 1997 1204b.

75. Seligmann writes back diplomatically, "It is too bad that you are not standing the climate and that you do not like the Mexican food. I think that nevertheless your stay in Mexico will be fruitfull [*sic*] for your artistic development, that Matta will give you many good suggestions for your work and that you, Matta and Barbara will stimulate one another with your perseverance in painting." Seligmann to Motherwell, July 19, 1941, Seligmann Papers, Accession number 1997 1204b.

76. Motherwell stayed at Kitigawa House, named after Tamiji Kitagawa, a Japanese artist trained at New York's Art Students League. Kitagawa moved to Mexico in 1921 and became director of the *Escuelas de Pintura al Aire Libre*. This pension was founded by Natalie Vivian Scott of New Orleans, c. 1930, as lodging for creative people. A staff member of Frances Toor's magazine, *Mexican Folkways*, Scott (a social worker and anthropologist) interacted with Rivera, Kahlo, Brenner, and other notable Mexicans and expatriates: http://specialcollections.tulane.edu/NVS/NVS_3.htm.

77. By contrast, Barbara Reis writes around the same time that she has not done any work yet, what with all the teas, cocktails, and dinner parties in Taxco, as well as horseback riding. Letter to Kurt and Arlette Seligmann, June 26, 1941, Seligmann Papers, Accession number 1997 1204b. Reis also states she and the Mattas rented a house in Taxco, but Bob does not live there: "He has rented an adorable three room studio where he paints and sleeps. He eats two meals a day at the pension and the third with us." While she is at the moment sunning herself on the porch, she calls the climate in Taxco uncertain ("one never knows when it is going to rain") and deplores the other Americans who, she says, they are going out of the way to avoid. "Poor Bob hates Mexico because he says he is bored to tears." Despite their unpleasant stay in Mexico City, "I for one am faithful to my first opinion and still love it." The group must still have been hoping the Seligmanns would join them; Reis questions when they might arrive and suggests Kurt bring canvases, expensive in Mexico. Response: n. 67.

78. Letter to Kurt and Arlette Seligmann, June 26, 1941, and undated letter, Reis to Kurt and Arlette Seligmann (written c. June 28, 1941, after being in Taxco for one week). On September 10, Reis writes from Hotel El Mirador, Acapulco, that she and the Mattas left Taxco September 7. They expect to stay in Acapulco until September 20, "or maybe leave sooner if our money doesn't hold out. Once I leave I expect to make a bee line for New York." Seligmann Papers, Accession number 1997 1204b. Motherwell's remaining: Mattison, conversation, November 8, 1979, "Art of Motherwell."

79. Title explanation: Letter, María Runyon to Phyllis Braff, Monterey, California, May 14, 1996. I thank Braff for sharing this and several other excerpts Runyon provided from *Mr. Motherwell's Ghost*, including description of Motherwell on the ship and her feeling about something missing in her life. Braff was guest curator of *The Surrealists and Their Friends on Eastern Long Island at Mid-Century*, Guild Hall Museum, East Hampton, New York, August 10–October 13, 1996. Runyon died in late 2010.

80. Motherwell, "Provincetown and Days Lumber Yard: A Memoir," *Days Lumber Yard Studios, 1914–1971* (Boston: ACME Fine Art, 2009), written July 21, 1978; Terenzio, *Collected Writings*, 224–27. Motherwell recalls his mother's "distaste for María's being a Chicano," but notes that his father "adored her." They wed after María's innocent letter to her mother in Mexico City about "the sinking of a German submarine (off Long Island Point was it?)" resulted in an FBI visit. Motherwell received an early number in the war draft; they "married, friendless, in the beautiful old Universalist Church, so that María might become my legal heir." He was never inducted, however, likely due to his chronic asthma.

81. Motherwell: "Actually in the portrait of Maria (*La Belle Mexicaine*), done in Mexico, the primary automatism is largely covered with a portrait of its own structure. But the portrait would have had a different figuration if it were not being worked out in relation to the primary automatism." "Robertson Addenda," Terenzio, *Collected Writings*, 146.

82. As Motherwell recalled, Onslow-Ford "demonstrate[d] automatism on the blackboard, in a most unexpected way" at the New School. He wrote, "The usual forms of automatism, as were practiced by Masson or Tanguy (in his preliminary drawings) and above all Miró, possess an absolute autonomy. Onslow-Ford began with lines seemingly at random and very rapidly drawn. At a certain critical moment, with the addition of several more lines, to my stupefaction, there appeared a typical classical de Chirico before one's eyes.—It never would have occurred to me that de Chiricos were made automatically, and to this day I am inclined to doubt it." "Letter to Lindberg": Terenzio, *Collected Writings*, 290.

83. "Young and brutal": Kozloff, "An Interview with Matta," 25. Motherwell on Matta: letters to Lindberg, October 19, 1988, and Edward Henning, October 18, 1978; Terenzio, *Collected Writings*, 290, 229. Matta "was also extremely generous and impartial in his artistic counsel. That is, if he was looking at an inexperienced artist's work of varying imagery and quality, he would invariably pick out the best expression by the artist and vehemently encourage him to move in that direction."

84. "Fourth Lecture, March 5, 1941," Sawin, *Onslow Ford*, 70. "The barriers that for our intelligence separate the differ-

ent parts of space as they separate the different parts of time have shown their artificial character," Onslow-Ford explained. Martica Sawin, "The Cycloptic Eye, Pataphysics and the Possible: Transformations of Surrealism," *The Interpretive Link: Abstract Surrealism into Abstract Expressionism, Works on Paper, 1938–1948* (Newport Beach, Calif.: Newport Harbor Art Museum, 1986), 37.

85. Soby, "Matta Echaurren," 104. Matta's reaction to volcanic eruption: Ferrari, *Entretiens morphologiques*, 108: "I saw everything in flames, but from a metaphysical point of view. . . . The light was not a surface but interior fire. . . . I painted that which burned in me and the best image of my body was a volcano."

86. Abel, "Surrealists in New York," 46, comments that Anne did not like this nickname: "'He's trying to make me smaller,' she said once, when someone asked her why she objected to that name. But I have heard other, more violent explanations of why that name should have been disliked, and why it was chosen by Matta." Matta and Anne Clark had twin sons in 1943, but they divorced shortly after.

87. While Motherwell professed not to have particularly admired Matta's finished paintings, his drawings in colored pencil, where the richness of imagery was less adulterated, hinted that his friend might turn out "the heir to Miró." "Letter to Lindberg," Terenzio, *Collected Writings*, 290. "Comic and plastic": Simon, "Motherwell Interview," 21–22. "I loved [Matta's] pencil drawings, but I never really liked his paintings. For me they were theatrical and glossy, too illusionistic for my taste. But I do think the drawings he made in those years—in the late 1930's and 1940's—are among the most beautiful, if not *the* most beautiful work made in America at that time."

88. Robert Mattison, "A Voyage: Motherwell's Earliest Works," *Arts Magazine* 59 (February 1985), 90–93. The sketchbook was found in 1979. Basic assumptions already present: "the predominant use of black and white, and restricted palette; the experimentation with different pictorial syntaxes and spatial modes; the use of automatism, to generate imagery; the limited technical means employed, so that the importance of the syntax of the imagery is never overwhelmed by technique for technique's sake; and finally, the tendency of the artist, when faced with a moving experience, to turn inward and to depict not the physical experience but his reaction to it." Jack Flam, "Robert Motherwell's Drawings," *Robert Motherwell Drawings: A Retrospective, 1941 to the Present* (Houston: Janie C. Lee Gallery, 1979), Part III, n.p. Mattison analyzes differences between the sketchbook drawings and later *Elegies to the Spanish Republic*.

89. Janis, "European Artists Come to New York," 95.

90. William Rubin, "A Personal Note on Matta in America," *Matta in America*, 36, describes the artist's introduction of deep space as suggesting "a kind of electrical system of the mind," a realm where "perspective devices project spatial metaphors for the tensions, ambiguities, contradictions and frustrations of psychic reality."

91. Instructions to himself in *The Mexican Sketchbook* include notations about the adjustment of spaces within and around forms and silhouettes of forms, and fine-tuning colors ("model white globular form," "make alizarin recede," etc.). These may relate to works not in the sketchbook, although amoebic forms sketched on this page are analogous to drawings included.

92. Robert Buck, "With Robert Motherwell," *Robert Motherwell* (New York: Abbeville, 1984), 25. Language needing to be found must "adequately express the complex physical and metaphysical realities that modern science and philosophy had made us aware of, that could more adequately reflect the nature of our understanding of how things really are."

93. Onslow-Ford, who moved to Mexico with Johnson in 1941 (to a village in Michoacán not far from Guston and Kadish's Morelia mural) described Los Cedros as "a nucleus of creative activity" with books all over the place, plus tables, walls and floors covered with primitive objects: a Cycladic figure, Olmec stone carved with a Baby-Jaguar, Quetzalcóatl in Plumed Serpent and Human form, a small Kawkiutl totem pole, etc. In addition to a huge whale penis, dominating Paalen's studio across the courtyard was "one of the world's masterpieces, a Tlingit totem screen 15 feet high of a brown bear with eyes in the joints, paws and head" that Paalen had moved from the Pacific Northwest. Illustrated by Covarrubias in the Amerindian Number of *Dyn* (4–5), this screen is now in the Denver Art Museum. Gordon Onslow-Ford, "Paalen the Messenger," *Hommage to Wolfgang Paalen the pioneer* (Mexico City: Museo de Arte Moderno, 1967), 39. Growing up with vacations on a family farm on Washington's seacoast "filled with the stuff," Motherwell stated that his prior familiarity with Northwest Coast art had rendered Paalen's collection less exotic to him: Ann Gibson, "Theory Undeclared: Avant-Garde Magazines as a Guide to Abstract Expressionist Images and Ideas," Ph.D. diss., University of Delaware, 1984, 263, from a telephone interview, April 21, 1983.

94. Martica Sawin, unpublished interview with Edward Renouf, June 4, 1988, Washington, Connecticut. Some of the points Renouf made are incorporated into *Surrealism in Exile*, 250–53. I thank Sawin for sharing the entire interview. Mexico, Renouf states, was uncongenial to Paalen, who disliked the Spanish language: "In no sense of the word was he assimilated."

95. The version in Wittenborn's compendium of Paalen's essays, *Form and Sense*, is illustrated by Alice Rahon-Paalen and Onslow-Ford. Letter from Paalen to Motherwell with instructions on how this essay and others should be presented, collection of the Dedalus Foundation. Undated, but probably 1944 or early 1945, this is one of four extant letters written from 1945–47, Paalen to Motherwell.

96. Quotes: "The New Image": *Problems of Contemporary Art Number 1: Wolfgang Paalen Form and Sense* (New York: Wittenborn, 1945), 31–41. Italics: Paalen and Motherwell's. First publication: *Dyn* 1, no. 1 (April–May 1942), 7–15.

97. Paalen separated from the Surrealists in 1940. Based on conversations with Motherwell, 1983–86, Terenzio, in *Collected*

Writings, 183, n. 3 states, "Although Motherwell was never officially part of the group, his work on Paalen's essay nearly caused his excommunication from the surrealist contingent in New York."

98. In view of this, it is curious that Motherwell would later attempt to allege more of a quid pro quo of reciprocity between them, insisting he'd educated Paalen about "contemporary philosophy in the English-speaking world, particularly the American pragmatic tradition of James, Pierce and Dewey, and also of Russell and Whitehead" merely in return for "factual information" about the origins and nature of Surrealism. "Letter to Irving Sandler," February 23, 1970, Terenzio, *Collected Writings,* 182. Further downplaying Paalen's impact, Motherwell wrote, "What we did do, as then isolated western intellectuals in Mexico, was to encourage each other in our various aspirations and with our various bits of knowledge and intuitions." Winter and Mattison have challenged such statements since Motherwell was as yet an unaccomplished artist. Amy Winter, *Wolfgang Paalen Artist and Theorist of the Avant-Garde* (Westport, Conn.: Praeger, 2003), 111, terms them an instance of "the anxiety of influence," referring to Bloom's book of that title (see Chapter 3). Motherwell objected to Sandler's statement in "The Surrealist Emigrés in New York" that the "influence of Paalen in part prompted Motherwell to modify his ideas." Andreas Neufert, in *Wolfgang Paalen's Implicit Spaces* (San Francisco: Frey Norris Gallery, 2007), 12, states that Motherwell also played down Paalen's influence in correspondence to him, October 16, 1986, writing that he and Paalen had a gentleman's agreement to destroy letters to each other (according to Neufert, sent almost weekly 1942–45). Motherwell wrote Onslow-Ford, October 2, 1984, "Hope your Paalen file contains no letters by me," perhaps referring to this agreement (Paalen Archive Berlin and Lucid Art Foundation, Inverness).

99. On his editorship, Motherwell said he'd decided "to repay my debt quietly to some of the artists in exile." "Parisian Artists in Exile: 1939–1945," typescript, 5–6, 1977, Dedalus Foundation.

100. Quotes in this section, unless otherwise identified: Paalen, "Surprise and Inspiration," *Form and Sense,* 43–50. On the relationship of Motherwell's painting of that title to Paalen's essay: Winter, *Artist and Theorist,* 109; Robert Mattison, *Robert Motherwell: The Formative Years* (Ann Arbor: UMI Research Press, 1987), 80–81, 92. Before leaving Mexico, he may have helped translate "Surprise and Inspiration" into English for *Dyn* 2.

101. Quoted material: taped interview, Motherwell and Ann Gibson, April 13, 1982. I thank Gibson for sharing this. Motherwell states that Paalen was "very elegant and charming" and that he had accompanied Paalen to buy Indian artifacts near Veracruz and borrowed money from him when funds sent by his father were stolen. He asserts that Paalen invited him to work in one of the O'Gorman studios (it's unclear whether that took place) and explains María was with him in San Angel for only part of the time because when they met she was engaged to a Broadway director and had first to go home and break it off.

102. Space in Paalen's works at this time was "less tectonic and not as ontologically framed" as in Matta's more pictorial Surrealist dreamscapes. Generating "a sort of magnetic field of emotion" to better visualize the "surprising" duality of science and art, in works like *Somewhere in Me* and *Space Unbound,* Paalen attempted to express the interactivity of spectator and universe rhythmically. See Gustav Regler, *Wolfgang Paalen* (New York: Nierendorf Editions, 1946), 52–53. (According to Winter and Sawin, Paalen himself probably wrote all or part of Regler's text.) See also Andreas Neufert, "Wolfgang Paalen's First Mexican Period (1939–1949): A Synthesis of Jewish Iconoclasm and Eschatology in the Gleam of the First Gaze," *Estudios de arte y estetica,* no. 49 (1998), 420. Supposedly not viewing Paalen's paintings, Motherwell told Neufert (letter, October 16, 1986), "and so our conversation had not to be about painting." It is difficult to know how much credence to give this and other statements Motherwell later made about Paalen's influence in light of visual evidence to the contrary. See also Neufert, "Art and the Science of Consciousness: Contributions of a Lesser-Known Surrealist," *Art Journal* 64 (Summer 2005), 103–4.

5 | Abstract Expressionism and Modernist Identity

1. Michael Leja, *Reframing Abstract Expressionism: Subjectivity and Painting in the 1940s* (New Haven: Yale University Press, 1993), 269.

2. E. A. Carmean, Jr. and Eliza E. Rathbone, *American Art at Mid-Century: The Subjects of the Artists* (Washington, D.C.: National Gallery of Art, 1978). A newer approach, for example: Barbara Cavaliere and Robert Hobbs, "Against a Newer Laocoon," *Arts Magazine* 51 (April 1977), 110–17.

3. "The American Action Painters," *Art News* 51 (December 1952), 22–23, 48–50.

4. My italics. Greenberg/Rosenberg rivalry: Ellen G. Landau, *Reading Abstract Expressionism: Context and Critique* (New Haven: Yale University Press, 1995), 9, 14–17, 19–22; *Action/Abstraction: Pollock, de Kooning and American Art, 1940–1976,* Norman L. Kleeblatt, ed. (New Haven: Jewish Museum, New York, and Yale University Press, 2008).

5. Paalen, "Farewell au Surréalisme," *Dyn* 1 (April 1942), 26. Motherwell, "The Modern Painter's World," Stephanie Terenzio, ed., *The Collected Writings of Robert Motherwell* (New York: Oxford University Press, 1992), 32: "Painting is a reality, among realities, which has been felt and formed. It is the pattern choices made, from the realm of possible choices, which gives a painting its form. The content of painting is our response to the painting's qualitative character, as made apprehendable [*sic*] by its form. This content is the feeling

'body-and-mind.' The 'body-and-mind,' in turn, is an event in reality, the interplay of a sentient being and the external world. The 'body-and-mind' being the interaction of the animal self and the external world, is just reality itself. It is for this reason that the 'mind,' in realizing itself in one of its mediums, expresses the nature of reality as felt."

6. However, both Motherwell and Rosenberg's wife, May Natalie Tabak, recalled Harold naming the magazine. Ann Gibson, "Theory Undeclared: Avant-Garde Magazines as a Guide to Abstract Expressionist Images and Ideas," Ph.D. diss., University of Delaware, 1984, 76.

7. A year after *Dyn* 6, Paalen wrote to Motherwell from Los Cedros, February 16, 1945: "I shall send you a detailed plan for the future development of Dyn and tell you how I think we could share the direction of the magazine." Dedalus Foundation, file marked "Wolfgang Paalen."

8. Motherwell : "What we tried to do in *Possibilities* and *Modern Artists in America* [a later publication he coedited] was not theoretical; we wanted to present the *evidence:* very factual descriptions presenting the thing—without theory." Gibson interview with Motherwell, November 13, 1982, "Theory Undeclared," 68. Surrealist and Dada attitudes: Aurélie Barnier, "Une revue de l'expressionisme abstrait amèricain: *Possibilities* (1947–1948)," *Les cahiers du Musée national d'art moderne* 71 (Spring 2000), 104–21.

9. Nicolas Calas, letter to Gerome Kamrowski, c. 1947, Gerome Kamrowski Papers, Archives of American Art, Smithsonian Institution; hereafter AAA.

10. *Indians* title: Gibson interview with Motherwell, June 11, 1984. Photographs of Native American art were included in *VVV. Dyn*'s Special Amerindian Number, 4–5 (1943), focused on Mexican indigenous art, but Paalen's "Totem Art," featured Northwest Coast examples, mostly Haida, Tsimshian, and Kwakiutl. Eva Sulzer's photos from British Columbia ran throughout several issues.

11. Motherwell states he was interested in folk art "atavistically, like Punch and Judy and Commedia dell'Arte or gypsies. The idea that there is some ritualistic lore behind it all touches me, but less than the immediate attraction of its bright and playful quality. When I was young, I needed joy above all. I was so sad!" "Interview with Bryan Robertson, Addenda," 1965: typescript, Dedalus Foundation; section not included in Terenzio, *Collected Writings.*

12. Typical discussion of *Three Personages Shot* comprises remarks on its horizontal multifigural format as common for Motherwell at that time, and on the influence of Picasso. Jack Flam states its "subject matter and graphic manner" are "still clearly related to Picasso," although he cites no examples of persons being murdered in the latter's oeuvre to back up similar themes. "Robert Motherwell Drawings," *Robert Motherwell Drawings: A Retrospective 1941 to the Present* (Houston: Janie C. Lee Gallery, 1979), Part III, n.p. William Seitz explains the work's structure as "reminiscent of Picasso's constructivist drawings, suggesting

structural rods or plane edges." *Abstract Expressionist Painting in America* (Cambridge, Mass.: Harvard University Press, 1983), 22. Robert Hobbs is an exception; see n. 13.

13. Robert Carleton Hobbs, "Motherwell's Concern with Death in Painting: An Investigation of his *Elegies to the Spanish Republic;* Including an Examination of his Philosophical and Methodological Considerations," Ph.D. diss., University of North Carolina, Chapel Hill, 1975, 133; hereafter Hobbs dissertation.

14. "The Modern Painter's World," *Dyn*, 6 (November 1944), 12. Robert Mattison comments only, "Many of Motherwell's early works embody feelings which are equivalent to the humane struggle in the Mexican Revolution. These include *Pancho Villa, Dead and Alive* and *Three Personages Shot.*" *Robert Motherwell: The Formative Years* (Ann Arbor: UMI Research Press), 42.

15. Andreas Neufert speaks of Paalen's dilemma as an assimilated (half-) Jewish intellectual "who had to rediscover identity as a permanent self-reflection, self-questioning and continuous invention. This questioning also contained the question of identification as such, as a necessary human means but also— in its possible distortions—as a moral problem." "Wolfgang Paalen's First Mexican Period (1939–1949): A Synthesis of Jewish Iconoclasm and Eschatology in the Gleam of the First Gaze," *Estudios de arte y estetica*, no. 49 (1998), 400.

16. Lionel Abel, "The Bow and the Gun: A Play," *Possibilities* 1 (Winter 1947–1948), 74. Abel's descriptions of Breton, "The Surrealists in New York" *Commentary* 72 (October 1981), 46– 50, suggest he may have patterned Chief Joseph's ambiguity on him. Abel introduced Rosenberg to Breton, leading to the former also contributing to *VVV.*

17. Abel collaborated with Matta, 1945–48, to produce *Instead*, another existentially oriented "little magazine." Breton relieved Motherwell of his *VVV* editorial duties after discovering (like Paalen) that he had no connections to potential financial backers. Motherwell proposed Abel as a substitute, but he lasted only a short while. Sculptor David Hare took over, leading to the unraveling of Breton's marriage. Oral History Interview Conducted by Cummings, 1971; Terenzio, *Collected Writings,* 18, n. 1. Hare and Motherwell agreed that Breton wanted an American frontman (Motherwell says "cover") to "do the legwork," not a real editor, "so that he wouldn't be held responsible and shoved back to Europe." Interview of David Hare conducted by Dorothy Seckler for the Archives of American Art, January 17, 1968," typescript, 28–29. Motherwell told Breton, "The United States government doesn't take poets and painters very seriously as subversive elements." Opinions of *VVV* by various Surrealists: Martica Sawin, *Surrealism in Exile and the Beginnings of the New York School* (Cambridge, Mass.: MIT Press, 1995), 214–20. In "Interview with Bryan Robertson, Addenda," 1965: typescript, Dedalus Foundation, n.p.), Motherwell states, "I would like to give an image here: my aspirations in the early forties and the resultant art that I created was a vision of the Parthenon in the midst of the gothic novel that I was then living, among the surrealists."

18. André Breton, "Situation of Surrealism Between the Two Wars": "I insist on the fact that Surrealism can be understood historically only in relation to the war. I mean—from 1919 to 1939—in relation to the war from which it extends and the war to which it extends." *What Is Surrealism?" Selected Writings*, Franklin Rosemont, ed. (New York: Monad, 1978), 243. Breton intended *VVV* (pronounced "triple vee") as a twenty-seventh letter of the alphabet, but Motherwell explained that English speakers do not pronounce W "doubleh vay," so this would make no sense. "Interview about Motherwell and Surrealism," Provincetown, Massachusetts, 1990, Mary Ann Caws, *Robert Motherwell: What Art Holds* (New York: Columbia University Press, 1996), 187.

19. Until that realization, he wrote, "I had been an observer, like a character in James, but with the advantage of having logical and plastic weapons with which to test my observations. Now I have taken a partisan stand, in the creative sense that the surrealist automatism is the basis of my painting, and in the theoretical sense that I find myself intellectually in accord with them." Motherwell, letter to William Carlos Williams, December 3, 1941; Terenzio, *Collected Writings*, 17–18, Motherwell's emphasis.

20. Abel, "Surrealists in New York," 50.

21. Marie Mauzé, "Totemic Landscapes and Vanishing Cultures Through the Eyes of Wolfgang Paalen and Kurt Seligmann," *Journal of Surrealism and the Americas* 2, no. 1 (2008), n. 43.

22. After a year on Perry Street, Motherwell and María moved to Eighth Street facing MacDougal Alley and stayed there until moving to East Hampton in 1945.

23. Random objects: Robert Motherwell, letter to Ed Henning, May 15, 1979; Terenzio, *Collected Writings*, 233. Groceries: Caws, *Robert Motherwell: What Art Holds*, 191. As a beginning painter, Motherwell said, he was treated as "a pet dog" by the Surrealists. Breton liked to put down Motherwell by calling him "le petit philosophe": John Bernard Myers, *Tracking the Marvelous* (New York: Random House, 1985), 35. Gossipy description of Breton's arrogance in New York and dismissive treatment of Motherwell: Steven Naifeh and Gregory White Smith, *Jackson Pollock: An American Saga* (New York: Clarkson N. Potter, 1989), 418–24, 428–30, 860–61.

24. Abel on *Possibilities:* "Unhappily, the review was limited to just one issue, and the reason, as Rosenberg told me with some glee, was that Motherwell had decided to undergo psychoanalysis, and his analyst had found Rosenberg bad for his ego. It struck me that someone who would drop you for the sake of his ego would have to be someone who had taken you up for his ego's sake." "Surrealists in New York," 44. Motherwell stated there was no second issue because interest waned after one of its publishers, Heinz Shultz, died in a plane crash. Robert C. Hobbs, "Re-Review: *Possibilities*," *Art Criticism* 1, no. 2 (1979), 103.

25. David Porter, *Personal Statement, Painting Prophecy 1950* (Washington, D.C.: Gallery Press, 1945); Robert Motherwell, *The Writings of Motherwell*, Dore Ashton and Joan Banach, eds. (Berkeley: University of California Press, 2007), 46. Busa also recalled Motherwell saying, "'Let's pretend we're not afraid.' Always with good humor, of course": "An Interview with Peter Busa and Matta conducted by Sidney Simon in Minneapolis in December 1966," *Art International* 11 (Summer 1967), 19. "Being nobody": "A Discussion on Surrealism and the Modernist Condition," Aldrich Museum of Art, Ridgefield, Connecticut, 1987, typescript, 39, Dedalus Foundation.

26. Mondrian's work "has the value of a *demonstration. . . .* His work has the value like that of an experimental scientist, *whether it is successful or not,* of showing us with permanent subjectivity what lies in a certain direction. But seizing the laboratory freedom of a scientist Mondrian has fallen into a natural trap—loss of contact with historical reality . . . he created a rational art when art was the only place man could find irrational sensual release": Motherwell, "Notes on Mondrian and Chirico," *VVV* 1 (June 1942), 59; Ashton and Banach, *Writings of Motherwell*, 15–19.

27. Other artists included Calder, Leonora Carrington, Chagall, Masson, Ernst, Seligmann and Tanguy. Hare contributed a photograph and Breton a collage incorporating a French postcard, string and sequins. Date and Miró influence: Mattison, *Formative Years,* 75.

28. Dore Ashton, *The New York School: A Cultural Reckoning* (Berkeley: University of California Press, 1992), 161–63.

29. "Robertson Addenda," Terenzio, *Collected Writings,* 145–46.

30. Motherwell told Mattison that, once structural clarity was "*driven home* by Mondrian," he saw its evidence in Picasso and Matisse. Interview, June 4, 1980; Robert Mattison, "The Art of Robert Motherwell during the 1940s," Ph.D. diss., Princeton University, 1985, 72. On Motherwell's New York art viewing, 64–68.

31. Dore Ashton, "Robert Motherwell, Passion and Transfiguration," *Studio International* 167 (March 1964), 100–5. He considered the Spanish-speaking world "a place where feelings dominated and impersonal mechanization had not yet taken over": Mattison, "Art of Motherwell," 81–82.

32. Re: mask that was chalk white with prominent yellow ochre accents (also scarlet red, purple, black and turquoise blue) "that became the origin of my color": Hobbs dissertation, 123, August 18, 1969, interview. Motherwell, "Statement on the 'Open' Series," *Art Now: New York* 1 (May 1969); Ashton and Banach, *Writings of Motherwell,* 243.

33. Quote to Gibson, taped interview, April 13, 1982. Relation to Guggenheim's Picasso and Mondrian: Mattison, *Formative Years,* 56–59.

34. "Interview with Bryan Robertson, Addenda," 1965: typescript, Dedalus Foundation; abridged from Terenzio, except Matta's Indian quote (Terenzio, *Collected Writings,* 144).

35. Asked to comment on *The Little Spanish Prison*, Motherwell provided a deeply emotional characterization: "the basic feel-

ing is oppressive, compassionate, and yet the picture displays a certain assertiveness." H. H. Arnason, *Robert Motherwell* (New York: Abrams, 1977), 97. Despite the title's obvious political resonance, Matta reacted defensively to it: "I remember when I painted *The Little Spanish Prison,* Matta saying to me, 'I don't know if Breton will go for a painting of a flag." Motherwell added, "What neither of us knew was that we were looking at one of the earliest of what nowadays would be called color-field paintings": "Interview with Robert Motherwell by Barbaralee Diamonstein," *Inside New York's Art World* (New York: Rizzoli, 1979), 241. "I knew it was a marvelous painting, that part of its impulse was the unconscious influence of Mondrian. He was the only one, and I fought against it, so I made the lines more hand-made, more sensitive, more I don't know what. In another sense it wasn't abstract at all, in the Mondrian way of being an assertion of universal principles and so on": Caws, *Robert Motherwell: What Art Holds,* 189.

36. Bryan Robertson, "On the Forties: An Unpublished Interview with Robert Motherwell," 1965, 18, Dedalus Foundation. Queried on political and social conditions in Mexico, Motherwell avoided responding whereas Matta commented, "I had come across considerable class violence in Mexico. The silence between foreigner, Spaniard and Indian was quite frightening, with daggers drawn." Germana Ferrari, *Entretiens morphologiques; Notebook No. 1, 1936–1944* (London and Lugano-Svizzera: Sistan, 1987), 226, n.7.

37. "Statement," *Motherwell,* exhibition catalogue (New York: Samuel Kootz, 1947); Ashton and Banach, *Writings of Motherwell,* 57. Weldon Kees, "Robert Motherwell," *Magazine of Art* 41 (March 1948), 88, quotes this statement, but nevertheless judges Motherwell's only subject matter as "paint itself."

38. Other examples in his 1944 Art of This Century exhibition: *Untitled (Mexico), The Door (Mexico), Mexican Air (Mexico), Configuration (Mexico)* of 1943, and *The Blue-Nosed Mexican, The Peasant Actors* (also known as *The Actors*), *The Indians,* and *Personage (el toro),* all 1944. *The Red Sun,* 1941, a tempera loaned by Motherwell's mother, dates to his first Mexican trip, as well as two 1941 drawings titled *Landscape,* lent by Mr. and Mrs. L. Gearhart and "Mme. Matta Echaurren." *Structure of Space,* 1944 (lent by Darius Milhaud) exhibits visual parallels with works Motherwell made in San Angel. Well over a third of the works on view had obvious Mexican connections.

39. Greenberg found Motherwell's watercolor drawings "of an astonishing felicity" but too uniform, "pouring directly from post-Cubism," and overly Picassoesque. "Review of Exhibitions of William Baziotes and Robert Motherwell," *Nation,* November 11, 1944; *Clement Greenberg: The Collected Essays and Criticism,* vol. 1 "Perceptions and Judgments, 1939–1944, John O'Brian, ed. (Chicago: University of Chicago Press, 1986), 239–41.

40. Mattison identifies the horizontal magenta bar in *The Little Spanish Prison* as originally a "window" revealing spontane-ous underpainting. Motherwell recalled the geometry of this work as "deliberately freehand emphasizing sensibility": "Art of Motherwell," 78, 80. A top layer of black added in 1942–43 to the "viewer's slot" was removed in the 1960s by a MoMA conservator, revealing the magenta beneath: Hobbs dissertation, 118. Katy Rogers considers the "window" in *Recuerdo de Coyoacán* to expose Motherwell's emphasis on "expression of a passageway between the conscious and the subconscious, the human and the cosmos. It is here that Motherwell internalizes this rhetoric and re-forms it to fit his own abstract mode." "To Transform the World: Matta and Motherwell in New York and Mexico," *Nexus New York: Latin/American Artists in the Modern Metropolis* (New York: El Museo de Barrio and Yale University Press, 2009), 191.

41. Robertson, "Conversation with Motherwell," 2. He also said, "I treat a canvas as though it were a wall. In another era I might have made Cretan or Egyptian wall tombs. . . . Texture, I like the kind of texture and chalkiness of whitewashed plaster. As for space, space that feels like a wall. Not architecture, but facades. How I repeat myself. Could one's style be one's obsessive repetitions?"

42. "Parisian Artists in Exile: 1939–1945," Musée nationale d'art moderne, 1977, typescript, 12; Dedalus Foundation.

43. Quotes: Motherwell to Mattison, March 10, 1980; *Formative Years,* 57. Automatism vs. geometry: Robert S. Mattison, "A Voyage: Robert Motherwell's Earliest Works," *Arts Magazine* 59 (February 1985): 92.

44. Inscription: undated folder marked "Motherwell and Barbara Reis"; Dedalus Foundation.

45. John Gruen, *The Party's over Now* (Wainscott, N.Y.: Pushcart, 1989), 194. Motherwell to Gruen on David Smith: "We both knew damn well the black abyss in each of us . . . the demons of guilt and depression that largely destroyed in one way or another the abstract expressionist generation."

46. "Robertson, Addenda," Terenzio, *Collected Writings,* 145.

47. Nevertheless, Motherwell confessed, once his peers in New York "had been shown the way by the Surrealists, it was 'like King Arthur finding that he could pull the sword from the stone. . . . I still shake when I think how that opened the door.'" Malone/Gill Projects, taped interview with Robert Motherwell, Surrealist Festival, Case Western Reserve University, Cleveland, 1979.

48. Motherwell adds, "There are not three other young Americans of whom this could be said," echoing Greenberg's judgment citing Pollock, Baziotes and himself. Greenberg stated of Motherwell in 1944, "Let him find his personal 'subject matter' and forget about the order of the day," concluding positively: "But [Motherwell] has already done enough to make it no exaggeration to say that the future of American painting depends on what he, Baziotes, Pollock, and only a comparatively few others do from now on." "Review of Exhibitions of William Baziotes and Robert Motherwell," *Nation,* November 11, 1944; O'Brian, *Collected Essays,* 1: 241.

49. See Claude Cernuschi, *Jackson Pollock: "Psychoanalytic" Drawings* (Durham, N.C.: Duke University Press, 1992) and summary of Jungian interpretations of Pollock in Landau, *Reading Abstract Expressionism*, 37–38.

50. [Joseph L. Henderson], "How a Disturbed Genius Talked to His Analyst with Art," *Medical World News* 12 (February 5, 1971), 18–28. Recommending that Pollock be classified 4-F, de Laszlo wrote the Selective Service that he exhibits "a great deal of emotional instability" and "finds it difficult to form or maintain any kind of relationship" because of a "certain schizoid disposition." Jackson Pollock Papers, AAA. As noted in Chapter 3, his brothers and doctors considered Jackson's psychological issues related to his "hell of a mother problem."

51. Jonathan Fineberg, "Death and Maternal Love: Psychological Speculations on Robert Motherwell's Art," *Artforum* 17 (September 1978), 52–57.

52. Naifeh and Smith, *Jackson Pollock: An American Saga*, 425, 861. They ridicule Motherwell's claim of "introducing" automatism to Pollock and other peers. Motherwell's recollection of these evenings: "in the beginning each of us wrote a line and then they were simply set down in turn, in no logical order." When it was concluded that this would not work, he arranged the lines in sequence. Still not satisfied, the group decided to choose a common topic. On one rainy night, the weather was their subject resulting in "an extremely beautiful poem," a copy of which Motherwell said he kept for years (with everyone's contribution acknowledged) but subsequently lost: "Robertson Addenda," Dedalus Foundation. See also Cavaliere and Hobbs, "Against a Newer Laocoon," 111.

53. Author's interview with Ethel Baziotes, New York, February 21, 1980, and Emily Wasserman, "Interview with Lee Krasner," January 9, 1968, typescript, 8, Lee Krasner Papers, AAA. See also Ellen G. Landau, *Jackson Pollock* (New York: Abrams, 1989), 90–92; David S. Rubin, "A Case for Content: Jackson Pollock's Subject Was the Automatic Gesture," *Arts Magazine* 53 (March 1979), 128–37. "Common meeting": Rubin, conversation with Ethel Baziotes, June 16, 1976.

54. Quoted in Sawin, *Surrealism in Exile*, 241, from an unidentified 1985 videotape.

55. Other American artists included John Goodwin, Ralph Nelson, Barbara Reis, Kay Sage, Jimmy Ernst, Alexander Calder and David Hare, all associated with Art of This Century. Dickran Tashjian, *A Boatload of Madmen: Surrealism and the American Avant-Garde 1920–1950* (New York: Thames and Hudson, 1995), 215–21; Sawin, *Surrealism in Exile*, 225–30. Motherwell's abstract painting is identified at far right in a photo reproduced in Lewis Kachur, *Displaying the Marvelous: Marcel Duchamp, Salvador Dali and Surrealist Exhibition Installations* (Cambridge, Mass.: MIT Press, 2001), 176. Pollock's refusal: Rubin, "Case for Content," 104.

56. Motherwell, letter to William Baziotes, September 6, 1944, William and Ethel Baziotes Papers, AAA; Sawin, *Surrealism in Exile*, 360.

57. Rubin, "Case for Content," 105. See also Mattison, "Art of Motherwell," 83–89; *Formative Years*, 71–73; "Concerning the Beginnings of the New York School: 1939–1943; "An Interview with Robert Motherwell Conducted by Sidney Simon in New York in January 1967," *Art International* 2 (Summer 1967); Terenzio, *Collected Writings*, 155–68; and Simon, "Busa/Matta Interview," 17–20.

58. Ferrari, *Entretiens morphologiques*, 226.

59. Matta, letter to Mattison, September 24, 1979: "Art of Motherwell," 87.

60. These meetings consisted of "aleatory games, explorations of improvisational techniques, discussions about reality as an ongoing transformation, and references to the simultaneous worlds that could be accessed through occultist practices, as well as Motherwell's impromptu lectures on aesthetics." Robert Hobbs, "Surrealism and Abstract Expressionism: From Psychic to Plastic Automatism," *Surrealism USA*, Isabelle Dervaux, ed. (New York: National Academy Museum and Hatje Cantz, 2005), 57. Busa recalled that Matta "would look at our work and make comments as to what dimension we were reflecting. He also had organizing attitudes and was interested in whether you were reflecting a rhythm that would be associated with water or with fire or with rock forms. . . . One didn't have an image to begin with, but rather a hand and motor ability." Sawin, *Surrealism in Exile*, 239–41.

61. Paul Haim, *Matta, agiter l'oeil avant de voir: Errances, souvenirs et autres divagations* (Paris: Séguier, 2001), 52. Matta told Haim, 47: "It is often said that I greatly influenced American artists. Absolutely false! We never understood each other. The only thing they grasped was the freedom of the gesture."

62. Each had a different take on what happened. Matta disagreed with Motherwell's emphasis on aesthetics and theory and said he left "when the thing was getting too 'painting' for me. I mean I was more and more involved in giving a material picture of history, of events. And all of that sounded to them, literary. To me it wasn't literary at all . . . art has always been a reflection of the need to re-present reality." Max Kozloff, "An Interview with Matta—These things were like rain catching up with a man who is running," *Artforum* 4 (September 1965), 26. Matta told Simon, "With Motherwell especially I had a terrific incompatibility of ideas." Simon, "Busa/Matta Interview," 18. Motherwell told Sawin, "I was as close to Matta then as anybody. He is a kind of intellectual Don Juan who seduces and then moves on." *Surrealism in Exile*, citing a November 1987 conversation, 186, n. 27. He also implies that Matta gravitated back to the Europeans after his new marriage to a wealthy woman, Patricia Connelly.

63. "Modern Painter's World," Terenzio, *Collected Writings*, 33–34.

64. Action of the imagination: Simon, "Busa/Matta Interview," 19. Adventurous: Simon, "Motherwell Interview," 23. Motherwell tells Simon, "What happened in American painting after the war had its origins in automatism assimilated to the particular New York situation, that is, the Surrealist tone and literary

qualities were dropped and the doodle transformed into something plastic, mysterious and sublime."

65. Busa in Simon, "Busa/Matta Interview," 19. Motherwell recalled making a similar work to *The Little Spanish Prison* based on Matta's recommendation to paint the hours of the day: conversation with Mattison, October 23, 1980, "Art of Motherwell," 89.

66. D'Arcy Wentworth Thompson, *On Growth and Form* (Cambridge, Eng.: Cambridge University Press, 1942), including reproductions of cells, snowflakes, liquid jets of water, and the like, as well as energy flow patterns, mathematical equations and other notations illustrated.

67. Melvin P. Lader, unpublished interview with Peter Busa, Minneapolis, May 26, 1976. "It was neither Picasso nor Orozco—it was something entirely different," Busa remarked.

68. Breton on Matta: "Genesis and Perspective of Surrealism," *Art of This Century: Objects-Drawings-Photographs-Paintings-Sculpture-Collages 1910 to 1942*, Peggy Guggenheim, ed. (New York: Art of This Century, 1942), 27. Haim, *Matta, agiter l'oeil*, 47: "I spoke of morphology . . . to the Americans, but all they absorbed was the way I started. I started from a stain that looked like a flow."

69. WPA experiments: Simon, "Busa/Matta Interview," 19. "Stick with hairs": Siqueiros's term for the brush, and other techniques: see Axel Horn, "Jackson Pollock: The Hollow and the Bump," *Carleton Miscellany* 7 (Summer 1966), 80–87.

70. Naifeh and Smith, *Jackson Pollock: An American Saga*, 415, 417. See also Martica Sawin, "'The Third Man,' or Automatism American Style," *Art Journal* 47 (Fall 1988), 181–86. More emotional: Motherwell to Robertson on what developed into Abstract Expressionism: Terenzio, *Collected Writings*, 147.

71. Frank O'Hara, *Jackson Pollock* (New York: George Braziller, 1959), 17.

72. Robert Mattison, "Robert Motherwell's First Collages: 'All My Life I Have Been Obsessed by Death,'" *Studies in Iconography* 2 (1988), 171–86; Gregory Gilbert, "Robert Motherwell's World War Two Collages: Signifying War as Topical Spectacle in Abstract Expressionist Art," *Oxford Art Journal* 27, no. 3 (2004), 311–37.

73. Greenberg, *Nation*, November 11, 1944, 599. Robert Motherwell, letter to James Valliere, August 31, 1964; Jackson Pollock Papers, AAA.

74. "The war was on everybody's mind. In the beginning, the *New York Times*, every day they would have a map of Europe, and every day it was blacker and blacker, and by the third year it seemed as though Germany was actually going to conquer all of Europe": Caws, *Robert Motherwell: What Art Holds*, 191. Gilbert, "Robert Motherwell's World War Two Collages," 321–22, points out that Motherwell's 1944 painting *View from a High Tower* also includes a military map cutting, and *The Joy of Living* could likewise be read as an aerial view.

75. Autobiographical: Cummings Motherwell AAA interview. Symbolic murder: E. A. Carmean, Jr., *The Collages of Robert Motherwell* (Houston: Museum of Fine Arts, 1972), 63; Hobbs dissertation, 170–71.

76. Thomas McEvilley, "Aspekte des Internationalismus im Werk von Siquieros und Pollock," *Siqueiros/Pollock; Pollock/Siqueiros*, Jürgen Harten, ed. (Düsseldorf: Kunsthalle Düsseldorf, 1995), 2: 67–72. "As Hegel articulated it, in the early 19th century, even though history was going some place, it needed concrete assistance in order to get there. This assistance would come from specially awakened and committed individuals (Geniuses) who could sense the direction history is inevitably taking and lend the force of their wills to push it that way. It needed, in short, World Historical Individuals: specially insightful, sensitive, and passionately motivated statesmen and leaders who would dedicate their lives to boosting History onward towards its goal." English translation provided by Hiltrud Eichelmann, Kunsthalle Düsseldorf, October 10, 1995.

77. "I remember I called it 'Wounded Personage.' Meyer Schapiro saw it; we discussed titles; and I still recall the look of revelation on his face when I told him its title. Somehow splashed paint on rice paper reminded me of blood-stained bandages." Mattison, "Formative Years," 92.

78. Mattison, "Formative Years," 178; from a telephone conversation with Motherwell, June 6, 1979. Encoding of self as other: Hobbs, "Surrealism and Abstract Expressionism," 63–64. Motherwell told Robertson, "The Figure interests me when it fills the picture as in a full-length portrait. It never occurs to me to have the figure do anything, its presence is sufficient; and I suppose it rarely occurs to me to do anything except feel my own presence" ("Formative Years," 93).

79. Clement Greenberg, "Review of a Group Exhibition at the Art of This Century Gallery, and of Exhibitions of Maria Martins and Luis Quintanilla," *Nation*, May 27, 1944; O'Brian, *Collected Writings*, 1: 209.

80. As late as 1979, Motherwell titled a painting *Posada*. This and other later works with Mexican references in their titles are illustrated in Katherine Manthorne, "Robert Motherwell in Mexico," *Latin American Art* 2, no. 4 (1990), 66–69.

81. Roberto Berdecio and Stanley Appelbaum, "Introduction," *Posada's Popular Mexican Prints* (New York: Dover, 1972), vii. Motherwell's quote: Terenzio, *Collected Writings*, 145.

82. Gibson, "Theory Undeclared," 373.

83. Hobbs dissertation, 134–38. Hobbs considers *Pancho Villa, Dead and Alive* to symbolize Motherwell's changing relationship with his father and that castration played a psychological role. Motherwell used pieces of the same German Christmas wrapping in other collages such as *La Résistance*, 1945.

84. Mattison, "First Collages," 176; from a conversation with Motherwell, June 5, 1980.

85. Motherwell explained, "Making an *Elegy* is like building a temple, an altar, a ritual place. . . . Unlike the rest of my work, the *Elegies* are, for the most part, public statements. The *Elegies* reflect the internationalist in me, interested in the histori-

cal forces of the twentieth century, with strong feelings about the conflicting forces in it." He added, "The *Elegies* use a basic pictorial language, in which I seem to have hit on an 'archetypal' image. Even people who are actively hostile to abstract art are, on occasion, moved by them, but do not know "why." Jack D. Flam, "With Robert Motherwell," *Robert Motherwell* (New York: Abbeville, 1983), 22.

86. Fineberg, "Death and Maternal Love," 55: from a conversation with Motherwell, January 8, 1977, Greenwich, Connecticut. Motherwell once described his home as "a little WASP prison": James E. B. Breslin, "From WASPism to Modernism," *Threepenny Review* 61 (Spring 1995), 25. Simple expression of the complex thought: Mark Rothko, Adolph Gottlieb [and Barnett Newman], "Letter to the *New York Times*, 1943," quoted in abbreviated form in Edward Alden Jewell, "'Globalism' Pops into View: The Realm of Art. A New Platform," *New York Times*, June 13, 1943, sec. 2, 9.

Conclusion

1. Robert Motherwell, *Seventeen Modern American Painters: The School of New York* (Beverly Hills, Calif.: Frank Perls Gallery, 1951).

2. See *The Interpretive Link: Abstract Surrealism into Abstract Expressionism, Works on Paper 1938–1948*, Paul Schimmel, ed. (Newport Beach, Calif.: Newport Harbor Art Museum, 1986); Martica Sawin, "Abstract Surrealism: The Uneasy Synthesis," *Les Surréalistes en exil et les débuts de l'école de New York* (Strasbourg: Musée d'art modern et contemporaine, 200), 359–70. Myth-maker category: Michael Leja, *Reframing Abstract Expressionism: Subjectivity and Painting in the 1940s* (New Haven: Yale University Press, 1993), 49–120; Gregory Gilbert, "Robert Motherwell's World War Two Collages: Signifying War as Topical Spectacle in Abstract Expressionist Art," *Oxford Art Journal* 27, no. 3 (2004), 332. Motherwell as Color-Field painter: Irving Sandler, *The Triumph of American Painting: A History of Abstract Expressionism* (New York: Praeger, 1970), 202–10.

3. Thomas W. Leavitt and Tom Armstrong, "Introduction," *Abstract Expressionism: The Formative Years* (New York: Herbert F. Johnson Museum of Art, Cornell University, and the Whitney Museum of America Art, 1978), 7. Robert Carleton Hobbs, "Early Abstract Expressionism: A Concern with the Unknown Within," 8.

4. Sawin, "Abstract Surrealism," 398; Ann Eden Gibson, *Abstract Expressionism: Other Politics* (New Haven: Yale University Press, 1997), xx, xxvi. Gibson uses this methodology to expand the canon of Abstract Expressionism to include women, homosexuals and people of color.

5. David Anfam, "Interrupted Stories: Reflections on Abstract Expressionism and Narrative," *American Abstract Expressionism*, David Thistlewood, ed. (Liverpool, Eng.: Liverpool University Press and Tate Gallery Liverpool, 1993), 21; includes quote below in text.

6. Harold Rosenberg, "The American Action Painters," *Art News* 51 (December 1952), 22.

7. Robert Motherwell, "The New York School," *The Collected Writings of Robert Motherwell*, Stephanie Terenzio, ed. (New York: Oxford University Press, 1992), 77. Motherwell's social approach was no doubt influenced by his relationship with Meyer Schapiro. See Gilbert, "Robert Motherwell's World War Two Collages," and Stephen Polcari, "The Psychology of Crisis: The Historical Roots of Abstract Expressionism," *Abstract Expressionism and the Modern Experience* (Cambridge, Eng.: Cambridge University Press, 1991), 3–30.

8. Wolfgang Paalen, "Introduction," *Problems of Contemporary Art 1: Form and Sense* (New York: Wittenborn, 1945), 6. See also Andreas Neufert, *Wolfgang Paalen: Implicit Spaces* (San Francisco: Frey Norris Gallery, 2007), 9–10 and other articles by Neufert cited in notes to Chapter 4. Neufert repeats Ethel Baziotes's statement to Amy Winter, "Paalen was very much discussed in the forties and it rivaled the discussion of Matta. . . . He was in the air, and he was also doing something revolutionary and new." Bultman: Steven Naifeh and Gregory White Smith, *Jackson Pollock: An American Saga* (New York: Clarkson N. Potter, 1989), 534.

9. Robert Motherwell, "Preface," *The Dada Painters and Poets* (New York: Wittenborn, Schultz, 1951), xii.

10. Martin Friedman, *Noguchi's Imaginary Landscapes* (Minneapolis: Walker Art Center, 1978), 8. Noguchi's Abstract Expressionist status: Lisa Phillips, *The Third Dimension: Sculpture of the New York School* (New York: Whitney Museum of American Art, 1984), 10; Stephen Polcari, "Martha Graham and Abstract Expressionism," *Smithsonian Studies in American Art* 4 (Winter 1990), 3–28.

11. *Noguchi at the Dance* (New York: Dance Collection at the New York Public Library for the Performing Arts, 1995), n.p., artist's comments to frames 1–2. Flaming nimbus: Robert Tracy, "Noguchi: Collaborating with Graham," *Ballet Review* 13 (Winter 1986), 12.

12. "Very often what I did in the theater had a carry-over from what I was actually doing in sculpture. . . . It's kind of a carry-over of similar themes or similar ways of doing things—to a certain extent; not altogether. It's my sculpture coming to life in the theater, in actuality of a setting, of relationships." "Nothing," he said, "is done in isolation from other activities and interests that one has . . . I was just doing the same thing all the time, more or less, whether I was doing it in the theater or not." Tobi Tobias, "Interview with Isamu Noguchi," 1979; transcript, New York Public Library for the Performing Arts, MGMT 3–5581, 22, 65.

13. Neil Printz, "'A Nearer Function than that of the Eye': Noguchi, Graham and the Physicality of the Dance," *Noguchi/Graham: Selected Works for Dance* (Long Island City: Noguchi Museum, 2005), 50. "I was interested in getting a certain

plasticity of form, like something alive—and I wanted it to imply a certain imminent motion. . . . I consciously sought after a counteraction to collapse—with collapse dominant." Isamu Noguchi, *A Sculptor's World* (New York: Harper and Row, 1968), 18. In *Seraphic Dialogue*, Joan of Arc "is assumed by St. Michael into the frame of the great gold icon as a figure of eternity": John Martin, "Dance: 'Acrobats of God,'" *New York Times*, April 28, 1960, L3.

14. *The Isamu Noguchi Garden Museum* (New York: Abrams, 1987), 216.

15. In July 1951 Graham wrote to Frances Wickes: "I wonder how long one can stay on fire. It is a curious fire. Perhaps it is good for Joan. I wonder. At least I think I know what it does mean to burn slowly from within . . . to feel so possessed by flame as to be infinitely hot and about to disintegrate into ash at any instant. It may be beautiful to watch." Martha Graham, *Blood Memory* (New York: Doubleday, 1991), 187. Elsewhere Graham wrote of Joan, "Hers is the triumph over the oblivion which is death whether it be physical death or the oblivion of the soul." *The Notebooks of Martha Graham* (New York: Harcourt Brace and Jovanovich, 1973), 238. Such ruminations were likely shared with Noguchi. See also Elizabeth Forsyth Harris, "Sculptural Theatre: Isamu Noguchi's Sets for Martha Graham," Ph.D. diss., University of Virginia, 2000, 129–35. "Like the womb": Tobias interview, 60; female psyche analogy: Harris, "Sculptural Theatre," 135.

16. Friedman, *Noguchi's Imaginary Landscapes*, 27.

17. John Martin, "The Dance: Noguchi, Designing the Stage for Modern Movement," *New York Times*, February 29, 1948, X3. Noguchi explained his use of props as spatial adjuncts to Graham's dancing as stemming in part from his experience with Japanese gardens in 1931 and said also that they had an impact on his own later garden sculpture designs: "Ordinary people looking around are themselves the actors and audience combined." Tobias interview, 26, 35. In his public outdoor works, it could be argued, Noguchi updated his desire to bring art to the masses.

18. Meyer Schapiro told Sawin that "it wasn't automatism that the Americans learned from the Surrealists, but how to be heroic." *Surrealism in Exile*, ix.

19. Hobbs, "Early Abstract Expressionism," 25.

20. Letter of June 7, 1951: *Jackson Pollock: A Catalogue Raisonné of Paintings, Drawings and Other Works*, Francis Valentine O'Connor and Eugene Victor Thaw, eds. (New Haven: Yale University Press, 1978), 4: 260; hereafter *JPCR*.

21. Francis V. O'Connor, interview with Dr. Elizabeth Hubbard, February 22, 1964, and letter from Hubbard to O'Connor, May 14, 1964, quoted in *The Black Pourings 1951–53* (Boston: Institute of Contemporary Art, 1980), 20. Also, Ellen G. Landau, *Jackson Pollock* (New York: Abrams, 1989), 217–18.

22. Elizabeth Langhorne, "Jackson Pollock's 'The Moon Woman Cuts the Circle,'" *Arts Magazine* 53 (March 1979), 128–37; Landau, *Pollock*, 113–17, 218; *JPCR* 90,1: 80–81. Others include *The Mad Moon Woman*, 1941 (*JPCR* 84); *The Moon Woman*, 1942 (JPCR 86).

23. Ann Gibson, "The Rhetoric of Abstract Expressionism," *Abstract Expressionism: The Critical Developments*, Michael Auping, ed. (New York: Abrams and Buffalo, N.Y.: Albright-Knox Gallery, 1987), 85–88.

24. Craig Owens, "The Allegorical Impulse: Toward a Theory of Postmodernism," *Beyond Recognition: Representation, Power and Culture* (Berkeley: University of California Press, 1992), 54.

25. Clement Greenberg, "Review of Exhibitions by Jean Dubuffet and Jackson Pollock," *Nation*, February 1, 1947, 137–39.

26. B. H. Friedman, "An Interview with Lee Krasner Pollock," *Jackson Pollock: Black and White* (New York: Marlborough-Gerson Gallery, 1969) reprinted in *Jackson Pollock: Interviews, Articles, Reviews*, Pepe Karmel, ed. (New York: Museum of Modern Art, 1999), 35–36.

27. Jackson Pollock, "My Painting," *Possibilities* 1 (Winter 1947/8), 79.

28. Pepe Karmel, "Pollock at Work: The Films and Photographs of Hans Namuth," *Jackson Pollock*, Kirk Varnedoe and Pepe Karmel, eds. (New York: Museum of Modern Art, 1998), 87–137.

29. Ellen G. Landau, "Jackson Pollock: The Body and Nature," *Jackson Pollock: The Irascibles and the New York School* (Milan: Skira Editore, 2002), 73–90, where points discussed here are elaborated. Motherwell's interest in Joyce: Evan R. Firestone, "James Joyce and the First Generation New York School," *Arts Magazine* 56 (June 1982), 116–21.

30. James Coddington, "No Chaos Damn It"; Carol Mancusi-Ungaro, "Jackson Pollock: Response as Dialogue," *Jackson Pollock: New Approaches*, Pepe Karmel, ed. (New York: Museum of Modern Art, 1999), 101–120, 145–53.

31. Dylan Thomas quoted in Thomas B. Hess, *American Masters: Art Students League* (New York, 1967), 96: "I make one image—though 'make' is not the word, I let, perhaps an image be 'made' emotionally in me and then apply to it what intellectual and critical forces I possess—let it breed another, let that image contradict the first, make of the third image bred out of the other two a fourth contradictory image, and let them all, within my imposed formal limits, conflict."

32. Francine du Plessix and Cleve Gray, "Who Was Jackson Pollock?" *Art in America* 55 (May–June 1967), 58.

33. Undated notation by Pollock: *JPCR*, 4: 253.

34. Robert Motherwell, "Notes on Bradley Walker Tomlin," in John I. H. Baur, *Bradley Walker Tomlin* (New York: Macmillan and Whitney Museum of American Art, 1957), 11–12.

35. Ideas expressed in Gilbert, "Robert Motherwell's World War Two Collages," 335–36, were very helpful in developing this argument. *Joy of Living* as prototype: Mary Ann Caws, *Robert Motherwell: What Art Holds* (New York: Columbia University Press, 1996), 36.

36. Leja, *Reframing Abstract Expressionism*, 275–83. He sees the relationship of Pollock's tension between control/uncontrol

as related to "Modern Man subjectivity" evident in popular culture books like Harvey Fergusson's 1936 *Modern Man: His Belief and Behavior* (which Pollock owned) and films noir of the 1940s and early '50s that share the web metaphor.

37. E[ugene] C. Goosen, "Robert Motherwell and the Seriousness of Subject," *Art International* 3, nos. 1–2 (1959), 34. Objection to Goosen's interpretation (which was endorsed by Hobbs): E. A. Carmean, Jr., "Robert Motherwell: The Elegies to the Spanish Republic," *American Art at Mid-Century: The Subjects of the Artists* (Washington, D.C.: National Gallery of Art, 1978), 106–9. Fragmentation as allegorical strategy: Benjamin H. D. Buchloh, "Allegorical Procedures: Appropriation and Montage in Contemporary Art," *Artforum* 21 (September 1982), 43.

38. Jonathan Fineberg, "Death and Maternal Love: Psychological Speculations on Robert Motherwell's Art," *Artforum* 17 (September 1978), 52. Blunt force: Goosen, "Motherwell and the Seriousness of Subject," 35.

39. Robert Motherwell, "Beyond the Aesthetic," *Design* 47 (April 1946), 14–15.

40. Robert Motherwell, Notebook, February 1977–February 1979, Dedalus Foundation; Stephanie Terenzio, *Robert Motherwell and Black* (Storrs, Conn.: William Benton Museum, University of Connecticut, 1980), 59. In *Black or White: Paintings by European and American Artists* (New York: Samuel Kootz Gallery, 1950), n.p., Motherwell wrote, "Sometimes I wonder, laying in a great black stripe on a canvas, what animal's bones (or horns) are making the furrows of my picture." He frequently discussed his fondness for yellow ochre as related to his California upbringing.

41. Terenzio, *Motherwell and Black*, 136–37. Barbara Catoir, "The Artist as a 'Walking Eye': Fragen an Robert Motherwell," *Bruckmanns Pantheon* 38 (1980), 285.

42. Lorca wailed, "Oh, white wall of Spain!/Oh black bull of sorrow!/Oh, hard, blood of Ignacio!"

43. Ann Eden Gibson, "Theory Undeclared: Avant-Garde Magazines as a Guide to Abstract Expressionist Images and Ideas," Ph.D. diss., University of Delaware, 1984, 168–69.

44. Fineberg, "Death and Maternal Love," 55, conversation with Motherwell, January 8, 1977. Fineberg discusses the emotional basis of Motherwell's *Je t'aime* pictures (1954–58), which coincided with the end of his second marriage, and the psychological basis for Motherwell's vulnerable relationships with women as located in his mother's lack of nurturance. After divorce from his third wife, the painter Helen Frankenthaler, Motherwell married Renate Ponsold, Guston's former lover.

45. *Robert Motherwell* (Northampton, Mass.: Smith College Museum of Art, 1983), n.p. "My Mexican wife": Carmean, *American Art at Mid-Century*, 98; from conversation with the artist, August 17, 1977. In his 1950 Kootz Gallery catalogue, Motherwell described the more spartan composition, *Spanish Prison (Window)*, as the first *Elegy* and *Pancho Villa, Dead and Alive* as the initial *Capriccio*, his designation for companion paintings with subtle differences in meaning and form that were "intimately connected" to the *Elegies* (Carmean, 100).

46. Quote: Philip Roth, "Breast Baring," *Vanity Fair*, October 1989, 99. Relationship of Guston's late works to his earliest: Robert Slifkin, "Philip Guston's Return to Figuration and the '1930s Renaissance' of the 1960s," *Art Bulletin* 92 (June 2011), 220–42. Slifkin does not mention the impact of the Morelia mural or Guston's Jewishness.

47. Guston, letter of December 7, 1977: Ross Feld, *Guston in Time: Remembering Philip Guston* (New York: Counterpoint, 2003), 124–25.

48. Jerry Talmer, " 'Creation' Is for Beauty Parlors," *New York Post*, April 9, 1977.

49. Woodstock neighbors by 1970, both artist and writer moved to the country to escape the Manhattan scene—Guston because of the sour reception of his so-called "new paintings" shown at Marlborough and Roth after the remarkably similar, somewhat more vituperative critical imbroglio over his scandalous (and, many alleged, self-loathing and anti-Semitic) sex-crazed novel *Portnoy's Complaint*.

50. While Pollock and Motherwell both had mother problems, all four artists in this study had serious father issues. Guston's was a failure and a suicide; Motherwell's "methodically cruel," judgmental and overbearing; Pollock's a poor provider, ineffectual and browbeaten by his wife; and Noguchi's famous poet father rejected his bastard son. Motherwell seems to have been drawn to Hispanic culture at least in part by his objection to the "externally directed, status derived, puritanical, materialistic" world of his father. Noguchi told Paul Cummings, "Yes, well to find one's own identity you cannot borrow from anyone else. Also one has to revolt against one's parents— Yes? And I had that very strongly in me in any case because I hated my father." Tape-recorded Interview with Isamu Noguchi, Long Island City, N.Y., November 7, 1973, Archives of American Art, Smithsonian Institution; hereafter AAA.

51. Bill Berkson, "The New Gustons," *Art News* 69 (October 1970), 85. Author's conversation with Berkson, October 19, 2012.

52. Sigmund Freud, *Jokes and Their Relation to the Unconscious*, James Strachey, trans. (New York: Norton, 1960. Also Martin Grotjahn, "Jewish Jokes and Their Relation to Masochism," *A Celebration of Laughter*, Werner M. Mendel, ed. (Los Angeles: Mara, 1970), 135–144; *Semites and Stereotypes: Characteristics of Jewish Humor*, Avner Ziv and Anat Zajdman, eds. (Westport, Conn.: Greenwood, 1993).

53. Gilbert Seldes, "The Krazy Kat That Walks by Himself," *The Seven Lively Arts* (New York: A. S. Barnes, 1971); Arthur Asa Berger, "Krazy Kat: The Social Dimensions of Fantasy," *The Comic-Stripped American: What Dick Tracy, Blondie, Daddy Warbucks, and Charlie Brown Tell Us About Ourselves* (New York: Walker, 1973), 60–71.

54. A typed page of notes includes the following dream (or nightmare)-like entry dated September 1970, where Guston catalogues preoccupations harking back to Krazy Kat: "In a drawer I find scraps of paper with these notes. Thickness of

things. Shoes. Rusted iron. Mended rags. Seams. Dries blood stains. Pink paint. Bricks. Bent nails and pieces of wood. Brick walls. Cigaret butts. Smoking. Empty booze bottles. /How would bricks look flying in the air—fixed in their gravity—falling? A brick fight. /Pictures hanging on nails in walls. The hands of clocks. Green window shades. Two- or three-story brick buildings. Endless black windows. Empty streets." Dore Ashton Papers, AAA.

55. "What if" question as Jewish: Andrew Furman, "What Drives Philip Roth," *Contemporary Jewish American Writers and the Multicultural Dilemma: The Return of the Exiled* (Syracuse, N.Y.: Syracuse University Press, 2000), 30; Lawrence E. Mintz, "Devil and Angel: Philip Roth's Humor," *Studies in American Jewish Literature* (Fall 1989), 157. Roth directly explored the implications of "What if?" in *The Counterlife* (1986) returning to it with devastating consequences after 9/11 in *The Plot Against America* (2004) which visualizes a different outcome for U.S. Jews to World War II.

56. "Ku Klux Komix," *Time*, November 9, 1970, 62–63. "I have *never* been so close to what I've painted, not pictures—but a substitute world which comes *from* the world": Philip Guston, letter to Bill Berkson, September 15, 1970: Debra Bricker Balken, *Poor Richard by Philip Guston* (Chicago: University of Chicago Press, 2001), 94. *If This Be Not I, Who Then May it Be?,* which is arguably Guston's most important composition of the early 1940s, makes explicit reference to the parable of substitution in a favorite fairy tale.

57. Roth, "Breast Baring," 98. Musa Mayer quotes poet Stanley Kunitz's description of her father, "Volcanic is another word I think of in connection with Philip. He did not so much occupy his physical frame as seethe within it. His rage was always periously close to the surface, ready for instantaneous eruption." *Night Studio: A Memoir of Philip Guston by His Daughter* (New York: Alfred A. Knopf, 1988), 235.

58. "Philip Guston Talking," *Philip Guston Paintings, 1969–1980* (London: Whitechapel Art Gallery, 1982), 54. Mark Harris, "Twilight of the Tummlers," *New York Magazine,* June 1, 2009, 39: "Jewish humor has always struggled between two extremes: the excluded outsider is also the smarty pants, self-mockery tussles with self-aggrandizement; the prideful intellectual is also a slave to his basest appetites and most uncontrollable body functions. And every era has found its own mode of angst."

59. Guston, notation of April 24, 1966; Ashton Papers, AAA. Gene Baro, "The Ethics of Risk," *Arts Magazine* 40 (January 1966), 41, 37. Motherwell's statement to Baro has slightly different implications than Pollock's assertion to Selden Rodman, "Every good artist paints what he is."

60. Discussing the guilt induced in him by his overbearing mother, Portnoy complains to his psychiatrist, "I'm living in the middle of a Jewish joke!" Philip Roth, *Portnoy's Complaint* (New York: Random House, 1969), 36–37. Redeeming the past for the present: Owens, "Allegorical Impulse," 53.

61. Antonin Artaud, *México y Viaje al país de los tarahumaras* (Mexico: Fondo de Cultura Económica, 1984), 176; Roger Bartra, *The Cage of Melancholy: Identity and Metamorphosis in the Mexican Character* (New Brunswick, N.J.: Rutgers University Press, 1992), 62.

62. Noguchi, *Sculptor's World,* 219.

63. Octavio Paz, *The Labyrinth of Solitude: Life and Thought in Mexico* (New York: Grove, 1962), 175.

Index